Cooperation and Competition
in humans and animals

The Comparative Psychology of Animals and Humans

Series Editor: Professor W. Sluckin, University of Leicester

The comparative perspective — viewing animals and human beings side by side — is best suited to a range of topics within psychology. The nature/nurture issue has traditionally been considered in this way, and more narrowly circumscribed areas of study, such as conditioning, have for a long time been investigated in animals as well as in humans. In more recent times, developments in the related fields of ethology and sociobiology have focused attention on the comparative approach to selected psychological topics.

The aim of this series is to produce books dealing in a comparative manner with a variety of topics. The multiple authorship of each book ensures a thorough and in-depth coverage of the topic, while at the same time great care is taken that the chapters cohere according to an overall structure provided by the book's editor. Each volume is under the separate editorship of a specialist in the given field. All the books review and evaluate research in the respective fields, and give an up-to-date summary of the present state of knowledge.

Sluckin	Fear in animals and man
Colman	Cooperation and Competition in humans and animals
Archer & Birke	Exploration in animals and humans
Mayes	Memory in humans and animals

Cooperation and Competition in humans and animals

Edited by

Andrew M. Colman
Department of Psychology
University of Leicester

Van Nostrand Reinhold (UK) Co. Ltd.

Published by Van Nostrand Reinhold (UK) Co. Ltd.,
Molly Millars Lane, Wokingham, Berkshire, England

Library of Congress Cataloging in Publication Data
Main entry under title:

Cooperation and competition in humans and animals.

(The Comparative psychology of animals and humans)
Includes bibliographical references and index.
1. Cooperativeness. 2. Competition (Psychology)
3. Psychology, Comparative. 4. Social behavior in
animals. I. Colman, Andrew. II. Series.
BF637.C58C66 302'.14 82-6985
ISBN 0-442-30521-4 AACR2

Preface

Cooperation and competition are the very foundation stones of social life. It is difficult to think of any form of social behaviour, whether primitive or sophisticated, simple or complex, that is neither cooperative nor competitive at its most basic level. This is because a person's or an animal's behaviour, if it affects others, is generally calculated either to promote the common interest or to give an advantage to the individual at the expense of others.

The various approaches to the study of cooperation and competition discussed in this volume have never before been assembled in one place. Each chapter centres on a different line of investigation, and the theories and research findings on which they are based are drawn from disciplines as diverse as psychology, biology, welfare economics, social anthropology, and moral philosophy. The book is intended primarily for advanced undergraduate and postgraduate psychology students, but readers from other disciplines may also find it interesting and useful. It is often surprisingly instructive to examine a problem, especially a familiar problem, from several entirely fresh angles.

Part I focuses on social behaviour in animals. Competition and conflict over food, territory, mates, and positions in dominance hierarchies are well known and readily understood features of animal life; but many species of animals manifest cooperative and altruistic forms of behaviour — even in the throes of combat — which present a real challenge to the theory of evolution and for which, until recently, there were no satisfactory explanations. A number of species have evolved efficient systems of communication, and some of the methods that are used — chemical and electrical signalling for example — have no natural human counterparts; human language, however, seems to be unique in certain fundamental ways. All of these matters are thoroughly discussed in the first three chapters and are commented on further in Chapter 11.

Part II is devoted to critical reviews of six areas of research into cooperation and competition in human societies. These range from voting as a method of resolving differences of opinion, and behaviour in experimental games, to bargaining and negotiation, helping behaviour, intergroup conflict and cooperation, and cross-cultural comparisons of cooperation and competition. Many of the ideas and empirical findings mentioned in this section have potential applications to social, economic, and political problems of everyday life, and each of the contributors has something to say about practical problems of conflict resolution.

Part III contains an examination, in the light of the ideas presented in some of the earlier chapters, of the ethics of cooperation and competition, a field in which interesting advances are currently taking place. This is followed by a brief concluding chapter devoted to a few of the fundamental similarities and differences between animal and human social behaviour and their implications.

Since the part of any book that is most widely read and quoted is its title, a great deal of soul-searching went into the christening of this book. Some linguistic purists may object to the title on the grounds that 'human' is still principally an adjective in educated English usage — in contrast to 'animal' which is equally acceptable as a noun — and some evolutionists may disapprove of the implicit suggestion that humans are not animals. These critics may have more sympathy with the title if they appreciate the hard road that led to it. 'Cooperation and Competition in Animals' would have had the virtues of simplicity and formal accuracy, but it would have been misleading, because there is more human psychology than zoology in the book. 'Cooperation and Competition in Human Beings and Other Animals' might have pleased the sticklers, but it does not go trippingly on the tongue. Darwin himself called one of his books *Expression of the Emotions in Man and Animals*, but I declined to use his formula as a model because, to many contemporary ears, it has a disagreeably sexist ring about it. After considering a number of other suggestions I eventually arrived, by a long process of elimination, at *Cooperation and Competition in Humans and Animals*.

I have to end this preface on a sad note by recording the death of one of the contributors, John Mackie, a great philosopher and a lovable man. The depth and clarity of his thinking, qualities that will be familiar to those who know his books, are evident in his contribution to this volume, which is among his last publications.

A.M.C.
January 1982

Contents

I Biological Perspectives

CHAPTER 1

The Evolution of Cooperation and Altruism

Felicity Huntingford

In *The Origin of Species* Darwin (1859) presented the theory that evolution is the result of a process which he called natural selection. Very simply, individual members of a species are not uniform but differ from one another in a variety of ways, some of which influence their chances of surviving and reproducing. Thus in any generation, some individuals by virtue of possession of particular characteristics such as large size or bright plumage produce more offspring than others. Where these characteristics are hereditary and offspring tend to resemble their parents, individuals with these characteristics become more common in the species and, as the generations pass, evolutionary change occurs. It is as if nature selects for breeding those individuals whose characteristics give them a competitive edge over their contemporaries. Thus evolution came to be viewed as the result of a 'struggle for existence'.

Since Darwin's time, the theory of natural selection has been modified and extended in the light of developments in biological knowledge, in particular in the field of genetics, but its essence remains the same and it is widely accepted as the major driving force in the evolutionary process. This being so, one might expect that of the two topics dealt with in this book, competition would be the more conspicuous in the animal kingdom. Although competition and conflict are indeed common (Chapter 2), animals regularly show behaviour which, if performed by a human being, could legitimately be called cooperation or even altruism. In this chapter, cooperation implies acting conjointly with another or working towards a common end. Altruism is defined purely in terms of the consequences of behaviour; an animal is described as altruistic if it performs an action which is not in its own best interest but which benefits others. This definition says nothing about the motivation underlying such behaviour and thus ignores an essential aspect of altruism as it refers to human beings, namely genuinely unselfish motives. It is not easy to see how performance of altruistic behaviour could increase an animal's contribution to subsequent generations and thus be favoured by natural selection. The fact that it does occur clearly poses a problem for the evolutionary biologist, especially as we are not talking about a few exceptional cases but a common aspect of animal life.

1.1 Some Examples of Cooperation and Altruism among Animals

(a) Small fish such as minnows spend their life in dense groups or schools with a highly ordered structure; the fish swim at fixed distances and bearings from their neighbours and move about in a highly coordinated manner (Pitcher, 1973, 1979).

Nectar-feeding bats forage in flocks which circle rapidly around the large flowers on which they feed, each bat waiting its turn to swoop in for a brief feed. The flock members follow any bat that changes feeding site or flies off to roost and are reluctant to feed alone (Howell, 1979).

In both these examples, to the extent that the animals concerned constrain their actions according to what others are doing, they may be said to be acting cooperatively.

(b) In other species, communal living is carried further, with different individuals playing different roles and combining together for a particular purpose. For example, lions live in groups or prides of several adult males and females and their cubs. The females, which do most of the hunting, track down prey in groups, searching and stalking together and often setting up elaborate ambushes. Following a successful hunt the kill is shared by all members of the pride (Schaller, 1972; Bertram, 1976). These animals are showing cooperative behaviour in the stronger sense of working together towards a common goal.

(c) Many species are noted for the care they lavish on their young; to give just one example, ring doves build nests for their eggs, spend many days incubating them, feed the chicks with a milky secretion produced by their crop for several weeks and at all stages defend them against attack by predators. The young are thus reared at great cost to their parents, in terms of energy expenditure, depleted food reserves and increased risk of injury (Lehrman, 1964). According to the definition given above, therefore, parent birds are acting altruistically.

(d) In addition, in ring doves, as in many other species, the two parents cooperate with each other in caring for the young. Thus the doves, having undergone a period of courtship and mating select a nest site together and cooperate in the building of the nest; generally the male gathers and the female builds. The female necessarily lays the eggs but both birds incubate them and both produce crop milk to feed the hatchlings (Lehrman, 1964).

(e) In yet other species, groups of several males and females cooperate to perform these functions. For example, in the groove billed ani (a species of bird) groups of two or three monogomously mated pairs defend a communal feeding territory, construct a single large nest and share the work of incubating, feeding and defending the young (Vehrencamp, 1978).

(f) Lorenz (1966) describes how, at the climax of a fight between two wolves, the loser averts its head, exposing its vulnerable neck to the victor who refrains from biting its defeated rival. This is one of many examples which have led to the view that aggression between animals normally takes the form of an elaborate but harmless ritual rather than a bloody fight. The idea can be overstated, and animals do often damage themselves seriously in fights but the fact remains that in many cases these stop short of overt violence (Chapter 2). Such restrained behaviour has been described as altruistic since while the loser obviously benefits from it, the winner is apparently acting against its own best interests. Any member of the same species, as long as it remains alive, is a potential competitor for resources. In addition, failing to kill a rival may allow the latter to reproduce; this reduces the relative contribution the self-restrained animal makes to the next generation.

(g) Within social groups, animals sometimes come to each other's aid during a fight. For example, male turkeys join together in groups to fight with other such groups, the one that wins being the most successful at attracting females (Watts & Stokes, 1971). In troops of savanna baboons, which consist of a number of adult males and females and their young, a male competing with another for a female may solicit help from a third animal. If the two together are successful in driving off the rival, the initiator of the attack mates with the female while the helper protects the couple from interference (Packer, 1977).

(h) In groups of animals that are vulnerable to predation, an individual that sees an approaching predator may give a warning call or display and thus alert its neighbours to the danger. For example, ground squirrels live in dense colonies of burrows, and the first animal to sight a predator produces a chattering call which is continued for some time. This causes nearby squirrels to hide or to run for their burrows but may result in the calling animal being stalked and killed by the predator (Sherman, 1977).

(i) In other cases, animals living in groups may support one another in attacking a predator; for example, elands and buffaloes assist each other in defence against hunting hyenas (Kruuk, 1972).

In (g), (h) and (i) above, animals are reducing their own chances of surviving while conferring an advantage on others.

(j) Lastly, there are many examples of animals foregoing their reproductive rights, either temporarily or permanently, to the advantage of other members of the species. Thus although all members of a wild turkey group join in the struggle for dominance, only one member of the group actually mates with any females (Watts & Stokes, 1971). Groups of Florida scrub jays defend territories in which all the resident birds feed but in which only one pair breeds, assisted in rearing their chicks by the other birds (Wolfenden, 1975). The most extreme example of a sacrifice of reproductive potential is the occurrence of completely sterile castes in termites, ants, bees and wasps (Wilson, 1971).

These examples illustrate three kinds of problems that arise when interpreting animal behaviour in evolutionary terms. The first problem relates to cooperative behaviour: examples (a), (b), (d) and (e). If natural selection is all about getting a competitive advantage over contemporaries, why should a minnow constrain its swimming according to what its neighbour is doing, why should bats wait their turn at a food source and why should one lioness help another in her search for food? Even when such behaviour may bring no actual disadvantage to the performer, if it increases in any way the survival or reproductive potential of other individuals, it reduces the performer's relative contribution to the next generation and therefore should not, on the face of it, be favoured by natural selection.

The same problem arises even more acutely in cases where animals fail to press home an advantage: example (f). Why do so many animals fail to destroy a defeated rival when the opportunity presents itself. Such restraint would seem to put the animal at a relative disadvantage and it is hard to see why natural selection has not eliminated it.

If failure to damage another animal and cooperating at no cost to the performer pose problems for classical evolutionary theory, this is much more the case when animals seem to be putting themselves at an absolute disadvantage for the benefit of others: examples (c), (g), (h), (i), (j). Here again, the bahaviour would seem to be the complete opposite to that predicted by the theory of natural selection.

The aim of this chapter is to look briefly at the ways in which students of the evolution of behaviour have tried to solve these problems and in doing so to review some current ideas about cooperation and altruism in animals.

1.2 Problem 1: Cooperation

There are many disadvantages that automatically result from living in groups, for example increased competition for limited resources and heightened risk of infectious disease. Since this way of life is very common in the animal kingdom, we must look for compensatory advantages. One possibility is that living in groups reduces vulnerability to predation: by schooling, individual fish may reduce the likelihood of ending their lives in the stomach of a predator. Several lines of evidence support this idea; for example, guppies living in streams and rivers where predators are abundant school more strongly than those from sites where predators are rare. Thus there is a correlation between the strength of this supposed anti-predator response and the vulnerability of the fish to predation (Seghers, 1974). In addition, experimental manipulation of the size of schools shows that single fish are very vulnerable to predation compared to even quite small schools (Neill & Cullen, 1974). Similar evidence indicates that individuals living in more complex groups also benefit from cooperating in this way.

In the communally breeding anis, there is in fact a great deal of competition among the females during egg laying, each one pushing existing eggs out of the nest as she lays. In the end, most of the surviving eggs belong to the dominant female and, because of their position in the nest, these hatch first and are better equipped to compete for food than the young of other females. Thus in terms of reproductive success, the subordinate birds do rather badly out of the communal nesting; however, comparison of the number of birds taken by predators from groups of different sizes shows that, in some habitats at least, birds living in large groups have greater chances of survival. The dominant male is an exception here, since he incubates at times when the nest is most vulnerable to predation and renders himself particularly conspicuous during territorial defence. Thus overall, the individual birds benefit from communal brooding, either in terms of increased reproduction (breeding males), or by reduced predation (subordinate males and females) or by both (dominant females)

(Vehrencamp, 1978).

In other cases, the individual animal living in a group gets more food than it would get on its own. Lions hunting communally make more and larger kills than those hunting alone. Bats foraging in groups are more likely to locate a source of food since the flowers on which they feed, although providing an abundant supply of nectar, are patchily distributed. By foraging systematically in flocks, the bats are also less likely to search for food in sites that have already been cleaned out. They thus forage more thoroughly and more efficiently than would the same number of animals feeding independently. In addition, they all fly off to roost close together when they are full and communal roosting makes temperature regulation easier and digestion and absorption of food more efficient (Howell, 1979).

Thus although it may not be possible to identify one advantage which inevitably and on its own causes animals to live and/or breed in groups, when all the gains and losses are taken into account it is clear that by living in groups, which may be large and complex and involve a fairly sophisticated level of cooperation, animals are acting in their own best interests. Many important questions about the precise ecological conditions under which group living confers an overall advantage and the mechanisms by which cooperation and cohesion are maintained (Chapter 3) remain to be answered. However, once it is established that the animals mentioned above benefit from living and cooperating in groups, these examples cease to present a problem for classical evolutionary theory and therefore require no further discussion here.

The previous statement is not quite true, since the possibility exists that animals might cheat. Why does natural selection not favour the lioness who puts a little less effort into the hunt than her companions but still shares in the kill? To illustrate one way of looking at this question, take the example of two parents rearing a brood of young. It would seem that as the parents have equal genetic shares in the offspring, the conflict of interest between them should be minimal. The traditional picture of courtship and reproduction stresses this cooperative aspect. The complex interactions of courtship in ring doves, for example, are seen as a way of allowing the animals to select a mate of the appropriate species, to synchronize their sexual arousal and to suppress inappropriate tendencies so that mating can take place. Following mating, since the offspring cannot survive without care, it is in the parents' mutual interest to help each other in rearing them. However, this picture tends to obscure the fact that there is a basic conflict of interest between the two parents; why does one not desert the brood to get on with the business of conceiving more babies while leaving the other partner to look after the existing young? Surely such behaviour would be favoured by natural selection. In fact, this often does happen and one parent rears the offspring alone; in the case of most species of duck it is the female who rears the young while in fish such as the stickleback it is the male. In order to understand why in some species both male and female participate in brood care it is necessary to discover what determines whether an animal deserts its young. Trivers (1972) has suggested that the critical factor is the amount of time and energy that each partner has invested in a particular brood of offspring; the parent that has invested more in the offspring will be the least likely to desert. Since by definition females produce larger and more energetically expensive sex cells or gametes, the scales are tipped in favour of maternal care from a very early stage in evolution. However, what really matters is not what each animal has invested in the past but how much reinvestment would be necessary to bring a new batch of young up to the same stage as the one that might be deserted (Dawkins & Carlisle, 1976). Thus if another mate is hard to come by, and a lot of work is needed to start a new brood, it will not necessarily pay an animal to cheat by deserting.

This is a case in which several courses of action are open, the precise consequences of which depend on how other animals behave. Such situations lend themselves to analysis by game theory (see Chapter 5), a branch of mathematics developed for the study of human conflict and applied to the evolution of animal behaviour by Maynard Smith (1972). Put simply, the possible course of action that the animals might pursue are identified; for example, both male and female might have a choice between guarding a batch of young and deserting them. These alternative courses of action are called strategies though this need not imply that the animals are making rational decisions about what to do. Next, the costs (in terms of energy expenditure, etc.) and benefits (in terms of expected numbers of progeny) of each strategy are defined depending on what the other animal does. These can then be used to investigate the circumstances under which one strategy will replace another; it may be possible to identify strategies which, once established in a population, cannot be replaced by any other through natural selection. These are called evolutionarily stable strategies (or ESSs) and are those we would expect to prevail in nature. Maynard Smith (1977) has applied this technique to the problem of mate desertion; the following description of one of his theories or models illustrates the kinds of insight that this approach can provide.

The model assumes that there is a limited breeding season and that the number of offspring produced depends on how much energy is available for egg production. (In particular, females who have produced a lot of large eggs are assumed to be less effective in guarding the eggs and vice versa). In Fig. 1.1, W represents the number of eggs a female can lay if she deserts and w the number if she guards, where $W \geqslant w$. In addition, the number of offspring successfully reared depends on the effectiveness of the care they receive from different numbers of parents (P_0, P_1 and P_2 represent the chances of survival of those guarded by no parents, by one or by two respectively, ($P_0 \leqslant P_1 \leqslant P_2$).

Other assumptions are that the female on deserting does not attempt a second brood and that a deserting male has a chance, M, of finding a new mate whom he will also desert. Fig. 1.1 illustrates the four possible combinations of male and female strategies and the net payoff (in terms of number of offspring reared) to each, given these various combinations. Taking the case we are interested in at the moment where both male and female guard, the payoff for the female is the product of the number of eggs she can lay, given that she also guards, and the chance that these eggs will be reared with two parents to care for them, i.e. the payoff is wP_2. This is shown in the 'north-eastern' half of the

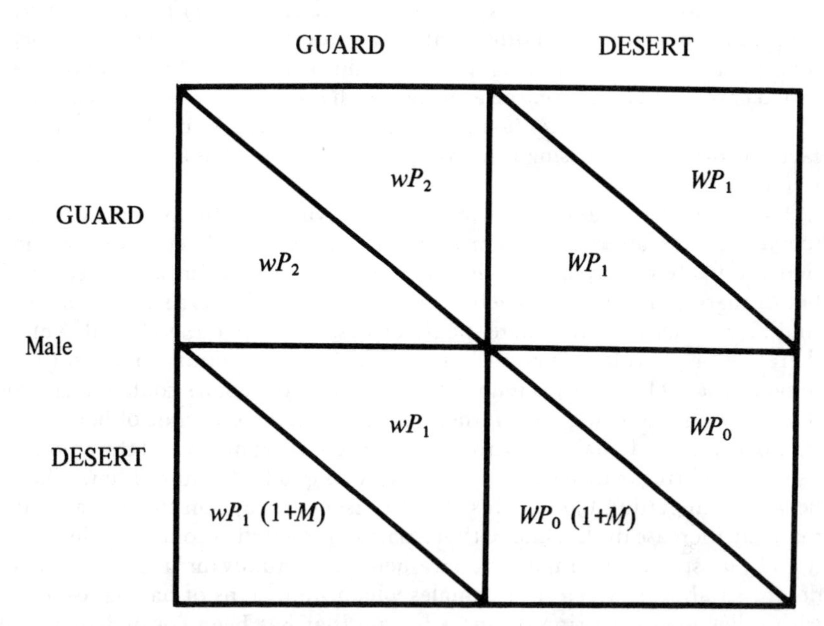

Fig. 1.1 Payoff matrix showing outcomes (in terms of evolutionary fitness) of guarding and deserting strategies by male and female parents. For example, wP_1 is the payoff to the female as a result of guarding if the male deserts; the corresponding payoff to the male is $wP_1(1 + M)$. A full explanation of payoff matrices can be found in Chapter 5.

GUARD-GUARD box in Fig. 1.1. For the male, the payoff is the same, since he is restricted by the number of eggs his faithful mate can lay, as shown in the 'south-western half of the same box. This strategy pair will be stable only if neither the male nor the female could increase his or her payoff by deserting. If the female deserted, while the male stayed, her payoff would now be WP_1 since her egg production would not be restricted by the need to guard, but her eggs would now belong to a one-parent family. If the male deserted, leaving the female to guard, his payoff would be, from his first brood, wP_1 since not only are his offspring reared by one parent but the female could not lay so many eggs and from his second brood wP_1M, as before, but corrected for his likelihood of finding another mate (whom he will desert). Thus his payoff is $wP_1 + wP_1M$ which simplifies to $wP_1(1 + M)$.

The conditions under which it will favour both partners to guard, and which will therefore favour the evolution of communal rearing can now be spelled out. For the female, wP_2 must be greater than WP_1, and for the male P_2 must be greater than $P_1(1 + M)$. Thus key factors determining whether communal parental care will evolve are the effectiveness of care by different numbers of parents (is one parent almost as good as two or much worse?) and the chances of a deserting male finding another mate. By applying the logic of game theory to this question, we can investigate the conditions under which monogamous brood care could evolve on the assumption that each individual is behaving in such a way as to maximize the number of viable young he or she produces. In fact, the predictions arising from Maynard Smith's models are borne out quite well in real life.

The animals themselves can influence the values of the parameters in the inequalities discussed above. For example, females could actively select males that are likely to stay around by forcing them to perform a long courtship before mating. If all females behave in this way, a male has a smaller chance of finding another receptive mate should he desert (the parameter M above) and therefore, as is evident from the payoff table, his temptation to desert (determined by $wP_1 (1 + M)$) is reduced. Alternatively, females could select males that show signs of being good fathers, thus increasing the value of both P_1 and P_2. For example, female terns are fed fish by courting males and the amount of fish a male brings during courtship provides a good indicator of how efficient he will be in getting food for his chicks (Nisbet, 1973). On the other hand, a male can increase the likelihood that a particular batch of young is indeed fertilized by his sperm (an important parameter not actually included in the model described above) by rejecting females which show signs of having associated with other males. In ring doves, a female that has been courted by a male becomes more receptive; if a male is presented with such a female, will he reject her rather than getting on with mating as the classic theory of courtship would predict (Erickson & Zenone, 1976)?

1.3 Problem 2: Failing to Press Home an Advantage

In Lorenz's (1966) explanation of ritualized fighting, animals refrain from inflicting serious damage on each other for the good of the species. This explanation is based on group selection, which will be discussed below and is no longer considered adequate. Looking at the problem more closely, it is clear that fighting is likely to incur costs as well as benefits both in expenditure of time and energy and in risk of injury. In addition the size of these costs and benefits will depend on how the opponent reacts. These facts were combined by Maynard Smith in his game theoretical analysis of the problem (Maynard Smith, 1974) which is discussed more fully in Chapter 2. Briefly, all-out war with destruction of the defeated rival is often not the best strategy that an animal can employ, and those that engage in ritualized fights are maximizing their gains and minimizing their losses, which is completely in line with the classical theory of natural selection.

1.4 Problem 3: Altruistic Behaviour

The self-sacrificing behaviour of a parent caring for its young, while qualifying as altruism as defined above, obviously presents no problem for evolutionary theory, since by showing such behaviour the parent increases its contribution to the next generation. It is as much in the parent's as in the offspring's interests that the latter should survive and flourish, provided that by caring for its present brood the parent is not decreasing its chances of producing others. This proviso does not always apply, and there is a conflict of interest between a parent and its offspring; it may pay the parent to withdraw care from potentially self-sufficient young in order to start work on another brood at a time when continued care would still benefit the first offspring. Trivers (1974) analysed such conflicts with reference to both the length of time a parent continues to care for a brood and the amount of care that it devotes to the individual members of a single brood. Parker and MacNair (1978) have extended this analysis by using game theory; here again, an apparently harmonious system turns out to be riddled with conflict, and both participants behave in such a way as to maximize their reproductive potential.

Thus many of the examples described above turn out to be understandable in classic evolutionary terms; the animals concerned live in groups, cooperate and avoid overt fighting because this is to their overall advantage, and parents care for their babies and cooperate with their mates in the process because in this way they leave the maximum number of offspring. However, in the other examples animals seem to reduce their own chances of surviving and reproducing for the benefit of some other individual. Why, for example, should animals get involved in other individuals' fights, why risk their lives by warning of the approach of a predator or even by trying to fight it off and why care for the young of others instead of rearing their own? Various theories have been proposed to explain such behaviour, one of the best known being the theory of group selection.

1.4.1 Group Selection

This theory suggests that evolutionary change may occur as a result of selection at the level of groups or populations as well as of the individual animal. This process could work for any trait but has mostly been applied to characteristics that are disadvantageous to the animal possessing them but that benefit the group to which it belongs. The idea has been around for a long time in the form of 'the good of the species' arguments but was stated most explicitly by Wynne-Edwards (1962). He proposed that groups whose members show altruistic behaviour, such as refraining from breeding when times are hard, benefit as a result, in this case by avoiding over-exploitation of food supplies; they may thus escape extinction while other groups die out. The disadvantageous consequences for the individual altruist are outweighed by the advantageous consequences for the group, and animals that show the behaviour pattern concerned will become the most common type in the species as a whole.

We know that many species exist in relatively distinct populations or groups, and we know that there is often behavioural variation between such groups. In addition, some do become extinct while others survive, and their fate must depend in part on the behaviour of their individual members. Thus the conditions for selection at this level might seem to exist. However, a major stumbling block to the theory, when it is applied to characteristics disadvantages to the individual animal, is understanding how such a trait could become sufficiently common within a group for its members to benefit in the first place. Put another way, what could possibly prevent an individual which cheats by failing to limit its reproductive rate from leaving more offspring (also selfish) than those which do not cheat, thereby reversing the effect of group selection?

There is an enormous literature on this subject, most of it devoted to attempts to establish whether it is theoretically possible for extinction and survival at the group level to effect evolutionary change when it is counteracted by the effects of similar pressure at the individual level, and if so, under what circumstances. The question of how frequently such conditions prevail in nature and thus how important the process might be in real life can then be settled by empirical observation. To give just one example, Maynard Smith (1964, 1976) developed a model in which local populations of a species are established and maintained in a transient resource for a limited number of generations during which they develop in a manner dictated by their original genetic constitution; mice living in haystacks are usually quoted as an example here. From time to time, when the limited resource fails, the populations disintegrate and individuals or small groups disperse to colonize new sites. Altruistic behaviour is assumed to be controlled by a pair of alleles segregating at a single locus (that is, by alternative versions of the same gene), *AA* and *Aa* individuals being selfish and *aa* individuals altruistic. Within a single population, selfish individuals will always do better than altruistic ones and therefore the *a* allele (altruistic) will always be eliminated from mixed populations. However, populations will exist which by chance start off with altruistic (*aa*) individuals only and these are assumed to have a particularly rapid growth rate, on account of the uniformly altruistic behaviour of their members. Thus such groups provide more founders of new populations when they disperse, and although the altruistic trait always disappears from mixed groups, it can still become the dominant one in the species. The process would be exaggerated if there were a tendency towards inbreeding since this increases the proportion of homozygote animals in the population and thus the number of groups being founded by altruists alone.

Of the stumbling blocks to the acceptance of group selection theory, Maynard Smith sees random colonization aided by inbreeding as the source of groups with a sufficiently large number of altruistic individuals to benefit from their behaviour. He does not postulate any mechanism to prevent the spread of selfish individuals in a mixed population; this is seen as inevitable and incorporated into the model. A number of other theories (Levins, 1970; Boreman & Levitt, 1973) also reached the conclusion that evolution of an altruistic trait by group selection is theoretically possible, but all these models indicate that the conditions under which it could happen are rarely met in nature. It is therefore generally believed that group selection has not played a significant role in the evolution of behaviour. However, there are dissenting voices; for example, Wade (1977) proved experimentally that group selection can occur in artificial populations of beetles, and also pointed out a number of assumptions made by all these theoretical models which he considers unreasonable and which are inherently unfavourable to the operation of group selection (Wade, 1978). Other authors (e.g. D.S. Wilson, 1977) argue that the conditions required by these models may well occur quite frequently in nature. The discussion is not over yet, but we still probably need to look for alternative explanations for the evolution of apparently altruistic behaviour. One possibility which has received considerable attention is Trivers' (1971) theory of reciprocal altruism.

1.4.2 *Reciprocal Altruism*

On this scheme an animal may put itself at risk in order to benefit another if the act is likely to be reciprocated in the future; in other words, the loss is only a short-term one and on a longer time scale animals that behave 'altruistically' actually benefit. For the idea to work, the costs incurred must be low, the benefits received high and the likelihood of reciprocation strong. The latter is increased if the animals concerned have long lives, low dispersion rates and some mechanism for detecting and punishing cheats. Stated verbally in this way, the idea seems rather obvious, but in the logical semi-mathematical form in which it was developed it does provide one mechanism by which an altruistic trait could evolve. In at least one case something along these lines seems to be happening. Not all the males in a baboon troop help others in a fight when such help is needed. There is a strong correlation between the frequency with which a male goes to the aid of others and the frequency with which it is itself successful in enlisting help. In other words, individuals that do not reaily give help are less likely to get it (Packer, 1977). Given the relatively low cost of the act, the great benefit derived from it, the long life and cohesiveness of the baboon troop and this apparent sanction against cheats, Trivers' theory of reciprocal altruism may be sufficient to explain how this type of cooperative fighting originaled. However, even if it does work for baboons, the theory requires fairly sophisticated mental capacities (are turkeys really up to the task of recognizing and discriminating against group members that do not pull their weight in a fight?) and is therefore unlikely to provide an explanation of the other examples of altruism discussed above.

1.4.3 *Kin Selection*

Any inherited characteristic that causes its bearer to leave more offspring will increase in frequency, because in subsequent generations there will be more individuals which have inherited the gene controlling its development. This is the basis of the classical theory of evolution by natural selection. However, in addition to such effects exerted via production of direct descendants, an animal may, by virtue of a particular characteristic, alter the breeding potential of other individuals. If the latter carry the gene for the same character, this indirect effect can also influence the frequency of the trait in question. Thus in assessing the relative genetic contribution to subsequent generations of an individual of a particular type it is necessary to consider the effect of its properties not only on its own breeding success but also on that of other animals with some of the same genes. Hamilton (1964) called this combined contribution the inclusive fitness of a particular type of animal, in order to distinguish it from fitness measured merely in terms of direct descendants.

There are a number of behavioural mechanisms whereby a particular inherited action could benefit primarily individuals that carry the genetic material coding for the same character. For example, animals might behave altruistically only towards those individuals that have been observed to behave altruistically themselves (towards any other animal). However, perhaps the simplest way to achieve this is to direct altruism towards relatives.

The mechanism of heredity is such that two animals are likely to share the same genes if they are related to each other. In most species the genetic material consists of a characteristic number (the diploid number) of chromosomes; the genetic material divides during the formation of the sex cells or gametes so that each contains half the chromosomes (the haploid number) of the parent organism. When the gametes are fertilized, the diploid chromosome is reconstituted and each member of the new generation inherits half its genetic material from each parent. The probability that an individual and its parents carry the same gene in a particular chromosomal slot (or locus) is therefore 50%. By similar reasoning, siblings have a 50% probability of carrying the same gene, half-siblings 25%, cousins 12.5% and so on. Thus two related individuals are more likely both to have the same gene at a given locus than are unrelated individuals and the closer the relationship the more likely they are to do so. Inherited altruistic behaviour directed at relatives could therefore increase in frequency in a population even though it reduced the breeding success of the altruistic animal. Maynard Smith (1964) has called selection acting in such a way 'kin selection'.

This extension of natural selection theory to include effects on the breeding potential of related individuals could be applied to the evolution of any characteristic. However, as in the case of group selection, it is most frequently used in discussions of characteristics which put the performer at a disadvantage. Thus just as the tendency for an animal to sacrifice itself for its offspring will spread to the extent that the latter are likely to have inherited the same tendency from their parents, so altruism towards other individuals could increase in frequency if the beneficiaries are relatives and therefore also likely to possess the gene responsible for this behaviour. In other words, by acting altruistically towards a relative, an individual may endanger its own life (and therefore its likelihood of producing offspring in the future), but may thereby increase its inclusive fitness in terms of the number of other copies of its genes that will survive.

Hamilton's (1964) creative contribution was to recognize these facts and to formulate precisely the conditions under which this process could lead to the evolution of altruistic traits. Briefly, if K represents the benefit of an altruistic act to the recipient divided by the cost incurred by the performer (both defined in terms of expected numbers of surviving offspring) and if r represents the chances that they possess the same genes, then the character in question could increase in frequency as a result of kin selection if $K > 1/r$. In other words, evolution of a characteristic by kin selection is favoured if the likelihood of genes being shared between aided and aiding individuals is high, if the cost is small or if the benefit is large. 'To express the matter more vividly . . . we expect to find that no one is prepared to sacrifice his life for any single person but everyone will sacrifice it when he can thereby save more than two brothers, or four half-brothers, or eight first cousins'. (Hamilton, 1964, p. 16)

The idea of kin selection is attractive in its simplicity and on paper it works as a mechanism by which altruistic behaviour could evolve. What evidence is there that it has played an important role in the evolution of behaviour? This question can be answered by seeing how well the predictions that arise from Hamilton's formulation are realized in nature. Taking first the effects of degree of relatedness on the likelihood of altruism, the prediction is that the more closely two animals are related, the more likely they are to behave altruistically towards each other. To give some examples, the eland and buffalo, which were described above as defending their neighbours against attack from predators, live in small cohesive groups whose members are likely to be related to each other. In contrast, Thompson's gazelles which live in large amorphous herds and are unlikely to be related to their neighbours do not behave in this way (Kruuk, 1972; West-Eberhard 1975). In turkeys, where groups of males cooperate in fights for dominance over other groups but a single animal gets all the matings, the key to the puzzle may lie in the fact that the members of a group are all brothers. Although the chance of a subordinate animal mating is small, the likelihood that copies of his genes will be passed on to the next generation in the offspring of his dominant brother is quite high (Watts & Stokes, 1971). Taking the example of the squirrels' alarm calls, it has been found that while females in a colony are closely related to their neighbours, males are not. Females are much more inclined to give alarm calls then are males (Sherman, 1977). In a related species of squirrel the males do give alarm calls quite frequently, but only when they are young enough to remain in their mothers' home range surrounded by relations (Dunford, 1977). Thus, there is a close fit between what these animals would be expected to do if their alarm calls had evolved as a result of kin selection and what they actually do.

In these examples, the prediction that the closer the relationship between two animals the more likely they are to behave altruistically towards each other is confirmed. However, perhaps the most compelling piece of evidence in favour of kin selection as an important force in the evolution of altruism comes from consideration of the peculiar genetic system of the Hymenoptera, the group of insects containing the ants, bees and wasps. In this group, whether an egg develops into a male or a female depends on whether it is fertilized, and this is under the control of the female who keeps a store of sperm for this purpose. During production of eggs, the number of chromosomes is halved as it is for other sexually reproducing species. If an egg is fertilized, it develops into a female with the normal diploid set of chromosomes and the normal 50% proportion of genes shared with its mother. If, on the other hand, the egg is left unfertilized it develops into a male with a haploid set of chromosomes. There is no need for a reduction division in the production of sperm which are therefore of uniform genetic constitution. This means that sisters produced as a result of a single mating have on average 75% of shared genes; on the other hand, their average relationship with their haploid brothers is only 25%. Thus female Hymenoptera are more closely related to their sisters than they are to their own offspring but less closely related to their brothers. This has a number of implications for the evolution of altruism by kin selection; in the first place, the close relationship between female hymenopterans should mean that altruism is very likely to evolve by kin selection in this group. In fact highly developed social life with cooperative brood care and sterile worker castes has evolved at least 11 times among the Hymenoptera but only once in all other insect groups, namely, in termites (Wilson, 1971). Second, the altruistic animals are likely to be female in hymenopteran societies. This is in fact the case, the sterile worker castes being female; in termites sterile castes come in both sexes. A third prediction stems from the fact that although female Hymenoptera are very closely related to their sisters, they are especially unrelated to their brothers. The kin selection argument only works if the females are able to expend care differentially on their brothers and sisters so that the latter get three times as much. Worker bees do give most care to their sisters and this prediction has been put to a quantitative test by Trivers and Hare (1976). In 20 species of ant the actual weight of adult flesh produced as a result of care by workers in the form of reproductive males and females was measured. In all but two species, which were slave makers and therefore subject to different selective forces, the ratio of male to female weight was about 1 : 3. This result can be seen as evidence in favour of the action of kin selection.

The other predictions from Hamilton's formulation of kin selection have to do with the costs and benefits of altruistic acts. Thus where the benefits are very high, the value of K will be high and the conditions for the evolution of altruism by kin selection may be met even for low levels of relatedness. In some primitive species of wasps, groups of probably related adult females share a nest but provision the cells containing their own young. In times of need only, females are allowed to steal prey from cells stocked by other nest members. At such times, stolen food may make the difference between life and death to the larvae concerned and thus the benefit from the altruistic act is very high (Eberhard, 1972).

Equally, when the loss incurred by the altruist is very low, K will be large and again altruism could evolve without very close relationship between the aided and the aiding animal. For example, the adult and juvenile helpers at the nests of breeding scrub jays are known to be the offspring of previous broods from the same pair. They are therefore related both to the breeders and to the brood, and kin selection could potentially explain their altruistic behaviour. The animals that benefit from the helpers' activity are the parents; the nestlings do not get any more food than they would in the absence of helpers, whose main effect is to reduce the time and effort spent in foraging by the breeding pair. In consequence the breeding female is able to produce more eggs in the breeding season while both male and female end the season with better energy reserves. A number of factors combine to make costs of helping low; these birds mature rather slowly so that for part of their time as helpers they might not be physiologically capable of breeding anyway. Ecological conditions are such that suitable breeding territories are hard to come by; thus the chance of breeding successfully in their own right is low even for mature helpers (Brown, 1974). Finally, the helpers may derive benefits from their activities that offset the losses. Thus larger groups can maintain better territories providing more food for all the inhabitants, and if a member of the breeding pair dies one of the helpers takes over its role (Wolfenden, 1975). Since the helpers may not lose all that much by feeding and defending their siblings such behaviour may well have evolved by kin selection.

1.4.4 Problems with the Theory of Kin Selection

Several predictions of Hamilton's theory of kin selection are borne out in nature and this, together with the simple elegance of the idea, has resulted in its being widely accepted. If it has not revolutionized the study of behaviour, the theory has at least given it a very different look. However, the idea is not without its critics, and it is worth spelling out some of the points on which it has been attacked; many of these apply not so much to Hamilton's original formulation as to the way others have applied it.

(a) There are several cases in which the predictions about the effect of relatedness on the evolution of altruism are not met. For example, an extraordinarily high level of complex social life with division of labour and sterile castes is seen in the termites, yet these insects have a conventional sex-determining mechanism which does not result in their being more closely related to their sisters than to their own offsprings. They therefore appear to lack the predisposition that the Hymenoptera have towards evolution of sibling altruism by kin selection. However, a peculiar rearrangement of the chromosomes has recently been reported for a number of termite species — technically, a series of translocations including the sex chromosomes which join in a ring during gamete formation (Syren & Luykx, 1977). As a consequence, a large fraction of the genome is functionally sex-linked, which means that these termites share significantly more than 50% of their genes with their like-sexed siblings while retaining a normal genetic relationship with their offspring. Thus both males and females of these species may well increase their inclusive fitness by caring for their like-sexed siblings rather than breeding themselves (Lacy, 1980). If this genetic peculiarity is widespread among termites, then far from providing evidence against the role of kin selection in the evolution of altruism, this group of insects provides unexpectedly strong evidence in its favour. An additional factor favouring the evolution of social life may have been the fact that in order to digest the wood on which they feed, these beasts need gut bacteria which are lost at each moult and can only be regained by feeding from another animal (Cleveland *et al.*, 1934).

There are also many Hymenoptera that share nests and rear the young of other females who are not their mothers but, at best, their sisters. The young on which the helpers expend this care share on average no more than 37.3% of their genes. Why then do these females not set up on their own and rear their own eggs? The answer seems to lie in the susceptibility of the nests of solitary females to predation and parasitism (Alexander, 1974). In addition a number of insect groups, including some beetles and many Hymenoptera, have a haplo – diploid sex-determining mechanism but a poorly developed social life.

Clearly, none of these examples proves that kin selection has not led to the evolution of altruism; they do indicate that other factors may be sufficient or at least necessary for it to occur. This is not a surprising conclusion and it is certainly not one with which Hamilton would disagree; however, it is a slightly different picture from that presented by the most enthusiastic proponents of kin selection. For example Wilson (1975) writes 'How can altruism . . . possibly have evolved by natural selection? *The* answer is kinship' (italics mine).

(b) Calculating the relationship between two individuals presents a number of problems. For example, all the figures given above for the relatedness of Hymenoptera depend on the assumption that the mother mates with a single male. We know that this is often not the case and each new batch of sperm reduces the degree to which sisters are related. Having arrived at an estimate of this figure, there is no simple relationship between it and the likelihood that the individuals concerned will carry the same gene at a particular locus. This depends on factors such as the degree of inbreeding, the frequency of the gene concerned and the rate at which this is changing as a result of selection. Unless these complications are taken into account when calculating the probability of shared genes, we cannot come up with really precise predictions about expected degrees of altruism which can then be used as critical tests of the action of kin selection in any particular case.

(c) On a related point, the arguments developed above are in terms of what animals should do in order to maximize their inclusive fitness. An alternative approach, using the techniques of population genetics, is to calculate the changes in frequency of alternative alleles under particular selection pressures, spelling out the conditions under which an altruistic gene could spread. When these two approaches are applied to the problem of kin selection, they do not always come up with the same predictions. For example, as already mentioned, Hamilton's treatment of the problem suggests that, given a haplo – diploid sex-determining mechanism, sterile castes would evolve more readily in females than in males. Several population genetics models (e.g. Scudo & Gheselin, 1975) come up with the opposite prediction; and if this is correct, the hymenopteran social systems are less likely to be the result of kin selection.

(d) As Hamilton realized, his theory encounters difficulties in explaining the selection of genes for altruism following an initial mutation; siblings may or may not carry the mutant depending on the stage of gamete production at which the mutation took place. The problem is a profound one if presented in terms of all-or-nothing genes for altruism; at its most extreme, if it stops its carrier breeding how could the gene initially get itself into the bodies of other animals so that kin selection has an opportunity to work? One way round the problem is to suggest that only a certain proportion of individuals carrying the gene show altruistic behaviour; the gene could then reach sufficiently high levels sheltered in the bodies of non-altruists (Charlesworth, 1978).

(e) Most models of the evolution of altruism by kin selection consider a single gene for altruism: substitution of one allele for another at a single locus is sufficient to produce an altruistic rather than a selfish animal. There are problems in imagining how this large behavioural difference could be brought about in such a way (this is discussed in more detail below). Thus the fact that models using this picture of the inheritance of altruism work on paper may tell us little about what happens in the real world. More sophisticated models, in which altruism and selfishness are extremes on a continuum controlled by the concerted action of a number of genes, have therefore been developed. Under these conditions, kin selection could still result in the evolution of altruism (Yokoyama & Felsenstein, 1978).

None of these criticisms poses insuperable problems, and the points they raise can be incorporated into a revised, more sophisticated theory of kin selection which will remain one possible route by which altruistic behaviour may have evolved.

1.4.5 Parental Manipulation

An alternative theory for the origin of altruism towards siblings is that this may evolve as a result of manipulation by parents of the behaviour of their offspring. Animals are assumed to produce progeny with an arrangement of altruistic tendencies that maximize the parents' reproductive potential. The altruists themselves would do better to devote all their energies to rearing their own young but parents evolve mechanisms for preventing them from doing so (Alexander, 1974). On this theory, the evolution of altruism does not depend on there being an especially close relationship between altruist and beneficiary but in practice it is difficult to distinguish between the results of parental manipulation and kin selection. In a general way, the predictions about the effect of low costs and large benefits are the same for both, and on paper, both could result in the evolution of altruism between siblings. However, the critical benefit : cost ratio at which an altruistic gene could spread is lower for models using parental manipulation than for those using kin selection (Charlesworth,

1978; Craig, 1979). Therefore this alternative mechanism for the evolution of altruism seems to warrant more interest than it has yet received.

1.5 Sociobiology

The picture of the evolution of cooperation and altruism that has been developed here is the result of intellectual activity in three different academic fields. These are: classical ethology (where the question of the survival value and evolution of behaviour has always had an important place); evolutionary ecology (as developed by MacArthur, 1972, to investigate the extent to which animals have developed optimal solutions to the problems posed by their environment); and evolutionary biology (where the challenge posed by the existence of apparently altruistic behaviour has resulted in the development of many of the theories discussed above).

The end product is a fairly complex theoretical framework within which the behaviour of animals can be interpreted. Wilson (1975) has elevated the part of this framework that applies to social behaviour to the status of a new discipline with the evolution of altruism as its central theoretical problem and which he calls sociobiology. His definition ('the systematic study of the biological basis of all social behaviour', p. 4) does not specifically restrict the new discipline to the function and evolution of behaviour, but in practice this seems to be what it is about. Wilson makes fairly extravagant claims for the new discipline; for example, he sees one of its aims as 'to reformulate the foundations of the social sciences in a way that draws these subjects into the Modern Synthesis (i.e. evolutionary biology)' (p. 4). Such claims, together with the fact that sociobiology has received a great deal of attention, make a discussion of its merits necessary in a book such as this one.

One can question whether Wilson's approach to the evolution of social behaviour is sufficiently distinct, either from earlier treatment of the problem or from studies of the same questions where non-social behaviour is concerned, to warrant this grand new name. However, this is mainly a matter of definition; the vital question about sociobiology is whether the theories that it embraces provided us with a satisfying and coherent picture of the forces moulding behaviour in general and, in the present context, of cooperative and altruistic behaviour in particular.

1.5.1 Does Sociobiology Work?

A number of examples of cooperation and altruism in animals have been described whose origins seemed inexplicable within the theoretical framework of earlier decades but which we are now beginning to understand. In addition, the theoretical approach characterized by sociobiology has provided a different way of looking at behaviour, a new slant on old facts and old problems and stimulating questions to be answered. Provisionally, therefore, sociobiology can be said to work. However, there are a number of weaknesses in the approach and some of these will be discussed briefly.

The first is the naïveté of the aims of sociobiologists. Wilson (1975) says 'When the same parameters and quantitative theory are used to analyse both termite colonies and rhesus monkey troops, we will have a unified science of sociobiology' (p. 4). To many people, this ideal is not only naïve but positively misleading as any generalizations which are broad enough to cover such disparate examples are likely to be trivial. To continue the quotation, 'The details of organization have been evolved by an evolutionary optimization process of unknown precision, during which some measure of added fitness was given to individuals with cooperative tendencies' (p. 5). This seems to mean that natural selection works and that animals cooperate when it is to their advantage to do so. This is undoubtedly true, but as a theoretical principal from which to make useful predictions about social structure it is not very powerful; as Wilson himself says 'The comparison may seem facile' (p. 5).

A number of serious criticisms of sociobiology centre upon the simple-minded approach of much of its literature to the factors controlling the development of complex behavioural traits. Sociobiological theories tend to deal with superficial and global classifications of behaviour rather than pin-pointing, for example, exactly what it is that an altruist does that its selfish conspecifics do not do, what cues the former is sensitive to that the latter is not, and so on. The next step is to assume that a single gene exists whose presence makes a selfish animal altruistic. Genes certainly do influence behaviour, and a great deal is known about how they do this. It is known, for example, that in many cases the inheritance of behaviour depends on the combined and complex effects of a number of genes. In addition, even when genetic differences have been shown to underlie a particular behavioural difference, this does not rule out a vast number of complex interactions with the environment, ranging from non-specific experience during development through learning during the lifetime of the individual animal to the cultural background in which it develops. Thus by building models which postulate a single gene deterministically converting one complex behavioural trait into another, the subtlety of the behavioural effects of single genes, the complexity of interactions between genes, and the pervasive influence of the environment on behaviour are all being ignored in a way which makes the models useless as anything but intellectual jumping-off points.

In defence of single-gene models as used in kin selection theory, Dawkins (1979) points out that it is not impossible for differences in the tendency of two individuals to behave altruistically to depend in part on their genetic constitution. A gene might well exist that '*tends* to make individuals in a normal environment *more likely* to show sibling altruism' (p. 189; italics mine). This suggests a continuously variable characteristic probably developing under the influence of a number of genes; such a genetic system is more complex than those used in most models of the evolution of altruism. He goes on to 'suppose' that a simple rule of thumb might exist mediating maternal care, namely 'feed anything that squawks inside your nest' and suggests that this could be a starting point for the evolution of altruism (p. 189). This is an interesting suggestion since it postulates a precise behavioural mechanism but the 'suppose' is a give away. When it comes to pinning down just what behavioural differences selection has to work on, sociobiologists are too ready to suppose rather than to find one. Techniques exists which are sufficiently sensitive to determine where the differences between altruistic and selfish animals lie; used properly, they might come up with something that behaviour geneticists could profitably study.

The 'Just-So' aspect of sociobiology has come in for a great deal of criticism. It has been described as adaptive story-telling scarcely more rigorous than Kipling's tale of how the elephant got his trunk. An initial assumption is made that the process of selection has moulded all aspects of an animal's behaviour. The possibility that it may be the result of random processes or a by-product of selection in some other system is never seriously considered. It is then all too easy to dream up ideas about what function a particular behaviour pattern might serve. What is difficult is to work out exactly what consequences, beneficial or otherwise, it does have. Vehrencamp's (1978) careful study of the effects of communal brood care in the groove-billed anis shows that, though difficult, the task is not impossible. Having established the various costs and benefits, it is even more difficult, though again not impossible, to decide how these should be compared and combined to establish the overall consequences of the behaviour. For example, how is the loss of one year's output of babies to be compared with a reduced risk of predation or an improved food supply? In theory, because all three must ultimately effect the genetic contribution of the animal concerned to subsequent generations, comparison should be easy. However, in practice, it is very difficult to determine the precise effect of, for example, an increase in food intake on inclusive fitness; the usual practice is simply to assume that some relationship exists between them (Parker, 1978). Attempts are being made to tackle these issues (Sibly & Mcfarland, 1976) but as yet there are few, if any, cases for which we have sufficient information about all the selective forces acting on animals to be able to build precise and useful models about how altruistic behaviour evolved.

1.5.2 Sociobiology and Human Behaviour

Briefly, then, sociobiology is easy to do badly but very difficult to do well and this is particularly the case when it is applied to human behaviour. Wilson (1975, 1978) feels that the concepts developed to explain the evolution of cooperation and altruism in animals can and should be applied to our own species. Our undoubted animal origins are seen as imposing upon the way we behave fairly precise constraints which we urgently need to understand.

Unfortunately, all the weakness of sociobiology as it is usually practised are accentuated where human behaviour is concerned. There are two additional problems: in the first place we describe much of animal behaviour in anthropomorphic terms, talking about altruism, selfishness and so on. There is a real danger that, having done this, we will inevitably find what seem to be the precursors of human social institutions when we look at animal behaviour. Second, there is a strong tendency in much sociobiological writing to accept as the norm the conditions prevailing in modern Western society. It becomes more than a political point if it involves, as it often does, neglecting the anthropological data on the diversity of human cultural systems. This is not to say that the ideas and methods used by sociobiologists cannot usefully be applied to human behaviour; their value is shown by Blurton-Jones and Sibly's (1978) demonstration that the !Kung Bushmen time the production of children so as to maximize their overall reproductive potential under the constraints of the environment in which they live. However, if we wish to use sociobiology to help us understand cooperation and altruism in human society, it needs to be good sociobiology and cautiously applied. This issue is discussed further in Chapters 10 and 11.

1.6 Conclusions

The examples discussed in this chapter fail to capture the full complexity of social behaviour in the animal kingdom. However, they suffice to show that animals do sometimes cooperate with and behave altruistically towards each other, at least in terms of the definitions used here.

The theory of natural selection, augmented to include selection via relatives other than direct descendants and, possibly, at levels higher than that of the individual animal, can explain how such behaviour may have evolved. At least for the examples described here, the postulate that animals behave in such a way as to maximize their inclusive fitness (the central tenet of sociobiological theory) seems a reasonable one. However, the way in which it does so is often highly complex and, inevitably, much more research is needed before we have a complete picture of the selective forces at work.

There are a number of difficulties which seriously limit the value of sociobiology as a tool in the analysis of cooperation in humans, but these may not be insuperable.

References

ALEXANDER, R.D. (1974). The evolution of social behaviour. *Annual Review of Ecology and Systematics*, 4, 325 – 383.

BERTRAM, B.R. (1976). Kin selection in lions and in evolution. In P.P. BATESON and R.A. HINDE (Eds.), *Growing Points in Ethology*. Cambridge: Cambridge University Press. Pp. 281 – 301.

BLURTON-JONES, N. and SIBLY, R.M. (1978). Testing adaptiveness of culturally determined behaviour. In V. REYNOLDS and N. BLURTON-JONES (Eds.), *Human Behaviour and Adaptation*. London: Taylor and Francis. Pp. 135 – 162.

BOREMAN, S.A. and LEVITT, P.R. (1973). Group selection at the boundary of a stable population. *Theoretical Population Biology*, 4, 85 – 128.

BROWN, J.L. (1974). Alternative routes to sociality in jays — with a theory for the evolution of altruism and communal breeding. *American Zoologist*, **14**, 63 – 80.

CHARLESWORTH, B. (1978). Some models of the evolution of altruistic behaviour between siblings. *Journal of Theoretical Biology*, **72**, 297 – 319.

CLEVELAND, L.R., HALL, S.R., SANDERS, E.P. and COLLIER, J. (1934). The wood-feeding roach *Cryptocercus*, its protozoa and the symbiosis between protozoa and roach. *Memoirs of the American Academy of Arts and Sciences*, **17**, 185 – 342.

CRAIG, R. (1979). Kin selection and the evolution of altruism. *Evolution*, **33**, 319 – 336.

DARWIN, C. (1859). *The Origin of Species by Means of Natural Selection*. London: John Murray.

DAWKINS, R. (1979). Twelve misunderstandings of kin selection. *Zeitschrift für Tierpsychologie*, **51**, 184 – 200.

DAWKINS, R. and CARLISLE, T.R. (1976). Parental investment and mate desertion: a fallacy. *Nature*, **262**, 131 – 133.

DUNFORD, C. (1977). Kin selection for ground squirrel alarm calls. *American Nature*, **111**, 782 – 785.

EBERHARD, W.G. (1972). Altruistic behaviour in a Sphecoid wasp: support for kin selection theory. *Science*, **172**, 1390 – 1391.

ERICKSON, C.J. and ZENONE, P.G. (1976). Courtship differences in male ring doves: avoidance of cuckoldry? *Science*, **192**, 1353 – 1354.

HAMILTON, W.D. (1964). The genetical theory of social behaviour. *Journal of Theoretical Biology*, **7**, 1 – 52.

HOWELL, D.J. (1979). Flock foraging in nectar feeding bats: advantages to the bats and to the host plants. *American Naturalist*, **114**, 23 – 49.

KRUUK, H. (1972). *The Spotted Hyena*. Chicago: University of Chicago Press.

LACY, R.C. (1980). The evolution of eusociality in termites: a haplodiploid analogy. *American Naturalist*, **116**, 449 – 451.

LEHRMAN, D. (1964). the reproductive behaviour of ring doves. *Scientific American*, **211** (5), 48 – 51.

LEVINS, R. (1970). Extinction. In 'Some Mathematical Questions in Biology'. *American Mathematics society*, **2**, 75 – 108.

LORENZ, K. (1966). *On Aggression*. London: Methuen.

MACARTHUR, R.H. (1972). *Geographical Ecology*. New York: Harper and Row.

MAYNARD SMITH, J. (1964). Group selection and kin selection. *Nature*, **201**, 1145 – 1147.

MAYNARD SMITH, J. (1972). Game theory and the evolution of fighting. In *On Evolution* by JOHN MAYNARD SMITH. Edinburgh: Edinburgh University Press.

MAYNARD SMITH, J. (1974). The theory of games and the evolution of animal conflicts. *Journal of Theoretical Biology*, **47**, 209 – 221.

MAYNARD SMITH, J. (1976). Group selection. *Quarterly Review of Biology*, **51**, 277 – 283.

MAYNARD SMITH, J. (1977). Parental investment: a prospective analysis. *Animal Behaviour*, **25**, 1 – 12.

NEILL, S.R., ST.J. and CULLEN, J.M. (1976). Experiments on whether schooling by their prey affects the hunting behaviour of cephalopod and fish predators. *Journal of Zoology*, **172**, 549 – 569.

NISBET, I.C.T. (1973). Courtship feeding, egg size and breeding success in Common Terns. *Nature*, **241**, 141 – 142.

PACKER, C. (1977). Reciprocal altruism in olive baboons. *Nature*, **265**, 441 – 443.

PARKER, G.A. (1978). Searching for mates. In J.R. KREBS and N.B. DAVIES (Eds.), *Behavioural Ecology*. Oxford: Blackwell.

PARKER, G.A. and MACNAIR, M.R. (1978). Models of parent-offspring conflict. I. Monogamy. *Animal Behaviour*, **26**, 92 – 110.

PITCHER, T. (1973). The three dimensional structure of schools in the minnow, *Phoxinus phoxinus*. *Animal Behaviour*, **21**, 263 – 286.

PITCHER, T. (1979). Sensory information and the organization of behaviour in a shoaling cyprinid fish. *Animal Behaviour*, **27**, 126 – 149.

SCHALLER, G.B. (1972). *The Serenghetti Lion*. Chicago: University of Chicago Press.

SCUDO, F.M. and GHESELIN, M.T. (1975). Familial selection and the evolution of social behaviour. *Journal of Genetics*, **62**, 1 – 31.

SEGHERS, B.H. (1974). Schooling behaviour in guppies: an evolutionary response to predation. *Evolution*, **28**, 486 – 489.

SHERMAN, P.W. (1977). Nepotism and the evolution of alarm calls. *Science*, **197**, 1246 – 1253.

SIBLY, R.M. and MCFARLAND, D.J. (1976). On the fitness of behavioural sequences. *American Naturalist*, **110**, 601 – 617.

SYREN, R.M. and LUYKX, P. (1977). Permanent segmental interchange complex in the termite *Incisitermes schwarzi*. *Nature*, **266**, 167 – 168.

TRIVERS, R.L. (1971). The evolution of reciprocal ultruism. *Quarterly Review of Biology*, **46**, 35 – 57.

TRIVERS, R.L. (1972). Parental investment and sexual selection. In B. CAMPBELL (Ed.), *Sexual selection and the Descent of Man*. Chicago: Aldine. Pp. 136 – 179.

TRIVERS, R.L. (1974). Parent – offspring conflict. *American Zoologist*, **14**, 249 – 264.

TRIVERS, R.L. and HARE, M. (1976). Haplodiploidy and the evolution of the social insects. *Science*, **191**, 249 – 263.

VEHRENCAMP, S.L. (1978). The adaptive significance of communal nesting in the groove-billed Anis (*Crotophaga salcirostris*). *Behavioural Ecology and Sociobiology*, **4**, 1 – 19.

WADE, M.J. (1977). An experimental study of group selection. *Evolution*, **31**, 134 – 153.

WADE, M.J. (1978). A critical review of the models of group selection. *Quarterly Review of Biology*, **53**, 101 – 114.

WATTS, C.R. and STOKES, A.W. (1971). The social order of turkeys. *Scientific American*, **224**(6), 112 – 118.

WEST-EBERHARD, M.J. (1975). The evolution of altruism by kin selection. *Quarterly Review of Biology*, **50**, 1 – 33.

WILSON, D.S. (1977). Structured demes and the evolution of group-advantageous traits. *American Naturalist*, **111**, 157 – 185.

WILSON, E.O. (1971). *The Insect Societies*. Cambridge, Massachusetts: Harvard University Press.

WILSON, E.O. (1975). *Sociobiology: The New Synthesis*. Cambridge, Massachusetts: Harvard University Press.

WILSON, E.O. (1978). *On Human Nature*. Cambridge, Massachusetts: Harvard University Press.

WOLFENDEN, G.E. (1975). Florida scrub jay helpers at the nest. *Auk*, **92**, 1 – 15.

WYNNE-EDWARDS, V.C. (1962). *Animal Dispersion in Relation to Social Behaviour*. Edinburgh and London: Oliver and Boyd.

YOKOYAMA, S. and FELSENSTEIN, J. (1978). A model of kin selection for an altruistic trait considered as a quantitative character. *Proceedings of the National Academy of Science*, **75**, 420 – 425.

CHAPTER 2

Competition and Conflict in Animals

John Lazarus

2.1 Introduction

Competition is at the heart of the evolutionary process. Whenever animals have access to the same resource the potential for competition exists and those more successful in the competition are the ones favoured by natural selection. In this sense the evolution of competitive behaviour is readily understood and, not surprisingly, such behaviour is ubiquitous in the animal kingdom. When individuals cooperate or behave altruistically, on the other hand, we need to seek rather more carefully for the evolutionary forces involved (see Chapter 1 of this volume).

Although the notion of competition may conjure up a picture of animals in combat, the concept is in fact much broader than this. For example, if the early bird catches the worm then an early start to the feeding day is a simple strategy for successful competition. Again, the bird with the best designed bill can obtain prey more efficiently than others and in this respect may outcompete even the earliest bird. In both cases competition is indirect, however, in that it does not involve behavioural interaction. Direct competition, on the other hand, involves some degree of social interaction between the competitors and it is this type of interaction which is the subject of the present chapter.

The concept of a resource is obviously of central importance to a discussion of competition and for present purposes can be defined simply as something in the environment that is utilized by an animal; normally it will be utilized in order to increase biological fitness. Not all resources are the objects of direct competition (e.g. oxygen to breathe, heat from the sun) but among the most ubiquitous that are must be included food and mates; the first for survival, the second for reproduction. Space is another resource directly competed for, often as a means to the end of procuring a mate or feeding in an efficient manner.

Direct competition essentially involves an attempt to gain a resource by 'persuading' the competitor to give it up. Such persuasion may take many subtle forms in man but in other animals is generally effected by physically driving off or injuring the competitor, or threatening to do so. Direct competition therefore involves aggressive or agonistic behaviour (the latter term encompassing the spectrum of responses from attack and threat to fleeing). Aggression is seen outside the context of competition too, of course (see Johnson, 1972, Ch. 1; Hinde, 1974, Ch. 16), for example in self-defence and defence of offspring in the face of predatory attack. Conflict too is not only competitive since individuals can be said to be in conflict whenever they desire a different outcome to some interaction. Thus, males and females often conflict over their reproductive goals (see Chapter 1 and the section on 'Competition for Mates' in the present chapter) and parents conflict with their offspring over the level of investment to be made in parental care (Trivers, 1974). I am concerned here only with the conflict that arises from competition for possession of a resource.

The nature of competition in animals is best understood in an evolutionary framework and this will be the approach adopted in the following sections, where the characteristics of competitive behaviour are considered. I shall also discuss the concepts of *dominance* and *dominance hierarchy*, which describe the pattern of agonistic relationships within a group. A dominance relationship between two individuals implies that one commonly wins when they compete and the existence of such relationships raises various questions. The dominance hierarchy in turn describes the pattern formed by the set of dominance relationships within a group, and raises its own questions for consideration. I shall conclude with some comments on the implications of the concepts discussed in this chapter for an understanding of human competition.

2.2 The Nature of Competitive Behaviour

In seeking general principles to explain *why* animals behave as they do in competitive encounters we must look to the predictions of natural selection theory. The separate question of *how* individuals effect their competitive behaviour, a question of proximate mechanism, requires a rather different approach and will not be pursued here.

In the most general terms selection can be said to favour the behavioural strategy that provides the greatest increase in fitness for the individual. Since behaviour has consequences that may be both beneficial and detrimental to fitness, this statement can be more precisely formulated in terms of the greatest *net benefit* to the individual, where net benefit equals benefit minus cost, both measured in units of fitness. For example, while competing successfully for a female (a benefit) a male will be using up energy (a cost) and may be exposing itself to predation (another cost). Using this approach we would predict, for example, that an animal will invest more in an encounter when the value of the resource being fought for is high or when alternative resources are scarce.

While defining the action of natural selection on individuals in this way is a straightforward matter, predicting the outcome of the process is far more difficult since we need to understand the changes occurring over an evolutionary time scale to a whole population of individuals. In particular we need to ask, in any particular case, whether the change brought about by natural selection is likely to reach a stable end-point or to pass through a series of unresolvable cycles (see Dawkins & Krebs, 1979). Where a particular stable end-point is predicted we would expect many populations to have reached this point and can therefore seek examples from nature to test our prediction. But for a cycling outcome there is the problem of deciding where in the cycle present populations are situated.

Although it is unlikely that the evolution of competitive behaviour *necessarily* produces stable individual strategies, many stable theoretical solutions have been found to questions about the evolution of competitive conflict, as we shall see. Cyclic outcomes, on the other hand, have been predicted for conflicts, under some conditions, between parent and offspring (Parker & Macnair, 1979) and between the sexes (Parker, 1979), and, in the present context, as a possible pattern for the evolution of threat displays (Andersson, 1980).

The importance of the concept of stability for an understanding of the evolution of social behaviour has only recently been realized, this new insight coming with the theoretical work of Maynard Smith (1972, 1974; Maynard Smith & Price, 1973) on the evolution of aggressive behaviour, an insight foreshadowed, however, by Gadgil (1972) and even by Darwin (1871). Maynard Smith and Price's (1973) aim was to find an 'evolutionarily stable strategy' (ESS) for aggressive behaviour and the analytical tool they used was the theory of games, developed originally to deal with human competitive encounters (see Chapter 5). This approach allows analysis of the outcome of a behavioural strategy when that outcome depends on the strategies employed by other members of the population, as it must do for competitive and, indeed, all other types of social encounter. The approach has now been fruitfully applied to a number of questions about competition (Maynard Smith, 1979) and will provide a theoretical framework for much that follows in this section.

2.2.1 *The Conventional Nature of Animal Conflict*

The striking feature of animal conflict that Maynard Smith & Price (1973) sought to explain was its conventional, non-injurious nature. Although competing animals do sometimes inflict serious injury (Geist, 1974) they tend not to employ the weaponry they possess to its full potential. The large carnivores, for example, refrain from attacking each other in the way that they treat their prey; deer use their antlers for pushing but rarely for piercing; rattlesnakes wrestle but do not bite. In many encounters animals merely display at each other, without making physical contact (see Geist, 1978, on mammals). At first sight this is difficult to explain, since a more aggressive individual would seem to be favoured in the midst of such restraint, and it had earlier been argued that animal conflict had evolved in this way since it reduced the amount of injury that was borne by the population as a whole (Wynne-Edwards, 1962, p. 131; Huxley, 1966). However, since this explanation relies on the process of group selection, which is now understood to be at best a very weak evolutionary force (see Maynard Smith, 1976a and Chapter 1), a satisfactory solution must be sought elsewhere.

The game theory approach to the problem can be introduced by a simple example (Maynard Smith, 1976b). Imagine a populaion in which individuals employ one of two strategies in competitive encounters, 'Hawk' and 'Dove', which involve three behavioural components: display, escalate (with a consequent risk of injury) and retreat. The Hawk always escalates until it is injured or until its opponent retreats; the Dove only displays, and retreats before getting injured if its opponent escalates. We shall assume that when two Hawks meet each is equally likely to be injured or to win and that winning the resource increases the individual's fitness by a value V and injury reduces fitness by a value W (for wound). Similarly when two Doves meet they are equally likely to win, but only after a long period of display which costs them T units of fitness due to lost time and energy. We can now calculate the consequences for fitness of all types of encounter and display these in a 'payoff matrix' as in Table 2.1.

Table 2.1 The Payoff Matrix for Encounters Between Hawks and Doves

		When competing against:	
		HAWK	DOVE
Payoff to:	HAWK	$\frac{1}{2}(V-W)$	V
	DOVE	0	$\frac{1}{2}V-T$

Each cell in the matrix shows the average payoff for the encounter in question. For example, a Hawk encountering another Hawk will either win (V) or lose ($-W$) and so on average gain $\frac{1}{2}(V-W)$ from the encounter. Is either Hawk or Dove an ESS? This depends on the relative magnitude of the fitness values involved. If $W < V$ (meaning W less than V) then Hawk is an ESS, since Doves gain less against Hawks than Hawks do (i.e. $\frac{1}{2}(V-W)$ is positive and therefore greater than 0) and also gain less against each other than Hawks do (i.e. V is always greater than $\frac{1}{2}V-T$). This means that over a number of generations Doves will decrease in frequency in the population and eventually become extinct. The Dove strategy might arise again by mutation but will never spread in a population composed of Hawks. This result is intuitively obvious; it means that if a prize brings a reward that outweighs the cost of fighting for it, then it is better to fight than retreat.

What if the cost of injury outweighs the benefit of the prize ($W > V$)? Then neither strategy is stable (i.e. there is no 'pure ESS') because in a population consisting almost entirely of Hawks, Doves will spread (since $0 > \frac{1}{2}(V-W)$), and in a population of Doves, Hawks will spread ($V > \frac{1}{2}V-T$). The population structure will therefore converge towards a stable mixture of the two strategies (a 'mixed ESS') *at which the average payoffs to Hawk and Dove are equal*. Any departure from this equilibrium is, by definition, accompanied by a decrease in average payoff for the strategy increasing in frequency so that the equilibrium is soon regained by *frequency-dependent selection*. The mixed

ESS may be realized as a mixture of individuals, some always playing Hawk and the remainder Dove (a stable polymorphism); alternatively it may consist of a population of identical strategists, playing Hawk and Dove with fixed probabilities. A combination of these two alternatives is also theoretically possible.

Do mixed ESSs occur in nature? There is little critical evidence bearing on this question, largely because it required the development of ESS theory to show that the question was an interesting one in the first place. Alternative strategies are certainly seen in nature, and particularly in competition for mates (discussed in a later section). However, it is rarely known whether these alternatives are equally successful — as required for a mixed ESS — or whether one is simply a second-best strategy taken up by less able individuals in the face of superior competitors.

Particularly clear evidence for the existence of a mixed ESS in nature comes from Brockmann's study of the great golden digger wasp, *Sphex ichneumoneus* (Brockmann *et al.*, 1979). Females of this species dig burrows in the summer, provision them with insects which they capture and paralyse, and lay a single egg on this food store which will later provide nourishment for the developing larva. Some burrows are abandoned before the egg is laid, however, due to invasion by ants or some other natural disaster and such nests may be used later by other wasps when they are safe again. There are therefore two nesting strategies; a female may either 'dig' her own burrow or 'enter' a burrow prepared by another female. These two strategies are not the result of a genetic polymorphism since each individual may both dig and enter at different times during the summer. This is not the whole story however. It seems that entering females cannot tell an abandoned nest from one whose occupier is away on a provisioning trip and, since these trips occupy a large proportion of the wasp's time, two females may provision the same brood chamber for some time without meeting. If they do meet, however, they fight, the loser leaves the burrow and only the winner lays an egg on the food store. For the 30 wasps in Brockmann's New Hampshire study area (though not for her Michigan wasps) there seemed to be a mixed ESS of diggers and enterers since the two strategies resulted in very similar rates of egg laying.

The Hawk – Dove game is a very simple one and was only a part of Maynard Smith & Price's (1973) original computer simulation model. Among others they introduced the strategy of 'Retaliator' which plays Dove against a Dove and Hawk against a Hawk. The payoff matrix for these three strategies is shown in Table 2.2. With the addition to the original analysis of a cost S (from possible injury) to a Dove meeting a Hawk (Dawkins & Krebs, 1978; Dawkins, 1980) there is now a pure ESS when $W > V$ and it is Retailator, since only in a population consisting mostly of Retaliators is the commonest strategy also the most successful. This conclusion accords well with reality since retaliation is a common feature of animal combat (Geist, 1974, 1978).

This game theory analysis has shown that the intuitive notion that selection acting at the individual level would necessarily favour hawkish tactics is misconceived, because it fails to account for the fact that when most of the population are competing in this injurious manner a more peaceful tactic has the

Table 2.2 The Payoff Matrix for Encounters Between Hawks, Doves and Retaliators

		When competing against: HAWK	DOVE	RETALIATOR
	HAWK	$\frac{1}{2}(V-W)$	V	$\frac{1}{2}(V-W)$
Payoff to:	DOVE	$-S$	$\frac{1}{2}V-T$	$\frac{1}{2}V-T$
	RETALIATOR	$\frac{1}{2}(V-W)$	$\frac{1}{2}V-T$	$\frac{1}{2}V-T$

advantage. Hawk is a stable strategy only when the cost of injury is outweighed by the value of the resource.

Let us be clear about the status of this kind of theoretical modelling. The arguments presented so far cannot and do not claim to provide a full explanation for the existence of conventional and ritualized competitive strategies. For one thing the models are very simple, omitting reference to a number of properties of animal competition, and I shall consider shortly whether the conclusions reached so far still hold when the models are elaborated to take account of these real-life features. More generally, though, the game theory approach is clearly an appropriate one, being a direct extension of the neo-Darwinian theory of natural selection (Dawkins, 1980). As such it merits further application and is currently being used to explore various aspects of competition as well as other types of social interaction.

So, how do the conclusions reached from these simple models stand up when the analysis is elaborated to make it more realistic? One variable that turns out to be important is the initial proportions of the different strategies in the population on which the analysis is carried out. With some initial proportions of the five strategies in Maynard Smith & Price's (1973) original analysis, for example, computer simulation shows that strategies more hawkish than Retaliator can be stable (Gale & Eaves, 1975; Maynard Smith, 1975). On the other hand if Hawks and Doves tend to encounter their own kind more often than by chance (e.g. in groups of kin), rather than encounters being random as asumed so far, then Dove-like tactics will sometimes be stable (Treisman, 1977; Grafen, 1979, Fagen, 1980). In the extreme, when Doves compete only against Doves and Hawks only against Hawks, Dove will be the pure ESS as long as $\frac{1}{2}W > T$ (see Table 2.1), a not unreasonable condition. Recently, Caryl (1980) has explored the effects of escalation between these artificial extremes of Hawk and Dove.

When two Doves meet they display at one another until one gives up. In this 'War of Attrition' it is interesting to seek the ESS for display time. There can be no pure ESS here since in a population displaying for a constant period any mutant that displays for a bit longer will win all its encounters (and if the cost of display is greater than the average gain from winning then a mutant not displaying at all will do better). There, however, a mixed ESS with a random distribution pattern of display times (Maynard Smith & Price, 1973; Maynard Smith, 1974), which makes the opponent's display time unpredictable.

This kind of mixed ESS is seen in the mating strategy of the male dung fly, *Scatophaga stercoraria*, studied by Parker (see Maynard Smith & Parker, 1976; Parker, 1978). Female dung flies are attracted to fresh cow pats to lay their eggs and males mate with them on the pats and in the surrounding grass. Males compete for mates and one element of their strategy is the length of time they stay on a pat searching for and mating with females. Their success obviously depends on what other males do; if others leave early it pays to stay longer since competition is diminished; if most males stay it pays to leave early and search elsewhere. The situation is therefore analogous to the war of attrition except that the 'game' is being played by a large number of males and not just two. Parker found that the distribution of stay times on the pat was that predicted by the war of attrition model and that, as required for a mixed ESS, all stay times resulted in an equivalent rate of fertilization. The data also fit a more complex mixed ESS that takes account of the continuous arrival of females at the pat (Parker, 1978).

The game theory analysis of competitive behaviour has been extended in a number of directions, which I now want to consider; not only for their own sake but also because they have generated new and interesting predictions about animal conflict, casting fresh light on old data and stimulating new empirical studies.

2.2.2 Asymmetries in Competitive Encounters

So far we have assumed that contestants are equal in all respects apart from their competitive strategies. This is obviously an oversimplification, there being three important ways in which contestants may differ (Parker, 1974; Maynard Smith & Parker, 1976). First, there may be an imbalance in the payoff to the winner, a hungry animal will gain more from an encounter over food than a satiated rival, for example. Second, there may be an asymmetry in fighting ability or strength, or more generally what Parker (1974) has termed 'resource holding power' (RHP). The third type of asymmetry is 'uncorrelated' with either payoff or RHP; common examples would be the distinction between the 'discoverer' of a resource and a 'latecomer' or between the 'resident' of a territory and an 'intruder'.

Although contestants will almost always differ to some extent in payoff and RHP it is instructive to look first at the effect that an uncorrelated asymmetry might have on the outcome of an encounter, since it might be influential even when these more ubiquitous asymmetries are present in addition.

The question arises whether an uncorrelated asymmetry could be used to settle encounters. Would such a conventional agreement be an ESS? Maynard Smith (1979) imagines such a strategy, 'Bourgeois', which in company with Hawks and Doves plays Hawk when it is the 'owner' or discoverer of a resource and Dove when it is the 'interloper'. The payoff matrix for this population is shown in Table 2.3. Assuming a Bourgeois to be an owner as often as it is an interloper its payoff is the average for Hawk and Dove when playing against these strategies. When pitted against another Bourgeois, however, the owner assumes the Hawk role and the interloper the Dove, so that on average a Bourgeois wins half of its encounters without ever getting injured or wasting any time displaying. This makes Bourgeois the pure ESS in such a population (for $W > V$) as can be seen from Table 2.3; only when Bourgeois is in the majority is the commonest strategy also the most successful.

Table 2.3 Payoffs for Encounters Between Hawk, Dove and Bourgeois

		When competing against: HAWK	DOVE	BOURGEOIS
	HAWK	$\frac{1}{2}(V-W)$	V	$\frac{1}{4}(V-W)+\frac{1}{2}V$
Payoff to:	DOVE	O	$\frac{1}{2}V-T$	$\frac{1}{2}(\frac{1}{2}V-T)$
	BOURGEOIS	$\frac{1}{4}(V-W)$	$\frac{1}{2}(\frac{1}{2}V-T)+\frac{1}{2}V$	$\frac{1}{2}V$

Just such a Bourgeois convention seems to be at work in the territorial behaviour of the speckled wood butterfly, *Pararge aegeria* (Davies, 1978a; see also Austad *et al.*, 1979; Davies, 1979). Male speckled woods take up mating territories in woodland sun spots and when another male enters the territory it always retreats again after a spiral display flight with the owner that lasts just a few seconds. Davies cleverly showed that this outcome was not due to the resident having a greater RHP, which might have been how it won the territory in the first place. Capturing two males, he could make either the winner simply by giving it owner status for a few moments before introducing the second as interloper. This finding also makes it unlikely that residents have a greater payoff, an asymmetry which could account for their success. He was also able to exploit the Bourgeois convention by introducing a male into an occupied territory without the resident noticing. When one male eventually noticed the other they went into a spiral flight as usual. Now, however, both males assumed the role of owner and the flight lasted 10 times longer than normal. A similar convention has also been described for captive male hamadryas baboons, *Papio hamadryas*, competing for a female (Kummer, 1971, pp. 104 – 105). Since the cue employed to settle encounters in uncorrelated asymmetries is purely conventional, the converse 'Anarchist' strategy — 'if interloper escalate, if owner retreat' — is also theoretically possible.

We might expect that an asymmetry in RHP — in size or strength for example — could also be used to settle encounters since the cue here is not merely conventional but provides information about the likely outcome of an escalated contest. A game theory analysis does indeed show that an asymmetry of RHP can provide the basis for a pure ESS with, for example, the stronger escalating and the weaker retreating (Maynard Smith & Parker, 1976). Animal combat often does seem to involve assessment of the opponent's fighting ability and it is common, for example, for larger animals to dominate smaller, as in species as diverse as sunfish, crayfish, mice and ponies (see Parker, 1974). This type of pure ESS should not be confused with a mixed ESS; although two strategies are involved they are the result of a pure *conditional* ESS. Given the condition, only one strategy is possible; for example, 'if big escalate, if small retreat'.

A cue which might be signalling a more unusual type of RHP asymmetry is stridulation by male locusts, *Locusta migratoria*. This noise is produced by males guarding females when the pair is approached by another male, and is effective in deterring attack. Parker *et al.* (1974) suggest that stridulation might signal that the opponent's approach has been detected and that its chance of successfully displacing the guarding male is thereby greatly reduced. If so, this would be a case in which the RHP asymmetry did not exist until the signal was given.

In nature a number of asymmetries will generally be operating simultaneously and Hammerstein (1981) and Parker and Rubenstein (1981) have examined theoretically the consequences of a combination of asymmetries. Consider, for example, the asymmetries of size and ownership in the fiddler crab *Uca pugilator* (Hyatt & Salmon, 1978). Male crabs resident in burrows are generally successful in warding off the attacks of 'wanderers', seeking burrows for themselves, irrespective of relative size. However, out of the 54 occasions on which a resident was observed to lose it was the larger animal only once. Both ownership and relative size therefore influence the outcome of encounters, ownership being the more powerful influence. Not surprisingly wandering males tend to pick on residents smaller than themselves. I should point out that residency in the fiddler crab cannot be assumed to be an uncorrelated asymmetry since it may have consequences for the payoff of the encounter, an issue I shall return to later.

If matters were as simple as the above argument about RHP asymmetry suggests, escalation would never occur since the weaker individual would retreat as soon as it had made an assessment of relative fighting abilities. Once again reality is more complex than our model suggests and the analysis must be extended.

In the first place there are two kinds of uncertainty to be taken into account. First, the larger or stronger animal may not *always* win the encounter, but only be more likely to do so. Use of an asymmetric cue can theoretically remain the pure ESS in spite of this type of uncertainty (Maynard Smith & Parker, 1976) but another uncertainty has a more far-reaching effect. Suppose, quite naturally, that contestants are not always able to judge correctly which of them has the greater RHP and which is consequently more likely to win if the contest is escalated. Then, not surprisingly, analysis predicts escalation to be more likely (Maynard Smith & Parker, 1976; Rand & Rand, 1976). The asymmetric cue may still be used to determine a pure ESS but now escalation will sometimes occur 'by mistake' due to an incorrect judgement.

Escalation should be most common when contestants are closely matched since predictability of the outcome of the encounter on the basis of RHP difference will then be low and it will also be more difficult for the individuals involved to assess their RHP difference accurately. This prediction is borne out by a study of the mantis shrimp, *Gonodactylus viridis*, in which individuals won contests consistently against opponents 50% to 90% of their own size but won only half the time against equal-sized rivals. Most important in the present context was the finding that outright attack was most frequent in the unpredictable encounters between like-sized animals. The outcome of encounters was probably determined in part by visual RHP assessment before the shrimps first made contact since at the outset larger animals were more likely to attack and smaller animals more likely to display or retreat (Caldwell & Dingle, 1979). North American rams of the species *Ovis dalli* also behave differently when approaching larger and smaller rivals, and if a strange ram enters a band he is most likely to interact agonistically with a ram of the same horn size class (Geist, 1966). The same phenomenon is seen also in several species of fish (Rubenstein, 1981).

Apart from the uncertainties just discussed the simple conditional strategy 'if higher RHP escalate, if lower retreat' meets with another type of problem. Since the point of RHP assessment is to judge one's chances of winning a competitive encounter *without actually fighting*, by employing a cue that is predictive of RHP, the system is vulnerable to cheating. That is, individuals would benefit by signalling a higher level of RHP than they actually possessed. Sheer size is a potentially good predictor of RHP and many agonistic displays which increase apparent size could be interpreted as just such a bluff. Dogs and other mammalian species erect their hair, for example; birds erect their feathers; fish raise their fins or gill covers.

The important question to ask here is whether such cheating is evolutionarily stable and therefore likely to be a common feature of signalling behaviour. Up to the present time this question has been analysed theoretically only for a very simple situation (Maynard Smith & Parker, 1976), but the results are intriguing. If the bluff cannot be detected then a bluffing mutant is predicted to spread through the population and is evolutionarily stable, as might be expected. But selection will then favour individuals that are able to see through the bluff and adjust their assessment mechanism accordingly. This in turn would favour ever more extreme or more subtle methods of deception and consequently ever more discriminating opponents. What is the evolutionarily stable state now? It seems that discrimination of bluff can be evolutionarily stable but that the bluff itself can also be stable. The erection of hair and feathers might therefore have arisen initially as effective bluff but now be maintained even though it fools no one.

It might be possible to investigate empirically whether a bluff is effective or transparent. If effective, individuals would be expected to escalate more cautiously against a bluffer than is good for them; if transparent, escalation should closely match the individual's chance of winning.

For an assessment cue to be successfully bluffed it must be taken at face value and rarely challenged. This point is nicely illustrated by Rohwer's (1977) experiments with Harris sparrows, *Zonotrichia querula*, which signal their fighting ability by the extent of black plumage on the throat, breast and crown. When Rohwer extended the black plumage of some individuals with dye and returned them to the wild they did not win more encounters than before, but instead were persecuted by the truly dominant birds of the flock. The failure of the dyed birds to increase their status may have been because, when challenged, their fighting prowess failed to live up to their plumage signal. Their persecution was perhaps an unnatural response to the unnatural discrepancy between appearance and behaviour. When plumage and fighting prowess were made compatible, by both dyeing and administering testosterone, the experimental birds increased their dominance status in the wild flock (Rohwer & Rohwer, 1978).

A factor militating against the evolution of bluff is individual recognition (van Rhijn & Vodegel, 1980). If the same individuals encounter one another regularly, know their neighbours as individuals, and at least occasionally penetrate any bluffed signal by escalation, then it is unlikely that bluff will be successful. The problem of bluff does not arise at all, of course, if the assessment cue is not bluffable; that is, if it is not able to develop independently of the RHP variable it is signalling. For example, a male common toad, *Bufo bufo*, competing with another male for possession of a female assesses its opponent by the depth of his croak; deeper croaks are reliably emitted by larger males and a larger male can generally beat a smaller one. If a male in possession of a female is temporarily rendered croakless he is attacked less by another male when accompanied by a tape-recorded low-pitched croak than by a high-pitched croak (Davies & Halliday, 1977, 1978). Croaking in toads would seem to be an unbluffable cue since its depth depends on the size of the vocal cords and the larynx, which are correlated with body size. However, we can still ask why small males have not developed large vocal cords, since we know in general that there is a certain amount of developmental plasticity which allows different parts of the body to develop at different rates. The answer may be that they have; that is that small males today have larger vocal cords than their small ancestors.

The roaring of male red deer, *Cervus elaphus*, may be an assessment cue that is truly unbluffable. Stags competing for hinds during the rut commonly engage in roaring 'contests' which may escalate into fights in which antlers are locked in a pushing contest (Clutton-Brock & Albon, 1979). The rate of roaring is significantly correlated with fighting ability which is more a function of body condition and agility than simply of size; old males, for example, are fully grown but are often poor fighters. Stags will increase their roaring rate in response to an increased rate from a loudspeaker and a roaring contest may be physically tiring or even exhausting for the combatants. It would then be a very difficult signal to bluff, demanding the same stamina that makes for success in fights.

We come now to the third type of asymmetry, that of payoff. Employing the cost – benefit approach introduced earlier, we can see that natural selection will favour greater investment in an encounter (in terms of fitness) the greater is the payoff of winning the resource and each individual can be thought of as possessing a 'fitness budget' (Parker, 1974) which it is willing to invest in an encounter before it withdraws. If opponents have equal RHP the one with the greater fitness budget will persist for longer, or sustain greater injury, before it is willing to withdraw. Likewise, the individual that brings the lower fitness budget to an encounter must have the higher RHP if it is to win. Whereas resource holding power represents the ability of an individual to win an encounter in terms of intrinsic, and relatively stable, properties such as strength and agility, the fitness budget is represented by the strength of the motivational tendency to fight and is expected to vary in an adaptive fashion from encounter to encounter. The two properties are unlikely to be entirely independent though since fighting tendency may affect not only persistence and willingness to escalate but also the strength and agility that are displayed in a fight.

Fitness budgets may differ between two competing individuals for a variety of reasons. A food resource will provide a greater payoff for a hungry than for a satiated animal, for example, so that the former will be expected to fight more persistently for it. Parental geese accompanying their offspring consistently dominate pairs without young (Boyd, 1953; Lazarus & Inglis, 1978) and, since winning an encounter assures uninterrupted feeding, this probably reflects a greater payoff for parents through an increase in fitness to their young.

Payoff asymmetries may also occur between the holder of a resource and an intruder in terms of the additional investment which must be made before the resource can be exploited (Parker, 1974). Consider territorial behaviour, for example. Before an intruder can exploit the food resources of a territory it may need to invest time in learning where the food sites are; if there is a female to be won she may need to be courted before she is willing to mate. If the attacker succeeds in taking over the territory he therefore has to invest more than the holder from that point on before he can benefit from it and this investment must be subtracted from the value of the resource to obtain its true (net) value to each individual. Such cases, in which the holder has the greater fitness budget, are common and may explain the fact that territorial owners commonly beat intruders with a minimum of display. Alternatively, or additionally, residency might be acting here as an uncorrelated asymmetry.

It would clearly benefit an individual to be able to assess its oppenent's fitness budget — just as it would for RHP assessment — but would it benefit an individual to *give* this information? For the sort of holder/intruder imbalances I have just been discussing it would not be necessary for individuals to 'calculate' their own and their opponent's budget (assuming this was possible) and withdraw or persist on the basis of which was the greater. Natural selection would favour holders which, more simply, persisted *longer* than their intruders and intruders which withdrew while the holder was still displaying; a stable situation. More generally though, when there is no such simple cue to relative fitness budgets, would natural selection favour an individual that gave some clue to its fitness budget or, in motivational terms, its persistence and willingness to escalate? Would such behaviour be evolutionarily stable?

These questions have been analysed by Maynard Smith (1974) and raise similar problems to the mutual assessment of RHP. Suppose contestants were to indicate their intended degree of persistence by the form or intensity of their agonistic display. We would then expect the individual signalling the lower persistence to withdraw immediately. Such a convention would be vulnerable to cheating, however, since selection would favour the signalling of maximum persistence in every encounter, and when all individuals were signalling in this fashion no information would be transmitted by the display at all. Even if we suppose that intentions cannot be bluffed in this way Maynard Smith argues (for symmetric contests) that the stable state is still for individuals to display in a constant fashion and not give away their intentions.

This conclusion is currently causing ethologists some concern since it seems to conflict with the fact that agonistic displays, particularly in birds and mammals, contain a variety of signals which reflect the motivational balance of fear and aggression in the performer. Such signals also allow the observer to predict the likelihood of attack or withdrawal in the signaller and the same information is potentially available to an opponent. The agonistic displays of the blue tit, *Parus caeruleus*, for example, involve crest raising, body position, feather fluffling, wing raising, beak movements and tail fanning (Stokes, 1962). How can such behaviour be reconciled with the theoretical prediction of the concealment of aggressive intentions?

2.2.3 The Information Content of Aggressive Displays

The traditional ethological view of the evolution of displays was that selection favours efficient information transfer, for the benefit of both actor and reactor (see Dawkins & Krebs, 1978). The existence of a display repertoire was compatible with this view but the view itself had mistaken the point at which natural selection acts. It acts not on actor and reactor together, as a cooperative unit, nor on the signal itself as a disembodied entity, but on the signalling individual. In line with the general account already given, natural selection can be seen to favour signalling behaviour that benefits the signaller (Dawkins & Krebs, 1978). At the same time, the consequence of the signal for the reactor will influence the evolutionary stability of the signaller's behaviour.

Some resolution of the predicted concealment of intentions with the existence of display repertoires is achieved when one looks in detail at the information content of agonistic displays. Caryl (1979) has recently reassessed and reanalysed some of the most relevant data, from four bird species, and concludes that very little information about attacking intentions are in fact contained in the displays. Even when different display components are combined there is a maximum probability of only about one-half that any display combination will be followed by an attack. Correspondingly, the display most predictive of attack in the actor had no effect on the behaviour of the rival (in terms of attacking, escaping or staying) in three species out of four (although results of a more recent study (Bossema & Burgler, 1980) are in line with those for the fourth, odd, species). While these results provide some support for the theoretical prediction it should be remembered that the prediction concerned *symmetric* contests (Maynard Smith, 1974). Where contestants differ in RHP, and particularly where there is individual recognition, van Rhijn & Vodegel (1980) argue — with support from computer simulations — that threat by the stronger animal, signalling unwillingness to give up the resource, can be a stable strategy. This would not explain the existence of display *repertoires*, of course, a point to which I shall return.

Caryl's analysis of displays predictive of escape (about which game theory models make no clear prediction) presents rather a different picture. The maximum probability that a combination of displays would be followed by escape in the actor was between 0.80 (i.e. 8 occasions out of 10) and 0.94 for three species. Furthermore the degree to which a display predicted escape in the actor was a consistently better predictor of the opponent's response than was the degree to which a display predicted attack in the actor. While there are some problems with this kind of evidence (Caryl, 1979; Bossema & Burgler, 1980; van Rhijn, 1980), one current challenge is to understand why an individual should signal to an opponent that it is about to flee. One widely held view has been that signalling that one is about to flee reduces the probability of being attacked (e.g. Smith, 1977, p. 269; Maynard Smith, 1979). However, although some submissive signals have this effect (e.g. Manning, 1979, p. 98), Caryl's analysis does not support this idea for escape signals since in two species out of four a bird exhibiting the display most reliably signalling its escape was as likely to be attacked as a bird not so displaying, and in the other two species the former was far *more* likely to be attacked. In the light of these results I offer the speculation that the purpose of a fleeing display might be for an individual reaching the end of its fitness budget to 'provoke' the opponent into showing its escalation intentions. As long as being attacked is not too costly this may be a better strategy than simply fleeing, since if the opponent fails to attack the encounter may not yet be lost. The explanation of escape signals clearly remains a challenge; there is a need for further theoretical work here and for more data of the sort discussed by Caryl.

Another unanswered question is this: if displays predictive of attack have in fact only low predictive power, and don't always influence the opponent, why are there often a number of such displays in a species' repertoire? In contrast to Maynard Smith's (1974) contention that bluffing would not be favoured by natural selection, Andersson (1980) argues that a variety of threat displays is to be expected if they are used as bluff. In line with the traditional view of the origin of threat signals from intention movements of attack he proposes that such signals are successful initially as 'honest' predictors of attack. However, they are soon exploited by cheaters who use them as bluff. When the deception associated with one threat signal is uncovered a second, still honest, signal may then become more efficient at deterring opponents but like the first will eventually be taken up by cheaters. In this way a succession of threat signals may arise. Andersson's new insight is that these signals could all be maintained in the population by frequency-dependent selection since each display becomes less efficient as a deterrent (and is therefore selected against) as it becomes more frequently used as bluff and is consequently ignored. A signal which had increased in frequency as bluff and later decreased as it came to be ignored would then become more reliable again (i.e. coupled more frequently with subsequent attack), and open once again to exploitation by cheaters. Whether the resulting equilibrium of displays would be stable or cycling is at present an open question.

A second approach to the problem is provided by Rand and Rand (1976) who argue from the results of their iguana study that, where displaying is costly, low cost displays will be favoured but escalation to higher cost signals may be necessary to win the contest.

Thirdly, distinguishing between signals on the basis of their predictability of attack may sometimes be a red herring. As Caryl (1979) points out, displays predictive of attack are also predictive, to a different degree, of escape (after all, the actor must either attack, escape or stay put after displaying) and it may be escape that is being signalled. This answer at least has the merit of leaving only one unsolved problem: the evolution of escape signals!

2.3 Competition for Mates

I have dealt at some length with evolutionary predictions about competitive behaviour, and with the relevant evidence, since work in this area is progressing particularly rapidly and has already radically altered the way in which we view the agonistic behaviour of animals. I want now to consider in more detail competition for two types of resource: mates and space. The special interest of these resources is that competition for them involves long-term strategies and raises functional issues that don't apply to competition over, say, a single food item. A full consideration of mating strategies and territorial behaviour would take us outside the scope of this chapter but fuller accounts of these topics can be found in the articles by Halliday (1978), Rubenstein (1980) and Davies (1978b).

Perhaps the first question to ask about mate competition is why it should occur at all. In populations with a roughly equal number of mature males and females why is monogamy not the rule, with each individual having a single mate? The answer is that the number of offspring that natural selection favours an individual to produce is generally greater for males than for females, since the male generally invests less in each of his offspring than does his mate (see Trivers, 1972, for a fuller account of this argument). To produce this greater number of offspring the male must obviously take more mates than the female, and where the sex ratio is roughly equal this inevitably leads to competition between males for access to females. Monogamy tends to occur, as in most birds (Lack, 1968), where parental investment by the two sexes is more equitable.

2.3.1 Male Mating Strategies

Competition between males for females is usually characterized by high levels of investment in terms of time and energy, and often risk of injury and predation, as well as structural investment in various types of weaponry. Natural selection favours such high investment since the potential prize is so great. Whereas losing a fight over a food item will generally have only a negligible effect on survival to the next breeding period, loss of a fight for access to a female strikes directly at reproductive success and therefore at fitness.

The great variety of competitive mating strategies used by males can be classified in terms of just a few important variables (Emlen & Oring, 1977). In the first place females may be acquired by males either simultaneously or sequentially. In simultaneous polygyny males either defend females directly, as in the harem-holding elephant seal, *Mirounga angustirostris* (Le Boeuf, 1974), and gelada baboon, *Theropitchecus gelada* (Dunbar & Dunbar, 1975), or compete for resources which females require for reproduction, as in damsel flies of the genus *Calopteryx* in which males defend oviposition sites (Waage, 1973). Where it is uneconomic for males to attempt to maintain sole access to a group of females they either compete anew for each female, as in the solitary bee *Centris pallida* (Alcock *et al.*, 1977), for example, or compete in advance of female availability for a dominance status that will later go unchallenged by subordinate males, as occurs in many multi-male primate societies. In a variant of this latter strategy males hold small territories on a communal display ground or 'lek' and females come to the area purely to mate. Male ruffs, *Philomachus pugnax* (van Rhijn, 1973), and Uganda kob antelopes, *Adenota kob* (Leuthold, 1966; Buechner & Roth, 1974), compete in this manner.

The female often plays a passive role in mate choice, simply accepting the advances of the male that wins the competition; in this way she is likely to produce sons that are similarly successful. In other contexts — on the lek for example — females make an active choice among the available males and in simultaneous resource defence polygyny there is evidence that females select the males with the best resources (see review by Davies, 1978b).

Alongside these major types of male strategy there coexists, in some species, an alternative strategy, which can be characterized as either 'sneak' or 'satellite' (Rubenstein, 1980). The sneaky male attempts to steal a female from a harem for long enough to copulate with her, often while the harem owner is otherwise occupied. This tactic is observed in horses (Rubenstein, 1980) and in red deer (Clutton-Brock *et al.*, 1979), for example. The satellite male has a longer-term relationship with a male employing the major strategy. In many anuran amphibians the males compete for calling stations, sites from which they call to attract females (e.g. Perrill *et al.*, 1978). However, a calling male may share his station with a silent satellite male who attempts to intercept females as they approach the caller. A satellite gelada baboon may accompany a harem for many months, associating with the immature females of the group and eventually leading them away to form a new harem. Less subtly, a male gelada may attempt to win the whole harem by attack its owner (Dunbar & Dunbar, 1975).

The coexistence of two qualitatively different male strategies in a population raises an interesting evolutionary question: do such strategies represent equally successful alternatives maintained at a mixed ESS by frequency-dependent selection, or is one of them an inferior 'best of a bad job' strategy taken up in the face of superior rivals? In the latter case the two strategies could represent a pure conditional ESS, like the 'if big escalate, if small retreat' case considered earlier. To answer this question we need to know the fertilization rates achieved by the two strategies. For a mixed ESS, involving males genetically constrained to a single strategy, the *lifetime* reproductive success for the two strategies must be equal; it will rarely be sufficient to measure success per season since although the major strategy often wins out on this measure it is probably more costly to maintain, resulting in a lowered reproductive success in the future. Where males switch readily between two strategies it becomes more useful to examine the fertilization rate of each as a measure of success (although the strategy costs may still differ). Calling and satellite green tree frogs, *Hyla cinerea*, fit this pattern and do have similar mating success (Perrill *et al.*, 1978), so that frequency-dependent selection could be at work here, maintaining the two strategies in coexistence.

Although the evidence is often inconclusive, many cases probably fit into the 'best of a bad job' category. Young males, which are weaker and less experienced than their elders, must often adopt a second-best strategy and be content with lower reproductive success until they mature. Young male red deer (Clutton-Brock *et al.*, 1979) and elephant seals (Le Boeuf, 1974) are examples here.

Rubenstein (1980) has reviewed these and other cases and has also developed a theoretical model to examine the conditions favouring the existence of a mixed ESS of mating strategies. For a complete understanding of the evolution of male strategies, one must also take account of the female; the stable evolutionary state involves not only stability among male strategies and among female strategies but also a stable mix of the two, often conflicting, sets of strategies. Maynard Smith (1977) has outlined a general theoretical approach to this complex problem but a full analysis has not yet been attempted.

2.3.2 Sperm Competition

Success in competition for a female is only assured when her ova are fertilized and males have evolved many adaptations to ensure that it is their sperm, and not that of another male, that wins this competition. Such adaptations trade off to differing degrees the opposing advantages of promiscuity and fidelity. The promiscuous male inseminates many females but since he stays with them for only a short time fertilization is often achieved by an earlier or a later competitor. The faithful male, on the other hand, has access to fewer females but in keeping off competitors is assured of a higher certainty of paternity.

In insects the male's sperm remains viable within the female's body for months or even years so that 'sperm competition' commonly occurs, within the female, between sperm from two or more males (Parker, 1970). This has resulted in the strategy, adopted by males mating with previously inseminated females, of displacing the earlier sperm in favour of their own. It has also led to the evolution of various adaptations whereby males reduce subsequent competition from the sperm of another male (Parker, 1970). One such adaptation is the production of a mating plug, a male secretion which coagulates within the female's genital tract and prevents further insemination, as well as sperm leakage. This adaptation (seen also in bats and rodents) allows the male to leave the female in search of new mates, in contrast to the other major class of competitive adaptations which involves some type of female guarding after copulation. Parker (1971) has shown for the dung fly that the advantage of post-copulatory guarding in reducing sperm competition far outweighs the cost in terms of lost inseminations.

In mammals, and other animals in which sperm remains viable within the female for a matter of days rather than months, sperm competition is a much weaker evolutionary force. However, males now have the problem of the uncertainty of whether their short-lived sperm have been successful in fertilization. Such uncertainty favours the evolution of repeated mating and responsiveness to signs of female fertility, such as oestrus in mammals. However, female guarding to reduce sperm competition is less important than in insects, unless the male provides parental care for his offspring. Assurance of paternity then gains additional importance and favours guarding of the female both before and after copulation.

Competition for a female is not necessarily lost even when another male has fertilized her. For example, the odour of male mice can induce abortion in females (Bruce, 1967), which then come into oestrus again. Intervening at an even later stage, male lions, *Panthera leo* (Bertram, 1975), and langurs (an Asian primate), *Presbytis entellus* (Hrdy, 1974), will often kill the infants of a troop that they take over from other males. This brings unreceptive females back into oestrus and gives the male's future offspring better survival prospects than if older offspring were also present in the group.

2.4 Competition for Space: Territoriality

Up to now I have been concerned largely with competition for a tangible resource of some kind. Territoriality, however, concerns competition for a fixed space, and although a resource may be involved its relationship to the space that contains it may take a number of forms; in two different cases that I shall consider there is no resource at all.

2.4.1 Territories and Resources

The two commonest resources contained in a territory are food and mates.

When food is the resource it is essentially the food that is being defended rather than the space *per se* and the same holds for male mating territories containing resources such as nests or oviposition sites. When males defend resources to be used by their mates they are often also competing in an indirect way for those mates themselves. Mating territories on a lek, however, contain no tangible resource; here males are competing indirectly for mates by competing directly for particular areas of ground on which females will preferentially converge; usually the central territories on the lek (Davies, 1978b).

2.4.2 *Conditions Favouring Territoriality*

I have referred to a number of these cases earlier in the chapter but the more general question I want to consider briefly here is this: Why do some species, under some conditions, defend a fixed space while others either move about in search of resources or share them amicably, without competition? The crucial concept here, introduced by Brown (1964), is that of 'economic defendability'. This concept is an early example of cost–benefit reasoning in ethology and says simply that territoriality involves both benefits and costs and should only be expected where the net benefit is positive (or, more strictly, where the net benefit is greater than that of alternative available strategies). Thus, we would be surprised to find a gannet, *Sula bassana*, attempting to defend acres of sea in the hope of monopolizing a school of fish but perhaps not surprised to see a pied wagtail, *Motacilla alba*, defending a stretch of river where it regularly catches insects (Davies, 1976). These examples illustrate the conditions under which territoriality is most likely to be adaptive: the resource should be plentiful, and also predictable in time and space, and defence costs should be small. Territory size will be determined by the optimal trade-off between defence costs and resource quantity.

Territoriality necessarily results in a spacing out of individuals and consequently may provide a benefit that has nothing to do with resources at all. Once a predator has located the first of a population of territorial individuals others will be at greater risk the closer they are together, and particularly so if the predator concentrates its search in the vicinity of its last find, as has been observed. This phenomenon has been demonstrated experimentally (Tinbergen *et al.*, 1967; Croze, 1970) and it has also been found for some territorial birds that nest predation decreases at great inter-nest distances (Murton, 1958; Horn, 1968; Krebs, 1971).

2.4.3. *Territorial Advertisement and Defence*

I have discussed the principles governing the evolution of territorial and other forms of defence and we have seen that conventional display can be a stable means of effecting such defence. It may often be sufficient simply to 'advertise' that a piece of ground is occupied, so that the uncorrelated asymmetry of ownership prevents trespass. Experiments show that bird song can function in this way: when great tits, *Parus major*, were removed from their territories and replaced by loudspeakers, those territories in which the loudspeakers broadcast recorded song remained uninvaded for longer than those in which the loudspeakers played a control sound (Krebs, 1977a). Scent marking by mammals sometimes functions in the same manner and is an efficient means of continuous defence, having the added advantage of advertising the territory while concealing the position of the resident from predators.

Where territorial encounters are decided not by the uncorrelated asymmetry of residence but by payoff or RHP asymmetries, advertisement will often be insufficient to deter intruders and must be replaced by defence. Mere advertisement would not require the great richness and variety of many bird songs, for example, and Dawkins and Krebs (1978), drawing on the analogy of human oratory, propose persuasion as a possible function of song elaboration. More specifically Krebs (1977b) has argued, with evidence (Krebs *et al.*, 1978; see also Yasukawa 1981), that a repertoire of songs might be employed in order to deceive newcomers into overestimating the density of residents in an area and therefore underestimating its suitability as a place in which to settle.

Where territoriality functions *only* to reduce predation by spacing out we would expect to see not defence but rather the minimal amount of advertisement necessary to signal the resident's presence. The reason is that spacing out is here of mutual benefit to all territory holders, there is no resource to compete for and in no functional sense is there a boundary to be defended. However, it would be difficult to test this prediction since territories are generally multifunctional. Even in gull colonies, for example, in which the territories contain no resources, other gulls pose the very real threat of accidentally damaging the eggs or even deliberately taking them for food (Tinbergen, 1953).

2.5 Dominance and Hierarchy

When two individuals compete repeatedly a number of new questions arise. For example, what is the pattern of wins and losses between them and what determines this pattern? What consequences does this relationship have for other aspects of their lives? What is the pattern of all such dyadic relationships within a population, how is this pattern maintained and what are its consequences for the social structure of the group?

2.5.1 Determinants of Dominance

When one individual repeatedly beats another the first is said to be *dominant* and the second *subordinate*. We have already seen that differences in RHP and payoff, as well as uncorrelated differences such as residency, commonly determine the outcome of encounters. The more stable such a difference is, therefore, the more likely it is that one individual will consistently dominate the other. A difference in RHP is an obvious candidate here: larger animals consistently dominate smaller ones; mature males dominate juveniles; males often dominate females.

Such asymmetries produce dominance relationships by influencing the outcome of each encounter independently. But with repeated encounters animals also have the opportunity of modifying their behaviour in the light of past experience. To the extent that individuals cannot innately recognize RHP or intention cues they must rely on their earliest encounters to learn these signals; learning which can usefully be applied in all future encounters. Beyond this, however, animals might learn the individual identity of competitors and assess their chances of winning an encounter on the basis of past experience with the same individual. Whether animals actually do this is difficult to determine although it probably occurs in many mammalian societies which are small in size and of constant membership. Barnard and Burk (1979) make the point that as far as competitor assessment is concerned, individual recognition is not qualitatively different from anonymous assessment of fighting ability since both involve recognition of some set of cues by which the ability of the opponent is assessed.

A further way in which past experience can increase the stability of dominance relationships is by self-assessment of fighting ability as a result of the outcome of previous encounters. An individual that had won encounters consistently in the past would be behaving adaptively if it fought more persistently in the future. This process would cause individuals to diverge increasingly in competitive strategy, winners becoming more likely to win and losers less so, and there is evidence for this 'confidence effect' in mice, rats (Scott & Fredericson, 1951), iguanas, *Iguana iguana* (Rand & Rand, 1976), and field crickets *Teleogryllus oceanicus* (Burk, 1979).

2.5.2 The Dominance Hierarchy

When the dominance relationships within a social group are examined collectively the pattern of these relationships can be defined. This pattern may take many forms, one extreme of which is the *linear hierarchy* in which individual A dominates all others, B dominates all except A, C dominates all except A and B and so on to the individual lowest in the hierarchy who is dominated by all others in the group (Fig. 2.1). In its stronger form 'dominates' here means 'beats every time', in its weaker form 'beats more than half the time'. Fig. 2.1 also shows some patterns of dominance relationships which are not linear hierarchies; in practice the term 'hierarchy' is used rather broadly to refer to any such pattern, even though it may depart considerably from linearity.

Just as RHP differences are important determinants of dominance relationships so absolute RHP is a very common correlate of an individual's position in the hierarchy. For example, larger individuals are ranked higher in fish of the genus *Xiphophorus* (Wechkin, 1975) and comb size (itself determined by testosterone levels) correlates with rank in domestic hens (Collias, 1943).

Linear hierarchy

A → B → C → D → E → F

Linear hierarchy with two reversals

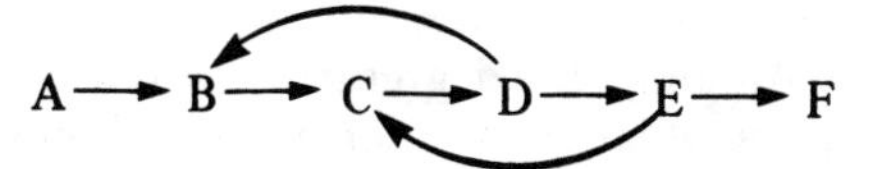

Weakly hierarchical organization

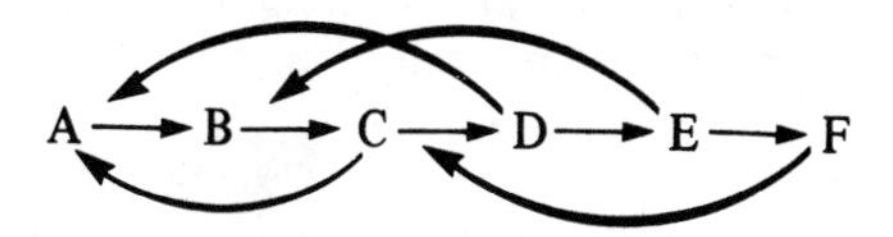

Fig. 2.1 Patterns of dominance relationships within a group. The arrow means 'dominates'. Unless otherwise indicated an individual dominates all those to its right.

Linear or near-linear hierarchies (with dominance used in the stronger sense) have in fact been commonly found in both captive and wild populations (e.g. Sabine, 1949; Marler, 1955), ever since the pioneering studies of Schjelderup-Ebbe (1922, 1935) on hens. The formation and maintenance of such a regular pattern of relationships has interested ethologists for some 60 years, but is still not fully understood.

2.5.3 How is a Linear Hierarchy Produced?

It should be remembered that a hierarchy is a group concept, one which organizes the information about dyadic interactions. What the individuals in the group *experience* is simply a series of interactions; they are unlikely to have a concept of the hierarchy itself (although individuals in some mammalian groups may have a knowledge of the dominance relationships between other pairs). How then might such a precise organization as a linear hierarchy arise?

Differential fighting ability and the use of associated cues will tend to produce a weak hierarchy but it requires an unrealistically high correlation between these intrinsic qualities of individuals and position in the hierarchy to produce a linear or near-linear ranking (Chase, 1974; Fagen, 1977; Wade, 1978). Remembering the uncertainties involved in competitive encounters (p. 34) it is not surprising that such correlations usually fall below the required level.

Additional processes must therefore be invoked to explain the formation of linear hierarchies. Although there is little firm evidence on the matter there would seem to be several possibilities. First, animals may be using RHP cues that are too subtle for the ethologist to measure. Similarly they may be using a *combination* of characters that, taken together, correlate highly with rank in the hierarchy (Collias, 1943); in the extreme each competitor may be distinguished individually by all others. These processes, together with the confidence effect, would be expected to increase the stability and linearity of the hierarchy over time, a trend that is commonly observed.

Although the degree of hierarchy stability varies a good deal from species to species it is common for the central positions to be less stable than those at the top and bottom (e.g. Butterfield & Crook, 1968, on the weaverbird *Quelea quelea*). The simplest explanation of this finding is that individuals differ less from their companions in fighting ability, on average, the closer they are to the centre of the hierarchy.

2.5.4 Correlates and Consequences of Dominance

Dominance status is only one facet of a social relationship, but one that influences and is influenced by many other aspects of social behaviour. This is particularly true of the primates, which form long-term stable groups and lead a complex social life. There is now a large primate literature reporting correlations – some high, some low – between various measures of dominance and between these measures and others such as grooming, proximity and gestures of fear and submission (see Hinde, 1974, Ch. 22; Richards, 1974 on primates; and Syme, 1974 on other species). Dominance rank in primates can itself be dependent on a social relationship, as in the cases of alliance between adults (Bernstein, 1976; Dunbar, 1980) and the 'dependent rank' of a young animal, which is predictable from its mother's rank (Hinde, 1974, Ch. 22). Of particular interest is the observation that high ranking individuals may threaten others outside the context of resource competition, presumably in order to reinforce the dominance relationship so as to facilitate success in future competitive interactions (e.g. Rowell, 1974; Deag, 1977).

Dominance status also has consequences for the maintenance of the social group. Particularly in times of food shortage subordinate individuals may benefit by leaving the group and seeking alternative feeding sites at which competition is less severe (Gauthreaux, 1978), although this benefit may have to be set against the lost advantages of group living (Rubenstein, 1978). Further, Gurney and Nisbet (1979) predict that the existence of a hierarchy will increase the stability of the size of the population.

From an evolutionary point of view it is interesting to examine the possibility that a high dominance status confers greater fitness. The relationship between male dominance and sexual access to females has often been examined in primates, some studies finding high positive correlations between the two measures and some not (Bernstein, 1976; Packer, 1979). In gelada baboons higher ranking females have more offspring and this is probably due to their harassment of more subordinate oestrus females (Dunbar, 1980). We should not be surprised that dominance rank in one context does not always predict rank in another, reproductive, context. Copulation frequency and other measures of sexual behaviour will be partly determined by female choice (Bernstein, 1976) and sneaky male strategies may increase the mating success of subordinate males. Further, a difference in RHP between two individuals sufficient to settle encounters conventionally over, say, food items or resting places may be inadequate for the higher prize of access to an oestrous female. In any case a measure such as copulation frequency during some short time period may be a poor indicator of lifetime reproductive success, or even of fertilization rate during the same period (Deag, 1977).

The relationship between dominance rank and fitness has also been examined in bird populations, and here winter survival has been found to be higher in the more dominant individuals of populations of juncos, *Junco hyemalis* (Fretwell, 1969), and silvereyes, *Zosterops lateralis* (Kikkawa, 1980). The process mediating this effect is likely to be success in encounters over food.

2.5.5 Do Hierarchies Have a Function?

It has often been suggested that the function of the dominance hierarchy is to reduce aggression (e.g. Huxley, 1966; Lorenz, 1966, p. 35) and Wynne-Edwards (1962, p. 139) proposed that its function was to channel resources to the fittest individuals, at the same time helping to match population size to the available resources.

The common error of these proposals is to treat the hierarchy as a unit of functional significance. Once we remember that natural selection acts on genes, via individual phenotypes, we can see that the question 'What is the function of a hierarchy?' is in fact misguided; it is not a sensible question to ask. Hierarchy formation is often *accompanied* by a reduction in overt aggression (as dominance relationships become established) and often has the *consequences* discussed by Wynne-Edwards, but neither of these can be thought of as functions. The hierarchy itself has no function since it represents a pattern of dyadic relationships, each one of which is the outcome of individual strategies and decisions. In order to understand these strategies and decisions, and ultimately the formation of hierarchies, we must return to the questions with which this chapter began. Under what circumstances will natural selection favour escalation? When will it favour withdrawal? And most important, is there a *stable* combination of such strategies in the population?

2.6 Implications for Human Competition

If the road of extrapolation from animals to man is paved with good intentions it is also littered with false constructions and muddled thinking. I shall do no more here than point to some of the more obvious pitfalls and indicate the potential application of one concept — stability — discussed in the present chapter. These issues are discussed further by Mackie, from a philosophical standpoint, in Chapter 10 of this book, and commented on further in Chapter 11.

Perhaps the greatest source of error has been confusion between different types of enquiry. Questions concerning eliciting stimuli, physiological mechanisms, development and function must be kept distinct; a similarity between man and other species along one of these dimensions does not necessarily imply similarity along another. For example, two species may share the same agonistic physiological mechanism but their aggressive responses may be elicited differently, develop differently and may have evolved under different selection pressures. In addition, there is the question of *which* species man is to be compared with. For problems of mechanism and development, which I have not dealt with here, extrapolations from other species to ourselves have been evaluated by Hinde (1972, 1974), Johnson (1972) and Montagu (1976).

Turning to functional and evolutionary issues, the major concepts discussed in this chapter should be applicable to aspects of human competitive behaviour that have arisen and are maintained by natural selection. The problem is, of course, to distinguish such aspects from others which are remote from selective forces, a problem for human behaviour in general which is currently taxing both anthropologists and sociobiologists (e.g. Gregory *et al.*, 1978; Chagnon & Irons, 1979; Barlow & Silverberg 1980; Crook, 1980; and Huntingford, Chapter 1 in this volume).

For those aspects of human competitive behaviour which have no obvious consequences for fitness (e.g. recreational game playing) the evolutionary concepts of this chapter may not apply. In the first place, the costs and benefits of action will not be measurable on the common scale of fitness and the most valid scale may be one based on a subjective assessment of penalties and values. In addition it may be difficult to define the limits of the competitive population for which stability conditions might be sought. Nevertheless it is still important to ask whether human competitive strategies in a particular context form a stable or an unstable set. Indeed, the concept of stability may provide one of the strongest continuities between our own competitive behaviour and that of other species.

Acknowledgement

I am grateful to Chris Barnard, Peter Caryl, Ian Inglis, Tom Jennings and Rebecca Torrance who read this chapter and provided valuable suggestions for its improvement.

References

ALCOCK, J., JONES, C.E. and BUCHMANN, S.L. (1977). Male mating strategies in the bee *Centris pallida* Fox (Anthophoridae : Hymenoptera). *American Naturalist*, **111**, 145 – 155.

ANDERSSON, M. (1980). Why are there so many threat displays? *Journal of Theoretical*

Biology, **86**, 773 – 781.

AUSTAD, S.N., JONES, W.T. and WASER, P.M. (1979). Territorial defence in speckled wood butterflies: Why does the resident always win? *Animal Behaviour*, **27**, 960 – 961.

BARLOW, G.W. and SILVERBERG, J. (Eds.) (1980). *Sociobiology : Beyond Nature/Nurture? Reports, Definitions and Debate*. AAAS Selected Symposium 35. Boulder, Colorado: Westview Press.

BARNARD, C.J. and BURK, T. (1979). Dominance hierarchies and the evolution of 'individual recognition'. *Journal of Theoretical Biology*, **81**, 65 – 73.

BERNSTEIN, I.S. (1976). Dominance, aggression and reproduction in primate societies. *Journal of Theoretical Biology*, **60**, 459 – 472.

BERTRAM, B.C.R. (1975). Social factors influencing reproduction in wild lions. *Journal of Zoology, London*, **177**, 463 – 482.

BOSSEMA, I. and BURGLER, R.R. (1980). Communication during monocular and binocular looking in European jays (*Garrulus g. glandarius*). *Behaviour*, **74**, 274 – 283.

BOYD, H. (1953). On encounters between wild white-fronted geese in winter flocks. *Behaviour*, **5**, 85 – 129.

BROCKMANN, H.J., GRAFEN, A. and DAWKINS, R. (1979). Evolutionarily stable nesting strategy in a digger wasp. *Journal of Theoretical Biology*, **77**, 473 – 496.

BROWN, J.L. (1964). The evolution of diversity in avian territorial systems. *Wilson Bulletin*, **76**, 160 – 169.

BRUCE, H.M. (1967). Effects of olfactory stimuli on reproduction in mammals. In G.E.W. WOLSTENHOLME and M. O'CONNOR (Eds.), *Effects of External Stimuli on Reproduction*. London: Churchill.

BUECHNER, H.K. and ROTH, H.D. (1974). The lek system in Uganda kob antelope. *American Zoologist*, **14**, 145 – 162.

BURK, T.E. (1979). Unpublished D. Phil. Thesis. University of Oxford.

BUTTERFIELD, P.A. and CROOK, J.H. (1968). The annual cycle of nest building and agonistic behaviour in captive *Quelea quelea* with reference to endocrine factors. *Animal Behaviour*, **16**, 308 – 317.

CALDWELL, R.L. and DINGLE, J. (1979). The influence of size differential on agonistic encounters in the mantis shrimp, *Gonodactylus viridis*. *Behaviour*. **69**, 255 – 264.

CARYL, P.G. (1979). Communication by agonistic displays: What can games theory contribute to ethology? *Behaviour*, **68**, 136 – 169.

CARYL, P.G. (1980). Escalated fighting and the war of nerves: games theory and animal combat. In P.P.G. BATESON and P.H. KLOPFER (Eds.), *Perspectives in Ethology, Volume 4, Advantages of Diversity*. New York: Plenum.

CHAGNON, N.A. and IRONS, W. (Eds.) (1979). *Evolutionary Biology and Human social Behaviour: An Anthropological Perspective*. North Scituate, Massachusetts: Duxbury Press.

CHASE, I.D. (1974). Models of hierarchy formation in animal societies. *Behavioral Science*, **19**, 374 – 382.

CLUTTON-BROCK, T.H. and ALBON, S.D. (1979). The roaring of red deer and the evolution of honest advertisement. *Behaviour*, **69**, 145 – 170.

CLUTTON-BROCK, T.H., ALBON, S.D., GIBSON, R.M. and GUINNESS, F.E. (1979). The logical stag: adaptive aspects of fighting in red deer (*Cervus elaphus* L.). *Animal Behaviour*, **27**, 211 – 225.

COLLIAS, N.E. (1943). Statistical analysis of factors which make for success in initial encounters between hens. *American Naturalist*, **77**, 519 – 538.

CROOK, J.H. (1980). *The Evolution of Human Consciousness*. Oxford: Oxford University Press.

CROZE, H. (1970). Searching image in carrion crows: hunting strategy in a predator and some anti-predator devices in camouflaged prey. *Zeitschrift für Tierpsychologie, Beiheft 5*. 85pp.

DARWIN, C. (1871). *The Descent of Man and Selection in Relation to Sex*. London: John Murray.

DAVIES, N.B. (1976). Food, flocking and territorial behaviour of the pied wagtail (*Motacilla alba yarrellii* Gould) in winter. *Journal of Animal Ecology*, **45**, 235 – 253.

DAVIES, N.B. (1978a). Territorial defence in the speckled wood butterfly (*Pararge aegeria*): the resident always wins. *Animal Behaviour*, **26**, 138 – 147.

DAVIES, N.B. (1978b). Ecological questions about territorial behaviour. In J.R. KREBS and N.B. DAVIES (Eds.), *Behavioural Ecology: An Evolutionary Approach*. Oxford: Blackwell.

DAVIES, N.B. (1979). Game theory and territorial behaviour in speckled wood butterflies. *Animal Behaviour*, **27**, 961 – 962.

DAVIES, N.B. and HALLIDAY, T.R. (1977). Optimal mate selection in the toad *Bufo bufo*. *Nature, London*, **269**, 56 – 58.

DAVIES, N.B. and HALLIDAY, T.R. (1978). Deep croaks and fighting assessment in toads *Bufo bufo*. *Nature, London*, **274**, 683 – 685.

DAWKINS, R. (1980). Good strategy or evolutionarily stable strategy? In G.W. BARLOW and J. SILVERBERG, (Eds.), *Sociobiology: Beyond Nature/Nurture? Reports, Definitions and Debate*. AAAS Selected Symposium 35. Boulder, Colorado: Westview Press.

DAWKINS, R. and KREBS, J.R. (1978). Animal signals: information or manipulation? In J.R. KREBS and N.B. DAVIES, (Eds.), *Behavioural Ecology. An Evolutionary Approach*. Oxford: Blackwell.

DAWKINS, R. and KREBS, J.R. (1979). Arms races between and within species. *Proceedings of the Royal Society of London B*, **205**, 489 – 511.

DEAG, J.M. (1977). Aggression and submission in monkey societies. *Animal Behaviour*, **25**, 465 – 474.

DUNBAR, R.I.M. (1980). Determinants and evolutionary consequences of dominance among female gelada baboons. *Behavioral Ecology and Sociobiology*, **7**, 253 – 265.

DUNBAR, R.I.M. and DUNBAR, E.P. (1975). *Social dynamics of Gelada Baboons*. (Contrib. Primatol. Vol. 6). Basel: Karger.

EMLEN, S.T. and ORING, L.W. (1977). Ecology, sexual selection, and the evolution of mating systems. *Science*, **197**, 215 – 223.

FAGEN, R.M. (1977). Animal hierarchies and repeated comparisons. *Behavioral Science*, **22**, 307 – 308.

FAGEN, R.M. (1980). When doves conspire: evolution of nondamaging fighting tactics in a nonrandom-encounter animal conflict model. *American Naturalist*, **115**, 858 – 869.

FRETWELL, S. (1969). Dominance behavior and winter habitat distribution in juncos (*Junco hyemalis*). *Bird Banding*, **40**, 1 – 25.

GADGIL, M. (1972). Male dimorphism as a consequence of sexual selection. *American Naturalist*, **106**, 574 – 580.

GALE, J.S. and EAVES, L.J. (1975). Logic of animal conflict. *Nature, London*, **254**, 463 – 464.

GAUTHREAUX, S.A., Jr. (1978). The ecological significance of behavioral dominance. In P.P.G. BATESON and P.H. KLOPFER (Eds.), *Perspectives in Ethology, Volume 3, Social Behaviour*. New York; Plenum.

GEIST, V. (1966). The evolution of horn-like organs. *Behaviour*, **27**, 175 – 214.

GEIST, V. (1974). On fighting strategies in animal combat. *Nature, London*, **250**, 354.

GEIST, V. (1978). On weapons, combat, and ecology. In L. KRAMES, P. PLINER and T. ALLOWAY (Eds.), *Aggression, Dominance and Individual Spacing*. Advances in the Study of Communication and Affect, Volume 4. New York: Plenum.

GRAFEN, A. (1979). The hawk–dove game played between relatives. *Animal Behaviour*, **27**, 905 – 907.

GREGOR, M.S., SILVERS, A. and SUTCH, D. (Eds.) (1978). *Sociobiology and Human Nature*. San Francisco: Jossey-Bass.

GURNEY, W.S.C. and NISBET, R.M. (1979). Ecological stability and social hierarchy. *Theoretical Population Biology*, **16**, 48 – 80.

HALLIDAY, T.R. (1978). Sexual selection and mate choice. In J.R. KREBS and N.B. DAVIES (Eds.), *Behavioural Ecology. An Evolutionary Approach*. Oxford: Blackwell.

HAMMERSTEIN, P. (1981). The role of asymmetries in animal contests. *Animal Behaviour*, **29**, 193 – 205.

HINDE, R.A. (1972). Aggression. In J.W.S. PRINGLE (Ed.), *Biology and the Human Sciences. The Herbert Spencer Lectures 1970*. Oxford: Oxford University Press.

HINDE, R.A. (1974). *Biological Bases of Human Social Behaviour*. New York: McGraw-Hill.

HORN, H.S. (1968). The adaptive significance of colonial nesting in the Brewer's blackbird (*Euphagus cyanocephalus*). *Ecology*, **49**, 682 – 694.

HRDY, S.B. (1974). Male–male competition and infanticide among the langurs (*Presbytis entellus*) of Abu, Rajasthan. *Folia Primatologica*, **22**, 19 – 58.

HUXLEY, J. (1966). Introduction (to 'A discussion on ritualization of behaviour in animals and man'). *Philosophical Transactions of the Royal Society B*, **251**, 249 – 271.

HYATT, G.W. and SALMON, M. (1978). Combat in the fiddler crabs *Uca pugilator* and *U. pugnax*: quantitative analysis. *Behaviour*, **65**, 182 – 211.

JOHNSON, R.N. (1972). *Aggression in Man and Animals*. Philadelphia: W.B. Saunders.

KIKKAWA, J. (1980). Winter survival in relation to dominance classes among silvereyes *Zosterops lateralis chlorocephala* of Heron Island, Great Barrier Reef. *Ibis*, **122**, 437 – 446.

KREBS, J.R. (1971). Territory and breeding density in the great tit *Parus major* L. *Ecology*, **52**, 2 – 22.

KREBS, J.R. (1977a). Song and territory in the great tit *Parus major*. In B. STONEHOUSE and C. PERRINS (Eds.), *Evolutionary Ecology*. London: Macmillan.

KREBS, JR. (1977b). The significance of song repertoires: the Beau Geste hypothesis. *Animal Behaviour*, **25**, 475 – 478.

KREBS, J.R., ASHCROFT, R. and WEBBER, M. (1978). Song repertoires and territory defence in the great tit. *Nature, London*, **271**, 539 – 542.

KUMMER, H. (1971). *Primate Societies: Group Techniques of Ecological Adaptation*. Chicago: Aldine-Atherton.

LACK, D. (1968). *Ecological Adaptations for Breeding in Birds*. London: Methuen.

LAZARUS, J. and INGLIS, I.R. (1978). The breeding behaviour of the pink-footed goose: parental care and vigilant behaviour during the fledging period. *Behaviour*, **65**, 62 – 88.

LE BOEUF, B.J. (1974). Male–male competition and reproductive success in elephant seals. *American Zoologist*, **14**, 163 – 176.

LEUTHOLD, W. (1966). Variations in territorial behavior of Uganda kob *Adenota kob thomasi* (Neumann 1896). *Behaviour*, **27**, 215 – 258.

LORENZ, K. (1966). *On Aggression*, London: Methuen.

MANNING, A. (1979). *An Introduction to Animal Behaviour*, 3rd edn. London: Edward Arnold.

MARLER, P. (1955). Studies of fighting in chaffinches (1) behaviour in relation to the social hierarchy. *British Journal of Animal Behaviour*, **3**, 111 – 117.
MAYNARD SMITH, J. (1972). Game theory and the evolution of fighting. In J. MAYNARD SMITH, *On Evolution*. Edinburgh: Edinburgh University Press.
MAYNARD SMITH, J. (1974). The theory of games and the evolution of animal conflicts. *Journal of Theoretical Biology*, **47**, 209 – 221.
MAYNARD SMITH, J. (1975). Logic of animal conflict: reply to Gale and Eaves. *Nature, London*, **254**, 464.
MAYNARD SMITH, J. (1976a). Group selection. *Quarterly Review of Biology*, **51**, 277 – 283.
MAYNARD SMITH, J. (1976b). Evolution and the theory of games. *American Scientist*, **64**, 41 – 45.
MAYNARD SMITH, J. (1977). Parental investment: a prospective analysis. *Animal Behaviour*, **25**, 1 – 9.
MAYNARD SMITH, J. (1979). Game theory and the evolution of behaviour. *Proceedings of the Royal Society of London B*, **205**, 475 – 488.
MAYNARD SMITH, J. and PARKER, G.A. (1976). The logic of asymmetric contests. *Animal Behaviour*, **24**, 159 – 175.
MAYNARD SMITH, J. and PRICE, G.R. (1973). The logic of animal conflict. *Nature, London*, **246**, 15 – 18.
MONTAGU, M.F.A. (1976). *The Nature of Human Aggression*. New York: Oxford University Press.
MURTON, R.K. (1958). The breeding of wood-pigeon populations. *Bird Study*, **5**, 157 – 183.
PACKER, C. (1979). Male dominance and reproductive activity in *Papio anubis*. *Animal Behaviour*, **27**, 37 – 45.
PARKER, G.A. (1970). Sperm competition and its evolutionary consequences in the insects. *Biological Reviews*, **45**, 525 – 568.
PARKER, G.A. (1971). The reproductive behaviour and the nature of sexual selection in *Scatophaga stercoraria* L. (Diptera: Scatophagidae). VII. The origin and evolution of the passive phase. *Evolution*, **24**, 791 – 805.
PARKER, G.A. (1974). Assessment strategy and the evolution of fighting behaviour. *Journal of Theoretical Biology*, **47**, 223 – 243.
PARKER, G.A. (1978). Searching for mates. In J.R. KREBS and N.B. DAVIES (Eds.), *Behavioural Ecology: An Evolutionary Approach*. Oxford: Blackwell.
PARKER, G.A. (1979). Sexual selection and sexual conflict. In M.S. BLUM and N.A. BLUM (Eds.), *Sexual Selection and Reproductive Competition in Insects*. New York: Academic Press.
PARKER, G.A., HAYHURST, G.R.G. and BRADLEY, J.S. (1974). Attack and defence strategies in reproductive interactions of *Locusta migratoria* and their adaptive significance. *Zietschrift für Tierpsychologie*, **34**, 1 – 24.
PARKER, G.A. and MACNAIR, M.R. (1979). Models of parent–offspring conflict. IV. Suppression: evolutionary retaliation by the parent. *Animal Behaviour*, **27**, 1210 – 1235.
PARKER, G.A. and RUBENSTEIN, D.I. (1981). Role assessment, reserve strategy, and acquisition of information in asymmetric animal conflicts. *Animal Behaviour*, **29**, 221 – 240.
PERRILL, S.A. GERHARDT, H.C. and DANIEL, R. (1978). Sexual parasitism in the green tree frog (*Hyla cinerea*). *Science*, **200**, 1179 – 1180.
RAND, W.M. and RAND, A.S. (1976). Agonistic behaviour in nesting iguanas: a stochastic analysis of dispute settlement dominated by the minimization of energy cost. *Zietschrift für Tierpsychologie*, **40**, 279 – 299.

VAN RHIJN, J.G. (1973). Behavioural dimorphism in male ruffs, *Philomachus pugnax* (L.). *Behaviour*, **47**, 153 – 229.
VAN RHIJN, J.G. (1980). Communication by agonistic displays: a discussion. *Behaviour*, **74**, 284 – 293.
VAN RHIJN, J.G. and VODEGEL, R. (1980). Being honest about one's intentions: an evolutionary stable strategy for animal conflicts. *Journal of Theoretical Biology*, **85**, 623 – 641.
RICHARDS, S.M. (1974). The concept of dominance and methods of assessment. *Animal Behaviour*, **22**, 914 – 930.
ROHWER, S. (1977). Status signalling in Harris sparrows: some experiments in deception. *Behaviour*, **61**, 107 – 129.
ROHWER, S. and ROHWER, F.C. (1978). Status signalling in Harris sparrows: experimental deceptions achieved. *Animal Behaviour*, **26**, 1012 – 1022.
ROWELL, T.E. (1974). The concept of social dominance. *Behavioral Biology*, **11**, 131 – 154.
RUBENSTEIN, D.I. (1978). On predation, competition, and the advantages of group living. In P.P.G. BATESON and P.H. KLOPFER (Eds.), *Perspectives in Ethology, Volume 3, Social Behaviour*. New York: Plenum.
RUBENSTEIN, D.I. (1980). On the evolution of alternative mating strategies. In J.E.R. STADDON (Ed.), *Limits to Action: The Allocation of Individual Behaviour*. New York: Academic Press.
RUBENSTEIN, D.I. (1981). Combat and communication in the Everglades pygmy sunfish. *Animal Behaviour*, **29**, 249 – 258.
SABINE, W.S. (1949). Dominance in winter flocks of juncos and tree sparrows. *Physiological Zoology*, **22**, 64 – 85.
SCHJELDERUP-EBBE, T. (1922). Beiträge zur Sozialpsychologie des Haushuhns. *Zeitschrift für Psychologie*, **88**, 225 – 252.
SCHJELDERUP-EBBE, T. (1935). Social behavior of birds. In C. MURCHISON (Ed.), *Handbook of Social Psychology*. Worcester, Massachusetts: Clark University Press.
SCOTT, J.P. and FREDERICSON, E. (1951). The causes of fighting in mice and rats. *Physiological Zoology*, **24**, 273 – 309.
SMITH, W.J. (1977). *The Behavior of Communicating: An Ethological Approach*. Cambridge, Massachusetts: Harvard University Press.
STOKES, A.W. (1962). Agonistic behaviour among blue tits at a winter feeding station. *Behaviour*, **19**, 118 – 138.
SYME, G.J. (1974). Competitive orders as measures of social dominance. *Animal Behaviour*, **22**, 931 – 940.
TINBERGEN, N. (1953). *The Herring Gull's World: A Study of the Social Behaviour of Birds*. London: Collins.
TINBERGEN, N., IMPEKOVEN, M. and FRANCK, D. (1967). An experiment on spacing-out as a defence against predation. *Behaviour*, **28**, 307 – 321.
TREISMAN, M. (1977). The evolutionary restriction of aggression within a species: a game theory analysis. *Journal of Mathematical Psychology*, **16**, 167 – 203.
TRIVERS, R.L. (1972). Parental investment and sexual selection. In B.G. CAMPBELL (Ed.), *Sexual Selection and the Descent of Man 1871 – 1971*. Chicago: Aldine.
TRIVERS, R.L. (1974). Parent – offspring conflict. *American Zoologist*, **14**, 249 – 264.
WAAGE, J.K. (1973). Reproductive behavior and its relation to territoriality in *Calopteryx maculata* (Beauvois) (Odonata: Calopterygidae). *Behaviour*, **47**, 240 – 256.
WADE, T.D. (1978). Status and hierarchy in nonhuman primate societies. In P.P.G. BATESON and P.H. KLOPFER (Eds.), *Perspectives in Ethology, Volume 3, Social*

Behaviour. New York: Plenum.
WECHKIN, S. (1975). Social familiarity and nip dominance in male swordtails (*Xiphophorus helleri*) and platys (*Xiphophorus maculatus*). *Psychological Reports*, **37**, 435 – 438.
WYNNE-EDWARDS, V.C. (1962). *Animal Dispersion in Relation to Social Behaviour*. Edinburgh: Oliver & Boyd.
YASUKAWA, K. (1981). Song repertoires in the red-winged blackbird (*Agelaius phoeniceus*): a test of the Beau Geste hypothesis. *Animal Behaviour*, **29**, 114 – 125.

CHAPTER 3

Animal Communication

Julia C. Berryman

3.1 The Problem of Definition

A generally agreed definition of communication is hard to find because definitions vary greatly with the context within which communication is to be used. Some students of animal communication have classified animal 'signals' on the basis of what messages they seem to the human observer to contain, rather than what they appear to convey to a member of the same species (a conspecific). Clark (1926) suggested that animal sounds contain messages such as 'keep away' and 'here I am', but he was not altogether clear on the effect of such messages on conspecifics. He noted that 'among the song birds there is little evidence in most cases that the females pay much attention to the songs of males' (p. 45), although he believed that songs probably serve as a 'sex stimulus'.

Stevens' (1950) definition of communication excluded any notion of a signal affecting a conspecific; he merely defined communication as 'the discriminatory response of an organism to a stimulus' in its environment (p. 689). Thus the response of an animal to a clap of thunder, or the rustle of wind, could be termed communication on this basis, since all Stevens believed that an animal must do was show that it had responded to some stimulus. Such a definition is far too wide to be of use in the context of animal communication, since our chief concern is to identify signals used between conspecifics.

Cherry (1957) gave a definition which emphasized the part played by conspecifics. He restricted communication to 'the establishment of a social unit from individuals, by the use of language or signs. The sharing of a common set of rules, for various goal-seeking activities' (p. 363). Thus, unlike Stevens, Cherry did not include in his definition the response of an individual to stimuli from inanimate objects.

A number of writers have attempted to include within a definition of communication the notion of intention or purpose (for example Révész, 1944; Hebb & Thompson, 1954). This poses a problem for the student of animal behaviour since purposive behaviour is hard for the observer to identify. Indeed Révész claimed that intentional communication is possible only in man; Hockett (1960), on the other hand, avoided the problem of intention, even in language, by defining the latter in terms of a number of properties that can be tested for in all species; purposiveness is actually left out of his analysis.

Marler (1967) suggested, like Rowell (1972), that clues to the occurrence of communication between two animals are to be found in the behaviour of one upon its perception of a signal from another. This view is similar to that of Scott (1968), who stated that 'communication includes any stimulus arising from one animal and eliciting a response in another' (p. 17). This view of communication is a very broad one, since it enables the observer of animals to consider that any behaviour exhibited by one animal, and responded to by another, is communicatory. Other researchers in this area have tried to specify more precisely the nature of signals, as distinct from any behavioural change to which another animal shows a response. A number of authorities, including Deag (1980), have suggested that communication is 'the passing of information from one animal to another (and so influencing its behaviour) by means of signals that have evolved for the purpose' (p. 39). This definition limits the notion of a signal to only those stimuli from an animal that have evolved as signals. These have been termed 'functional' signals by Otte (1974).

Deag's (1980) view of communication is too restrictive for our purposes, since in this chapter I propose to include some discussion of signals that have clearly not 'evolved for the purpose'. Signals of this nature have been termed 'incidental' signals by Otte (1974). Brown (1979), in his review of chemical communication, noted that a number of what he considers to be chemical signals may be the result of incidental effects. For example, chemical stimuli (or signals) from faeces appear to be important in communication in many rodent species, and yet their precise nature may be determined by diet; thus they do not fall into the category of 'functional' signals. It will therefore be necessary to take a rather liberal view of what constitutes communication here in order to include those signals that are not clearly 'functional'.

Another view of communication which is of relevance in relation to cooperation and competition between animals is that of Dawkins and Krebs (1978). These authors suggested that 'Communication is said to occur when an animal, the actor, does something which appears to be the result of selection to influence the sense organs of another animal, the reactor, so that the reactor's behaviour changes to the advantage of the actor' (p. 283). Benefit to the actor may not always be evident, but Dawkins and Krebs indicated that on average this will be so. Similarly Otte (1974) believed that communication systems have evolved 'because such action fostered survival or reproduction' (p. 385). Dawkins and Krebs observed that the reactor (to a signal) may also benefit by responding to the signal, but this benefit is not central to their definition. Mutual benefit is, however, implied directly or indirectly by a number of other writers, as Dawkins and Krebs (1978) have pointed out. Tinbergen (1964) implied it, and Marler (1968) stressed it by noting that 'In true communication, however, both participants seek to maximize the efficiency of information transfer' (p. 103). Cherry's (1957) definition also hinted at mutual benefit. The occurrence of mutual benefit is a point of particular relevance to the theme of this book because communication can be seen, in an indirect sense, to be a cooperative form of behaviour. In terms of survival, communicatory signals have evolved, according to these latter writers, because members of a species sharing such a system benefit by using that system. In the 'selfish-gene' approach, in which an animal is conceived as 'a machine designed to preserve and propagate the genes which ride inside it' (Dawkins & Krebs, 1978, p. 282), mutual benefit is not a central characteristic of communication. In this case the mutual benefit or cooperative element is incidental, however frequently it may occur. What is important in this approach is the evolutionary benefit, to the individual communicator, in promoting the survival of its genes.

Before considering the types of signals used in animal communication it is necessary to note that animal signals can be divided roughly into two types: 'discrete' and 'graded' signals (Wilson, 1975), or as Sebeok (1962) termed them, 'digital' and 'analog'. Discrete (digital) signals are those that can be presented in a simple on/off manner: they are present or absent and are not shown at varying intensities. The red belly of the male three-spined stickleback, which evokes aggressive responses in other males, is an example of a discrete signal, as are the flashing signals of fireflies (Lloyd, 1975) which are used during pair formation. Graded or analog signals, on the other hand, show variability which often reflects the degree of motivation of the actor. Many vocalizations are graded rather than discrete signals; for instance many mammal calls become higher in pitch, louder, and longer with increasing distress. Otte (1974) suggested that graded signalling becomes increasingly important among higher vertebrates, particularly in primates, as such signals make possible more complex social systems.

The following sections will explore five major types of communication among non-human animals. These are: chemical, visual, acoustic, tactile, and electric communication. Although these sections will deal with signals primarily in these categories, systems mesh together and in many cases displays incorporate signals of several types at any one time. A further section of the chapter will explore the controversy concerning linguistic communication among apes.

3.2 Chemical Communication

Chemical signals were probably the first to be put to service in the evolution of animal communication (Wilson, 1968); certainly among single-celled organisms primitive communication was most likely to have been chemical. Chemical signals may also be one of the first forms of communication used by many young altricial mammals (those whose young are very immature at birth); such mammals may not have fully functional ears and eyes at birth, and thus rely chiefly on olfactory and tactile communication during the first few days or even weeks of life. Although chemical stimuli are probably best known among the insects, they are also used by various other arthropods, such as crabs and spiders. Other animals utilizing chemical signals in communication include various nematodes, amphibians, reptiles, fish and mammals (see Shorey, 1977, for details).

Chemical signals are secreted as liquids and are transmitted either as liquids or gases. They may be detected at a distance, by olfaction, or at the surface of the body of the emitting animal by smell or taste. Other chemical signals may be encountered in the liquid phase as 'signposts' of the emitting animal. The capacity for discrete chemical signals is limited or non-existent, and unlike auditory or electric signals, chemical signals are hard to present in a simple on/off manner. Chemical signals have been classified (see Wilson & Bossert, 1963) on the basis of the speed of response which they produce in the recipient. Some stimuli may evoke immediate behavioural responses, called 'releaser' effects, while other chemical signals, which are said to have 'primer' effects, act on endocrine or other physiological processes, and may not have any observable effects on the recipient for some time.

The term 'pheromone' (coined by Karlson & Lüscher, 1959) has, in recent years, been widely used to refer to a variety of chemical signals. However, the precise meaning of this term has been much discussed, and some authorities (such as Beauchamp *et al.*, 1976; Brown, 1979) now feel that its use should be restricted to that for which it was first used. In this section, therefore, I propose to use the term 'chemical signals' to avoid any ambiguity that the term 'pheromone' now has.

Chemical signals have a wide variety of functions in animal communication. They are used in both cooperative and competitive contexts, and Wilson (1968) recorded their use in bringing animals together, sexual stimulation, territory and home-range marking, non-territorial dispersal, recognition of group and rank, recruitment and alarm. Signals from scent glands are well known for their use as aphrodisiacs, presented by the male in order to render the female more susceptible to his sexual approach (Wilson, 1968). Females may also release chemical signals at or before the time of sexual receptivity in order to attract males. Such signals play a large part in coordinating and synchronizing sexual behaviour, and thus signals are used to promote the cooperation of a conspecific during courtship and copulation. Chemical substances, such as those in vaginal secretions, appear to be important in sexual attraction in primates, and it is thought that chemical cues of this nature may also be influential in human sexual behaviour (Michael *et al.*, 1976; Sokolov *et al.*, 1976).

Brown (1979) suggested that the signalling function of chemical stimuli from urine and faeces have evolved from their excretory function and thus dietary factors are obviously important in determining the exact characteristics of these two sources of stimuli. Such stimuli contribute towards the fostering of efficient mother – young relationships (for example, Leon, 1975) and contribute to group or colony odour (for example, Mykytowycz, 1970). Chemical stimuli are also secreted from a variety of scent glands. Brown reported that as many as 40 different types of gland have been identified, and within a species a wide range of glands may be present.

The rabbit provides a good example of the variety of signals which may be used in chemical communication. Mykytowycz (1970) observed that the European rabbit has anal glands, chin glands, paired inguinal glands, and within the orbit of the eye Harderian, infra-orbital and lachrymal glands.

These are not the only sources of chemical stimuli in this species, since urine and faeces also play a part in rabbit chemical communication. Territory odour is contributed to by both urine and faeces. Males mark females by urinating on them during sexual behaviour, and in aggressive displays males urinate on each other. Young rabbits are marked with urine and are identified by the odour this produces. Marking with foreign urine provokes mothers to attack their own young. Faeces are used to mark out territory and these faeces distribute the rabbit's anal gland secretions. Dung hills are found all over rabbit territory and effectively mark out the area to intruders (Mykytowycz, 1968).

The dominance status of a rabbit is indicated by odour. The size of its anal gland and its place in the warren hierarchy are closely linked. Chin gland secretions deposited by chinning (marking with this gland), are also important in establishing dominance. Chinning is shown more by dominant animals and, as with the anal gland, dominant animals have larger chin glands. When strange animals meet, the animal showing most chinning establishes his place as dominant over the stranger. This competition over resources, for instance territory, or between individuals within the warren hierarchy, is in great part established via the use of chemical signals (Mykytowycz, 1968).

Wilson (1975) has drawn attention to the fact that aggression need not be direct, and chemical stimuli are used in indirect aggression in various rodent species. If a female mouse, recently inseminated by a male, is placed with a strange male strain she will usually abort and will then become again available for insemination. Bruce (1959, 1960) was first to demonstrate this pregnancy-blocking by a strange male. The stimulus producing this abortion or blocking of the pregnancy is the odour of male urine, and this odour activates the pituitary gland and corpora lutea (Bruce, 1966; Bronson, 1969). Even more susceptible to this phenomenon is the vole, *Microtus ochrogaster* (Stehn & Richmond, 1975). This animal shows the same blocking response at almost all stages of pregnancy, not just within the first few days. Stehn and Richmond found that unfamiliar males caused abortions in 81% of females ranging from 3 to 15 days pregnant. This form of aggression is obviously a highly efficient way for one male to compete with another. Clearly where social relationships within a population of voles are unstable, or where immigration has occurred, birth rates will drop until social stability returns. Thus this form of indirect aggression may have dramatic effects on the birth rate of a species.

A pattern of behaviour that may be of importance in the context of chemical communication is grooming. During self-grooming and mutual grooming animals often distribute chemical substances over their own body surfaces, and in mutual grooming each animal may be exposed to a variety of olfactory signals from its partner. Ewer (1968) included social grooming as one type of 'socially positive, friendly or amicable behaviour' (p. 186) and believed that it is highly important in maintaining social cohesion and fostering cooperation. It also enables an animal to have part of its coat groomed which it cannot itself reach. Interactions of this nature between members of a colony are also likely to increase the uniformity of individuals' odours. Chemical signals laid down by this means serve to identify group membership and further promote cohesion.

Brown (1979) has suggested that insufficient attention has been paid to this form of activity and its role in chemical communication. He also noted that in self-grooming the ingestion of an animal's own secretory products may have important feedback effects on that animal's behaviour, endocrine system and activity of the scent glands themselves. Chemical substances are likely to be made more volatile when body temperature increases. Thiessen *et al.*, (1976) showed that social grooming is elicited when body temperature is raised as a result of either a change in ambient temperature or through social interaction. Thus grooming activities may be functionally useful activities in thermoregulation as well as in fostering group cohesion and general care of the skin.

Chemical signals released when an animal is threatened or injured often function as alarm signals for many species, and they may promote dispersion of conspecifics in the vicinity. Many aquatic snails show escape reactions when they perceive the juices of crushed conspecifics (Shorey, 1977). Sea urchins move rapidly away from a location where a conspecific has been crushed; in such cases they may mount on their ventral spines and 'race' away for a metre or more (Snyder & Snyder, 1970). Termites lay chemical trails to the area of a threatening stimulus and the function of this trail in lower termites seems to be entirely to alarm conspecifics. In more highly evolved termites however, trail-laying also serves a recruitment function to attract conspecifics to a food source (Stuart, 1963).

When honey bees sting an enemy they emit iso-amyl acetate (probably together with other compounds) from glands near the base of the sting. This substance is in part responsible for promoting stinging of that same enemy by other bees (Boch *et al.*, 1962), and in this case the alarm substance promotes cooperative defensive responses by conspecifics.

Chemical stimuli can thus be seen to function as signals of warning or alarm, but while doing this they also make the signaller more conspicuous. This form of signalling may not always have obvious beneficial effects for the animal emitting the signals, but the survival value of responding to these signals is evident. This form of behaviour can be seen as cooperative (see Chapter 1 for discussion) because it promotes the survival of members of the same species.

To summarize briefly the role of chemical signals in animal life, it is clear that these signals serve a variety of functions. Chemical signals may be used in direct or indirect communication, and actor and reactor need not both be present in order to communicate. Signals may have primer effects in eliciting physiological changes within the reactor which in turn may have delayed effects such as pregnancy blocking. Signals have a role in both cooperative and competitive behaviour. In the former, examples were taken from reproductive behaviour, warning and grooming, while the latter was exemplified in dominance, aggression, and territorial behaviour.

3.3 Visual Communication

Visual communication is used widely by many animals. Among invertebrates it is important in cephalopods, for example the cuttle fish, and in arthropods it is particularly used among insects. In vertebrates it is of importance in fish, reptiles, birds, and certain mammals.

Optical systems can provide numerous kinds of visual signals which are perceptible to a greater or lesser degree by animals using this sensory modality. Visual stimuli may vary in brightness (intensity), colour (wavelength), spatial and temporal pattern, and the degree and plane of polarization (Marler, 1968). Most animals communicate visually by modulating reflected light, however a variety of animals generate their own light to provide signals — these include protozoans, various worms, snails, shrimps, beetles, and various deep sea fish, to name only a few (Lloyd, 1977). Where visual signals are to be transmitted over a considerable range, the visual displays found in animals are obviously designed to achieve conspicuousness in contexts in which the animal is signalling. Contrast with the environment is often essential in these signals.

A variety of patterns seem to have inherently high attention-catching qualities for some species. Many animals (fish, birds, and mammals) find the vertebrate eye pattern inherently conspicuous, and exhibit innate withdrawal or flight responses to two large eyes (Edmunds, 1974). The value of this innate response is shown by the large number of animals that have startle displays involving false eyespots; butterflies and moths are well-known examples (Blest, 1957). Conspicuousness is therefore not only employed in intraspecific communication; it is frequently used in interspecific communication in warning colouration.

Since many animals rely heavily on visual communication, it is not surprising to find that visual signals can have an enormous variety of functions in the social behaviour of animals. They are used in individual recognition, reproductive behaviour, aggression and dominance, cooperative hunting, grooming, and alarm. In dimorphic species, males and females are identified by conspicuous differences in shape, size, and frequently colouration. Familiar in this context are the many dimorphic bird species in which the male has brilliant plumage. In many cases colouration and pattern may serve to identify not only the sex, but also individual animals. The female guinea-pig recognizes her own young using both visual and olfactory cues (Porter *et al.*, 1973; Fullerton *et al.*, 1974), and the recognition of lambs by sight has also been shown in ewes, although, like guinea-pigs, olfaction is also used in recognition (Tschanz, 1962; Lindsay & Fletcher, 1968).

In aggression and dominance where animals compete for resources such as space, food, mate, or position in the hierarchy (which may then give them access to all kinds of resources) visual signals are frequently employed. A conspicuous colour such as red is often the salient stimulus or releaser in eliciting aggression or withdrawal in a variety of species. The English robin's red breast is one such example. Lack (1946) demonstrated that even a bunch of red feathers when placed in a robin's territory suffices to release attack from the resident robin; and similarly a crude model of a stickleback with a red belly elicits more attacks by a male stickleback than does an accurate model lacking red (Tinbergen, 1951). Colour changes may also be used in aggressive displays in the octopus. The aggressor octopus (*Octopus vulgaris*) in an aggressive encounter shows a dark red 'aggressive flush' (Packard & Sanders, 1971) which covers the whole surface of the body, and can be maintained for several seconds.

Increase in apparent size is another commonly used aggressive signal. The bristling of hair is shown by many mammals, for example the guinea-pig (Kunkel & Kunkel, 1964), the collared peccary (Schweinburg & Sowls, 1972), and the wolf (Mech, 1970), and expansion of the body may occur as in the lateral display shown by various lizards (Evans, 1961, cited by Marler, 1968). Marler suggested that many animals stretch and extend their head and limbs in a way that seems to be designed to increase apparent size. The 'head-up posture' found in many passerines and gulls may serve this function.

Unlike aggressive signals, submissive signals used by animals are not designed to elicit withdrawal but to enable one animal to remain close to another without provoking attack or avoidance. Such signals promote cooperation. Signals of this type are often the exact opposite of those employed in aggression, as Darwin (1872) proposed in his principle of antithesis. A submissive dog lowers his body to the ground in a manner opposite to that of a hostile one, as Darwin (and no doubt many before him) observed; in more extreme cases the dog may lie on his back with belly uppermost. This form of appeasement is also found in rats, hamsters, and the vole (*Microtus agrestis*), and lowering the head, lying down, or the intention movement of lying down may be used as visual signals of submission in various artiodactyls, for instance deer (Ewer, 1968). Postural changes are frequently used as indicators of submission. The facial expressions and tail postures in wolves (Schenkel, 1947, 1967; Mech, 1970) provide subtle indicators of mood and dominance status. Subordinate status is revealed in the wolf's face by slit-like eyes, smooth forehead, closed mouth with corners pulled far back, and ears drawn back and held close to the head; the tail is tucked in between the legs. The dominant wolf on the other hand has a wrinkled and swollen forehead, bared teeth and mouth corners pulled forward, ears erect and forward pointing, and the tail is held high. In aggressive interactions between high-ranking animals, wagging of the tail tip may also be observed. Thus position, shape and movements of the tail all play a part in communication in the wolf, and indeed most canids.

Aside from colour and posture, both playing an important role in visual communication systems, a number of structural elements such as antlers and horns have come to have a significant role in social behaviour, not just as weapons but also as indicators of status. Mountain sheep signal their rank by the size of their horns, as do red deer (see Geist, 1971, for further discussion). Thus animals can display their status without having to resort to physical combat.

Signals used in sexual behaviour are commonly visual signals, particularly in the pairing stage of reproductive behaviour when cues may need to be effective at a distance (these are distal cues) in order to attract males and females to one another. Several species of Florida fiddler crab (genus *Uca*) show a claw-waving display in courtship which is species specific (Salmon, 1967). Males make certain waving movements of the chela (or pincer) which differ in pattern and tempo from species to species, and waving rate is increased when females approach males. As with most displays, signals are not confined to one sensory modality, courtship sounds also play a part in the displays of these crabs.

Another visual display in which the temporal element is central is that of the firefly (genus *Photinus*) (Lloyd, 1977). Species each have their own characteristic flash pattern and flight path during light emission. During flight the male emits his characteristic flash pattern and then the female, on the ground or in vegetation, flashes in response to the male after a species-characteristic interval following the male's flash. This sequence is then repeated for up to 10 flash exchanges, before the male lands and approaches the female. Attraction of the male to the female depends entirely on these visual cues, and females flashing from airtight glass containers (thus emitting no chemical stimuli) are equally effective in attracting males. Not all visual signals used in courtship or sexual behaviour are highly conspicuous however. Simmons and Weidmann (1973) observed that male mallard ducks may show 'interest' in a particular female, by exhibiting a subtle directional bias in their head movements during shaking.

Grooming behaviour may be elicited by visual signals. This behaviour is, as has been already noted, an example of cooperative behaviour, and Stanley (1971) observed that it typically lacks agonistic elements, and usually involves a relaxed posture in both participants. Animals may solicit grooming using a variety of signals. A chimpanzee will often present itself for grooming by standing or sitting in front of its chosen partner, with slightly bowed head, and offering some portion of the anatomy to be groomed – typically the head, back or rump (Lawick-Goodall, 1968); such behaviour usually elicits grooming from another chimpanzee. In New Forest ponies mutual grooming of the neck, main, forelegs and withers is shown between animals within groups, although most ponies only have a small number of grooming partners (Tyler, 1972). Grooming is initiated by one pony approaching another with its ears forward and its mouth occasionally open with the lower teeth slightly exposed. If, however, a pony soliciting grooming is the dominant in a pair then it approaches the subordinate animals with its ears laid back.

In summary, it is clear that visual signals, like chemical signals, serve a variety of functions. Unlike the latter, visual signals cannot be left behind in the absence of the signaller, but they have an advantage over chemical signals in that they may be used to convey rapid changes in motivation. Visual signals are, as the example given here show, used to elicit cooperative and competitive behaviour in conspecifics. They are involved in reproductive and aggressive behaviour, as well as in individual recognition and in grooming.

3.4 Acoustic Communication

Acoustic communication occurs throughout the animal kingdom, although its value in relation to other means of communication varies greatly from species to species. It is generally considered to be of prime importance for many birds, and in some of these it is of particular significance in individual recognition.

In any communication system the efficiency of communication is determined by the nature of the signal, and the medium in which it is transmitted. Sounds travel faster in a dense medium and thus the acoustic signals of underwater animals can travel enormous distances before dying away. Background noise is another factor to be considered in relation to acoustic signalling. If sounds are to function as signals then they must have characteristics that make them conspicuous within the habitat of a given species.

Animal sounds are produced in an almost infinite number of ways and the larynx and vocal chords are only one solution to the problem of production. Numerous other parts of the body may be used to achieve a noisy effect; for example the teeth may be gnashed or rythmically brought together as in guinea-pigs; the hind legs may be thumped on the ground to produce drumming as in rabbits; and even the noisy blowing of intestinal gases may perhaps have a signalling effect in some species, for instance horses (Tembrock, 1968). Among the invertebrates, sounds are frequently produced by the friction of one part of the body against another (this is called 'stridulation'); the grasshopper, for example, rubs its specialized hind legs against its wings or abdomen. In fact almost any movable part of the body, brought into contact with any other part of the body, or surroundings, can be used to produce a sound which may serve as a signal for a conspecific; but, it must be emphasized, not all sounds necessarily serve a communicative function (Marler, 1967).

A particular advantage of acoustic communication is that it is one of the most rapid means (see section on electrical communication below) by which one animal can make contact with another when they are separated by distance, physical obstacles obstructing vision, or darkness. Evidence indicates that animals living in dense forest regions (Kiley, 1969, 1972) have more complex vocal repertoires than those living on open plains, where visual communication is also possible. Although chemical communication is effective in dense environments, its disadvantage is that it needs time.

Marler (1955) has pointed out that both mammals and birds locate sounds by making binaural comparisons of phase, intensity, and time of arrival. Phase differences are best detected at lower frequencies in which the wavelengths exceed the distance between the animal's ears, while intensity differences are better detected at higher frequencies in which sonic 'shadows' can be created by the animal's head. Clearly, the size of the animal is of some importance here, as the distance between its ears will be closely related to its overall size, and thus mice, for example, make more use of intensity differences at higher frequencies in locating sound sources than would larger mammals. Similarly, the size of the animal will to some extent limit the frequencies which it can produce vocally; the smaller the larynx and vocal cords the higher these will be (Sewell, 1970).

A considerable amount of information can be passed acoustically. Tembrock (1968) suggested that species, sex, individuality, age, physiological status, motivation of behaviour, space and time can all be communicated in this way; but typically a species does not use acoustic means alone to transmit all of these.

The function of sounds has been considered by a number of researchers. Tembrock (1968) used the notion of approach and withdrawal in his functional analysis. Among canids (for instance, the dog) he suggested that four types occur: these are sounds eliciting approach and withdrawal, warning sounds, and infantile sounds. Other researchers have also used this approach. Marler (1972) looked at calls in terms of their likelihood of producing increased or decreased approach in conspecifics in the black and white colobus monkey, as did Berryman (1976) in her analysis of guinea-pig sounds.

Of course in many instances animals attempt to conceal rather than reveal information about themselves while at the same time alerting conspecifics to danger. Warning calls, for instance, are most effective if they do not indicate the animal's location to its predator. Thus in dense undergrowth, or grassland, high sounds would be best used, since they reflect off small objects (Marler, 1955; Sewell, 1970) and make the location of the source more difficult. The warning call, given by birds in the presence of a flying predator, will thus ideally be heard easily, but will transmit minimal directional information, and will therefore be difficult to locate. Shalter (1978) has now shown, however, that certain birds of prey are able to orient towards the source of this type of call. This finding poses problems for students of animal communication since the warning calls may offer less concealment than was once thought. Catchpole (1980) has suggested that this ability on the part of the birds of prey may not always have been present but may have appeared relatively late in evolutionary terms. It may be that Shalter's findings do not apply in all natural contexts, and thus in certain situations alarm calls may still offer concealment to the prey, while warning nearby conspecifics.

Animal sounds can transmit a number of different types of information at the same time. For example Caldwell and Caldwell (1977) recorded that the dolphin's whistle can convey 'Attention! I am a dolphin with which you are (or are not) familiar. I am located on your left, and I am to some degree excited' (p. 797). The identification of specific individuals is possible in a number of species by sound alone. Catchpole (1980) reported that many parent sea birds breeding in densely packed colonies give special calls before landing, to which the young react before seeing their parents, suggesting that individual recognition does occur. Individual recognition by voice has been shown in many types of animals, such as northern elephant seals (Petrinovich, 1974), reindeer (Espmark, 1971), and it is likely in pigs, cattle, and horses (Kiley, 1972). Hutchison *et al.*, (1968) have demonstrated in the sandwich tern (*Sterna sandvicensis*), that clear and consistent differences between individuals' calls can be shown by means of spectrographic analysis. Individual birds' calls varied in the frequency and duration of each segment making up the call, thus each bird had its own distinctive call pattern.

Where animals are competing over essential resources, be they food, territory or mate, acoustic signals are often employed. Bird song is frequently used in the advertisement and defence of territory (see Jellis, 1977, for full discussion). Songs are distinguished from calls because they are generally longer, more complex in structure, and are produced by males in the breeding season, whereas calls are short, simple and are produced throughout the year by both sexes (Catchpole, 1980). Birds are not the only animals which sing. The fruit fly (*Drososophila*) also uses song in courtship (Ewing, 1977) and whales are well known for their exceedingly long songs (Payne & McVay, 1971), the function of which is uncertain.

The territorial function of bird song has been elegantly demonstrated by Krebs (1976) in the great tit (*Parus major*). In this study Krebs removed males from their territories and replaced their songs with a system of loudspeakers. Thus the effect of the song alone could be determined. Krebs used a number of controls in this study and was able to demonstrate that areas where songs were played were not invaded by males, whereas the control territories in which they were not played were soon occupied. Evidently the song itself, even in the absence of the singer, repels rival males.

In aggressive encounters acoustic communication is used widely by many species. Sounds often accompany other displays and frequently serve in territorial and/or mate defence (Bartholomew & Collias, 1962). In the elephant seal the most characteristic call is the 'clap-threat'. This sound, not unlike the exhaust noise of a diesel engine, is made with the use of this animal's enormously enlarged proboscis, and is a signal of incipient attack. It is usually sufficient to repel males of lower status, but fights may ensue between males where the dominance status of the bulls has not yet been fully established. Kiley (1972), in her review of vocalizations in ungulates, noted that vocal threats are not very characteristic of this group although bulls and bison, and some cervids, are reported to make threatening roars. Elaborate visual displays are more often used by ungulates. Canids use vocal threats (the well known bark of the dog is a typical instance) and felids also used vocalizations in defensive threat (Tembrock, 1968).

Acoustic signals often precede and accompany sexual behaviour. Male grasshoppers of some species stridulate just before beginning to approach and mount the female, and in other species there is an exchange of sounds between the male and female during pair formation (Alexander, 1968).

In birds, song may function in sexual attraction as well as territorial defence, as Catchpole (1973) has demonstrated in his study of the reed warbler (*Acrocephalus scirpaceus*). The males of these birds advertise their presence with much singing throughout the day. Once a female is attracted and pairing occurs, singing is restricted greatly to the dawn and dusk chorus. One interpretation that Catchpole has suggested to explain this change in behaviour is that the sexual and territorial parts of the song become separated after pairing. The dawn and dusk choruses are the territorial advertisement, whereas the singing during the day is concerned with sexual attraction, and once the female appears this function has been dealt with, and hence singing between dawn and dusk ceases. In many tropical birds the female also contributes to the song, forming a duet with the male. This behaviour seems to be important in maintaining the pair bond over long periods of time in dense habitats where visibility is poor (Thorpe, 1973). Thus bird song has a role in both cooperative and competitive behaviour.

Mammals frequently use vocalizations in courtship and sexual behaviour. For example guinea-pigs vocalize, giving a characteristic purr during courtship. Males purr when displaying to females while performing hip swaying movements (the 'rhumba'), and females purr when sexually receptive (Berryman, 1976). Vocalizations may be given just after copulation in some animals, and in the rat these are thought to be 'desist-contact' signals. Barfield and Geyer (1972) described the ultrasonic post-ejaculatory song of the male rat. The duration of the song corresponds to an 'absolute refractory period' during which the male cannot spontaneously initiate copulation.

Many acoustic signals function to maintain group cohesion in animals that cannot maintain visual contact with their colony or group. The common grunt of the pig, the 'mm' call (a type of moo) of cattle (Kiley, 1972), and the 'chut' of the guinea-pig (Berryman, 1976), all have this function; they are also used in greeting.

In reproductive behaviour the behaviour of parents (usually mother) and infants may often have to be closely synchronized to allow suckling in mammals, feeding, grooming, and care of the young. The chimpanzee, for instance, relies mainly on tactile and vocal communication during early maternal care. Lawick-Goodall (1968) described three clear-cut vocal sounds which are used by chimpanzee babies in this context. Noirot (1964) observed that ultrasonic cries (these are cries outside the human audible range) from mouse pups elicit maternal responses (for example retrieval) in both lactating and virgin females. Infant mice are not able to regulate their body temperature (they are thus poikilothermic) for some days after birth, and infants quickly cool down if they fall from the nest. Rapid retrieval of such infants is essential for survival, and 'aunt' behaviour (maternal care in animals which are not actually mothers) is common in many species particularly in response to infants' distress calls. Thus vocalizations may elicit cooperative care of infant animals.

It is evident from the examples given above that acoustic signals have a unique function in the social behaviour of animals. They are used to coordinate the behaviour of conspecifics to an extraordinary degree, because they have the quality of rapid fading which enables the transmission of many signals, each conveying subtle changes in motivation. In audition, unlike vision, the sense organs do not have to be 'focused' on the signaller, thus animals' signals can be perceived by all those in the vicinity. Acoustic signals serve the same wide variety of functions already noted in this chapter. Their advantage over visual signals is that, though discrete, they have immense carrying properites and can be used between widely separated animals. Reproductive, aggressive, territorial, and warning behaviour may all be controlled by auditory signals, and these signals may frequently be used in individual recognition.

3.5 Tactile Communication

Although tactile communication clearly plays a significant role in a variety of forms of behaviour, relatively little has been written about this form of animal communication. Indeed, as Geldard (1977) pointed out, this field of knowledge has not been systematically explored except in the field of human behaviour, and tactile communication in animals finds a very small place in many texts on communication (Sebeok, 1977). Montagu (1978) stressed the importance of tactile communication in man, and his observation that 'The skin, like a cloak, covers us all over, the oldest and most sensitive of our organs, our first means of communication' (p. 1) must certainly apply to most mammals. Argyle (1975) suggested that tactile signals are not really signals at all but 'basic social behaviour' (p. 29), and he believed that signals from other communication channels lead to tactile events. While it is undoubtedly true that much social behaviour is designed to promote close physical proximity, as in suckling or copulation, tactile signals still have an important role in initiating these and other forms of social behaviour, as the examples in the following paragraphs will show.

The importance of touch in animal life varies greatly from species to species. For many animals, physical contact is almost totally confined to reproductive behaviour. This is certainly the case in many solitary mammals, and in most birds it is the rule, except in roosting where animals may 'clump' together (Morris, 1956). In reptiles, fish, and many invertebrates, this relative lack of physical contact is also found. However, contact in social mammals plays an important part in many forms of behaviour, for instance greeting, grooming, fighting, reproductive behaviour, and play.

Touch is often used in greeting between animals; a strange animal may approach and touch a conspecific in a characteristic way which appears to have evolved to show friendly rather than aggressive intentions. Chimpanzees greet each other by holding out their hands, much like the human handshake, or by touching lips, or kissing (Lawick-Goodall, 1968). This latter form of behaviour is regarded as a ritualized form of feeding (as is shown, for instance, in maternal care; see Eibl-Eibesfeldt, 1970a). A variety of animals, for example many rodents, show kissing during greeting, but in these animals sniffing and nibbling around the conspecific's mouth may well provide useful information through the perception of olfactory and taste stimuli. Eibl-Eibesfeldt noted that seal mothers greet their young by rubbing snouts, and affectionate rubbing of noses is characteristic of many carnivores; like rodents, this behaviour probably provides a variety of other signals which may be used in individual recognition.

Since many greeting responses appear to arise out of patterns of behaviour characteristic of maternal care, the use of tactile stimuli in this form of behaviour is not unexpected. The young of higher animals typically spend their early life in close proximity to one or both parents, and thus signalling by this means is likely to be well developed. Young mammals suckle from their mothers, and tactile stimuli often play a large part in controlling this behaviour. It is well known to mothers that a touch on the cheek of a human baby will elicit head turning towards the source of the stimulus (the rooting reflex), and this is found in many other mammals (Prechtl & Schleidt, 1950, cited by Eibl-Eibesfeldt, 1970a). Tactile and olfactory cues are thought to play an important role in the establishment of suckling in many species, particularly those where the young are very immature at birth (altricial species). Rosenblatt (1971) in his study of kittens, suggested that these cues are important in establishing nipple preferences, since kittens tend to suckle regularly from one particular nipple, although a 'teat order' as rigid as that found in piglets (McBride, 1963) is not characteristic in kittens. Elimination of urine and faeces in young animals is often elicited by tactile stimuli. Mothers of many species, including the wolf (Mech, 1970), and the guinea-pig (Berryman, 1974), stimulate their infants by licking around the anogenital region, and this causes the urine and faeces to be passed. Infants may die if not stimulated to eliminate in this way.

Many animals beg for food from their parents during infancy, and this is often done by animals touching, or nuzzling, the parents around the mouth; in the wolf, for instance, pups nuzzle the corners of the mouth to stimulate the mother to regurgitate food (Mech, 1970). In the courtship of birds, ritualized food begging is often shown, and although food may be presented, in some cases a pair simply 'flirt with their beaks' but no longer exchange food — the bullfinch is one such example (Eibl-Eibesfeldt, 1970b, p. 108) — and thus the tactile stimuli in beaking form a central part of this display. Although clearly the goal of courtship is copulation, usually involving very close contact between mates, tactile signals may also be used in courtship prior to mounting in mammals, in the elicitation of the appropriate sexual posture in the female. Evidence for the role of tactile stimuli in sexual behaviour has been clearly demonstrated by Signoret (1970) in the pig. Sows exhibit a 'mating stance' or 'standing reaction' which enables the boar to mount and copulate. Standing can be elicited by a variety of cues, but 60% of sows respond to tactile stimuli on their backs by standing even in the absence of the boar (this occurs between the 24th and 36th hour of oestrus). Lordosis (the posture of the female rodent during copulation) in response to tactile stimuli is shown in various female rodents at oestrus; the hamster (Murphy, 1974) is one example.

Another form of behaviour in which contact frequently plays a major role is play. Although the identification of play behaviour is problematical it is thought to occur in many mammals. According to Miller (1968), it is shown by cats, dogs, lions, sheep, goats, horses, elephants, rhinoceroses, camels, rabbits, and hares. It is also prevalent in many primates. Lawick-Goodall (1968) reported that mother chimpanzees often initiate play with their infants by tickling, and older infants try to initiate play by pulling their mothers' hands towards them while also showing the 'play-face'. Adults often initiate play by tickling or thumping their chosen partner, and adult males may use 'finger wrestling', or patting under the chin. While it is clear that other signals are involved in the initiation of play behaviour, the non-aggressive nature of the tactile signals is clearly important in establishing the form of the social interaction which will follow. Bodily contact has a powerful soothing and calming effect on individuals. It represents comfort and protection and is not only confined to the parent–infant relationship, but is retained into adult life

(Eibl-Eibesfeldt, 1970b), although as has already been emphasized, much bodily contact is in fact initiated by the use of other non-tactile signals. The stimulation it affords in grooming, for instance, is clearly essential to the maintenance of social groups of animals.

Lastly in this section the use of tactile stimuli in honey bee communication should be noted. The honey bee is well known for the sophisticated dance which she performs when communicating the source of nectar to her fellow workers (von Frisch, 1954). This dance incorporates a number of features, including circular and figure-of-eight movements, wagging of the abdomen, and specific directional orientation on the honeycomb. Worker bees follow the dance by touching the dancer with their antennae and moving with her as she dances. The dance is performed in the dark interior of the hive, thus the bees receive information about the distance and direction of the nectar through the sense of touch. Acoustic and olfactory signals are also important in the bee dance.

To summarize: tactile communication is unlike all other methods described in this chapter in that it does not travel. This property necessitates that animals have come together as a result of some other form of communication, and thus tactile stimuli are often the essence of, rather than the initiation of, social interactions. Tactile stimuli are commonly used, as has been shown, in sexual, affiliative, and amicable contexts, and they play a vital role in cooperative behaviour. Group cooperation is often maintained via tactile events such as are found in greeting, protection, and grooming.

3.6 Electric Communication

Electric communication, which exists among only a few aquatic species, serves a variety of functions. Hopkins (1977), reviewing this field, observed that animals with powerful electric organ discharges (EODs) such as the electric eel, and electric catfish, use them to stun their prey, while animals with both electric organs and electric receptors can use this sense in the detection of objects (termed 'electrolocation'), and in communication with conspecifics. Others lacking electric organs, but sensitive to electric fields, use this sense in prey detection. Thus electric organs are not used for communication alone.

The ability to sense the presence of an electric current is more widespread than the ability to generate one. Electric production occurs in both freshwater and marine fish. The former include the gymnotid fish of South America, and the African myriform fish. Marine examples include the electric rays (*Torpedinidae*), electric skates (*Rajidae*), and stargazers (*Uranoscopidae*) (Hopkins, 1977). Electric currents are generated from organs that are similar in structure to either muscle or nerve tissue. The former are most common, and they may be localized in specific regions of the fish, or along the whole length of the animal (Hopkins, 1974a). All electric fish are capable of producing their own signal energy, they do not have to depend on other available sources of energy outside the body such as sunlight. Although the majority of animals do not perceive electric currents, Bullock (1973) has suggested that nearly all animals including humans emit d.c. (direct current) fields when immersed in water. These are thought to arise from differences in electrical potentials between body fluids and the water, and also between different parts of the body. A.c. (alternating current) fields (which are much smaller) are due to muscle and heart activity. Wounds increase the voltage gradient, and thus animals using the electric modality may not only detect a wide variety of species, but also determine their condition, by the means of electric signals.

Electric signals are transmitted only for short distances, perhaps up to 10 metres, and they fade out rapidly. This means that subtle and rapid changes in the motivation of an animal can be transmitted. Like sound and chemical signals, they are also capable of crooked line transmission. Suspended particulate matter in the water does not affect them, and they have the almost instantanous properties of visual signals, but are ideal in dark and muddy waters. Although the function of electric signals has not been studied to the extent that signal function has been explored in other sensory modalities, it is known that these signals are used in a variety of ways.

Signals may indicate the species of the signaller. Hopkins (1974b) demonstrated that the 'wave' discharges of *Eigenmannia virescens* (one of the common gymnotid fish) are clearly distinguishable from other 'wave' species. Signals are used in sexual behaviour, and Hopkins (1977) has shown that in *Sternopygus macrurus* (another species of gymnotid), sexually mature males and females have characteristically different discharge frequencies: females have higher frequencies than males. During the breeding season males produce a particular sort of modification in their discharge when a female passes nearby. Since these occur only in the breeding season, and only in the presence of females, they are thought to be signals which elicit approach on the part of the female (Hopkins, 1972). Indeed Hopkins (1974c) observed in two pairs of *Sternopygus* that the male and female discharges have a particular relationship to each other. When the male and female come together for pairing either one may change its frequency to be in an octave relation with the other, thereby imitating the partner and facilitating mate recognition.

Electric signals are sometimes used in aggressive interactions during threat and submission. Black-Cleworth (1970) has shown from her observations of the electric fish *Gymnotus carapo* that these animals exhibit dominance hierarchies and territoriality, and have well-developed aggressive behaviour. Her observations revealed that this species shows a particular electric display just prior to attack. This display consists of a *sharp increase* in the EOD frequency followed by a *decrease* back to the resting frequency (the SID display). SID displays rarely accompany threats, and frequently are followed by attacks and biting. Recipients are likely to retreat after SID displays. This form of display appears to be widespread in gymnotids and mormyrids (Hopkins, 1977). Submissive signals in *Gymnotus carapo* take the form of a discharge arrest, or a complete cessation in the EOD for up to three minutes. Black-Cleworth found that arrests were given exclusively by submissive fish and she suggested that these function as appeasement signals.

To summarize: although there is comparatively little research on this exotic form of animal communication, the few examples given here serve to illustrate that electric signals have functions in communication much like signals in other sensory modalities. Electrical signals may be used to facilitate mate recognition between pairs, and hence foster male–female cooperation in spawning behaviour, and they may also have a function in competition, between males fighting over territory, or their place in the dominance hierarchy.

3.7 Language Learning in Non-human Primates: The Controversy

Although the question of ape linguistic ability is a most interesting aspect of animal communication, its role in cooperative and competitive behaviour seems at first glance to be tenuous. Unlike other forms of communication discussed here, which have evolved within a species and thus have a genetic basis, linguistic ability in apes, if it can be shown to occur, would be an entirely acquired system of communication. If it can be acquired, this raises many important questions, two of which will be considered here. First, are the signs acquired by apes used linguistically in the same way that we use them in our language? And second, if the animals learn our signs, can they use them in communication with each other, and not just in interactions with humans? The following paragraphs will explore these two points.

First attempts at teaching non-human primates language centred on phonetic language. Hayes (1951) reported teaching Viki, a chimpanzee, several words, by moving her lips while she was making an 'ah' sound. By this means Viki learned four words, but the process was exceedingly laboured since chimps are mostly silent except when excited. This inability on the part of chimpanzees to articulate as we do is highlighted by Keleman (1948) who noted that they are unable to imitate human speech, as a chimpanzee's voice is made up of entirely different phonetic elements. Studies such as this one indicate that the phonetic aspect of language is probably unique to man (Healy, 1973).

Subsequent researchers have used manual and visual means in exploring the question of language learning by non-human primates. A number of researchers have used visual/manual techniques and of these, four especially notable examples will be considered: the Gardners' (1975a, 1975b, 1978) work on Washoe, a female chimpanzee; Premack's (1976) work on Sarah, a female chimpanzee; Rumbaugh *et al.*'s (1973) work on Lana, also a female chimpanzee; and Terrace's (1979) work on Nim, a male chimpanzee.

The Gardners' work (1975a, 1975b, 1978) on Washoe was concerned with teaching her American Sign Language (Ameslan) by a process which was termed 'moulding'. This involved showing the chimpanzee the relevant sign by guiding its hand to the sign used in Ameslan. Washoe learned a large number of words, and she used these singly and in combinations. If her words are to be considered as language then the word combinations should have particular grammatical relations to each other (Terrace *et al.*, 1979). The Gardners believed that Washoe's word combinations did have this quality. A further feature of Washoe's signing which has been widely discussed was her ability to create new meanings. through novel word combinations, in particular her coining of the term 'water-bird' when asked 'what that?' in the presence of a swan (Linden, 1976; Terrace *et al.*, 1979).

A number of criticisms have been aimed at the conclusions drawn from this work. Terrace (1979), and Terrace *et al.*, (1979) noted that the Gardners' work (1975a, 1975b, 1978) in general does not allow the reader to see the exact response made by Washoe. Washoe's responses were recorded in most cases in only one order, the order that would be followed in English, and this was not necessarily the order in which she signed. A record of 'more tickle' and 'tickle more' were both recorded as 'more tickle', and thus the reader cannot ascertain whether Washoe obeyed the language rules of sign order.

A series of double-blind tests were used during the training of Washoe (Fouts & Rigby, 1977) in which it was hoped that Washoe would not receive any clues from her trainers that might lead her to the correct answer. Evidence indicating just how sensitive animals can be to cues from their trainers comes from Clever Hans, the thinking horse owned by Herr von Osten of Berlin in the early part of this century. Clever Hans was thought to be able to perform arithmetical calculations (among other feats), by tapping out answers to questions with his hooves, until it was shown that he was responding to unintentional cues from his questioners (Sebeok & Umiker-Sebeok, 1979). However, Sebeok and Umiker-Sebeok noted that despite the care with which Washoe's tests were constructed (neither the trainer nor the observers in these tests could see the objects which Washoe was asked to name) there were loopholes in the system. Washoe's vocabulary was small, the possible answers available to her were limited, and her own non-verbal responses to the things in front of her may have indicated to her observers exactly what the objects were. Sebeok and Umiker-Sebeok reported that the two observers came to agree more and more on Washoe's signing as tests progressed, and some form of cuing, however subtle, seems to have been involved.

Washoe's ability to generate novel meanings is also in doubt (Terrace *et al.*, 1979). Washoe signed 'water' then 'bird' in the presence of water and a bird, but it is impossible to conclude that she related the two signs to the form of the swan in front of her. To the human observer this combination is meaningful, but we have no basis for applying our notion of its meaning to Washoe. Washoe is not reported to have subsequently called swans 'water-birds' in the absence of water. Perhaps if she had it might be concluded that she characterized the swan as a bird which inhabits water. A further point to consider is that Washoe did not generate these sorts of responses frequently; her language consisted of using and repeating many of the words given to her in the preceeding questions of her teachers. That she produced a single word combination of her own would not be considered significant in a statistical analysis, but would rather be attributed to chance.

Research on Sarah and Lana, both of whom were taught an artificial language, will be considered next. Sarah communicated using plastic chips of different colours and shapes (Premack, 1976) and Lana was taught to use Yerkish, an artifical visual language, using a computer (Rumbaugh *et al.*,

1973). Sarah could be shown to follow instructions such as 'Sarah insert apple pail' and 'Sarah insert banana dish' when confronted with both fruits and utensils, and Lana could press keys to ask 'please machine give juice' and similar requests.

Although both animals were impressive in the tasks that they could perform, the degree of comprehension achieved by each chimp is not clear, despite Premack's (1976) assertion that Sarah clearly could read and interpret sentences. Terrace *et al.* (1979) suggested that both chimps' multisign utterances, or responses to such utterances, were interpretable as responses arising from rote learned sequences of symbols arranged in particular orders. He suggested that the chimps' understanding of words, other than object names, was by no means established, and, apart from the object names, the chimps were not able to substitute other symbols in the correct positions in a previously learned sequence. Terrace *et al.* likened these chimps' behaviour to that of pigeons trained to peck colour arrays in a particular sequence. Symbols may be grammatically related in our eyes, but their significance to the chimpanzees may be quite different (Limber, 1977). Recent work by Thompson and Church (1980) lends further support to Terrace *et al.*'s views. These writers have shown that a simple computer program can do all that Lana was capable of. The program that was used had a stock of six standard sentences, each with variable elements, and the sentences produced accounted for almost all of Lana's utterances. Thus the learning of particular sequences seems to be all that is necessary in order to explain Lana's behaviour.

Terrace *et al.* (1979) have investigated in detail much of the chimp language claims made to date, and Terrace (1979) has spent some years on a project involving the teaching of both the expression and comprehension of signs to a chimpanzee called Nim. This project overcame some of the problems found in earlier studies. Exact records of Nim's signing were kept, and Nim was considered to have acquired a sign only when he used it spontaneously (without prior prompting) in the correct context, and was observed by three independent observers on separate occasions. Like the other chimps Nim soon acquired a large vocabulary, and he signed using various word combinations. These combinations were analysed in a variety of ways. Lexical regularities and semantic relationships were looked for and a discourse analysis was made of Nim's conversations with his teacher. Results indicated that Nim's signing showed regularities, and the vast number of word combinations produced by Nim tended to indicate that these were probably not simply learned by rote. However Terrace *et al.* suggested that these observed regularities were not sufficient to demonstrate that such combinations were sentences, and he noted that 'In the absence of additional evidence, the simplist explanation of Nim's utterances is that they are unstructured combinations of signs' (p. 893). Nim appeared to have position preferences for word combinations, but clearly a non-random positioning of words does not make them into sentences. Combinations of more than two words often included repetitions, and were not like children's utterances where such repeated elements would not be used: examples include 'banana Nim banana Nim' and 'me Nim eat me'.

The analysis of semantic relationships expressed in Nim's utterances was carried out by an observer relating the utterances' immediate context to its content. Enormous problems arise in attempting to do this (they are explained in detail by Terrace *et al.*, 1979) and Terrace *et al.* have indicated that such analyses have not progressed beyond 'the stage of unvalidated interpretation' (p. 895). The problem of Washoe's 'water-bird' has already been considered, and clearly there is no basis on which to distinguish between the use of 'me' and 'Nim' in the four word combination quoted in the preceding paragraph.

The discourse analysis revealed that Nim's utterances were greatly influenced by his teacher's preceding utterance. Thus semantic relationships and position preferences might both be influenced by the teacher's signing habits. Terrace *et al.* (1979) also noted that Nim imitated his teachers more than twice as much as is found in children at an equivalent stage, and where Nim expanded his teacher's signs, he frequently added little new information. 'Nim', 'me', and 'you' were often used as expansions, whereas children do not expand responses in this way. One extremely long utterance given by Nim contained 16 signs 'give orange me give eat orange me eat orange give me eat orange give me you' (Terrace *et al.*, p. 895) and clearly shows that utterance length does not indicate semantic or syntactic competence.

The nature of the chimp – teacher conversation was also found to be unlike that in human conversation. Nim signed simultaneously with his teacher and interrupted the teacher's signing in 71% of those utterances examined (Terrace *et al.*, 1979, also analysed films of Washoe and found this to be true of her conversations). Terrace *et al.* observe that despite little if any data on this behaviour in children and adults, the most comparable study which these authors found revealed virtually no interruptions on the part of a deaf baby signing with its mother.

Terrace *et al.* (1979) concluded that despite certain lexical regularities in Nim's utterances, his signing, and that in other apes, showed merely that they can learn many isolated symbols (as can dogs, horses, and other non-human species), but they show no unequivocal evidence of mastering the conversational, semantic, or syntactic organization of language. Thus in Terrace's mind the evidence so far is clear: we have not taught chimpanzees language.

The second question posed at the start of this section remains to be answered. It has been shown that apes can use signs in communicating (if not talking) with their human teachers, yet relatively little has been written concerning their use of these learned signs in ape – ape interactions. Linden (1976), and Fouts and Rigby (1977), reported that the interactions between chimps which have been taught Ameslan may incorporate these signs. Food dominates these 'conversations', as do signs for tickling and playing. Watson (1979) recorded that chimps use 'come tickle' and 'come play', but the more complex messages used in human – chimp interactions have not been reported. It is of interest to note that the messages used are only those that chimps can also convey in their own system of communication. It would appear that teaching chimpanzees Ameslan has not enhanced or widened the scope of chimp – chimp interactions.

In summary apes do not appear to have learned human language, but they have learned many signs which they use in non-random ways in communicating with man. The patience and skill of researchers such as the Gardners, Premack, Rumbaugh, and Terrace have been rewarded by man – chimp cooperation to the extent that chimps used these learned signals to communicate with their trainers. A little evidence suggests that signs once learned may be used in signalling with conspecifics who also have been taught to sign, but as yet it appears that the only messages passed between chimps are messages which they can already send effectively with their own species-characteristic signals. For a further discussion of the uniqueness of human language, see Chapter 11.

3.8 Conclusions

In this chapter five different naturally occurring methods of animal communication have been briefly surveyed, together with one artifically taught method. The different types of communication described here enable the user to communicate a wide variety of messages, and within any given species one message may be conveyed by signals from several different modalities. Such a system ensures that the message sent impinges on at least one type of sensory receptor in a conspecific.

Communication systems used by a species vary greatly with the habitat, activity rhythms, and social life of that species. Visual signals relying on reflected light are most appropriately used by diurnal social animals living in open spaces where signals will not be obscured, while olfactory, acoustic, and electric signals are all effective in the absence of light, and the latter two are highly efficient in a dense medium, or where objects obscure conspecifics from each other. Tactile signals are of course unaffected by light, or by the type of medium in which the animal lives, since animals must be close together for these signals to be effective.

Signals vary greatly in the distances over which they may travel. Whales' sounds can travel many hundreds of kilometres across the ocean, whereas electric signals in water are effective over only a metre or so. Olfactory signals may be detected over several kilometres, but generally they are detected over rather smaller distances than either visual or acoustic signals. Tactile signals are again the exception here in having no carrying properties.

As has been noted, signals generally fall into two major categories: graded or discrete. Olfactory signals are not well suited to the discrete category, while most signals in other sensory modalities may be either graded or discrete.

Signals used in animal communication do not always have immediate effects on conspecifics, indeed chemical signals may have a 'priming' effect (in promoting certain physiological changes within an organism) the effects of which are not immediately apparent. This effect is the exception rather than the rule in animal communication.

Chemical signals are also unique in that they can be deposited by the sender, and thus evoke a response in his absence. Other signal types are received instantaneously, or almost instantaneously. Although sounds take some finite time to arrive at the sense organs of a conspecific, such that the source can be located by making binaural comparisons of phase or intensity difference, once the signal has arrived the perception if it lasts no longer than its original duration at emission. A chemical stimulus, on the other hand, may be emitted in seconds, but may remain for all to perceive over a period of days or even weeks.

The extent to which the signaller can be located varies with the type of signal emitted. Sounds emitted in certain contexts are easy to locate, and yet they can be modified to make location more difficult. For example, high, short sounds emitted in dense undergrowth are hard to trace. Warning calls appear to have evolved to make location difficult, but even this system appears not to be foolproof. The density gradient of molecules from a chemical signal enables the animal emitting such signals to be located. However, electric signals do not reveal the precise location of the signaller, whereas visual signals, whether by reflected light or bioluminescence, inevitably give away the location of the signaller, as do tactile signals.

Since most animals use a number of different types of signals, the particular properties of each signal tend to be utilized according to the context in which the animal is signalling. For example, dogs may use scent marking by urination to indicate their territory to conspecifics when the latter are *not* in the vicinity, but when other dogs are visible they may show demonstration marking by performing the raised leg display without urinating (Bekoff, 1979). Similarly, separated dogs may communicate vocally, while dogs in close contact may use visual signals in the form of changed facial expressions, tail postures, and tactile signals. Thus a wide variety of signal types are utilized within the communication system of a given species.

The traditional view of animal communication is that signals have evolved to facilitate cooperation between species members. A variety of researchers writing on animal communication (for instance, Cherry, 1957; Tinbergen, 1964; Marler, 1968) have suggested that communication within a species is mutually beneficial to the communicators. Thus signals used even in highly competitive contexts, for example in aggression, dominance, and territoriality, have their basis in a system that is ultimately thought to have evolved for the benefit of all the users of that system within a species. On this basis it could be argued that signals of threat, or appeasement and submission, are used because they enable animals to resolve their conflicts without having to resort to physical combat, and thus both participants benefit by using a common set of signals which prevent (or reduce the chances of) either being hurt. Dawkins and Krebs (1978) explained the same sort of behaviour in rather different terms. These authors suggested that natural selection favours individuals who manipulate the behaviour of other individuals — whether or not those other individuals benefit. On this basis animal communication is not seen as cooperative, although elements of it may appear to have incidental beneficial effects on conspecifics.

In competitive contexts species members complete for resources (for example food, shelter, territory, or mate). In such circumstances highly ritualized forms of combat are often observed. Since all animals are in the business of survival, any type of signal that enables a battle to be resolved without danger or harm to participants is directly beneficial to the signaller, and incidentally beneficial to the reactor. In terms of survival, a threat display is better than a bite, and if the former prevents the reactor from attacking then it is obviously a signal that benefits the actor. Likewise if a weak animal can survive longer (and hence reproduce) by using submissive signals in the presence of a more dominant conspecific, such signals are clearly beneficial to the actor. They prevent battles in which the actor's life may be lost, or at the very least endangered (see Chapter 2).

The preceding pages contain a number of examples of signals used in competitive contexts. Signals used in these contexts are more varied in social animals: the domestic cat in an aggressive encounter merely attacks or defends, whereas the dog attacks, defends, or submits (Ewer, 1968). If a wolf competes and loses, it must still exist beside the winner. It must signal to the more dominant animal that it is inferior, and that it will not therefore initiate aggressive outbursts. By this means it can retain its place and live among other wolves. Signals eliciting cooperative behaviour have evolved because the actor benefits by this behaviour. In social species, more examples of cooperative acts are found because the survival of individuals depends to a greater extent on other conspecifics than does survival in solitary species. Thus both cooperative and competitive signals are likely to be more highly developed in social species — and it is no surprise to find the communication systems in social species are indeed more complex.

Animal communication is a highly efficient way of enabling an animal to control the behaviour of its conspecifics. In terms of survival, and the efficient use of an animal's energy resources, it is much more efficient to sing a song, or secrete a chemical substance, or wave a chela, or to emit an electric discharge in order to attract a mate than to go out and search for one at random. Dawkins and Krebs (1978) suggested that 'Communication, which we use interchangeably with 'signalling', could be characterized as a means by which one animal makes use of another animal's muscle power' (p. 283). Thus whether an animal appears to cooperate or to compete, it can be seen as efficiently manipulating the behaviour of others through the signals that it uses in communication.

Acknowledgements

I should like to thank Dr. U. Weidmann and Dr. D. Harper for their helpful comments on this manuscript.

References

ALEXANDER, R.D. (1968). Arthropods. In T.A. SEBEOK (Ed.), *Animal Communication: Techniques of Study and Results of Research*. Bloomington: Indiana University Press.

ARGYLE, M. (1975). *Bodily Communication.* London: Methuen.

BARFIELD, R.J. and GEYER, L.A. (1972). Sexual behaviour: ultrasonic post-ejaculatory song of the male rat. *Science*, **176**, 1349 – 1350.

BARTHOLOMEW, G.A. and COLLIAS, N.E. (1962). The role of vocalization in the social behaviour of the northern elephant seal. *Animal Behaviour*, **10**, 7 – 14.

BEAUCHAMP, G.K. DOTY, R.L., MOULTON, D.G. and MUGFORD, R.A. (1976). The pheromone concept in mammalian chemical communication: a critique. In R.L. DOTY (Ed.), *Mammalian Olfaction, Reproductive Processes, and Behaviour*. London: Academic Press.

BEKOFF, M. (1979). Ground scratching by male domestic dogs: a composite signal. *Journal of Mammalogy*, **60**, 847 – 848.

BERRYMAN, J.C. (1974). A study of guinea pig vocalizations: with particular reference to mother – infant interactions. Unpublished doctoral dissertation, University of Leicester.

BERRYMAN, J.C. (1976). Guinea-pig vocalizations: their structure, causation and function. *Zeitschrift für Tierpsychologie*, **41**, 80 – 106.

BLACK-CLEWORTH, P. (1970). The role of electrical discharges in the non-reproductive social behaviour of *Gymnotus carapo* (Gymnotidae, Pisces). *Animal Behaviour Monographs*, **3** (1).

BLEST, D. (1957). The function of eyespot patterns in the Lepidoptera. *Behaviour*, **11**, 209 – 256.

BOCH, R., SHEARER, D.A. and STONE, B.C. (1962). Identification of iso-amyl acetate as an active component in the sting pheromone of the honey bee. *Nature*, **195**, 1018 – 1020.

BRONSON, F.H. (1969). Pheromonal influences on mammalian reproduction. In M. DIMOND (Ed.), *Perspectives in Reproduction and Sexual Behaviour*. Bloomington: Indiana University Press.

BROWN, K. (1979). Chemical communication between animals. In K. BROWN and S.J. COOPER (Eds.), *Chemical Influences on Behaviour*. London: Academic Press.

BRUCE, H.M. (1959). An exteroceptive block to pregnancy in the mouse. *Nature*, **184**, 105.

BRUCE, H.M. (1960). A block to pregnancy in the mouse caused by proximity of strange males. *Journal of Reproduction and Fertility*, **1**, 96 – 103.

BRUCE, H.M. (1966). Smell as an exteroceptive factor. *Journal of Animal Science, Supplement*, **25**, 83 – 89.

BULLOCK, T.H. (1973). Seeing the world through a new sense: electroreception in fish. *American Scientist*, **61**, 316 – 325.

CALDWELL, D.K. and CALDWELL, M.C. (1977). Cetaceans. In T.A. SEBEOK (Ed.), *How Animals Communicate*. Bloomington: Indiana University Press.

CATCHPOLE, C.K. (1973). The function of advertising song in the sedge warbler (*Acrocephalus schoenobaenus*) and the reed warbler (*A. scirpaceus*). *Behaviour*, **46**, 300 – 320.

CATCHPOLE, C.K. (1980). *Vocal Communication in Birds: Studies in Biology No. 115.* Edward Arnold: London.

CHERRY, D. (1957). *On Human Communication: A Review, a Survey, and a Criticism.* London: Massachusetts Institute of Technology Press.

CLARK, A.H. (1926). Animal voices. *Scientific Monthly*, **22**, 40 – 48.

DARWIN, C. (1872). *The Expression of the Emotions in Man and Animals.* London: John Murray.

DAWKINS, R. and KREBS, J.R. (1978). Animal signals: information or manipulation? In

J.R. KREBS and N.B. DAVIES (Eds.), *Behavioural Ecology*. Oxford: Blackwell.

DEAG, J.M. (1980). *Social Behaviour of Animals: Studies in Biology No. 118*. London: Edward Arnold.

EDMUNDS, M. (1974). *Defence in Animals: A Survey of Anti-predator Defences*. Harlow, Essex: Longman.

EIBL-EIBESFELDT, I. (1970a). *Ethology: The Biology of Behaviour*. New York: Holt, Rinehart & Winston.

EIBL-EIBESFELDT, I. (1970b). *Love and Hate: On the Natural History of Basic Behaviour Patterns*. London: Methuen.

ESPMARK, Y. (1971). Individual recognition by voice in reindeer mother – young relationship: field observations and playback experiments. *Behaviour*, **40**, 296 – 301.

EWER, R.F. (1968). *Ethology of Mammals*. London: Logos Press.

EWING, A.W. (1977). Communication in Diptera. In T.A. SEBEOK (Ed.), *How Animals Communicate*. Bloomington: Indiana University Press.

FOUTS, R.S. and RIGBY, R.L. (1977). Man – chimpanzee communication. In T.A. SEBEOK (Ed.), *How Animals Communicate*. Bloomington: Indiana University Press.

FRISCH, K. VON (1954). *The Dancing Bees: An Account of the Life and Senses of the Honey Bee*. London: Methuen.

FULLERTON, C., BERRYMAN, J.C. and PORTER, R.H. (1974). On the nature of mother – infant interactions in the guinea-pig (*Cavia porcellus*). *Behaviour*, **48**, 145 – 156.

GARDNER, R.A. and GARDNER, B.T. (1975a). Early signs of language in child and chimpanzee. *Science*, **187**, 752 – 753.

GARDNER, B.T. and GARDNER, R.A. (1975b). Evidence for sentence constituents in the early utterances of child and chimpanzee. *Journal of Experimental Psychology: General*, **104**, 244 – 267.

GARDNER, R.A. and GARDNER, B.T. (1978). Comparative psychology and language acquisition. *Annals of the New York Academy of Science*, **309**, 37 – 75.

GEIST, V. (1971). *Mountain Sheep: A Study in Behaviour and Evolution*. Chicago: University of Chicago Press.

GELDARD, F.A. (1977). Tactile communication. In T.A. SEBEOK (Ed.), *How Animals Communicate*. Bloomington: Indiana University Press.

HAYES, C. (1951). *The Ape in Our House*. New York: Harper & Row.

HEALY, A.F. (1973). Can chimpanzees learn a phonetic language? *Journal of Psycholinguistic Research*, **2**, 167 – 170.

HEBB, D.O. and THOMPSON, W.R. (1954). The social significance of animal studies. In G. LINDSAY and E. ARONSON (Eds.), *Handbook of Social Psychology Vol 2*. New York: Addison-Wesley.

HOCKETT, C.F. (1960). Logical considerations in the study of animal communication. In W.E. LANYON and W.N. TAVOLGA (Eds.), *Animal Sounds and Communication*. Washington, D.C.: American Institute of Biological Sciences.

HOPKINS, C.D. (1972). Sex differences in electric signalling in an electric fish. *Science*, **176**, 1035 – 1037.

HOPKINS, C.D. (1974a). Electric communication in fish. *American Scientist*, **62**, 426 – 437.

HOPKINS, C.D. (1974b). Electric communication: functions in the social behaviour of *Eigenmannia virescens*. *Behaviour*, **50**, 270 – 305.

HOPKINS, C.D. (1974c). Electric communication in the reproductive behaviour of *Sternopygus macrurus*. *Zeitschrift für Tierpsychologie*, **35**, 518 – 535.

HOPKINS, C.D. (1977). Electric communication. In T.A. SEBEOK (Ed.), *How Animals Communicate*. Bloomington: Indiana University Press.

HUTCHISON, R.E., STEVENSON, J.G. and THORPE, W.H. (1968). The basis for individual recognition by voice in the sandwich tern (*Sterna sandvicensis*). *Behaviour*, **32**, 150 – 157.

JELLIS, R. (1977). *Bird Sounds and Their Meaning*. London: British Broadcasting Corporation.

KARLSON, P. and LÜSCHER, M. (1959). 'Pheromones': a new term for a class of biologically active substances. *Nature*, **183**, 55 – 56.

KELEMAN, G. (1948). The anatomical basis of phonation in the chimpanzee. *Journal of Morphology*, **82**, 229 – 256.

KILEY, M. (1969). A comparative study of some displays in ungulates, canids and felids, with particular reference to causation. Unpublished doctoral dissertation, University of Sussex.

KILEY, M. (1972). The vocalizations of ungulates, their causation and function. *Zeitschrift für Tierpsychologie*, **31**, 171 – 222.

KREBS, J.R. (1976). Bird song and territorial defence. *New Scientist*, **70**, 534 – 536.

KUNKEL, P. and KUNKEL, I. (1964). Beiträge zur Ethologie des Hausmeerschweinchens *Cavia aperea f. porcellus (L)*. *Zeitschrift für Tierpsychologie*, **21**, 603 – 641.

LACK, D. (1946). *The Life of the Robin*. London: Witherby.

LAWICK-GOODALL, J. VAN (1968). The behaviour of free-living chimpanzees in the Gombe stream reserve. *Animal Behaviour Monographs*, **1** (3).

LEON, M. (1975). Dietary control of maternal pheromone in the lactating rat. *Physiology and Behaviour*, **14**, 311 – 319.

LIMBER, J. (1977). Language in child and chimp? *American Psychologist*, **32**, 280 – 295.

LINDEN, E. (1976). *Apes, Men and Language*. Harmondsworth: Penguin.

LINDSAY, D.R. and FLETCHER, J.C. (1968). Sensory involvement in the recognition of lambs by their dams. *Animal Behaviour*, **16**, 415 – 417.

LLOYD, J.E. (1975). Aggressive mimicry in *Photuris* fireflies: signal repertoires by femme fatales. *Science*, **187**, 452 – 453.

LLOYD, J.E. (1977). Bioluminescence and communication. In T.A. SEBEOK, (Ed.), *How Animals Communicate*. Bloomington: Indiana University Press.

MARLER, P.J. (1955). Characteristics of some animal calls. *Nature*, **176**, 6 – 8.

MARLER, P.J. (1967). Animal communication signals. *Science*, **157**, 769 – 774.

MARLER, P. (1968). Visual systems. In T.A. SEBEOK, (Ed.), *Animal Communication: Techniques of Study and Results of Research*. Bloomington: Indiana University Press.

MARLER, P. (1972). Vocalizations of East African monkeys. **II**: Black and white colobus. *Behaviour*, **42**, 175 – 195.

MCBRIBE, G. (1963). The teat order and communication in young pigs. *Animal Behaviour*, **11**, 53 – 56.

MECH, L.D. (1970). *The Wolf: The Ecology and Behaviour of an Endangered Species*. New York: Natural History Press.

MICHAEL, R.P., BONSALL, R.W. and ZUMPE, D. (1976). Evidence for chemical communication in primates. *Vitamins and Hormones*, **34**, 137 – 187.

MILLER, S. (1968). *The Psychology of Play*. Harmondsworth: Penguin.

MONTAGU, A. (1978). *Touching: The Human Significance of Skin*. London: Harper & Row.

MORRIS, D. (1956). The feather postures of birds and the problem of the origin of social signals. *Behaviour*, **9**, 75 – 114.

MURPHY, M.R. (1974). Relative importance of tactual and nontactual stimuli in eliciting lordosis in the female golden hamster. *Behavioural Biology*, **11**, 115 – 119.

MYKYTOWYCZ, R. (1968). Territorial marking by rabbits. *Scientific American*, **218** (5), 116–126.

MYKYTOWYCZ, R. (1970). The role of skin glands in mammalian communication. In J.W. JOHNSTON, D.G. MOULTON and A. TURK (Eds.), *Advances in Chemoreception*. Vol. 1. New York: Appleton-Century Croft.

NOIROT, E. (1964). Changes in responsiveness to young in the adult mouse. The problematical effect of hormones. *Animal Behaviour*, **12**, 52–58.

OTTE, D. (1974). Effects and functions in the evolution of signalling systems. *Annual Review of Ecology and Systematics*, **5**, 385–417.

PACKARD, A. and SANDERS, G.D. (1971). Body patterns of *Octopus vulgaris* and maturation of the response to disturbance. *Animal Behaviour*, **19**, 780–790.

PAYNE, R.S. and MCVAY, S. (1971). Songs of humpback whales. *Science*, **173**, 587–597.

PETRINOVICH, L. (1974). Individual recognition of pup vocalization by northern elephant seal mothers. *Zeitschrift für Tierpsychologie*, **34**, 308–312.

PORTER, R.H. FULLERTON, C. and BERRYMAN, J.C. (1973). Guinea-pig maternal–young attachment behaviour. *Zeitschrift für Tierpsychologie*, **32**, 489–495.

PREMACK, A.J. (1976). *Why Chimps Can Read*. London: Harper & Row.

RÉVÉSZ, G. (1944). The language of animals. *Journal of General Psychology*, **30**, 117–147.

ROSENBLATT, J.S. (1971). Suckling and home orientation in the kitten: a comparative developmental study. In E. TOBACH, L.R. ARONSON and E. SHAW (Eds.), *The Biopsychology of Development*. London: Academic Press.

ROWELL, T. (1972). *Social Behaviour of Monkeys*. Harmondsworth: Penguin.

RUMBAUGH, D.M., VON GLASERFELD, E.D., WARNER, H., PISANI, P., GILL, T.V., BROWN, J.V., and BELL, C.L. (1973). Exploring language skills of Lana chimpanzee. *International Journal of Symbology*, **4**, 1–9.

SALMON, M. (1967). Coastal distribution, display and sound production by Florida fiddler crabs (genus *Uca*). *Animal Behaviour*, **15**, 449–459.

SCHENKEL, R. (1947). Expression studies of wolves. *Behaviour*, **1**, 81–129.

SCHENKEL, R. (1967). Submission: its features and function in the wolf and dog. *American Zoologist*, **7**, 319–329.

SCHWEINBURG. R.E. and SOWLS, L.K. (1972). Aggressive behaviour and related phenomena in the collared peccary. *Zeitschrift für Tierpsychologie*, **30**, 132–145.

SCOTT, J.P. (1968). Observation. In T.A. SEBEOK (Ed.), *Animal Communication: Techniques of Study and Results of Research*. Bloomington: Indiana University Press.

SEBEOK, T.A. (1962). Coding in the evolution of signalling behaviour. *Behavioural Science*, **7**, 430–442.

SEBEOK, T.A. (1977). *How Animals Communicate*. Bloomington: Indiana University Press.

SEBEOK, T.A. and UMIKER-SEBEOK, J. (1979). Performing animals: secrets of the trade. *Psychology Today*, **13** (6), 78–91.

SEWELL, G.D. (1970). Ultrasonic signals from rodents. *Ultrasonics*, **8**, 26–30.

SHALTER, M.D. (1978). Localization of passerine seeet and mobbing calls by goshawks and pygmy owls. *Zeitschrift für Tierpsychologie*, **46**, 260–267.

SHOREY, H.H. (1977). Pheromones. In T.A. SEBEOK, (Ed.), *How Animals Communicate*. Bloomington: Indiana University Press.

SIGNORET, J.P. (1970). Reproductive behaviour of pigs. *Journal of Reproduction and Fertility, Supplement*, **11**, 105–117.

SIMMONS, K.E.L. and WEIDMANN, U. (1973). Directional bias as a component of social behaviour with special reference to the mallard, *Anas platyrhynchos*. *Journal of Zoology*, **170**, 49 – 62.

SNYDER, N. and SNYDER, H. (1970). Alarm responses of *Diadema antillarum*. *Science*, **168**, 276 – 278.

SOKOLOV, J.J., HARRIS, R.T. and HECKER, M.R. (1976). Isolation of substances from human vaginal secretions previously shown to be sex attractant pheromones in high primates. *Archives of Sexual Behaviour*, **5**, 269 – 274.

STANLEY, M. (1971). An ethogram of the hopping mouse, *Notomys alexis*. *Zeitschrift für Tierpsychologie*, **29**, 225 – 258.

STEHN, R.A. and RICHMOND, M.E. (1975). Male-induced pregnancy termination in the prairie vole, *Microtus ochrogaster*. *Science*, **187**, 1211 – 1213.

STEVENS, S.S. (1950). Introduction: a definition of communication. *Journal of the Acoustical Society of America*, **22**, 689 – 690.

STUART, A.M. (1963). Origin of the trail in the termites *Nasutitermes corniger (Motschulsky)* and *Zootermopsis nevadensis (Hagen)*, Isoptera. *Physiological Zoology*, **36**, 69 – 84.

TEMBROCK, T. (1968). Communication in land mammals. In T.A. SEBEOK, (Ed.), *Animal Communication: Techniques of Study and Results of Research*. Bloomington: Indiana University Press.

TERRACE, H.S. (1979). *Nim*. London: Eyre Methuen.

TERRACE, H.S., PETITTO, L.A. SANDERS, R.J. and BEVER, T.G. (1979). Can an ape create a sentence? *Science*, **206**, 891 – 902.

THIESSEN, D.P., CLANCY, A. and GOODWIN, M. (1976). Harderian gland pheromone in the Mongolian gerbil *Meriones unguiculatus*. *Journal of Chemical Ecology*, **2**, 231 – 238.

THOMPSON, C.R. and CHURCH, R.M. (1980). An explanation of the language of a chimpanzee. *Science*, **208**, 313 – 314.

THORPE, W.H. (1973). Duet-singing birds. *Scientific American*, **229** (2), 70 – 79.

TINBERGEN, N. (1951). *The Study of Instinct*. London: Oxford University Press.

TINBERGEN, N. (1964). The evolution of signalling devices. In W. ETKIN (Ed.), *Social Behaviour and Organization Among Vertebrates*. Chicago: University of Chicago Press.

TSCHANZ, B. (1962). Uber die Beziehungen zwischen Muttertier und Jungen beim Mufflon (*Ovis airis musimon Pall*). *Experientia*, **18**, 187 – 190.

TYLER, S.J. (1972). The behaviour and social organization of the New Forest ponies. *Animal Behaviour Monographs*, **5** (2).

WATSON, P. (1979). How Moja the talking chimp learned to draw. *The Sunday Times Magazine*, *18 November*, 64 – 75.

WILSON, E.O. (1968). Chemical systems. In T.A. SEBEOK, (Ed.), *Animal Communication: Techniques of Study and Results of Research*. Bloomington: Indiana University Press.

WILSON, E.O. (1975). *Sociobiology: The New Synthesis*. Cambridge, Mass: Harvard University Press.

WILSON, E.O. and BOSSERT, W.H. (1963). Chemical communication among animals. *Recent Progress in Hormone Research*, **19**, 673 – 716.

II Human Social Behaviour

CHAPTER 4

Theory of Voting

Andrew M. Colman

4.1 Background

This chapter focuses on the problem of reaching a 'fair' and 'democratic' collective decision on the basis of a set of conflicting individual preferences. This is a familiar problem of cooperation in complex societies: it arises whenever a group of people whose tastes, interests, beliefs, attitudes, and values differ have to submit to a decision that will be binding on everyone. In such circumstances, any decision is likely to please some people and to disappoint others, and it is therefore desirable for political and ethical reasons that the collective decision should reflect majority opinion as fairly as possible. Any method of combining disparate preferences into a single choice is called a *collective choice rule*, and voting procedures are collective choice rules that are expressly designed to reflect majority opinion in a democratically acceptable way.

It has been known since classical times, however, that seemingly democratic voting procedures can sometimes produce obviously undemocratic collective choices, and a number of disturbing voting paradoxes were discovered by mathematicians and physicists at the time of the French Revolution. The first major contribution to collective choice theory was made by Borda (1781), whose ideas were developed by Condorcet (1785) and Laplace (1814). In spite of this promising start, collective choice theory attracted little attention until the 1960s and 1970s, though Lewis Carroll (writing under his real name, the Reverend C.L. Dodgson, 1876) and other isolated scholars independently rediscovered some of the paradoxes in the intervening period. Recent contributions, most of which have been made by economists and political scientists, are for the most part theoretical in character; social psychologists are still largely oblivious of collective choice theory in spite of their long-standing interest in group decision making, and many important empirical questions remain to be answered through controlled empirical investigations of voting behaviour.

The early history of collective choice theory has been outlined by Black (1958) and Riker (1961), and more recent summaries of what has become a vast and complex branch of mathematical decision theory are also available (e.g. Sen, 1970; Fishburn, 1973a; Kelly, 1978). The purpose of this chapter is to provide an introductory, non-technical review of the collective choice literature, with special emphasis on those aspects of the theory that seem to be most relevant to social psychology in general and to the problem of cooperation in particular. Associated empirical evidence — of which there is very little — is included in this review, and attention is drawn to potential areas of empirical research that have been neglected up till now. Some of the examples and ideas are taken from Colman (1982, Chs. 10 and 11), but they have been reformulated to fit in with the broader concerns of this volume and to avoid unnecessary mathematics.

4.2 Elements of Collective Choice Theory

The following hypothetical example will help to clarify the primitive terms and axioms of collective choice theory. A political office has fallen vacant and there are three candidates, Adams, Brown, and Carter, available to fill it. One of these candidates must be chosen, and the choice rests with a group of voters — a small committee or a large electorate. Adams is known to hold left-wing views, Brown is politically moderate, and Carter is extremely right-wing. Among the voters, there are three blocs of opinion. As might be expected, the left-wing voters prefer Adams to Brown and Brown to Carter; their preference scale can be written *ABC*. The moderate voters prefer Brown to Adams and Adams to Carter, so their preference scale is *BAC*; and the right-wing voters (naturally) prefer Carter to Brown and Brown to Adams, that is, *CBA*. These three preference scales, we shall assume, are the only ones represented among the voters; no one, for example, prefers Adams to Carter and Carter to Brown. A further assumption is that each of the voting blocs commands less than half the votes and can therefore be outvoted by the other two.

In this example, there are three *candidates* from among whom a collective choice must be made: *A* (Adams), *B* (Brown), and *C* (Carter). In general, the 'candidates' may be proposals or motions or possible courses of action or any other options from among which the choice must be made. The *voters* may be thought of as the members of the committee or electorate, but it is often simpler to identify them with the distinct opinion blocs; in the above example we need thus consider only three effectively distinguishable voters. Finally, each voter has *preferences* among the available candidates: we assume that each voter can express a preference between any pair of candidates. It is clear that preferences serve the function in the theory of relating voters to candidates.

For technical reasons, and also to incorporate certain basic assumptions about human rationality into the model, two restrictions are usually placed on the voters' preferences. The first is *completeness* or *connectedness*: it is assumed that, given any pair of candidates, a voter necessarily prefers either the first to the second or the second to the first, but not both. This restriction is sometimes modified to allow a voter to express indifference; but what is essential is the assumption that each voter can express a preference (or indifference) between *A* and *B*, *A* and *C*, and *B* and *C*. The second restriction is *transitivity*: any voter who prefers *A* to *B* and *B* to *C* must necessarily prefer *A* to *C*. According to this restriction a voter cannot, for example, prefer

Adams to Brown, Brown to Carter, and Carter to Adams.

Formally, the strong ordering relation P ('is preferred to') can be defined for each voter and for each pair of candidates by incorporating the restrictions into the model as axioms:

(i) *Completeness*: For every voter and for every pair of candidates x, y, either xPy or yPx (but not both);
(ii) *Transitivity*: For every voter and for any three candidates x, y, z, if xPy and yPz, then xPz.

The first axiom is quite innocuous; it simply states that the preference relation is defined for all voters over all pairs of candidates. The second, however, is based on an important assumption about human rationality, and it raises two interesting questions. The first is this: Can it ever be rational to prefer x to y, y to z, and z to x? Plausible examples of individual intransitivity are difficult to construct, but consider the following: in choosing where to live, a person may prefer the suburbs to the inner city because of the cleaner air, and the countryside to the suburbs for the same reason; but it is not obviously irrational for this same person to prefer the inner city to the countryside because of the relative convenience of travelling to work. The second question is: Do people commonly hold instransitive preferences? Empirical evidence (reviewed in Edwards & Tversky, 1967, pp. 44 – 47, 77 – 78) is consistent with the view that intransitivities usually arise from carelessness when numerous unimportant comparisons have to be made; when the intransitivities are pointed out, the voter usually proceeds to eliminate them (Niemi & Riker, 1976). Intransitivities can, of course, be avoided by requiring the voter to arrange all of the candidates in a single rank order of preference. Insufficient empirical research has been devoted to discovering the circumstances in which axiom (ii) is violated by human decision makers. It is worth pointing out, however, that the whole edifice of collective choice theory rests on it.

We now have all the necessary ingredients of a simple collective choice model representing the Adams – Brown – Carter election. The candidates, voters, and preferences are summarized compactly in Table 4.1.

Table 4.1 Relative Preferences of Three Voters or Voting Blocs For Three Candidates

	Voters (or voting blocs)		
	Left-wing	Moderate	Right-wing
Most preferred candidate	*A*	*B*	*C*
Second ranked candidate	*B*	*A*	*B*
Least preferred candidate	*C*	*C*	*A*

4.3 Voting Procedures

In this section, three of the simplest and most common voting procedures will be examined in the light of the assumptions built into Table 4.1. Each will be shown to have certain unexpected and undesirable properties and to provide imperfect solutions to the problem of resolving differences of opinion. The three voting procedures to be examined are called *successive*, *amendment*, and *plurality* voting respectively.

Successive voting is quite commonly used in committees, and it is the standard procedure in the legislatures of West Germany, Denmark, and Norway, and in the European Council. A vote is taken on each candidate in turn; if the majority votes in favour of it, then it is declared the winner; otherwise it is eliminated. The process of elimination continues, if necessary, until just two candidates remain, whereupon a final ballot between these two decides the issue. As we shall see, the order of voting can make all the difference: different orders of successive voting can produce different collective choices from a given set of voters' preferences.

We shall begin by assuming that voting is *sincere*, that is to say that the committee members or electors vote strictly according to their preference scales on every ballot. The left-wing voters in the example summarized in Table 4.1 accordingly vote for A as long as A is still in the running, and if A has been eliminated they vote for B. The assumption is that the moderate and right-wing voters also behave sincerely in this sense. Bearing in mind that each voter or voting bloc has less than half the total number of votes, the outcome of successive voting with A presented first is as follows:

First ballot: In favour of A, left-wing voters;
Against A, moderate and right-wing voters.
Result: A is eliminated. Therefore
Second ballot: In favour of B, left-wing and moderate voters;
In favour of C, right-wing voters.
Final result: B.

The collective choice is accordingly Brown, the candidate considered best by the moderate voters and second best by the left-wing and right-wing voters. Now let us examine what happens under successive voting if B is singled out for presentation in the first ballot:

First ballot: In favour of B, moderate voters;
Against B, left-wing and right-wing voters.
Result: B is eliminated. Therefore
Second ballot: In favour of A, left-wing and moderate voters;
In favour of C, right-wing voters.
Final result: A.

With this order of voting, Adams wins! It is easily verified that the third possible order of voting, in which C is singled out for the first ballot, leads to a victory for Brown. It is clear, therefore, that the order of voting under the successive procedure can be crucial in determining the final result.

It follows from this that the voters, if they are rational, are likely to have views about the order in which the votes should be taken. If they know one another's preference scales, then the left-wing voters will favour the order in which *B* is voted on first, because this ensures that *A*, their favourite candidate, will be the final winner. The moderate and right-wing voters, on the other hand, will prefer *A* or *C* to be voted on first, because this ensures that *B* will win and they prefer *B* to *A*. In terms of final outcomes, there are in effect only two distinguishable orders of voting: '*B* first' and '*A* or *C* first'. A single procedural vote could be used to decide between these alternative orders before voting on the candidates. The moderate and right-wing blocs would outvote the left-wing bloc on this procedural issue and '*A* or *C* first' would be chosen, thus ensuring that the final winner would be *B*. Procedural votes of this kind are permitted in some decision-making bodies but not in others; they are permitted, for example, in the Swedish Parliament or *Riksdag* (Rustow, 1955) and in British Labour Party Conferences: *The Times* (24 January 1981) reported that:

> a procedural strategy adopted by the moderate leaders of the Amalgamated Union of Engineering Workers (AUEW) could threaten the precariously balanced centre-left coalition supporting the compromise formula [for electing the party leader] favoured by Mr Michael Foot . . . by getting delegates to reject the standing orders committee recommendation [regarding the order of voting on the proposals].

The order of voting that was eventually adopted led to the 'compromise formula' being eliminated before the final ballot — as planned by the AUEW. On the final ballot, however, a left-wing motion granting trade unions the largest influence in the election of the party leader, rather than the AUEW's right-wing motion, was passed by a narrow majority (*The Times*, 26 January 1981).

We turn now to the *amendment* procedure, which is traditionally used in committees, legislative bodies, and parliaments in the United Kingdom and all her former colonies including the United States, and also in Sweden and Finland. A substantive motion is tabled and an amendment is proposed. The first ballot is on the issue of whether to amend the motion. If the amendment is adopted, the second ballot is on the amended motion; if the amendment is defeated, the second ballot is on the original substantive motion. Rejecting the motion (whether substantive or amended) on the final ballot is logically equivalent to choosing a third (default) option, which is usually the *status quo*.

In the example summarized in Table 4.1, let us assume that the default option is *A*, that is, Adams will be chosen unless a majority is in favour of some other candidate. The substantive motion might then be 'That Carter be appointed to the vacant post', and the amendment 'That the word "Carter" be replaced by "Brown" '. The first ballot is between *B* and *C*, and if the electors are sincere the voting proceeds as follows:

First ballot: In favour of *B* (the amendment), left-wing and moderate voters;
In favour of *C* (the substantive motion), right-wing voters.

	Result: *B* (the amendment is carried).
Second ballot:	In favour of *B* (the amended motion), moderate and right-wing voters;
	Against *B* (i.e. in favour of *A*, the default option), left-wing voters.
	Final result: *B*.

It is easily verified that, with the postulated preferences of the voters, Brown emerges as the winner under any order of voting. In other words, whether the substantive motion is *A*, *B*, or *C*, and whichever of the others is treated as the amendment, the final collective choice is B. With preference scales different from the ones shown in Table 4.1, however, the order of voting under the amendment procedure can make a difference. Had the preference scales been *ABC*, *BCA*, and *CAB*, for example, then the final outcome would depend on the order of voting, as the reader can easily check. This is an example of Condorcet's paradox, to which we shall return later.

There are many sequential voting procedures apart from successive and amendment voting in which the order of voting can influence the final outcome; several examples have been analysed by Brams (1976), Niemi and Riker (1976), Schelling (1967) and others. Riker and Ordeshook (1973) and Miller (1977) have specified the conditions that have to be satisfied for the order of voting in sequential procedures to affect the final outcome, and the way in which voters may be expected to vote on procedural issues if they are rational. Bjurulf and Niemi (1981) have provided a complete analysis of the effects of voting orders under successive and amendment procedures.

The last voting procedure to be considered here is the one that is most commonly used in committees and elections in all countries: this is the *plurality* procedure in which all the candidates are pitted against one another in a single ballot, the one receiving the largest number of votes being declared the winner. Plurality voting avoids the problems of voting orders inherent in other procedures because it is a single-ballot, non-sequential procedure; but it has certain other peculiarities if voting is not sincere, as we shall see later.

It is impossible to determine the outcome of plurality voting from the pattern of preferences summarized in Table 4.1 without knowing which of the three voting blocs is the largest. There is a further problem if the two largest blocs are of exactly equal size, for in that case a simple plurality vote would result in a tie and the collective choice would therefore remain indeterminate. To ensure that a decisive result is always reached, a special rule for resolving ties is required. To this end, it is customary in Britain and in most other English-speaking countries (though not in the United States and Canada) for the chairman to have a casting vote, to be used in addition to his ordinary deliberative vote in the event of a tie. In order to examine the workings of the plurality procedure, let us assume that the left-wing voters in Table 4.1 constitute the largest voting bloc or — if one of the other blocs is equally large — that one of the left-wing voters has an additional casting vote. The outcome is then as follows:

Three-Way ballot: In favour of A, left-wing voters;
In favour of B, moderate voters;
In favour of C, right-wing voters.
Final result: A.

The collective choice is obviously Adams, provided that the left-wing voters are most numerous or — if one of the other blocs is equally large — that one of the left-wing voters has a casting vote to resolve a tie. The outcome of strategic voting under the plurality procedure is, as we shall see later, less obvious.

The outcomes of sincere voting under the successive, amendment, and plurality procedures may be summarized as follows. With the pattern of preferences shown in Table 4.1, and assuming that the left-wing voting bloc is largest, the successive procedure results in the choice of Adams or Brown, depending on the order in which the votes are taken; the amendment procedure results in the choice of Brown; and the plurality procedure results in the choice of Adams. None of the procedures allows Carter to be elected.

In the interests of fairness, perhaps the voters themselves ought to be allowed to choose which of the voting procedures should be used. The left-wing voters would favour the successive procedure with B presented first or the plurality procedure, because if either of these procedures were used, their favourite candidate (A) would win. Both the moderate and the right-wing voters, on the other hand, would favour the successive procedure with A or C presented first or the amendment procedure, either of which would ensure that B would win, because they prefer B to A. But in order to choose one of the voting procedures democratically, some kind of voting procedure would have to be used, and there are cases in which the voters might not agree on the most desirable procedure for this preliminary procedural vote. If the voters were sincere and rational, an infinite regress of procedural votes might follow from this analysis, and the committee or electorate might never get round to deciding on the original issue. This problem has been discussed by Riker and Ordeshook (1973, pp. 14 – 16).

4.4 Strategic Voting

It is not always in a voter's best interests simply to vote for the candidate he considers best, without paying any attention to the likely outcome; a better outcome can sometimes be ensured by voting in a way that seems not to be strictly in accordance with the voter's scale of preferences. Voting in a manner calculated to produce the *outcome* one considers best, rather than simply voting for the *candidate* one considers best, is called *strategic* or *sophisticated* voting; its full complexities are beyond the scope of this chapter, but some of the main ideas can be illustrated quite simply (see Farquharson, 1969; Kramer, 1972; Brams, 1975, Ch. 2; Brams, 1976, Ch. 1; McKelvey & Niemi, 1978; Colman, 1982, Ch. 11 for more advanced presentations).

We have seen that the order of voting sometimes makes all the difference in sequential procedures if the voters are sincere; it is possible, for example, for a candidate to lose an election simply on account of an unfavourable order of voting that is against the interests of the majority of voters. In these circumstances, if procedural votes on the issue of voting order are not permitted, it is clear that the will of the majority will be thwarted. But it has been proved (Brams, 1975, pp. 83 – 85) that the candidate who would have won under sincere voting if the order had been chosen democratically is bound to win under the unfavourable order if strategic voting is used. This theorem is illustrated in the following example.

In the successive procedure, with the pattern of preferences shown in Table 4.1, the outcomes of sincere voting are as follows: if *B* is presented first, then *A* wins, and if *A* or *C* is presented first, then *B* wins. In a procedural vote, the proposal to present *A* or *C* first would win if the voters acted in their own self-interests. But suppose that *B* is presented first — an unfavourable order for the majority of voters — and strategic voting is used. According to the theorem, *B* will win in spite of the unfavourable order of voting. This can be shown quite simply: knowing the preferences of the other voters, it would be irrational for the right-wing voters to behave sincerely because to do so would be to ensure that the winner would be *A*, their least preferred candidate. Instead of voting sincerely against *B* on the first ballot, they could vote strategically in favour of *B*, thus ensuring that this candidate, whom they prefer to *A*, would win immediately:

First ballot:	In favour of *B*, moderate and right-wing voters;
	Against *B*, left-wing voters.
	Final result: *B*.

What would happen if the moderate and left-wing voters anticipated that their right-wing colleagues might vote strategically for *B* on the first ballot? It is easy to verify that they would be powerless to do anything to alter the final outcome in their favour. The strategic outcome, *B*, is the only one that gives none of the voting blocs cause to regret the way they voted: the outcome would be no better from the left-wing voters' point of view if they voted differently, and the same can be said of the moderate and (of course) the right-wing voters. And the strategic outcome is the same as the one that would have resulted from sincere voting if a procedural vote had first been held on the question of voting order. This shows that the resource of strategic voting allows the majority opinion to prevail when procedural votes are not permitted.

Under the plurality voting procedure, the largest voting bloc — or the voter with an additional casting vote if the largest blocs are of equal size — is of course at an advantage if the voters are sincere. In the example of Table 4.1, assuming that the left-wing votes are most numerous, *A* is bound to win because he is the favourite candidate of the strongest voting bloc. Farquharson (1969) proved, however, that the exact reverse is true if strategic voting is used. Once again it is the right-wing voters who are the only ones with a rational incentive to adopt strategic voting: they can vote strategically for *B* rather than *C* in order to ensure the election of their second-ranked than their third-ranked candidate (*B* rather than *A*), and the strategic outcome (*B*) gives none of the voters any cause to regret the way they voted since none could produce a preferable outcome by voting differently. Farquharson showed that, in the majority of cases, the largest voting bloc is bound to have to settle for a less-than-favourite outcome if strategic voting is used. A shrewd politician ought therefore to seek extra power in a sincere committee or legislature but shun extra power in one given to strategic voting; this provides a simple refutation of the dogma that the fittest always survive (for a more complicated example, see Shubik, 1954).

It is possible to make certain commonsense predictions about whether sincere or strategic voting will occur in a real decision-making body. In a complicated election, for example, with numerous candidates and voting blocs, strategic votes are relatively unlikely because it is difficult for the voters to calculate their effects. Second, if the outcome of the election is of little importance to the voters, they are relatively unlikely to devote the time and energy required to work out the optimal strategies, and sincere voting is therefore to be expected. Third, if the voters are ignorant of one another's preference scales, then they lack the necessary information to vote strategically and are relatively unlikely to try to do so. On the other hand, in a simple election on an issue of great importance to the voters in which the preference scales of the various voting blocs are generally known, strategic voting seems relatively likely to occur. These are merely conjectures, however; controlled experimental investigations are needed to test them and to discover other factors that encourage sincere or strategic voting in the real world. The existing empirical evidence is entirely anecdotal; but it tends to confirm the major hypothesis that strategic voting sometimes occurs and sometimes does not occur in everyday decision-making situations. The following empirical examples are particularly striking.

Strategic voting was apparently quite common in ancient Greece and Rome (Stavely, 1972). An interesting incident in the Roman Senate, referred to in the letters of Pliny the Younger, provides a clear instance. One of the consuls had been found slain, and it was unclear whether he had killed himself or been murdered by his freedmen. The freedmen were brought before the Senate. Pliny moved that they should be acquitted; another senator that they should be banished to an island; and a third that they should be condemned to death (Pliny's letter is reproduced in Farquharson, 1969, pp. 57 – 60). There appear to have been three opinion blocs in the Senate: the acquitters' preference scale was (obviously) *ABC*, that is, acquit, banish, condemn to death; the banishers' scale was *BAC*; and the condemners' scale was *CBA*. None of the voting blocs commanded more than half of the votes, and the situation was therefore formally identical to the case of Adams, Brown, and Carter shown in Table 4.1. The final decision was reached through a simple plurality vote and, since the acquitters constituted the largest voting bloc, the outcome of sincere voting would have been *A* (acquit); but the decision actually reached was *B* (banish), which corresponds to the outcome of strategic voting — it appears that the condemners voted strategically for banishment instead of voting sincerely for condemnation to death.

Several examples of sincere and strategic voting in modern American politics have appeared in the literature. In the 1912 presidential election, according to Riker and Ordeshook (1973, p. 98) and Brams (1975, Ch. 2), voting was generally sincere, but the voters' preference scales were such that Roosevelt would probably have defeated Woodrow Wilson had the voters adopted strategic voting. In the 1948 presidential election, on the other hand, strategic voting seems to have occurred on a large scale. According to Downs (1957), 'some voters who preferred the Progressive candidate to all others nevertheless voted for the Democratic candidate' because sincere voting would have 'increased the probability that the one they favored least would win' (p. 47). In the event, Truman (Democrat) narrowly defeated Dewey (Republican) in spite of the predictions of opinion pollsters to the contrary, and Wallace (Progressive) got only 2.4% of the popular vote. During the 1970 election of a senator in New York, Ottinger (Democrat), Goodell (Republican), and Buckley (Conservative) were the three candidates. Voting was generally sincere and Buckley was elected. But the Goodell supporters, who knew that they were in a minority, could have voted strategically for Ottinger, whom they preferred to Buckley; and if sufficient of them had done this, then Ottinger would have won the election (Niemi & Riker, 1976, pp. 24 – 25).

A number of other examples of sincere and strategic voting have been reported. Rosenthal (1974), for example, has provided indirect evidence of strategic voting in French labour elections, and further examples have been discussed by Brams (1975, 1976). The evidence is all anecdotal, however, and is based on *assumptions* about the preference scales of the voters, for which hard data are invariably lacking.

Strategic voting is considered deceitful or unethical by most political commentators, and this attitude has deep historical roots. Shortly before the outbreak of the French Revolution, Borda devised a new voting procedure which was supposed to avoid certain undesirable paradoxes. When it was pointed out to him that his procedure was vulnerable to strategic voting, he exclaimed 'My scheme is intended only for honest men!' (quoted in Kelly, 1978, p. 65). In Victorian times, C.L. Dogson (Lewis Carroll) complained about a tendency among voters to make an election 'more of a game of skill than a real test of the wishes of the electors' (quoted in Farquharson, 1969, p. 17). More recently, the well-known American political scientist William Riker (1961) suggested that 'there may be nothing wrong with lying as a political strategy, but one would not, I assume, wish to give a systematic advantage to liars' (p. 905). Several writers (most recently Steen, 1980) have therefore tried to devise voting procedures that are invulnerable to strategic manipulation. But the quest for a strategy-proof system is, in fact, entirely vain. A theorem has been proved independently by Gibbard (1973) and Satterthwaite (1973, 1975) to the effect that any strategy-proof voting procedure is bound to violate some more fundamental requirement of fairness. The ethical objections to strategic voting have, in any event, never been persuasively formulated, and it has been argued

(Colman, 1982, Ch. 11) that strategic voting often has the desirable effect of allowing the majority opinion to prevail in circumstances in which sincere voting generates patently unfair outcomes.

4.5 Condorcet's Paradox

The Marquis de Condorcet (1785) was apparently the first person to discover a paradox with grave implications for democratic theory and practice inherent in all voting procedures. Its simplest manifestation is in a group of three voters choosing among three candidates, *A*, *B*, and *C*. Assuming as before that the voters' preference scales are complete and transitive, consider the possible pattern shown in Table 4.2, which is called a latin square:

Table 4.2

	Voter		
	1	2	3
Most preferred candidate	*A*	*B*	*C*
Second ranked candidate	*B*	*C*	*A*
Least preferred candidate	*C*	*A*	*B*

Notice that each candidate appears exactly once in each position — first, second, third — in the three preference scales. The only other profile of preferences to which this applies (and which also generates the paradox) is *ACB*, *BAC*, *CBA*.

The paradox emerges if we assume that the voters are sincere, and then try to determine the collective choice according to majority rule. It is evident that *A* defeats *B* by a majority of two votes to one because Voters 1 and 3 prefer *A* to *B* while only Voter 2 prefers them in the opposite order. But *B* defeats *C* by two votes (Voters 1 and 2) to one (Voter 3), and *C* defeates *A* by two votes (Voters 2 and 3) to one (Voter 1). Thus a majority of the voters prefer *A* to *B*, *B* to *C*, and *C* to *A*! Starting from a set of transitive individual preferences, we have ended up with an intransitive collective preference, often called a *cyclic majority*. The unexpected ramifications of this will become apparent shortly.

In order to make a decision on the basis of a set of individual preferences, some form of collective choice rule is required. Each of the following is a possible collective choice rule: 'Choose the candidate who is preferred to each of the others by a majority of the voters'; 'Choose a candidate at random'; 'Choose the favourite candidate of the oldest voter'. In practice, the problem is usually to find a procedure that is not only workable but also fair. The random method is unfair because it does not depend in any way on the preferences of the voters — a candidate might be chosen even if all of the voters consider him worst — and it is therefore called, in the terminology of collective choice theory, an *imposed* rule. The method based on seniority is even more obviously unfair because the choice reflects the preference of only one of the voters; it is *dictatorial*. The method of majority decision seems fair, but unfortunately it is not always workable: it is impossible to make a choice according to this rule from the cyclic pattern of preferences shown earlier because none of the candidates is preferred to both of the others by a majority of the voters.

The possibility of cyclic majorities gives rise to the following elementary impossibility theorem (Colman & Pountney, 1975b). No collective choice rule ever devised, and no rule that could ever be devised in the future, can satisfy the following conditions of workableness and fairness:

(i) The collective choice rule must be capable of choosing a unique winner from any profile of individual preferences.
(ii) None of the losing candidates must ever be preferred to the winner by a majority of the voters.

The proof is transparently simple. In order to satisfy (i) the rule must choose a winner from the profile of preferences that generates the cyclic majority described above. It would therefore have to choose *A* or *B* or *C*. But *A* cannot be chosen so as to satisfy (ii) because a majority prefers *C* to *A*; similarly *B* is unacceptable because a majority prefers *A* to *B*; and *C* is unacceptable because a majority prefers *B* to *C*. No collective choice rule could satisfy (i) and (ii) with the postulated profile of preferences, therefore none could so so in all cases. Because of the severity of the second condition, this impossibility theorem is less worrying than some others, including Arrow's (1951, 1963) famous theorem to be considered shortly, but it has the virtue of simplicity, and, unlike Arrow's, its proof does not depend on the assumption that voting is necessarily sincere.

Nanson (1882) used the phrase 'the paradox of voting' to refer to cyclic majorities, and the name seems to have stuck. A better name for it is 'Condorcet's paradox', because a large number of voting paradoxes are now known; some are described in this chapter, and several others are discussed by Fishburn (1974a) and Brams (1976). Condorcet's paradox is not restricted to the simple case of three candidates and three voters; to show how it can arise in a more complex situation, and also to illustrate a set of circumstances in which it might plausibly occur in an election, the following hypothetical example will suffice.

A large group of voters — a constituency in an election, say — contains 30 000 members. Roughly one-third are poor, one-third are in the middle income bracket, and one-third are rich. The main election issue is taxation: some candidates favour increasing the tax burden on the poor or the rich or both. We shall assume that all voters are in favour of any tax increase that does not apply to their own group, because of the indirect benefits which might flow from increased government revenue. But all voters strongly object to their own taxes being increased. Thus about 10 000 middle income earners favour higher taxes on both the rich and the poor, 10 000 or so poor voters favour the rich tax and oppose the poor tax, and 10 000 rich voters favour the poor tax and oppose the rich tax. Four candidates contest the election on the following platforms:

A: Higher taxes on rich and poor.
B: Higher taxes on poor only.
C: Higher taxes on rich only.
D: No tax increases.

There is something for everyone here, and with one exception the preference scales of the three groups of voters are perfectly predictable. The preference scale of the poor voters is clearly *CDAB*, and that of the rich voters is *BDAC*. The preference scale of the middle income earners depends on whether they prefer the rich or the poor to pay higher taxes. Let us assume the latter: their preference scale is therefore *ABCD*.

A two-thirds majority of the voters (20 000 middle income and rich voters) favour higher taxes on the poor, and a similar majority (20 000 middle income and poor voters) favour higher taxes on the rich. Furthermore, none of the voters is in favour of no tax increases. Yet the candidate who combines both of the popular tax increases in his election platform (*A*) attracts only one-third of the votes under the plurality procedure if voting is sincere, and if *B* and *C* withdrew before the election, *A* would be defeated by *D*, the candidate who proposes neither of the tax increases! The reason for this is that 20 000 rich and poor voters all prefer *D* to *A*. The trouble arises from a cyclic majority; two-to-one majorities prefer *A* to *B*, *B* to *C*, *C* to *D*, and *D* to *A*. Each of the candidates could defeat one of the others by a two-to-one majority if the remaining candidates withdrew. Although this example is slightly artificial, it shows how cyclic majorities can arise in complex situations. For a detailed analysis of Condorcet's paradox arising from the combination of issues and platforms, see Downs (1957) and Hillinger (1971).

4.6 Probabilities of Cyclic Majorities

Whenever there are fewer than three candidates, or fewer than three voters, a cyclic majority obviously cannot arise. With three or more voters and candidates it is always possible, but how likely is it? This is ultimately an empirical question which needs to be answered through empirical observations under controlled conditions. Although it has important political, moral, and practical implications, it has attracted little attention from psychologists and sociologists. Some progress has none the less been made towards answering it by indirect methods.

First, a number of purely theoretical attempts have been made to calculate probabilities of cyclic majorities. The earliest calculations were devoted to the simplest case of three candidates and three voters. In order to compute theoretical probabilities, it is necessary to make assumptions about the distribution of preferences among the voters. The earliest calculations were based on the assumption of an *equiprobable culture*, that is, a profile of preferences that arises when the voters are equally likely to adopt any of the logically possible preference scales. In the three-candidate case, for example, an equiprobable culture is one in which each voter is equally likely to adopt any of the six possible preference scales *ABC*, *ACB*, *BAC*, *BCA*, *CAB*, *CBA*.

Since each voter may adopt any of six possible preference scales, there are $6 \times 6 \times 6 = 216$ possible profiles of preferences among three voters. For the paradox to occur, the profile must be either (*ABC*, *BCA*, *CAB*) or (*ACB*, *BAC*, *CBA*) as pointed out earlier. The probability of this event, given the assumption of an equiprobable culture, can be calculated quite easily. The number of different ways in which the first paradoxical profile can arise is $3 \times 2 \times 1 = 6$, because the first voter must adopt *ABC*, *BCA*, or *CAB*, and in each case there remain two possibilities for the second voter and one for the third if the paradox is to occur. There are similarly six different ways in which the second paradoxical profile can arise. Of the 216 possible profiles, 12 are thus paradoxical. If all individual preference scales are equally probable, it follows that the probability of a cyclic majority is $12/216 = 0.056$; in other words it may be expected to occur between five and six times in a hundred. The first to report this result were Guilbaud (1952) and Black (1958). The probabilities in equiprobable cultures with larger sets of candidates and voters were subsequently calculated by Niemi and Weisberg (1968), Garman and Kamien (1968), Gleser (1969), DeMeyer and Plott (1970), May (1971), Blin (1973), Kelly (1974) and others (see also Niemi & Weisberg, 1972, Part 3). The results are summarized in Table 4.3.

Table 4.3 Probabilities of Cyclic Majorities in Equiprobable Cultures

Number of candidates	Number of voters				
	3	5	7	...	∞
3	.056	.069	.075	...	.088
4	.111	.139	.150	...	.176
5	.160	.200	.215	...	.251
6	.202	.255	.258	...	.315
7	.239	.299	.305	...	.369
.	.	.	.	.	.
.	.	.	.	.	.
.	.	.	.	.	.
∞	1.000	1.000	1.000	1.000	1.000

Two things are particularly noteworthy about these results. On the one hand, the probability of a cyclic majority is evidently rather insensitive to increases in the number of voters: with three candidates, for example, it rises from 0.056, or about 1 in 18, to a limit of only 0.088, which is still less than 1 in 11. But on the other hand, the probability is extremely sensitive to increases in the number of candidates: it rises rapidly and tends towards certainty for groups of any size (larger than two) as the number of candidates increases.

The meaning of these results is, however, unclear because of the assumption of equiprobable cultures. The voters are assumed to be indifferent to the candidates to the point of adopting preference scales purely at random; but, as Colman (1980) has commented, objective interests and social pressures almost inevitably make some candidates appear preferable to others, at least in the opinions of some voters. It is hard to imagine a situation in which every voter would be as likely to choose one preference scale as any other: one is tempted to say that an equiprobable culture is highly improbable in practice.

Garman and Kamien (1968), Niemi and Weisberg (1968, 1973) and others have calculated probabilities of cyclic majorities in various non-equiprobable cultures, defined by non-uniform probability distributions over the set of logically possible preference scales. In the three-candidate case, for example, one such non-equiprobable culture is that in which the voters adopt the preference scales *ABC*, *ACB*, *BAC*, *BCA*, *CAB*, and *CBA* with respective probabilities of $\frac{1}{4}$, $\frac{1}{4}$, $\frac{1}{8}$, $\frac{1}{8}$, $\frac{1}{8}$, and $\frac{1}{8}$. The equiprobable (Garman & Kamien use the adjective 'impartial') culture is seen as a special case in which all of the probabilities are equal. In some non-equiprobable cultures — for example in what Colman (1980) calls a 'completely concordant' culture in which all but one of the probabilities are zero — the probability of a cyclic majority is zero. In other cultures — for example in a 'completely discordant' culture in which the only preference rankings with non-zero probabilities are *ABC*, *BCA*, *CAB* — the probability of a cyclic majority is high.

These results are, to say the least, difficult to interpret. To begin with, the probability with which people choose different preference scales is an essentially empirical question: it is not sufficient simply to postulate certain arbitrary probability distributions if one wishes to know how likely cyclic majorities are in practice. Second, even in non-equiprobable cultures, the calculations are based on the assumption that the probability distribution over the set of possible preference scales is the same for all voters. In a completely discordant culture, for example, all voters are supposed to adopt, *ABC*, *BCA*, and *CAB* with non-zero probabilities and *ACB*, *BAC*, and *CBA* with zero probabilities (or vice versa). This is a highly dubious factual assumption. In practice, no rational voter could have such a preference pattern and, in any event, the voters' preferences are likely to differ from one another. Most seriously of all, it is unclear what a probability distribution for a voter over a set of preference scales represents (Sen, 1970, pp. 165 – 166). 'In the long run', a voter is presumably expected to adopt each of the preference scales with relative frequencies specified by the probability distribution, but over time a voter's tastes and the set of available alternatives are bound to change. For all these reasons, attempts to estimate the probabilities of cyclic majorities by non-empirical methods have limited relevance to real-world committees and elections.

A more promising theoretical approach is to establish the conditions that a profile of individual preferences must satisfy in order to guarantee the occurrence or non-occurrence of a cyclic majority. There is one well-known condition that makes a cyclic majority impossible. This condition, known as *single-peakedness*, was discovered by Black (1948a, 1948b). It is satisfied if all the voters evaluate the candidates according to the same single criterion. In a political election, for example, the profile of preferences will be single-peaked if all the voters rank all the candidates according to how left-wing they are, as in the example of Adams, Brown, and Carter discussed in the previous sections. It is then always possible to arrange the candidates in order along a horizontal axis in such a way that each voter's preference scale, with degrees of preference represented by the vertical axis, emerges as a graph with a single peak corresponding to his favourite candidate. If Adams, Brown, and Carter are arranged in that order along the horizontal axis, for example, then the peak of the left-wing voters' preference scale will be on the left-hand side of the graph, the moderates' peak will be in the middle, an the right-wing voters' peak will be on the right. Had the preference scales been *ABC*, *BCA*, and *CAB*, on the other hand, no arrangement of the candidates would be possible in which all three curves are single-peaked. The example of candidates and platforms concerning taxation discussed earlier was specifically devised to violate the single-peakedness condition. In that case the voters evaluated the candidates according to two quite separate criteria — their proposals about taxing the rich and taxing the poor. Black proved that single-peakedness in a committee or electorate containing an odd number of votes rules out the possibility of cyclic majority, and Coombs (1964, Chs. 9, 19) later provided an interpretation of single-peakedness in terms of his unfolding theory.

Strict single-peakedness is seldom likely to prevail in complex voting situations. Attention has therefore recently tended to focus on degrees of single-peakedness. Niemi (1969) demonstrated through Monte Carlo simulation methods that the more closely a profile of voters' preferences approximates strict single-peakedness, the less likely a cyclic majority becomes. In other words, if most but not all the voters evaluate the candidates according to the same single criterion, Condorcet's paradox, though possible, is unlikely. Further results along the same lines have been reported by Grofman (1972), Fishburn (1973b, 1974b), Kugn and Nagatani (1974) and others. On the other hand, Kramer (1973) has proved that if the voters are required to express quantitative degrees of preference on a continous scale rather than discrete (yes/no) choices, cyclic majorities are bound to occur unless their preferences are virtually identical. This is not surprising in the light of the pattern of probabilities shown in Table 4.3 above, because a quantitative choice is, in effect, a choice from an infinite set of alternatives.

Condorcet's paradox has not been systematically investigated under laboratory conditions, but a number of empirical examples of it have come to light in the field of politics. Most of these examples are vitiated to a degree by the fact that the voters' preference scales were merely conjectured by the investigators, however plausibly, but not empirically established. Riker (1965) presented evidence suggesting that the paradox has occurred on more than one occasion in the United States Congress, and Bowen (1972) has estimated its frequency of occurrence in Senate roll call votes. Niemi (1970) has reported likely occurrences from faculty elections in universities. Brams (1976, Ch. 2) has summarized a number of further empirical examples, and Gardner (1974) has discussed several amusing examples of cyclic relations in sports and games.

4.7 Arrow's Impossibility Theorem

Arrow (1951) was the first to use Condorcet's paradox to prove that no collective choice rule can satisfy certain minimal conditions of workableness and fairness. His original proof was later found by Blau (1957) to be flawed; in fact Blau managed to construct a counterexample in the form of a collective choice rule that satisfied all of Arrow's conditions and was therefore apparently workable and fair. Unfortunately — or fortunately, depending on one's point of view — Arrow (1963) proceeded to modify his theorem in a way that not only removed the error but also strengthened the conclusion.

Arrow's theorem requires a collective choice rule to be a *social welfare function*. This is a method of producing a collective ranking of all of the candidates, from most preferred to least preferred (with ties allowed), on the basis of the individual voters' preference rankings. The simple plurality voting procedure, for example, is a social welfare function because it results in a collective preference ranking of the candidates: one of the candidates comes first, another comes second, and so on. Arrow (1963) suggested that any democratically acceptable social welfare function ought to satisfy the following four apparently mild and uncontroversial conditions:

- *U*: *Unrestricted domain*. The social welfare function must be capable of deriving a collective preference ranking from any logically possible set of individual preference rankings.
- *P*: *Pareto condition*. Whenever all of the voters prefer a candidate x to another candidate y, x must be preferred to y in the collective preference ranking.
- *I*: *Independence of irrelevant alternatives*. The collective ranking of any pair of candidates x and y must depend solely on the voters' rankings of these two candidates and must not be influenced by their rankings of 'irrelevant' candidates.
- *D*: *Non-dictatorship*. The collective ranking must not be dictated by the preferences of one voter alone. It must not be the case that whenever a certain voter prefers x to y, x is ranked above y in the collective preference ranking irrespective of the preferences of the other voters.

Most of these conditions are self-explanatory; the only one that requires further comment is *I*. Referring once again to the case of Adams, Brown and Carter, what is intended is this: whether Adams is ranked above or below Brown by the social welfare function must depend solely on how the individual voters rank these two candidates. The voters' opinions on the relative merits of Adams and Carter, Brown and Carter, or Carter and Mickey Mouse are irrelevant to the ranking of Adams relative to Brown; the collective preference ranking of Adams and Brown must be independent of the voters' rankings of such irrelevant pairs. If a certain profile of preferences leads to Adams being collectively preferred to Brown according to the social welfare function, and if one or more of the voters change their minds about the relative merits of irrelevant pairs, but not about the relative merits of Adams and Brown, then the collective ranking of Adams relative to Brown must not be affected.

Arrow's (1963) astonishing theorem asserts that no social welfare function can satisfy all four of the conditions *U*, *P*, *I*, and *D*. The essential idea behind the proof is as follows. Condition *U* allows any profile of preferences to be postulated; we may therefore assume a profile that generates a cyclic majority. It can then be proved routinely (though not very briefly) that any social welfare function satisfying *P* and *I* necessarily violates *D*.

A variety of alternative proofs of Arrow's impossibility theorem have been devised, and literally scores of related impossibility theorems have been proved. Kelly (1978) has provided an excellent 'field guide' to this difficult body of literature. People who are unfamiliar with recent work on collective choice theory often deny the significance of Arrow's result by arguing that one of his conditions (usually *I*) is not absolutely essential to a democratically acceptable collective choice rule. Kelly has pointed out, however, that '*for each of Arrow's conditions, there is now an impossibility theorem not employing that condition*' (p. 3, italics in original). The general conclusion is no longer even restricted to social welfare functions; impossibility theorems have been proved for all kinds of collective choice rules including voting procedures that merely select a single winner without ranking the other candidates (Blair *et al.*, 1976). The conclusion is quite inescapable: no collective choice rule could ever be devised in such a way as to satisfy a few mild and uncontroversial conditions of democratic acceptability.

4.8 The Borda Effect

Condorcet's paradox, which underlies Arrow's and most other impossibility theorems, cannot occur if the voters evaluate the candidates according to the same single criterion, because the profile of preferences is then bound to be single-peaked. A less well-known but equally disturbing paradox, originally discovered by Borda (1781), can arise even under conditions of single-peakedness. The Borda effect (Colman, 1979, 1980, 1981, pp. 70 – 71; Colman & Pountney, 1978) can be illustrated quite simply in terms of the familiar example of Adams, Brown, and Carter. Suppose that there are seven committee members — two left-wing, two moderate, and three right-wing — choosing among these three candidates. Adams is left-wing, Brown is moderate, and Carter is extremely right-wing, so (as before) the left-wing voters' preference scale is *ABC*, the moderate voters' scale is *BAC*, and the right-wing voters' scale is *CBA*. The complete profile of individual preferences is summarized in Table 4.4.

In a simple plurality vote, assuming that the voters were sincere, Carter would clearly be chosen because he is the favourite candidate of the right-wing voters (5, 6 and 7) who constitute the largest voting bloc. But it does not neces-

Table 4.4 The Borda Effect: Preference Scales of Seven Committee Members

	Committee members						
	1	2	3	4	5	6	7
Most preferred candidate	*A*	*A*	*B*	*B*	*C*	*C*	*C*
Second ranked candidate	*B*	*B*	*A*	*A*	*B*	*B*	*B*
Least preferred candidate	*C*	*C*	*C*	*C*	*A*	*A*	*A*

sarily follow that Carter is the fairest collective choice, given this profile of individual preferences. In particular, it does not follow that a majority of the committee members prefer Carter to the other two candidates. The results of plurality votes are almost universally misinterpreted in this way, but to do so is to commit a logical blunder.

An inspection of Table 4.4 reveals, on the contrary, that a majority of the committee members (1, 2, 3, and 4) prefer both Adams and Brown to Carter! The plurality winner (*C*) is the *least* preferred candidate according to the criterion of majority preference: a majority of the voters prefer both of the losing candidates to the plurality winner. A *minority* of the voters consider Carter *best*, and a *majority* consider him *worst*.

Colman and Pountney (1978) distinguished between the *strong Borda effect*, in which there is a unique plurality winner but all of the losing candidates are preferred to it by a majority of the voters — as in Table 4.4 — and the *weak Borda effect*, in which there is a unique plurality winner but at least one of the losing candidates is preferred to it by a majority. There must be three or more candidates for either effect to occur, and when there are exactly three the smallest number of voters necessary to produce the effect is seven. The Borda effect cannot (curiously) occur in a group of eight voters choosing among only three candidates, but in larger groups the possibility is always present, provided of course that there are three or more candidates.

Some theoretical probabilities of the strong and weak Borda effects have been reported by Colman and Pountney (1978) and by Colman (1980). In the simplest case of a seven-member committee choosing among three candidates, the probabilities of the strong and weak effects, assuming equiprobable

Table 4.5 Theoretical Probabilities of Strong and Weak Borda Effects: Three Candidates and Equiprobable Cultures

	Number of voters															
	7	8	9	10	11	12	...	100	101	...	200	201	...	300	301
Strong effect	.018	0	.012	.003	.006	.002	...	.017	.025	...	.020	.028	...	.023	.029
Weak effect	.126	0	.132	.050	.106	.056	...	.202	.247	...	.228	.269	...	.245	.276

cultures, are 0.018 and 0.126 respectively. Exact probabilities, again assuming equiprobable cultures, for groups of various sizes choosing among three candidates have been calculated by Gillett (see Colman & Pountney, 1978, pp. 16 – 17). The results are summarized in Table 4.5.

The results in Table 4.5 show that the probabilities tend to rise as the number of voters increases. The probability of the weak effect is considerably greater than that of the strong effect even in very large groups. Both effects are distinctly more probable when the number of voters is odd than when it is even, and this is true even in large groups.

Monte Carlo simulations reported by Fishburn (1974a, 1977) and Fishburn and Gehrlein (1976) have shown that the probability of the weak effect tends to increase as the number of candidates increases. These workers have also estimated probabilities, assuming various non-equiprobable cultures and various voting procedures apart from the simple plurality procedure, of a candidate being chosen in spite of not being preferred by a majority of voters to all other candidates. Calculations of theoretical probabilities such as these are, unfortunately, subject to the limitations mentioned earlier in connection with the theoretical probabilities of cyclic majorities.

Colman (1980) has attempted to determine some of the properties of profiles of preferences that may be expected to maximize and minimize the likelihood of the Borda effect. The property of single-peakedness is not critical in this case; the effect can occur in its strong form in spite of the profile being single-peaked, as in the example of the appointment committee summarized in Table 4.4. Any tendency towards uniformity of opinion — towards a completely concordant culture — renders the probability lower than it would be in an equiprobable culture, however, and even the weak effect cannot occur when there is a reasonably high degree of agreement among the voters' preferences. In a completely discordant culture, in which the preconditions of a cyclic majority exist, on the other hand, the probability of the effect is maximized. In a seven-member committee choosing among the candidates *A*, *B*, and *C*, for example, if the only preference scales represented among the voters are *ABC*, *BCA*, and *CAB*, then the probability of the weak effect is 0.288. The same probability applies to the other strictly discordant culture in which the only preference scales adopted by the seven voters are *ACB*, *BAC*, *CBA*. These are, of course, the individual preference scales that produce cyclic majorities when they are approximately evenly distributed among the voters. In a group of any size, the existence of a cyclic majority ensures the occurrence of the Borda effect at least in its weak form unless there is a plurality tie, because whichever candidate wins, one of the others is preferred to the winner by a majority of the voters. But the example of Table 4.4 shows that a cyclic majority is not a *necessary* precondition for the occurrence of the Borda effect.

The empirical frequency of the Borda effect has been investigated under laboratory conditions in seven-member groups of university students who were asked to rank triplets of female first names (*Adeline*, *Agnes*, *Alice*, etc.) according to attractiveness (Colman, 1980). A relatively wide diversity of opinion is to be expected in this attitudinal arena. The hypothesis was that the observed frequency of the Borda effect would nevertheless be smaller than the theoretical frequency calculated on the assumption of an equiprobable culture, because of the ubiquitous tendency towards uniformity of taste resulting from similar socialization experiences, mass media effects, and so on. This hypothesis was confirmed: the observed relative frequency of the weak effect was 0.020, which is significantly lower than the theoretical probability in an equiprobable culture (0.126). The strong effect was not observed in any of the 200 group decisions.

Colman and Pountney (1975a, 1975b, 1978) presented evidence suggesting that the Borda effect occurred in a number of constituencies in the 1966 British General Election. From the results of a large-scale opinion survey in which voters were asked to rank the three main political parties, the preference scales of the voters in the 261 constituencies contested by these parties were estimated. The election results, coupled with the estimated preference scales of the voters, enabled the occurrence or non-occurrence of the strong and weak Borda effects to be determined. No examples of the strong effect were found, but in 15 constituencies the weak effect occurred, and in all but one case it favoured the Conservative Party candidate. In an equiprobable culture the effect would have occurred much more frequently; so there is evidently a tendency towards concordance in political attitudes, as one might have expected. It is, however, disturbing to think that 15 candidates who failed to be elected to the House of Commons in 1966 were probably preferred by a majority of the voters in their constituencies to those who were elected.

4.9 Conclusions

The problem of reaching a democratic decision on the basis of a diversity of individual preferences is one that crops up frequently in everyday life. Collective choices have to be made, and they often have important social implications. The voting procedures discussed in this chapter are used by committees, electorates, legislatures, political parties, trade unions, boards of directors, colleges of cardinals, and many other decision-making bodies. We have seen how the most common voting procedures — and, alas, any others that could ever be devised — are liable to produce decisions that few would consider democratic or fair. Collective choice theory breathes new life into E.M. Forster's slogan 'two cheers for democracy!'.

Social life demands cooperation among people with conflicting opinions, and voting procedures are indispensable tools for resolving differences in the most democratic ways possible. Research into collective decision making has been mainly theoretical in character, and has revealed that voting procedures are fraught with paradox. But the occurrence of most voting paradoxes is contingent on certain 'pathological' patterns of preferences among the voters. The likelihood of an unfair decision under a particular voting procedure is an empirical question, which depends on the probability of a particular pattern of preferences occurring among the voters and on whether the voters choose to vote sincerely or strategically. Under what social and psychological conditions do particular types of preference patterns tend to arise in groups? And what factors influence people's decisions to vote sincerely or strategically? Social psychologists are best equipped to investigate questions like these through empirical studies; but most social psychologists are oblivious of collective choice theory, and very little is known about the social and psychological problems raised by the theory. There are discoveries of considerable importance waiting to be made by experimental investigators in this area.

References

ARROW, K.J. (1951). *Social Choice and Individual Values*. New York: Wiley.

ARROW, K.J. (1963). *Social Choice and Individual Values*. 2nd edn. New York: Wiley.

BJURULF, B.H. and NIEMI, R.G. (1981). Order-of-voting effects. In M.J. HOLLER (Ed.), *Power, Voting, and Voting Power*. Würzburg: Physica-Verlag.

BLACK, D. (1948a). The decisions of a committee using a special majority. *Econometrica*, **16**, 245 – 261.

BLACK, D. (1948b). On the rationale of group decision making. *Journal of Political Economy*, **56**, 23 – 34.

BLACK, D. (1958). *The Theory of Committees and Elections*. Cambridge: Cambridge University Press.

BLAIR, D.H., BORDES, G., KELLY, J.S. and SUZUMURA, K. (1976). Impossibility theorems without collective rationality. *Journal of Economic Theory*, **13**, 361 – 379.

BLAU, J.H. (1957). The existence of a social welfare function. *Econometrica*, **25**, 302 – 313.

BLIN, J.-M. (1973). Intransitive social orderings and the probability of the Condorcet effect. *Kyklos*, **26**, 25 – 35.

BORDA, J.-C. DE. (1781). Mémoire sur les élections au scrutin. *Mémoires de l'Académie Royale des Sciences*, 657 – 665. Trans. A. de Grazia, *Isis*, 1953, **44**, 42 – 51.

BOWEN, B.D. (1972). Occurrence of the paradox of voting in U.S. senate roll call votes. In R.G. NIEMI and H.F. WEISBERG (Eds.), *Probability Models of Collective Decision Making*. Columbus: Charles E. Merrill. Pp. 181 – 203.

BRAMS, S.J. (1975). *Game Theory and Politics*. New York: Free Press.

BRAMS, S.J. (1976). *Paradoxes in Politics: An Introduction to the Nonobvious in Political Science*. New York: Free Press.

COLMAN, A.M. (1979). The Borda effect: evidence from small groups and from a British General Election. *Bulletin of the British Psychological Society*, **32**, 221 (Abstract).

COLMAN, A.M. (1980). The likelihood of the Borda effect in small decision-making committees. *British Journal of Mathematical and Statistical Psychology*, **33**, 50 – 56.

COLMAN, A.M. (1981). *What is Psychology?* London: Kogan Page.

COLMAN, A.M. (1982). *Game Theory and Experimental Games: The Study of Strategic Interaction*. Oxford: Pergamon (In press).

COLMAN, A.M. and POUNTNEY, I. (1975a). Voting paradoxes: a Socratic dialogue. I. *Political Quarterly*, **46** (2), 186 – 190.

COLMAN, A.M. and POUNTNEY, I. (1975b). Voting paradoxes: a Socratic dialogue. II. *Political Quarterly*, **46** (3), 304 – 309.

COLMAN, A.M. and POUNTNEY, I. (1978). Borda's voting paradox: theoretical likeihood and electoral occurrences. *Behavioral Science*, **23**, 15 – 20.

CONDORCET, M.J.A.N.C. MARQUIS DE. (1785). *Essai sur l'application de l'analyse à la probabilité des décisions rendues à la pluralité des voix*. In M.J.A.N.C. MARQUIS DE CONDORCET, *Oeuvres Completes*. Paris, 1804.

COOMBS, C.H. (1964). *A Theory of Data*. New York: Wiley.

DEMEYER, F. and PLOTT, C. (1970). The probability of a cyclical majority. *Econometrica*, **38**, 345 – 354.

DODGSON, C.L. (1876). *A Method of Taking Votes on More than Two Issues*. Oxford: Clarendon. Reprinted in Black (1958).

DOWNS, A. (1957). *An Economic Theory of Democracy*. New York: Harper & Row.

EDWARDS, W. and TVERSKY, A. (Eds.) (1967). *Decision Making: Selected Readings*. Harmondsworth: Penguin.

FARQUHARSON, R. (1969). *Theory of Voting*. Oxford: Basil Blackwell.

FISHBURN, P.C. (1973a). *The Theory of Social Choice*. Princeton, NJ: Princeton University Press.

FISHBURN, P.C. (1973b). Voter concordance, simple majorities, and group decision methods. *Behavioral Science*, **18**, 364 – 376.

FISHBURN, P.C. (1974a). Simple voting systems and majority rule. *Behavioral Science*, **19**, 166 – 176.

FISHBURN, P.C. (1974b). Single-peaked preferences and probabilities of cyclical majorities. *Behavioral Science*, **19**, 21 – 27.

FISHBURN, P.C. (1977). An analysis of voting procedures with nonranked voting. *Behavioral Science*, **22**, 178 – 185.

FISHBURN, P.C. and GEHRLEIN, W.V. (1976). An analysis of simple two-stage voting systems. *Behavioral Science*, **21**, 1 – 12.

GARDNER, M. (1974). Mathematical games. *Scientific American*, **231**(4), 120 – 124.

GARMAN, M. and KAMIEN, M. (1968). The paradox of voting: probability calculations. *Behavioral Science*, **13**, 306 – 316.

GIBBARD, A. (1973). Manipulation of voting schemes: a general result. *Econometrica*, **41**, 587 – 601.

GLESER, L.J. (1969). The paradox of voting: some probabilistic results. *Public Choice*, **7**, 47 – 64.

GROFMAN, B. (1972). A note on some generalizations of the paradox of cyclical majorities. *Public Choice*, **12**, 113 – 114.

GUILBAUD, G.T. (1952). Les théories de l'interêt général et la problème logique de l'aggregation. *Economie Appliquée*, **5**, 501 – 584. Trans. and repr. in P.F. LAZARSFELD & N.W. HENRY (Eds.), *Readings in Mathematical Social Sciences*. Chicago: Science Research Associates. Pp. 262 – 307.

HILLINGER, C. (1971). Voting on issues and on platforms. *Behavioral Science*, **16**, 564 – 566.

KELLY, J.S. (1974). Voting anomalies, the number of voters, and the number of alternatives. *Econometrica*, **42**, 239 – 251.

KELLY, J.S. (1978). *Arrow Impossibility Theorems*. New York: Academic Press.

KRAMER, G.H. (1972). Sophisticated voting over multidimensional choice spaces. *Journal of Mathematical Sociology*, **2**, 165 – 180.

KRAMER, G.H. (1973). On a class of equilibrium conditions for majority rule. *Econometrica*, **41**, 285 – 297.

KUGN, K. and NAGATANI, K. (1974). Voter antagonism and the paradox of voting. *Econometrica*, **42**, 1045 – 1067.

LAPLACE, P.-S. (1814). Théorie Analytique des Probabilités. 2nd edn. Paris. In P.-S. LAPLACE, *Oeuvres Complètes*, Vol. 7, Supplement 1. Paris, 1878 – 1912.

MAY, R.M. (1971). Some mathematical remarks on the paradox of voting. *Behavioral Science*, **16**, 143 – 151.
MCKELVEY, R.D. and NIEMI, R.G. (1978). A multistage game representation of sophisticated voting for binary procedures, *Journal of Economic Theory*, **18**, 1 – 22.
MILLER, N.R. (1977). Graph-theoretic approaches to the theory of voting. *American Journal of Political Science*, **21**, 769 – 803.
NANSON, E.J. (1882). Methods of elections. *Transactions and Proceedings of the Royal Society of Victoria*, **18**.
NIEMI, R.G. (1969). Majority decision-making with partial unidimensionality. *American Political Science Review*, **63**, 488 – 497.
NIEMI, R.G. (1970). The occurrence of the paradox of voting in university elections. *Public Choice*, **8**, 91 – 100.
NIEMI, R.G. and RIKER, W.H. (1976). The choice of voting systems. *Scientific American*, **234**(6), 21 – 27.
NIEMI, R.G. and WEISBERG, H.F. (1968). A mathematical solution for the probability of the paradox of voting. *Behavioral Science*, **13**, 317 – 323.
NIEMI, R.G. and WEISBERG, H.F. (Eds.) (1972). *Probability Models of Collective Decision Making*. Columbus: Charles E. Merrill.
NIEMI, R.G. and WEISBERG, H.F. (1973). A pairwise probability approach to the likelihood of the paradox of voting. *Behavioral Science*, **18**, 109 – 118.
RIKER, W.H. (1961). Voting and the summation of preferences: an interpretative bibliographical review of selected developments during the last decade. *American Political Science Review*, **55** (4), 900 – 911.
RIKER, W.H. (1965). Arrow's theorem and some examples of the paradox of voting. In J.M. CLAUNCH (Ed.), *Mathematical Applications in Political Science*. Dallas: Southern Methodist University Press. Pp. 41 – 60.
RIKER, W.H. and ORDESHOOK, P.C. (1973). *An Introduction to Positive Political Theory*. Englewood Cliffs, NJ: Prentice-Hall.
ROSENTHAL, H. (1974). Game-theoretic models of bloc-voting under proportional representation: really sophisticated voting in French labor elections. *Public Choice*, **18**, 1 – 23.
RUSTOW, D. (1955). *The Politics of Compromise: A Study of Parties and Cabinet Government in Sweden*. Princeton, NJ: Princeton University Press.
SATTERTHWAITE, M.A. (1973). The Existence of a Strategy Proof Voting Procedure: A Topic in Social Choice Theory. Unpublished doctoral dissertation, University of Wisconsin.
SATTERTHWAITE, M.A. (1975). Strategy-proofness and Arrow's conditions: existence and correspondence theorems for voting procedures and social welfare functions. *Journal of Economic Theory*, **10**, 187 – 217.
SCHELLING, T.C. (1967). What is game theory? In J.C. CHARLESWORTH (Ed.), *Contemporary Political Analysis*. New York: Free Press. Pp. 224 – 232.
SEN, A.K. (1970). *Collective Choice and Social Welfare*. Edinburgh: Oliver & Boyd.
SHUBIK, M. (1954). Does the fittest necessarily survive? In M. SHUBIK (Ed.), *Readings in Game Theory and Political Behavior*. New York: Doubleday. Pp. 36 – 43.
STAVELY, E.S. (1972). *Greek and Roman Voting and Elections*. Ithaca, NY: Cornell University Press.
STEEN, L.A. (1980). From counting votes to making votes count: the mathematics of elections. *Scientific American*, **243**(4), 16 – 26.

CHAPTER 5

Experimental Games

Andrew M. Colman

5.1 Game Theory

Game theory is a branch of mathematics devoted to the analysis of interdependent decision making. It is applicable to any social interaction in which: (a) there are two or more decision makers, called *players*, each of whom faces a choice between two or more courses of action, called *strategies*; (b) the outcome of the interaction depends on the strategy choices of all the players; and (c) each player has preferences among the possible outcomes, so that a set of *payoffs* reflecting these preferences can be assigned to every outcome. Any social interaction that has these properties can be modelled by a game, and the primary goal of the theory is to discover, through purely logical reasoning within the model, what strategies rational players should choose in order to maximize their payoffs, that is, to produce the best outcomes for themselves. It is important to understand that the theory is primarily *normative* rather than *positive*: it seeks to show how players *ought* to choose in order to pursue their interests most effectively, but it makes no predictions about how people *will* behave in any actual interaction. The theory cannot, therefore, be tested and falsified by experimental methods, though it provides a useful formal framework for empirical studies of behaviour in situations involving interdependent choice.

A game is a purely imaginary idealization of a social interaction. A real social interaction is too complex and transitory to be clearly perceived and perfectly understood, so it is replaced by a deliberately simplified abstract structure whose basic elements — players, strategies, and payoffs — are explicitly defined and from which other properties can be deduced by formal reasoning. These deductions apply not to the social interaction itself but to the game, and they are true, provided only that the reasoning is sound, whether or not the game corresponds to the original social interaction. But if the game does not correspond to reality in important details, then its practical value is limited; and if it does not yield insights that transcend a commonsense understanding of interdependent decision making, then it serves no useful purpose at all. The models devised by game theorists are often criticized by psychologists and social scientists for failing to capture the full complexity of the social reality they are designed to represent; but this criticism stems from a misunderstanding of the fundamental purpose of a formal model, which is to reduce reality to its bare essentials by deliberately excluding unnecessary details. Simplified models have proved their usefulness in other fields of investigation: Euclidian geometry is a striking example of such wide applicability that many people confuse it with reality itself.

The groundwork of game theory was laid in a series of papers by the French mathematician Émile Borel between 1921 and 1927 (see Fréchet, 1953). The theory emerged in a fully developed form during the Second World War with the publication of von Neumann and Morgenstern's (1944) *Theory of Games and Economic Behavior*; but it was later text by Luce and Raiffa (1957) that made the fundamental ideas accessible to psychologists and social scientists. Experimental games began to appear during the 1950s, and 30 experiments had been published by the time the first review (Rapoport & Orwant, 1962) appeared. In 1965 the *Journal of Conflict Resolution* began to devote a separate section of every issue to experimental games, and by 1972 more than 1000 experiments had found their way into print (Guyer & Perkel, 1972; Wrightsman *et al.*, 1972). Most of these experiments were based on a handful of simple two-person games with interesting psychological properties. Towards the mid-1970s many researchers began to concentrate instead on multi-person games which seemed to model a wider range of everyday social problems. Multi-person experimental gaming expanded rapidly during the late 1970s and early 1980s, while research into two-person games continued at a diminished rate.

The enduring popularity of experimental games is not difficult to explain. One appealing feature from the researcher's point of view is the ease and flexibility with which subjects can be placed in precisely specified states of interdependence, corresponding at a formal level to any imaginable social situation. Second, experimental games provide a means of investigating fierce competition without the ethical problems usually associated with the study of potentially antisocial forms of behaviour. Third, the experiments are relatively economical and easy to perform, and they generate objective and quantitative data. Last and perhaps most important, there are many interesting phenomena associated with social interaction, including cooperation and competition, that are difficult or impossible to understand without the conceptual framework of game theory, and experimental games provide a natural and convenient method of investigating them.

But experimental games have attracted fierce criticism from some commentators. The criticism has focused chiefly on the highly abstract and artificial nature of the tasks with which the subjects are usually confronted. The ecological validity of experimental games — the degree of confidence with which the findings can be generalized to non-experimental, naturally occurring social interactions — has been questioned increasingly often in recent years (e.g. Nemeth, 1972; Plon, 1974; Pruitt & Kimmel, 1977). A price must be paid for replacing complex, naturally occurring social interactions with simple experimental games: the applicability of the findings to everyday life is open to conjecture. Recent evidence (Sermat, 1970; Eiser & Bhavnani, 1974; Young, 1977; Colman, 1982) suggests that behaviour in abstract games may be quite different from behaviour in structurally equivalent lifelike interactions.

This chapter contains a selective review of research into cooperation and competition based on experimental games. For a broader perspective on the experimental gaming literature, the reader is referred to the reviews by Gallo and McClintock (1965); Wrightsman *et al.* (1972); Tedeschi *et al.* (1973); Davis *et al.* (1976); Pruitt and Kimmel (1977); and Colman (1982); the last of these also provides a grounding in the theory of games. Before discussing empirical findings in detail, however, it is necessary to say a few words about the classification of two-person games.

5.2 Varieties of Two-Person Games

Three general classes of two-person games can be distinguished. A *strictly competitive* or *zero-sum* game is one in which the players' preferences are diametrically opposed: an outcome that is good for one player is correspondingly bad for the other and vice versa. At the opposite extreme is a *pure coordination* game, in which the players' preferences among the possible outcomes coincide exactly. Finally, a *mixed-motive* game is an intermediate case in which the players' preferences are neither strictly opposed nor strictly coincident, and which therefore possesses both competitive and cooperative features.

From a mathematical point of view, strictly competitive games are especially interesting. The fundamental minimax theorem of game theory, first proved by von Neumann (1928), shows that any finite, strictly competitive game has a rational solution, that is, a pair of optimal strategies through which the players can maximize their respective payoffs. (Standard proofs of the minimax theorem are extremely difficult for non-mathematicians to follow; the simplest presentation is in Colman, 1982.) But, for several reasons, this result has only limited relevance to real-world decision making. (a) Most real-life social interactions cannot be represented by strictly competitive games, because it is seldom the case that every possible outcome is as good for one of the players as it is bad for the other. Board games such as chess, and some political, military, and economic conflicts are strictly competitive, but in most other everyday interactions there are some outcomes that *both* players prefer to some others, and the corresponding games are therefore mixed-motive. (b) Although all finite, strictly competitive games have rational solutions, the computation of optimal strategies is extremely difficult except in the simplest cases. Human beings have bounded rationality and cannot be expected to find the optimal solutions in most cases. Thus although chess corresponds to a two-person, zero-sum game, a knowledge of game theory is of no use to a practical chess player because the game is far too complicated to solve, even with the help of a computer. The most powerful chess-playing computer currently available evaluates 160 000 positions per second, or about 29 million for each move it makes; but this enables it to 'think' only a few moves ahead, and it plays considerably below grandmaster strength (*Scientific American*, 1981). (c) A characteristic feature of strategic interactions in everyday life is that the players have incomplete knowledge of the available strategies and payoffs, and another is that the rules change — and are sometimes deliberately changed by the players — while the interaction is in progress. These features can be incorporated into game theory only at the cost of a vast increase in complexity, making the theory as a guide to practical action all the more vulnerable to (b).

Pure coordination games, whether two-person or multi-person, are theoretically trivial: since there is no conflict of interest between the players, their sole objective is to cooperate in such a way as to obtain the outcome that is best for all. But in practice, if the players cannot communicate with one another, coordination of strategies can be problematical. Suppose, for example, that a husband and wife accidentally lose each other during a shopping spree and are anxious to become reunited. Each should try to head for the spot where they are most likely to meet up again, and if both choose the same spot they will be rewarded. Any pair of strategies leads to an outcome that is either good for both or bad for both, and the problem therefore corresponds to a pure coordination game. The husband cold approach the problem non-strategically by simply choosing the spot that he considers most obvious as a meeting place. But he may have a better chance of success if he chooses the spot that he thinks his wife will consider most obvious, or the spot that he thinks she will expect him to consider most obvious, or the spot that he thinks she will expect him to expect her to consider most obvious, and so on, and his wife faces a similar infinite regress of expectations. A rather subtle form of strategic intuition is evidently required, but people are surprisingly adept at coordinating their strategies in circumstances like these, even when the range of options is vast or infinite.

Schelling (1960) has shown how successful cooperation in a pure coordination game often demands a recognition by the players of a *focal point*, which is a combination of strategies that is somehow prominent or conspicuous among the set of possibilities. Consider the following variation of the rendezvous problem mentioned in the previous paragraph. A pair of strangers have arranged to meet in the city of New York on a specified day but have forgotten to fix a time and place and cannot get in touch with each other before the rendezvous. Where should they go, and when? A majority of Schelling's subjects, when confronted with this dilemma, succeeded in coordinating by nominating 12 noon at the information booth in the Grand Central Station (they were Harvard University students). Considering the number of options from which they had to choose, these results, and others like them which Schelling reported, are remarkable. A majority of subjects must have considered the chosen time and place to be focal points of sufficient prominence that their unknown partners ought to recognize them as such and realize that they are the obvious choices. For the same reason, astronomers listen for radio signals from intelligent beings on other planets by tuning to 1420 megacycles; this is the obvious choice — and intelligent aliens would probably expect us to listen on this frequency — because it is the characteristic radio emission line of neutral hydrogen, and hydrogen is the most plentiful element in the universe.

Mixed-motive games, in which the players' preferences are neither diametrically opposed (as in strictly competitive games) not identical (as in pure coordination games) are especially interesting from a psychological point of view. A player in a mixed-motive game is motivated partly to cooperate and partly to compete, and has therefore to contend with an *intra*personal conflict arising from this clash of motives in addition to the *inter*personal conflict that is built into the game. The range of mixed-motive games is almost unimaginably vast, so theorists and experimentalists have tended to concentrate on the simplest cases only. The fundamental properties of the simple mixed-motive games that have been used in most experimental studies of cooperation and competition are outlined below.

5.2.1 Maximizing Difference Game

A two-person game can be specified most conveniently by a *payoff matrix*; and the Maximizing Difference Game (MDG) is represented in this form in Matrix 5.1.

Matrix 5.1 Maximizing Difference Game

		II	
		C	*D*
I	*C*	3,3	1,2
	D	2,1	1,1

The players are labelled I and II. The rules of the game specify that Player I must choose either row *C* (cooperate) or row *D* (defect) and that Player II must choose either column *C* or column *D*. The pair of numbers at the intersection of the chosen row and column are the payoffs to Players I and II respectively. Thus if Player I chooses *C* and II chooses *C*, then I's payoff is 3 and II's payoff is 3; if I chooses *C* and II chooses *D*, then I's payoff is 1 and II's is 2, and so on. The payoffs reflect the players' preferences among the possible outcomes: the best outcome for both is the top left-hand (*CC*) cell of the matrix. The absolute values of the payoffs are unimportant; any 2 × 2 (two-row, two-column) game is by definition an MDG if the players' rank orders of preferences from best to worst are the same as those shown in Matrix 5.1.

A generalized payoff matrix for any 2 × 2 game is shown in Matrix 5.2.

Matrix 5.2 Generalized 2 × 2 Matrix

		II	
		C	*D*
I	*C*	*R,R*	*S,T*
	D	*T,S*	*P,P*

The payoffs are symbolized by R (reward for joint cooperation), P (punishment for joint defection), T (temptation to defect), and S (sucker's payoff). These labels are merely suggestive; they do not apply equally well to all 2×2 games and are not intended to prejudge the meanings of the outcomes to the players. In this notation, the MDG can be defined compactly by the inequality $R > T > S = P$. The matrix with $R = 6$, $T = 5$, $S = 0$, and $P = 0$ is therefore also an MDG because $6 > 5 > 0 = 0$.

If both players in an MDG are motivated solely to maximize their individual payoffs, then it is obvious from an inspection of Matrix 5.1 that they will both choose C — provided that they are rational — and they will also choose C if they are motivated to maximize the joint payoff of the pair. The only intelligible motive for a D choice in this game is spite, that is, a competitive desire to do better than one's partner at the expense of a worse payoff for oneself. As we shall see, empirical studies have revealed surprisingly high levels of competitive spitefulness in subjects playing the MDG.

5.2.2 *Prisoner's Dilemma Game*

An example of the Prisoner's Dilemma Game (PDG) is shown in Matrix 5.3.

Matrix 5.3 Prisoner's Dilemma Game

		II	
		C	*D*
I	*C*	3,3	1,4
	D	4,1	2,2

In the notation of the generalized payoff matrix (Matrix 5.2), the defining inequality of the PDG is $T > R > P > S$; for technical reasons some authorities require also that $2R > S + T$. This game, first identified by Flood in 1951 and later explicitly formulated and named by Tucker, has attracted more attention from empirical researchers than any other on account of its intriguing properties. Its name derives from the following imaginary social dilemma to which it corresponds. Two people are arrested on suspicion of joint involvement in a serious crime which they have, in fact, committed. They are held in separate cells and prevented from communicating with each other. The police have insufficient evidence to obtain a conviction unless at least one of the prisoners discloses certain incriminating evidence. Each prisoner is confronted with a choice between concealing the evidence (C) and disclosing it (D). If both conceal the evidence, then both will be acquitted; if both disclose the evidence, then both will be convicted; but if only one prisoner discloses the information, then he will not only be acquitted but will also receive a reward, and his partner in cime will receive an especially heavy sentence on account of his obstructiveness. The prisoners know all this, and their preferences among the possible outcomes, taking into account moral attitudes, personal feelings of guilt and betrayal, and so on, are assumed to correspond to the numbers shown in Matrix 5.3. The cooperative strategy is obviously C, and the competitive or defecting strategy is D.

One of the reasons for this game's popularity is its paradoxical character. A sensible player will not choose C if he does not trust his partner to do likewise, but even if he does trust his partner to choose C, he can take advantage of this by choosing D and ensuring the best possible payoff for himself — and the worst for his partner. The essence of the paradox is as follows. Player I is better off choosing D than C irrespective of his partner's choice, and the same is true of Player II; in the terminology of game theory, the D strategy is *dominant* for both players. It would therefore appear that both players should choose D if they are rational. But if both 'irrationally' choose C, then the outcome is better from each player's point of view than if they both choose D! Individual rationality is self-defeating in the PDG; what is required is some principle of collective rationality such as the categorical imperative of the philosopher Immanuel Kant: 'Act only on such a maxim through which you can at the same time will that it should become a universal law'. Numerous strategic interactions in the real world correspond to the PDG; the arms race between the two superpowers is one familiar example.

5.2.3 Chicken

Matrix 5.4 shows a version of the game of Chicken.

Matrix 5.4 Chicken

		II	
		C	D
I	C	4,4	2,5
	D	5,2	1,1

This game bears a superficial resemblance to the PDG, and it is often confused with the PDG in the experimental gaming literature, but its properties are really quite different. In terms of the generalized matrix (Matrix 5.2), the defining inequality of Chicken is $T > R > S > P$, and some authorities include a further technical restriction $2R > S + T$. It is the archetypal *dangerous game* (Swingle, 1970), and it is named after a gruesome pastime which originated among Californian teenagers in the 1930s. The contestants drive towards each other at high speeds in motor-cars, and each has to choose between swerving to avoid a head-on collision and thus showing himself to be chicken (C) and driving straight ahead (D). If both players choose C the result is a draw, and if both choose D they may both be killed; but if one chooses C and the other D, then the first loses face — but remains alive — and the other receives the highest possible payoff in the form of a large ego-boost. In this game, C is really a *cautious* and D a *dangerous* strategy, though it is customary in the literature to call them *cooperative* and *competitive* (or *defecting*) strategies respectively. Chicken is a dangerous game because a player cannot go for the highest payoff without risking the worst possible payoff for both players.

One curious property of Chicken is its compulsive character: a person who declines a challenge to a game of Chicken has effectively played and lost. Another is the paradoxical advantage that it gives to a player who is known to be foolish, reckless, irrational, or lacking in self-control. Kahn (1965) pointed out that a 'skilful' player of automobile Chicken might get into his car in an obviously drunken state, wear very dark glasses, and throw the steering wheel out of the window ostentatiously when the car reaches high speed. 'If his opponent is watching, he has won. If his opponent is not watching, he has a problem; likewise if both playes try this strategy' (p. 11). In a lecture on 'The Political Uses of Madness', Daniel Ellsberg (1959) argued that Adolf Hitler won a number of military and diplomatic games of Chicken in Europe in the 1930s by virtue of his obvious irrationality.

5.3 Cooperation and Competition in Dyads

What follows is an introductory review of experimental studies of cooperation and competition based on two-person (dyadic) mixed-motive games. The major findings will be discussed under the following sub-headings: game structure, payoffs and incentives, mode of presentation, opportunities for communication, responses to programmed strategies, and attribution effects.

5.3.1 Game Structure

The PDG, on account of its puzzling strategic structure, has attracted more attention from empirical researchers than any other two-person game, and the findings have tended to confound the predictions of game theorists. In their classic textbook of game theory, Luce and Raiffa (1957) predicted that cooperative choices would predominate if pairs of subjects were to play several repetitions of the PDG: 'We feel that in most cases an unarticulated collusion between the players will develop. . . . This arises from a knowledge that the situation will be repeated and that reprisals are possible' (p. 101). Shortly after the publication of Luce and Raiffa's book, however, the *DD lock-in effect* was discovered. Flood (1958) reported that long runs of competitive (D) choices by both players tend to occur when the game is repeated over trials. This finding was replicated by Scodel *et al.* (1959) and has since been confirmed literally hundreds of times.

Rapoport and Chammah (1965) examined the choices of pairs of subjects over 300 repetitions of the PDG. On the very first trial the proportion of cooperative (*C*) choices was slightly greater than 50%; this was followed by a *sobering period* during which the percentage of cooperative choices declined rapidly and *DD* lock-ins were common, but after approximately 30 to 50 trials a *recovery period* characterized by a gradual increase in cooperation took place, and after 300 trials approximately 60% of choices were cooperative. The sobering period may be due to a decline in mutual trust or simply to a gradual realization that the competitive strategy is dominant — that it yields a higher payoff than the alternative cooperative strategy irrespective of the opponent's choice — and the recovery period is probably due to the partial growth of an unarticulated collusion as the players come to understand that joint cooperation pays better than joint competition.

When other factors are held constant, the game of Chicken elicits more cooperation than the PDG. This is in line with commonsense predictions because the competitive *D* strategy is not dominant in Chicken as it is in the PDG. Also in contrast to the PDG, a *D* choice is dangerous in so far as it exposes a player who makes it to the risk of the worst possible outcome; in the PDG it is a *C* choice that is risky. In a detailed empirical investigation of Chicken, Rapoport and Chammah (1969) found that approximately 65% of initial choices were cooperative. When the game was repeated many times, the percentage of cooperative choices declined very slightly over the first 30 to 50 trials and increased steadily thereafter, reaching more than 70% after 300 repetitions.

McClintock (1972) has distinguished between three possible motives for cooperation and competition in the PDG and Chicken. Subjects are usually instructed to *maximize individual payoffs*, but the appropriate strategy for realizing this goal is unclear in both games because either *C* or *D* choices might yield higher individual payoffs depending on the opponent's choices. Subjects who are motivated to *maximize joint payoffs*, on the other hand, will choose cooperatively if they are rational, and those who are motivated to *maximize relative payoffs* — that is, to beat the opponent — will choose competitively in both games. It is clearly impossible to infer the players' true motives from their choices in the PDG or Chicken: *C* choices may reflect attempts to maximize individual payoffs (on the basis of trust) or joint payoffs, and *D* choices may reflect attempts to maximize individual payoffs (on the basis of mistrust) or relative payoffs.

In the Maximizing Difference Game (MDG), on the other hand, the only intelligible motive for a *D* choice is relative payoff maximization. Several empirical investigations of the MDG (reviewed by McClintock, 1972) have revealed that *D* choices are frequently made. This suggests that many subjects, though instructed to try to maximize individual payoffs, adopt the spiteful policy of relative payoff maximization. McClintock and McNeel (1967), for example, reported that only about 50% of choices were cooperative in pairs of Belgian students who were given the opportunity of winning substantial sums of money by accumulating points over 100 repetitions of an MDG, and subjects who were offered smaller monetary incentives behaved even less cooperatively.

This suggests that some subjects were willing to forego tangible monetary gain in order to beat their opponents in this game. It is not unreasonable to assume that some subjects approach the PDG and Chicken in a similarly spiteful frame of mind.

5.3.2 *Payoffs and Incentives*

Numerous investigators have examined the effects on cooperation of varying the relative magnitudes of the payoffs within a specified game structure, and the results are broadly in line with commonsense predictions. In the PDG, for example, the proportion of cooperative choices tends to increase when the reward for joint cooperation (R) is increased relative to the punishment for joint competition (P), and to decrease when the temptation to defect (T) is increased relative to the sucker's payoff (S) – see Matrix 5.2. Rapoport and Chammah (1965) found that a cooperation index defined by the ratio $r = (R - P)/(T - S)$ is a reliable predictor of cooperation across PDG matrices: the correlation between log r and proportion of C choices was 0.641.

In a later investigation of cooperation in the game of Chicken (Rapoport & Chammah, 1969), five matrices were used. In all of the matrices the values of T, R, and S were 2, 1, and -2 respectively; the value of P, however, varied across matrices from -3 to -40. As predicted, a strong, positive relationship was found between the value of P and the proportion of competitive choices: the highest proportion occurred in the least dangerous game ($P = -3$) and the lowest in the most dangerous game ($P = -40$). These results cast doubt on the assumption of many penologists and child psychologists that certainty of punishment is a more effective deterrent than severity of punishment, a superstition which underpins the doctrine of limited nuclear war as a preferable alternative to mutual assured destruction (MAD) in American strategic thinking. But *fewer* competitive choices were made in the more dangerous than the less dangerous games, in spite of the fact that the disastrous DD outcome was objectively less likely. Rapoport and Chammah pointed out, on the basis of their findings, that 'more severe punishment seems to be a more efficient deterrent than more certain punishment' (p. 169).

In their early review of experimental games, Gallo and McClintock (1965) advanced the view that the surprisingly low proportion of cooperative choices typically observed might be attributable to the small or non-existent monetary incentives assigned to the payoffs in most experiments. Many subsequent studies (reviewed by Oskamp & Kleinke, 1970) have addressed this problem directly by comparing behaviour in low-incentive and high-incentive conditions, and the findings are thoroughly equivocal. Non-significant incentive effects have emerged from several studies of the PDG (e.g. Wrightsman, 1966) and Chicken (e.g. Sermat, 1967); in others, significantly more cooperation has been found in high-incentive than in low-incentive conditions (e.g. Stahelski & Kelley, 1969); and in a few, significantly less cooperation has been found in high-incentive than in low-incentive conditions (e.g. Gumpert *et al.*, 1969). It seems reasonable to conclude that incentive effects are neither very pronounced nor very consistent in the PDG and Chicken. In the MDG, on the other hand, monetary incentives have consistently been found to increase cooperation (e.g. McClintock & McNeel, 1967). The incentive effect in the MDG is easy to understand: the motive for competition in this game is a desire to beat the opponent, but the motive of monetary gain is likely to override it when large incentives are assigned to the payoffs and the rewards for cooperation are correspondingly great.

5.3.3 Mode of Presentation

A game can be presented to the players in various ways, and the mode of presentation has been found to have a powerful effect on their behaviour. The most important findings in this area of research concern *decomposed* PDGs. Matrix 5.5 shows a conventional PDG and two decomposed versions of it.

Matrix 5.5 PDG and Two Decomposed Versions

		II *C*	II *D*
I	*C*	3,3	1,4
	D	4,1	2,2

(a)

	My payoff	Opponent's payoff
C	0	3
D	1	1

(b)

	My payoff	Opponent's payoff
C	1	2
D	2	0

(c)

Suppose that both players are presented with the decomposed PDG shown in Matrix 5.5b. The numbers in the matrix represent the payoffs that each player awards to himself and to his opponent by choosing *C* or *D*. A player who chooses *C*, for example, awards himself 0 and his opponent 3; thus if both players choose *C*, each awards himself 0 and is awarded 3 by his opponent, so each receives a total payoff of 3. (The same payoffs for joint cooperation appear in the conventional presentation of the game – Matrix 5.5a.) If Player I chooses *C* and II chooses *D*, then I awards himself 0 and his opponent 3, while II awards himself 1 and his opponent 1; so I's total payoff is 1 and II's total payoff is 4, and so on. The total payoffs invariably correspond to those shown in the conventional matrix, and the other decomposed PDG (Matrix 5.5c) also corresponds to the original game. All three versions convey exactly the same information in different ways; but although they are logically equivalent they have quite different psychological properties.

Matrix 5.5c invites an interpretation in terms of generosity and stinginess, as Pruitt and Kimmel (1977, p. 373) have pointed out. Next-door neighbours, for example, frequently have to choose between leading (*C*) and refusing to lend (*D*) each other garden tools, eggs, the use of their telephones, and the like. Matrix 5.5c reflects this dilemma if we assume that lending yields little benefit to the lender, though considerable benefit to the recipient, and that refusing to lend may save a certain amount of trouble. But both neighbours are clearly better off in the long run if both consistently agree to lend than if both consistently refuse. Other decompositions of the same PDG highlight other aspects of the underlying dilemma. Matrix 5.5b, for example, shows in a particularly vivid way that neither player can obtain a high payoff without the cooperation of his opponent.

A number of investigators (e.g. Evans & Crumbaugh, 1966; Pruitt, 1967) have reported higher levels of cooperation in decomposed PDGs than in conventional PDGs with equivalent payoffs. Cooperative behaviour is most common in decompositions like Matrix 5.5b in which the players' payoffs seem to depend almost entirely on their opponents' choices. Decompositions of this type make plain the players' dependence on each other's goodwill, and this evidently facilitates the development of mutual trust and thereby encourages cooperative behaviour. Experiments have revealed that subjects are especially quick to reciprocate cooperative choices and slow to retaliate when their opponents choose competitively in decomposed PDGs that highlight their strategic interdependence (Pruitt, 1970; Tognoli, 1975).

Several attempts have been made to present two-person mixed-motive games in ways that are less abstract and meaningless than stark numerical payoff matrices. Deutsch and Krauss's (1960) *trucking game* is the most thoroughly researched of these non-matrix methods of presentation, and the major findings that have emerged from its use have been reviewed by Harvey and Smith (1977, pp. 311 – 323). In the trucking game, the players adopt the roles of truck drivers trying to deliver their consignments to different destinations as quickly as possible. Each player has a choice between two alternative routes, one of which is much shorter than the other. They travel in opposite directions, and the shorter route contains a stretch of single-lane road which can be used by only one truck at a time. If both players choose the shorter route simultaneously, then a head-on blockage occurs and both lose valuable time until one of them decides to back off and switch to the longer route. In some conditions, one or both of the players control gates which can be used to prevent their opponents' trucks from using the single-lane stretch of road without impeding the movement of their own trucks.

Some of Deutsch and Krauss's (1960, 1962) original subjects played repeated trials of the trucking game without gates, and in these circumstances they quickly learned to cooperate by alternating on the shorter route. The rest of the subjects played under conditions in which one or both members of each pair controlled gates, and much lower levels of cooperation were found, even when the threat potential of the gates was not actually used. In the *bilateral threat* condition, in which both subjects controlled gates, frequent head-on blockages occurred in the single-lane stretch of road and — somewhat surprisingly — no improvement occurred over trials. The *unilateral threat* condition, in which only one member of each pair controlled a gate, produced intermediate levels of cooperation. These findings seem to show that the availability of potential threats, whether or not they are actually used, makes cooperation more difficult. Deutsch (1969) believes that this conclusion casts doubt on the assumptions underlying conventional doctrines of military deterrence, the balance of power (or terror), and the nuclear arms race.

5.3.4 *Opportunities for Communication*

In naturally occurring social interactions, the participants are generally able to communicate with each other – to issue verbal threats, promises, commitments, and so on. In most experimental games, on the other hand, the subjects are forbidden to communicate, and some commentators (e.g. Nemeth, 1972, p. 213) have argued that this may account for the distinctly uncooperative behaviour usually displayed by experimental subjects. Common sense suggests that communication should facilitate cooperation in mixed-motive games, and several investigators have examined this hypothesis empirically.

Deutsch (1958) found that opportunities for communication led to increased cooperation in the PDG when the subjects were given instructions calculated to induce an individualistic motivational set, that is, to encourage them to maximize their own payoffs without regard to those of their opponents. But subjects given a competitive set (to beat their opponents) or a cooperative set (to act in the interests of both players) did not behave significantly more cooperatively when given opportunities to communicate. These findings, which have been replicated many times, can be explained in terms of McClintock's (1972) theoretical analysis (mentioned in Section 5.3.1) of the motivational sources of cooperative and competitive choices. Deutsch's competitive and cooperative motivational sets correspond to McClintock's motives of relative payoff maximization and joint payoff maximization, and the appropriate strategies are obviously *D* and *C* respectively. But the appropriate strategy for individualistically motivated subjects is indeterminate, and under this motivational set subjects are therefore most likely to be influenced by other factors. It is in these circumstances that communication can help to foster mutual trust, in the absence of which cooperation is unlikely to develop.

Evans (1964) compared the levels of cooperation in individualistically motivated subjects in three treatment conditions: enforceable promises with stiff penalties for breaking them, unenforceable promises, and no communication. The highest level of cooperation was found in the enforceable promises condition and the lowest in the no communication condition; unenforceable promises did not increase cooperation very much. These findings confirm and extend those of Deutsch (1958): mere promises are not much help, but promises that are coupled with sanctions against deceitfulness are more trustworthy.

An elaborate investigation of the effects of verbal and non-verbal communication was reported by Wichman (1972). Individualistically motivated subjects played 70 trials of a PDG under conditions in which they could either see their opponents but not hear them speaking, hear but not see them, see and hear them, or neither see nor hear them. The subjects behaved most cooperatively in the see-and-hear condition, less cooperatively in the hear-only condition, less cooperatively still in the see-only condition, and least cooperatively in the isolated condition. It was only in the sea-and-hear condition that subjects managed to establish anything resembling joint cooperative behaviour over the series of 70 trials. These results suggest that the effects of communication on the development of trust, trustworthiness, and cooperation are rather more subtle than was previously assumed.

5.3.5 Responses to Programmed Strategies

In many mixed-motive experimental games the subjects are pitted against human opponents or computers whose sequence of choices is programmed in advance. The subjects are usually led to believe that their opponents are genuine. The results allow conclusions to be drawn about the way people respond to various patterns of behaviour on the part of their opponents. Oskamp (1971) has provided an exhaustive review of the relevant findings, which will be only briefly summarized here.

The simplest programmed strategies are those in which a cooperative choice is made every trial (100% *C*) or a competitive choice is made on every trial (0% *C*). Sermat (1967) showed that, in the PDG, the unconditionally cooperative program elicits much more cooperation from subjects than the unconditionally competitive program, but that in the game of Chicken exactly the reverse is true. This is in line with common sense: in the PDG the best response to an expected *D* choice is *D*, whereas in Chicken the best response to *D* is *C*, so rational players are bound to compete against an unconditionally competitive program in the PDG and to play cooperatively against it in Chicken, and this difference alone could explain Sermat's finding.

Many subjects reciprocate the cooperation of the 100% *C* program in the PDG, but what is surprising is the fact that many others seize the opportunity of exploiting this unconditionally cooperative opponent by repeatedly choosing *D*. The tendency of a significant proportion of subjects to exploit their opponents' 'pacifist' strategies has been found in other games as well (Shure *et al.*, 1965), although their likelihood of doing so is now known to depend on various circumstantial factors (Reychler,.1979).

A great deal of research has been devoted to a conditional programmed strategy called *tit-for-tat* (TFT) in which, after an initial *C* choice, *C* is chosen whenever the subject's previous choice was *C*, and *D* is chosen whenever the subject's previous choice was *D*. This program can be interpreted as a way of signalling 'I'll cooperate if and only if you cooperate'. Crumbaugh and Evans (1967) were the first to show that TFT elicits significantly more cooperation in the PDG than a randomized program containing an equivalent number of *C* choices. This proves that the *pattern* of choices has an effect over and above the mere *frequency* of *C* or *D* choices in a programmed strategy.

Several experiments have focused on the effects of programmed strategies involving unconditional increases or decreases in the frequency of cooperative choices. Harford and Solomon (1967) examined what they called *reformed sinner* and *lapsed saint* programs. The reformed sinner chooses 0% *C* on the first few trials, switches to 100% *C*, and plays TFT in the final block of trials. The lapsed saint begins with 100% *C* and then switches to TFT. The reformed sinner program was found to elicit much more cooperation from subjects than the lapsed saint, and this finding has been replicated several times.

5.3.6 Sex Differences

Perhaps the most puzzling finding to have emerged from early research into mixed-motive games is the apparent tendency for men to choose more cooperatively in both the PDG and Chicken than women. This is very surprising since traditional sex-role norms would seem to encourage greater *competitiveness* in men. Rapoport and Chammah (1965), who discovered the sex difference, found an average of 59% cooperative choices in the PDG among male pairs compared with only 34% among female pairs; in mixed pairs the average was about 50%. The striking difference between same-sex pairs, which was replicated in all seven PDG matrices used in the investigation, was due largely to a steeper and longer lasting sobering period (see Section 5.3.1) among the women. A similar sex difference was later found in the game of Chicken (Rapoport & Chammah, 1969).

Numerous studies (e.g. Hottes & Kahn, 1974; Mack, 1975) have confirmed these findngs, but a few (e.g. Kanouse & Wiest, 1967) have failed to uncover a significant sex difference, and a handful (e.g. Tedeschi *et al.*, 1970) have reported significantly *less* cooperation in male than in female pairs. Skotko *et al.* (1974) have suggested that the sex difference might be an artefact attributable to the presence of male experimenters in most investigations, but Julia Gibbs (1982) found significantly more cooperation in men than in women in two experiments conducted by herself. Although the existing evidence is not entirely consistent, the sex difference is a sufficiently well-established finding to require an explanation.

Hottes and Kahn (1974) have argued that the generally greater competitiveness of women in the PDG is due to their tendency to behave more *defensively* than men. In the PDG, a policy of defensive safety first, that is, of avoiding at all costs the possibility of the worst possible payoff, would lead a player to choose *D* whenever there is any possibility that her opponent might choose *D*. Thus, according to Hottes and Kahn, women tend to choose *D* more frequently than men, not because they are more competitive, but because they are generally more cautious or defensive. This hypothesis is plausible inasmuch as it seems to fit in with conventional sex role stereotypes, but it collapses when the evidence from the game of Chicken is taken into account. In Chicken, a defensive player who adopts a cautious policy of safety first will choose cooperatively rather than competitively because the worst possible payoffs result from *D* choices. If women are generally more defensive than men, they should therefore appear more *cooperative* in Chicken; but, as indicated earlier, exactly the reverse is observed in practice.

Colman (1982, Ch. 7) has attempted to explain the sex differences in both the PDG and Chicken as follows. Perhaps women tend to be more strongly motivated than men to avoid making fools of themselves by receiving worse payoffs than their opponents. According to this hypothesis, women are generally more anxious than men to ensure that the *relative* payoffs do not mount up in favour of their opponents. A player who is motivated to avoid relative loss will tend to make frequent *D* choices in both the PDG and Chicken, because it is impossible (in both games) for a player who chooses *D* to receive a worse payoff than her opponent. If this hypothesis is correct – and it could be tested empirically without too much difficulty – then it is misleading to interpret the higher frequency of *D* choices in female than in male pairs as indicating that 'women have a greater tendency to respond suspiciously, resentfully, conservatively, and thus competitively than do men' (Bixenstine & O'Reilly, 1966, p. 263). The evidence may simply show that women are more anxious than men to avoid appearing foolish in comparison with their opponents.

5.3.7 Attribution Effects

A series of interesting studies by Kelley and Stahelski (1970a, 1970b, 1970c) have focused on the effects of players' beliefs about their opponents' intentions on cooperation in the PDG. In the first experiment, subjects were invited to indicate their cooperative or competitive intentions privately to the experimenter before playing 40 trials of the PDG in pairs. After each block of 10 trials they were questioned about their inferences regarding their opponents' intentions. Attributional errors were found to relate to cooperative and competitive behaviour in an intriguing way. Subjects whose own intentions were cooperative were generally able to infer their opponents' intentions correctly after only 10 trials, but subjects whose own intentions were competitive were generally unable to do so even after 40 trials.

The authors explained their findings as follows. Suppose that people tend to assume, in the absence of evidence to the contrary, that others are similar to themselves: cooperatively intentioned people tend to assume that others are generally cooperative, and competitively intentioned people that others are generally competitive. Now cooperative people are likely to discover through everyday mixed-motive interactions that their assumption is false, because some of the people with whom they interact are bound to exploit their cooperative behaviour by responding competitively. But competitive people are less likely to discover through everyday experience that some others are unlike themselves because their competitive behaviour in PDG-type encounters leaves their opponents no rational alternative but to respond competitively: no rational player responds cooperatively to an obviously competitive opponent because to do so would be to invite the worst possible payoff. Thus, in contrast to cooperative people, competitive people are likely to find their assumption that others are similar to themselves apparently confirmed by experience, and they are therefore unlikely to be able to infer the true intentions of their opponents.

Kelley and Stahelski (1970c) produced the following evidence in support of their hypothesis. Subjects who favoured competitive solutions to a wide range of problems, including bargaining conflicts, socio-political struggles, and PDGs, tended to attribute uniformly competitive motives to other people, whereas cooperative people tended to believe, correctly, that people vary greatly in cooperativeness/competitiveness. The relationship between cooperative or competitive intentions and attributions of intent to others is called the *triangle hypothesis* because of its geometric properties when depicted in the manner of Table 5.1.

Table 5.1 The Triangle Hypothesis

Own intentions	Attributions of intent to others		
	Cooperative	Neutral	Competitive
Cooperative	X	X	X
Neutral		X	X
Competitive			X

The first row of the table indicates that cooperative people attribute the full range of cooperative and competitive intentions to others; the bottom row indicates that competitive people attribute only competitive intentions to others. According to Kelley and Stahelski (1970c), competitive people have a cynical and authoritarian outlook on life. They believe that others are as competitive as themselves, and this belief operates as a self-fulfilling prophecy, forcing others to behave competitively in interactions with them. Cooperative people, on the other hand, have a less pessimistic outlook on life and a more realistic understanding of the diversity of human nature.

Indirect support for the triangle hypothesis has come from a study by Eiser and Tajfel (1972) in which cooperative subjects were shown to be more eager than competitive subjects to obtain information about their opponents' intentions in a non-PDG mixed-motive game. This finding harmonizes with the triangle hypothesis, according to which competitive people think they know what other people's intentions are, and therefore that they have no need for additional information. Other investigators (Miller & Holmes, 1975; Kuhlman & Wimberley, 1976) have corroborated the triangle hypothesis in the PDG but found it less applicable to certain other mixed-motive games.

5.4 Multi-Person Games

By the early 1970s a great deal had been learnt about cooperation and competition in dyads. At about this time, however, public concern was aroused in the

United States and Europe by a range of social and economic problems connected with cooperation and competition in larger groups — the energy crisis and other problems revolving around the conservation of scarce resources, inflationary wage settlements, environmental pollution, and the nuclear arms race — to which the conventional two-person models seemed hardly applicable. A multi-person game suitable for modelling problems such as these was developed simultaneously and independently by Dawes (1973), Hamburger (1973), and Schelling (1973). The *N*-Person Prisoner's Dilemma (NPD) as it is usually called, has been used as an experimental game in numerous investigations, and some interesting new discoveries about cooperative and competitive behaviour have emerged. The empirical findings have been reviewed by Dawes (1980) and Colman (1982, Ch. 9). Before summarizing and commenting on them, it is necessary to say something about the intuitive background and formal structure of the NPD.

5.4.1 Intuitive Background and Formalization

The following strategic problem was mentioned by Lloyd (1833) in a lecture on 'The Checks to Population' and discussed in detail by Hardin (1968). Suppose that six farmers have access to a common pasture on which to graze their cattle. Each farmer owns a single cow weighing 1000 lb, and each has the opportunity of increasing his wealth in livestock by adding a second 1000 – lb cow to the common. But the common cannot sustain any more cows without deterioration through overgrazing: for each cow that is added, the weight of every cow on the common will decrease by 100 lb. Thus if one farmer decides to add a cow, his own wealth in livestock will increase from 1 × 1000 lb to 2 × 900 lb, and it is in his individual self-interest to add a cow even if some or all of the other farmers decide to do so as well. But if every farmer does this, then each ends up poorer (with two 400 – lb cows) that if every farmer contents himself with one 1000 – lb cow. Non-cooperative pursuit of individual self-interest leads to a collectively deficient outcome, and some such process appears to have contributed to the impoverishment of small farmers in England in the 18th century, during the period of the enclosures.

The tragedy of the commons, as it is often called, can be modelled by a multi-person game with the following defining properties: (a) Each player faces a choice between two strategies, which may be labelled *C* (cooperate) and *D* (defect); (b) the *D* strategy is dominant for every player: it yields a higher payoff to the player who chooses it than the alternative *C* strategy, irrespective of the choices of the other players; (c) the payoff to each player is higher if every player chooses *C* than if every player chooses *D*.

The two-person Prisoner's Dilemma Game processes all these defining properties and can therefore be regarded as a special case of the NPD; it is for this reason that the general case is usually called the N-Person Prisoner's Dilemma, though the less specific terms 'commons dilemma' and 'social dilemma' are still sometimes used to describe it (Dawes *et al.*, 1977; Dawes, 1980). The NPD corresponds to an astonishingly wide range of everyday strategic interactions in which individual rationality is at odds with collective rationality. It is in the individual self-interest of a trade union to negotiate wage settlements above the national rate of inflation whether or not other unions do so as well, but a better outcome for all results from collective wage restraint; an individual householder or motorist may benefit by disregarding an appeal for energy or fuel conservation, but everyone may none the less be better off if all heed the appeal than if none does so; an individual nation may improve its security by increasing its expenditure on arms, but every nation may be more secure as a result of multilateral disarmament; and so on. In each case, the pursuit of individual rationality would clearly lead to universal defection or competitive choices, but the resulting outcome would not be in anyone's interest. Paradoxically, it would benefit all concerned to relinquish their freedom to choose by entering into a binding agreement, enforceable by law, to behave cooperatively. This seems to be the idea behind the social contract advocated by the philosophers Hobbes and Rousseau (see Chapter 11).

The abstract structure of the simplest type of three-person NPD is displayed in Matrix 5.6.

Matrix 5.6 Three-Person NPD

Number choosing *C*	Number choosing *D*	Payoff to each *C*-chooser	Payoff to each *D*-chooser
3	0	3	—
2	1	2	4
1	2	1	3
0	3	—	2

The first row of the matrix shows that the payoff to each *C*-chooser is three units if all three players choose *C*, and in this case, since there is no *D*-chooser, there is a dash in the last column. The second row shows what happens if two players choose *C* and one chooses *D*; in that case the payoff to each *C*-chooser is two units and the payoff to the solitary *D*-chooser is four units and so on.

The game can be depicted graphically without loss of information as shown in Fig. 5.1. The payoff to an individual *C*-chooser or *D*-chooser is measured on the vertical axis; the horizontal axis indicates the number of *other* players choosing *C*. The graph shows clearly that a *D* choice pays the player who chooses it better than a *C* choice irrespective of the number of other players choosing *C*; but the left-hand extremity of the upper line is below the right-hand extremity of the lower line, which shows that an individual player receives a smaller payoff when all choose *D* than when all choose *C*.

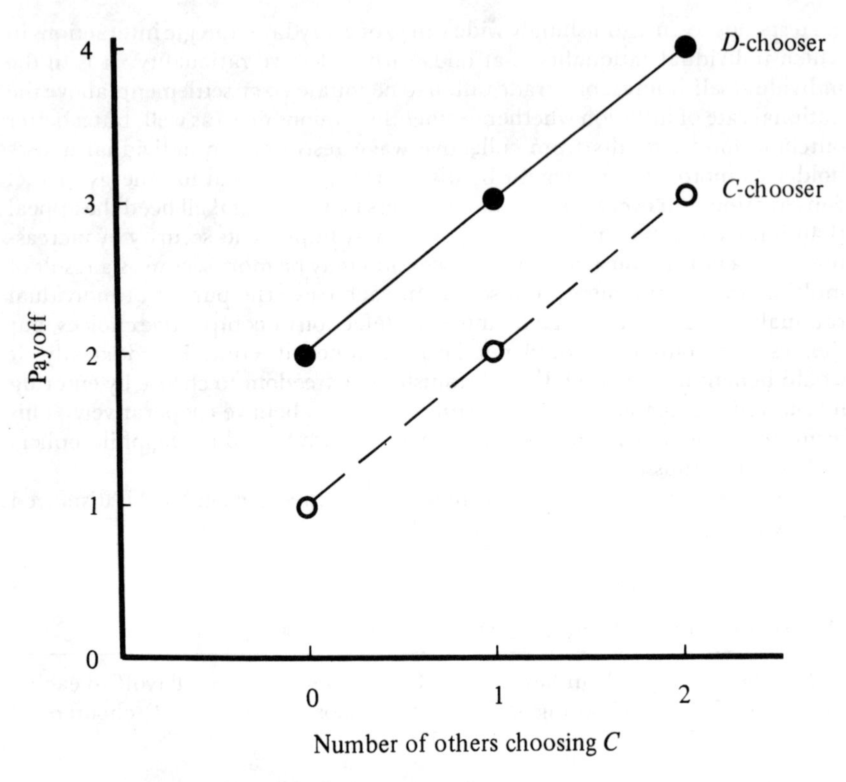

Fig. 5.1 NPD : Graphical representation.

5.4.2 Empirical Findings

The earliest forerunner of modern NPD research is Mintz's (1951) classic experiment on 'non-adaptive group behaviour', which was designed as a laboratory analogue of an escape panic. Each member of a group of subjects held one end of a string, the other end of which was attached to an aluminium cone. The cones lay in the bottom of a narrow-necked bottle, and the subjects' task was to remove them from the bottle as quickly as possible. The bottle was slowly filled with water from below, and a substantial monetary reward was offered to the subjects whose cones emerged from the bottle dry. There was just enough time for all the cones to pass through the neck of the bottle one by one, but whenever two or more cones arrived at the neck together a blockage resulted. The task corresponds to an NPD if the simplifying assumption is made that each subject faces a choice between two strategies: cooperative turn-taking (*C*) and competitive rushing towards the neck of the bottle (*D*). An analogous situation arises when a fire breaks out in a crowded theatre: Mintz's water represents the fire, the neck of the bottle is the theatre exit, and the cones are the members of the audience.

The invariable outcome in Mintz's (1951) experiment was a traffic jam at the neck of the bottle, preventing all or some of the cones from being removed in time. When the subjects were allowed to discuss and plan their strategies in advance there was some slight improvement, but a blockage was still the usual outcome. When the water and financial incentives were removed, however, and the subjects were instructed simply to withdraw their cones as quickly as possible, serious blockages never occurred. Under these conditions, of course, the task corresponds to a pure coordination game (see Section 5.2) rather than an NPD, and rushing for the exit is no longer a dominant strategy; the culturally prominent solution is first-come, first-served.

Recent experiments have been based on explicit NPD structures with the payoffs presented numerically, usually in the manner of Matrix 5.6. The most striking findings concern group size, opportunities for communication between players, and attribution effects. Attempts to link other variables with cooperation and competition have been less successful. The sex difference found in the two-person PDG, for example, does not emerge in the multi-person NPD (Caldwell, 1976; Goehring & Kahan, 1976; Dawes *et al.*, 1977).

With the exception of one of the games used by Bonacich *et al.* (1976), an inverse relationship has invariably been reported between group size and cooperation in the NPD. Marwell and Schmitt (1972), for example, reported significantly more cooperation in two-person than in three-person groups; Hamburger *et al.* (1975) found a similar difference between three-person and seven-person groups; and Fox and Guyer (1977) found significantly more cooperation in three-person than in seven-person or twelve-person groups. There are technical problems in this area of research that investigators do not always seem to appreciate: it is difficult to vary group size without at the same time altering other parameters of the game. But when, through the use of elaborate controls, everything is held constant except group size, the inverse relationship between number of players and cooperation still emerges (Hamburger, 1977).

Several hypotheses have been advanced to explain the effect of group size on cooperation. The *bad apple* hypothesis is based on the assumption that people are motivated to cooperate only when there is a reasonable likelihood that everybody else will cooperate. It takes only one 'bad apple' (competitive defector) in a group to initiate a spiral of disillusioned competitiveness, and the chances of a bad apple turning up in a group are obviously greater the larger the number of players in the group. Hamburger (1977) therefore compared the behaviour of subjects pitted against one or two stooge opponents whose choices were equally cooperative in the small and the larger groups. Although the number of bad apples was thus held constant, the genuine subjects still cooperated less in the larger groups, and this finding tends to undermine the bad apple hypothesis.

A second hypothesis focuses on the relatively smaller degree of *interpersonal control* that is possible in large groups. In a two-person group, a player can reward or punish an opponent by choosing cooperatively or competitively. This is essentially what lies behind the tit-for-tat programmed strategy, which is known to elicit rather high levels of cooperation in the PDG (see Section 5.3.5). But in a large group a player cannot reciprocate the others' choices in this way when — as is usually the case — some are cooperative and others competitive. If we assume that a major motive for cooperation in the two-person PDG is to reinforce the opponent's cooperative behaviour, then the relative lack of cooperation in multi-person groups is readily explained (Hamburger, 1979, p. 243). The interpersonal control hypothesis accounts satisfactorily for the difference between two-person and multi-person groups, but it cannot convincingly explain the difference between multi-person groups of different sizes: a player has scarcely any more scope for selectively reinforcing the others' behaviour in a three-person than a seven-person NPD, for example.

The most satisfactory explanation for the effect of group size on cooperation is the *de-individuation* hypothesis originally proposed by Hamburger *et al.* (1975). De-individuation is said to occur when individuality and personal accountability are submerged in a group and the group members are consequently less inhibited from behaving selfishly or antisocially than they might otherwise be. Hamburger, Guyer, and Fox aruged that 'deindividuation in a group increases as the size of the group increases since, everything else being equal, the individual appears more anonymous in a larger group than in a smaller one' (p. 524). Fox and Guyer (1978) tested this hypothesis in a four-person NPD in which subjects made their choices publicly or anonymously. Significantly more cooperation was observed in the public choice condition, as predicted by the hypothesis. This finding corroborates those of Kahan (1973) and Jerdee and Rosen (1974), which revealed extremely low levels of cooperation under anonymous choice conditions.

Opportunities for communication between players have generally been found to enhance cooperation in the NPD, as they do in the PDG. Mintz's (1951) findings have already been discussed; two other major investigations of the effects of communication are those of Caldwell (1976) and Dawes *et al.* (1977). Caldwell's subjects played a five-person NPD in which they could either communicate and penalize defectors by reducing their payoffs, communicate without sanctions, or not communicate at all. The effect of mere communication was non-significant, but communication coupled with sanctions led to increased cooperation. Caldwell describes this as a communication effect, but it is really an effect of altering the payoff structure of the game. Dawes *et al.*'s data, on the other hand, show clearly that mere communication can have a significant effect. Subjects were assigned to groups varying in size from five to eight, and the effects of four levels of communication were examined: no communication; communication only about matters unrelated to the game; relevant communication; and relevant communication plus non-binding public announcements of intended choices before every trial. The first two conditions yielded 30% and 32% cooperative choices respectively, and the last two 72% and 71% respectively. The effect of relevant communication was highly significant; but it is clear that irrelevant chatter has no noticeable effect, and that non-binding promises do nothing to increase cooperation, presumably because they do not enhance the players' trustworthiness. Promises without sanctions against breaking them are, after all, mere promises.

Several investigations have focused on attribution effects in the NPD. Tyszka and Grzelak (1976); Alcock and Mansell (1977); Dawes *et al.* (1977); and Marwell and Ames (1979) have all reported a strong, positive relationship between cooperation and attributions of cooperative intent to others. Alcock and Mansell reported that defectors predicted an average of 24% cooperation from the other players in the group while cooperators predicted an average of 68%. In the Dawes, McTavish, and Shaklee experiment, defectors predicted four times as many defecting choices from others as did cooperators, and the correlation between cooperation and attribution of cooperative intent to others was 0.60. These findings are readily intelligible in the light of Kelley and Stahelski's (1970c) triangle hypothesis, which was discussed in Section 5.3.7.

5.5 The Future of Experimental Games

Game theory is concerned with the deliberate choices of interdependent decision makers, and experimental games are based on the assumption that when people have the power to influence events, they normally try to obtain the outcomes that they consider best. In this respect experimental games are more akin to neo-classical economics than to traditional social psychology which, in spite of the vogue for cognitive rather than purely behavioural explanations, tends to view human beings as passive respondents to stimuli impinging on them from the external environment. Psychologists' predeliction for 'explaining' human behaviour in terms of external causes without invoking free will, by trying to specify the independent variables associated with various classes of behaviour, is no doubt due largely to the remarkable success of this approach in many branches of natural science. But unlike electrons, gases, planets, plants, and even perhaps some animals, human beings are capable of making deliberate choices; and any psychological theory that ignores this quintessentially psychological feature of human action is bound to fail, or at least to have only limited usefulness.

A second characteristic feature of game theory and experimental games is the irreducibly social character of the phenomena with which they are concerned. The outcome of a game is, by definition, contingent on the choices of all the players and cannot be specified in terms of the behaviour of a single individual. Much of traditional social psychology, on the other hand, deals with non-social behavioural phenomena – the effects of persuasive messages on an *individual's* attitudes, the effects of induced emotional states on an *individual's* non-verbal behaviour, the effects of television violence on an *individual's* aggressive behaviour, and so on. Cooperation and competition fall into the class of inherently social phenomena which cannot even be defined at the individual level, and which were largely neglected by social psychologists until the advent of experimental games, in spite of their important social, political, and economic implications.

Interdependent decision making is a significant and ubiquitous fact of life, and it is therefore unlikely that the experimental gaming tradition will ever die. But it is bound to change: application of the fundamental ideas of game theory to empirical problems has so far been extremely unimaginative and limited in scope, and the ecological validity of the results of experimental games has increasingly been challenged. For more than two decades empirical investigations of cooperation and competition focused almost exclusively on the PDG and a few other two-person games. The relative decline of two-person experimental games and the rise of the multi-person NPD since the mid-1970s has corrected this imbalance, but the danger remains of research in this area being dominated by a narrow range of theoretical models. There are many interesting strategic problems that cannot realistically be modelled by two-person or multi-person Prisoner's Dilemmas, and experimental studies based on other game structures are urgently needed.

Experimental games are traditionally presented to the subjects as abstract exercises, usually in the form of payoff matrices, in which the object is to accumulate small amounts of money, valueless tokens, or points. The payoff matrices are, it is true, formally identical to naturally occurring strategic interactions, but the decision contexts in which the subjects operate are so abstract and artificial that questions naturally arise about the generalizability of the findings to everyday life. Nemeth (1972), for example, has claimed that 'the seemingly irrational behavior of subjects in a Prisoner's Dilemma game is due primarily to the essential incomprehensibility of the situation in which the subject is placed' (p. 213). After an exhaustive survey of experimental games, Wrightsman *et al.* (1972) had this to say: 'What surprises us most, in our review of research, is that apparently no studies have compared the degree of cooperative behavior in a laboratory mixed-motive game with cooperation in different real-world tasks' (p. 277). There is no *a priori* reason to suppose that people behave identically in abstract laboratory games and lifelike interactions with equivalent strategic structures. In fact recent evidence (Colman, 1982) shows that they do not. More lifelike experimental games will have to be used in future research if the goal of enlarging our understanding of everyday cooperation and competition is to be achieved.

References

ALCOCK, J.E. and MANSELL, D. (1977). Predisposition and behaviour in a collective dilemma. *Journal of Conflict Resolution*, **21**, 443–457.

BIXENSTINE, V.E. and O'REILLY, E.F. JR. (1966). Money vs. electric shock as payoff in a Prisoner's Dilemma game. *Psychological Record*, **16**, 251–264.

BONACICH, P., SHURE, G.H., KAHAN, J.P., and MEEKER, R.J. (1976). Cooperation and group size in the N-Person Prisoners' Dilemma. *Journal of Conflict Resolution*, **20**, 687–706.

CALDWELL, M.D. (1976). Communication and sex effects in a five-person Prisoner's

Dilemma Game. *Journal of Personality and Social Psychology*, **33**, 273 – 280.
COLMAN, A.M. (1982). *Game Theory and Experimental Games: The Study of Strategic Interaction*. Oxford: Pergamon (In press).
CRUMBAUGH, C.M. and EVANS, G.W. (1967). Presentation format, other-person strategies, and cooperative behavior in the Prisoner's Dilemma. *Psychological Reports*, **20**, 895 – 902.
DAVIS, J.H., LAUGHLIN, P.R., and KOMORITA, S.S. (1976). The social psychology of small groups. *Annual Review of Psychology*, **27**, 501 – 542.
DAWES, R.M. (1973). The commons dilemma game : An *n*-person mixed-motive game with a dominating strategy for defection. *Oregon Research Institute Research Bulletin*, **13**(2).
DAWES, R.M. (1980). Social dilemmas. *Annual Review of Psychology*, **31**, 169 – 193.
DAWES, R.M., MCTAVISH, J., and SHAKLEE, H. (1977). Behavior, communication, and assumptions about other people's behavior in a Commons Dilemma situation. *Journal of Personality and Social Psychology*, **35**, 1 – 11.
DEUTSCH, M. (1958). Trust and suspicion. *Journal of Conflict Resolution*, **2**, 265 – 279.
DEUTSCH, M. (1969). Socially relevant science: reflections on some studies of interpersonal conflict. *American Psychologist*, **24**, 1076 – 1092.
DEUTSCH, M. and KRAUSS, R.M. (1960). The effect of threat upon interpersonal bargaining. *Journal of Abnormal and Social Psychology*, **61**, 181 – 189.
DEUTSCH, M. and KRAUSS, R.M. (1962). Studies of interpersonal bargaining. *Journal of Conflict Resolution*, **6**, 52 – 76.
EISER, J.R. and BHAVNANI, K.-K. (1974). The effect of situational meaning on the behaviour of subjects in the Prisoner's Dilemma Game. *European Journal of Social Psychology*, **4**, 93 – 97.
EISER, J.R. and TAJFEL, H. (1972). Acquisition of information in dyadic interaction. *Journal of Personality and Social Psychology*, **23**, 340 – 345.
ELLSBERG, D. (1959). The Political Uses of Madness. Lowell Lecture, Santa Monica, Ca.: The Rand Corporation.
EVANS, G. (1964). Effect of unilateral promise and value of rewards upon cooperation and trust. *Journal of Abnormal and Social Psychology*, **69**, 587 – 590.
EVANS, G. and CRUMBAUGH, C.M. (1966). Effects of prisoner's dilemma format on cooperative behavior. *Journal of Personality and Social Psychology*, **3**, 486 – 488.
FLOOD, M.M. (1958). Some experimental games. *Management Science*, **5**, 5 – 26.
FOX, J. and GUYER, M. (1977). Group size and others' strategy in an N-person game. *Journal of Conflict Resolution*, **21**, 323 – 338.
FOX, J. and GUYER, M. (1978). 'Public' choice and cooperation in N-Person Prisoner's Dilemma. *Journal of Conflict Resolution*, **22**, 469 – 481.
FRÉCHET, M. (1953). Émile Borel, initiator of the theory of psychological games and its application. *Econometrica*, **21**, 95 – 96.
GALLO, P.S. and MCCLINTOCK, C.G. (1965). Cooperative and competitive behavior in mixed-motive games. *Journal of Conflict Resolution*, **9**, 68 – 78.
GIBBS, J. (1982). Sex and Communication Effects in a Mixed-Motive Game. Unpublished doctoral dissertation, University of Durham.
GOEHRING, D.J. and KAHAN, J.P. (1976). The uniform N-Person Prisoner's Dilemma Game: Construction and test of an index of cooperation. *Journal of Conflict Resolution*, **20**, 111 – 128.
GUMPERT, P., DEUTSCH, M., and EPSTEIN, Y. (1969). Effects of incentive magnitude on cooperation in the Prisoner's Dilemma game. *Journal of Personality and Social Psychology*, **11**, 66 – 69.
GUYER, M. and PERKEL, B. (1972). *Experimental Games: A Bibliography*

(1945 – 1971). Ann Arbor, Mich.: Mental Health Research Institute, Communication 293.

HAMBURGER, H. (1973). N-person Prisoner's Dilemma. *Journal of Mathematical Sociology*, **3**, 27 – 48.

HAMBURGER, H. (1977). Dynamics of cooperation in the take-some games. In W.H. KEMPF and B.H. REPP (Eds.), *Mathematical Models for Social Psychology*. Bern: Hans Huber.

HAMBURGER, H. (1979). *Games as Models of Social Phenomena*. San Francisco: W.H. Freeman.

HAMBURGER, H., GUYER, M. and FOX, J. (1975). Group size and cooperation. *Journal of Conflict Resolution*, **19**, 503 – 531.

HARDIN, G. (1968). The tragedy of the commons. *Science*, **162**, 1243 – 1248.

HARFORD, T.C. and SOLOMON, L. (1967). 'Reformed sinner' and 'lapsed saint' strategies in the Prisoner's Dilemma game. *Journal of Conflict Resolution*, **11**, 104 – 109.

HARVEY, J.H. and SMITH, W.P. (1977). *Social Psychology: An Attributional Approach*. St Louis: Mosby.

HOTTES, J. and KAHN, A. (1974). Sex differences in a mixed-motive conflict situation. *Journal of Personality*, **42**, 260 – 275.

JERDEE, T.H. and ROSEN, B. (1974). Effects of opportunity to communicate and visibility of individual decisions on behavior in the common interest. *Journal of Applied Psychology*, **59**, 712 – 716.

KAHAN, J.P. (1973). Noninteraction in an anonymous three-person Prisoner's Dilemma Game. *Behavioral Science*, **18**, 124 – 127.

KAHN, H. (1965). *On Escalation*. New York: Praeger.

KANOUSE, D.E. and WIEST, W.M. (1967). Some factors affecting choice in the Prisoner's Dilemma. *Journal of Conflict Resolution*, **11**, 206 – 213.

KELLEY, H.H. and STAHELSKI, A.J. (1970a). Errors in perception of intentions in a mixed-motive game. *Journal of Experimental Social Psychology*, **6**, 379 – 400.

KELLEY, H.H. and STAHELSKI, A.J. (1970b). The inference of intentions from moves in the Prisoner's Dilemma Game. *Journal of Experimental Social Psychology*, **6**, 401 – 419.

KELLEY, H.H. and STAHELSKI, A.J. (1970c). Social interaction basis of cooperators' and competitors' beliefs about others. *Journal of Personality and Social Psychology*, **16**, 66 – 91.

KUHLMAN, D.M. and WIMBERLEY, D.L. (1976). Expectations of choice behavior held by cooperators, competitors and individualists across four classes of experimental game. *Journal of Personality and Social Psychology*, **34**, 69 – 81.

LLOYD, W.F. (1833). *Two Lectures on the Checks to Population*. Oxford: Oxford University Press.

LUCE, R.D. and RAIFFA, H. (1957). *Games and Decisions: Introduction and Critical Survey*. New York: Wiley.

MACK, D. (1975). Skirting the competition. *Psychology Today*, **8**, 39 – 41.

MARWELL, G. and AMES, R.E. (1979). Experiments on the provision of public goods I: Resources, interest, group size, and the free rider problem. *American Journal of Sociology*, **84**, 1335 – 1360.

MARWELL, G. and SCHMITT, D. (1972). Cooperation in a three-person Prisoner's Dilemma. *Journal of Personality and Social Psychology*, **21**, 376 – 383.

MCCLINTOCK, C.G. (1972). Game behavior and social motivation in interpersonal settings. In C.G. MCCLINTOCK (Ed.), *Experimental Social Psychology*. New York: Holt, Rinehart, & Winston. Pp. 271 – 297.

McCLINTOCK, C.G. and McNEEL, S.P. (1967). Prior dyadic experience and monetary reward as determinants of cooperative behavior. *Journal of Personality and Social Psychology*, **5**, 282 – 294.

MILLER, D.T. and HOLMES, J.G. (1975). The role of situational restrictiveness on self-fulfilling prophecies: a theoretical and empirical extension of Kelley and Stahelski's triangle hypothesis. *Journal of Personality and Social Psychology*, **31**, 661 – 673.

MINTZ, A. (1951). Non-adaptive group behavior. *Journal of Abnormal and Social Psychology*, **46**, 150 – 159.

NEMETH, C. (1972). A critical analysis of research utilizing the prisoner's dilemma paradigm for the study of bargaining. *Advances in Experimental Social Psychology*, **6**, 203 – 234.

NEUMANN, J. VON (1928). Zur Theorie der Gesellschaftsspiele. *Mathematische Annalen*, **100**, 295 – 320.

NEUMANN, J. VON and MORGENSTERN, O. (1944). *Theory of Games and Economic Behavior*. Princeton, NJ: Princeton University Press. 2nd edn., 1947; 3rd edn., 1953.

OSKAMP, S. (1971). Effects of programmed strategies on cooperation in the Prisoner's Dilemma and other mixed-motive games. *Journal of Conflict Resolution*, **15**, 225 – 259.

OSKAMP, S. and KLEINKE, C. (1970). Amount of reward as a variable in the Prisoner's Dilemma game. *Journal of Personality and Social Psychology*, **16**, 133 – 140.

PLON, M. (1974). On the meaning of the notion of conflict and its study in social psychology. *European Journal of Social Psychology*, **4**, 389 – 436.

PRUITT, D.G. (1967). Reward structure and cooperation: the decomposed prisoner's dilemma game. *Journal of Personality and Social Psychology*, **7**, 21 – 27.

PRUITT, D.G. (1970). Motivational processes in the decomposed prisoner's dilemma game. *Journal of Personality and Social Psychology*, **14**, 277 – 238.

PRUITT, D.G. and KIMMEL, M.J. (1977). Twenty years of experimental gaming: critique, synthesis, and suggestions for the future. *Annual Review of Psychology*, **28**, 363 – 392.

RAPOPORT, A. and CHAMMAH, A.M. (1965). *Prisoner's Dilemma: A Study in Conflict and Cooperation*. Ann Arbor: University of Michigan Press.

RAPOPORT, A. and CHAMMAH, A.M. (1969). The game of Chicken. In I.R. BUCHLER and H.G. NUTINI (Eds.), *Game Theory in the Behavioral Sciences*. Pittsburgh: University of Pittsburgh Press. Pp. 151 – 175.

RAPOPORT, A. and ORWANT, C. (1962). Experimental games: a review. *Behavioral Science*, **7**, 1 – 37.

REYCHLER, L. (1979). The effectiveness of a pacifist strategy in conflict resolution: an experimental study. *Journal of Conflict Resolution*, **23**, 228 – 260.

SCHELLING, T.C. (1960). *The Strategy of Conflict*. Cambridge, Mass.: Harvard University Press.

SCHELLING, T.C. (1973). Hockey helmets, concealed weapons, and daylight saving: a study of binary choices with externalities. *Journal of Conflict Resolution*, **17**, 381 – 428.

Scientific American (1981). Program Power. Vol. **244**(4). 71A – 72.

SCODEL, A., MINAS, J.S., RATOOSH, P. and LIPETZ, M. (1959). Some descriptive aspects of two-person non-zero-sum games. *Journal of Conflict Resolution*, **3**, 114 – 119.

SERMAT, V. (1967). The possibility of influencing the other's behavior and cooperation: Chicken vs. Prisoner's Dilemma. *Canadian Journal of Psychology*, **27**, 204 – 219.

SERMAT, V. (1970). Is game behavior related to behavior in other interpersonal situations? *Journal of Personality and Social Psychology*, **16**, 92 – 109.

SHURE, G.H. MEEKER, R.J. and HANSFORD, E.A. (1965). The effectiveness of pacifist strategies in bargaining games. *Journal of Conflict Resolution*, **9**, 106 – 117.

SKOTKO, V., LANGMEYER, D. and LUNDGREN, D. (1974). Sex differences as artifacts in the prisoner's dilemma game. *Journal of Conflict Resolution*, **18**, 707 – 713.

STAHELSKI, A.J. and KELLEY, H.H. (1969). The effects of incentives on cooperators and competitors in a Prisoner's Dilemma game. Paper presented at the Western Psychological Association Convention, Vancouver. [Cited in Wrightsman, O'Connor and Baker (1972), pp. 51 – 52.]

SWINGLE, P.G. (1970). Dangerous games. In P.G. SWINGLE (Ed.), *The Structure of Conflict*. New York: Academic Press. Pp. 235 – 276.

TEDESCHI, J.T., BONOMA, T.V. and NOVINSON, N. (1970). Behavior of a threatener: retaliation vs. fixed opportunity costs. *Journal of Conflict Resolution*, **14**, 69 – 76.

TEDESCHI, J.T., SCHLENKER, B.R. and BONOMA, T.V. (1973). *Conflict, Power, and Games*. Chicago: Aldine.

TOGNOLI, J. (1975). Reciprocation of generosity and knowledge of game termination in the decomposed Prisoner's Dilemma Game. *European Journal of Social Psychology*, **5**, 297 – 312.

TYSZKA, T. and GRZELAK, J.L. (1976). Criteria of choice in non-constant zero-sum games. *Journal of Conflict Resolution*, **20**, 357 – 376.

WICHMAN, H. (1972). Effects of isolation and communication on cooperation in a two-person game. In L.S. WRIGHTSMAN, J. O'CONNOR and N.J. BAKER (Eds.), *Cooperation and Competition: Readings on Mixed-Motive Games*. Belmont: Brooks-Cole. Pp. 197 – 205.

WRIGHTSMAN, L.S. (1966). Personality and attitudinal correlates of trusting and trustworthy behaviors in a two-person game. *Journal of Personality and Social Psychology*, **4**, 328 – 332.

WRIGHTSMAN, L.S., O'CONNOR, J. and BAKER, N.J. (Eds.) (1972). *Cooperation and Competition: Readings on Mixed-Motive Games*. Belmont: Brooks-Cole.

YOUNG, J.W. (1977). Behavioral and perceptual differences between structurally equivalent, two-person games: a rich versus poor context comparison. *Journal of Conflict Resolution*, **21**, 299 – 322.

CHAPTER 6

Bargaining and Negotiation

Maryon Tysoe *

6.1 Introduction

6.1.1 Definitions

What does 'negotiation' actually mean? According to Morley and Stephenson (1977), who surveyed the diverse uses of the term, its core meaning is the verbal communication which parties undertake in order jointly to resolve a conflict of interest between them. They define bargaining as 'the process of negotiating for agreement' (p. 26), although the two terms are usually used interchangeably.

These definitions rule out conflicts of attitudes (as opposed to interests) as the focus of negotiations; they would be resolved by debate or discussion. The notion of joint decision making is crucial to the definitions – hitting one another over the head or sending in the troops would definitely not be counted. Furthermore, it is implicit that the participants do genuinely wish to reach an agreement, the possible costs involved in negotiating being less than those involved in allowing the conflict to continue. Sometimes the participants have some other goal in mind, such as delaying tactics or propaganda (Kerr, 1954; Mack & Snyder, 1957; Nogee, 1960; Sawyer & Guetzkow, 1965). Although this is not common, when it does occur the behaviour is not considered to qualify as a negotiation (Kniveton, 1974).

Given that the parties would like to reach agreement, then, they have not only a motive to compete in order to gain a settlement maximally favourable to themselves, but also a motive to cooperate in order to reach a settlement at all. In other words, negotiation involves *mixed motives* (Morley & Stephenson, 1977).

Who are the 'parties' involved in such mixed-motive conflicts of interest? They can be individuals or they can be groups, such as management or union, communities, nations. Negotiations to resolve interpersonal conflicts have been termed 'informal' negotiations, as opposed to 'formal' negotiations between group representatives (Stephenson, 1971). Any number of parties can negotiate together, but most experimental research to date has concentrated

* This work was done while Maryon Tysoe was at the University of Kent at Canterbury. She is now a freelance writer on psychology.

on the two-party case. Work on more than two parties has mainly focused upon the formation of coalitions (see Murnighan, 1978, for a review) and third-party intervention (see Webb, 1979; Rubin, 1980, for reviews).

This chapter will attempt to outline the social psychological approach to the study of negotiations. This does not, of course, mean that 'economic, political and sociological factors' (Morley, 1979, p. 214) do not influence negotiations, or that conflict arises purely from psychological factors — it usually arises from 'objective' goal incompatibility (Sawyer & Guetzkow, 1965). However, it has been strongly argued that '*there is an irreducibly psychological component*' (Morley, 1979, p. 214) involved in negotiations, and that therefore social psychology does have a role to play in understanding bargaining processes (see, e.g. Druckman, 1971).

In the process of examining this approach, we shall see how emphasis has been shifting away from the cooperative and competitive motivations (the two primary motives investigated in this field) at work in negotiations, to the cognitive elements intrinsic to the task of finding a solution to a conflict of interest that is acceptable to one's opponent.

6.1.2 Early Work

Early work on negotiations fell into two main categories (Magenau & Pruitt, 1979). First, 'speculative writings by unsystematic empiricists' (*ibid.*, p. 181), particularly by political scientists and labour economists (see, e.g. Stevens, 1963; Iklé, 1964; Lall, 1966). These writers did, however, tend to take into account the context and history of disputes, a commonly cited failing of social psychology experiments.

The second major category of work was carried out mainly by economists and applied mathematicians. This consisted of describing conflicts mathematically, essentially in terms of choices between various utilities (values) assigned to the available outcomes and assessment of probabilities of one's opponent making certain choices. Once the conflict was described in these terms, it became possible to calculate the most 'rational' strategies which the participants would or should adopt (see, e.g. Young, 1975). It has, however, been argued that these approaches are insufficient as descriptions of the negotiation process and predictors of negotiation outcomes.

6.1.3 The Experimental Method

More recently, controlled experiments have come to the fore as the most popular way of investigating negotiations (Magenau & Pruitt, 1979). There are five dominant paradigms, where a 'paradigm' means 'a range of experimental procedures with something significant in common' (Dulany, 1974, p. 44). The labels of paradigms 3 – 5 below follow Morley and Stephenson (1977).

This type of experimental work has been conducted mainly by social psychologists. Matrix games, however, are very popular with political scientists also, particularly for testing aspects of game theory (originally developed by von Neumann & Morgenstern, 1944).

The paradigms reflect the definition of negotiation that was taken as a starting point. Having defined the behaviour one is trying to simulate, it is necessary to *'identify certain key components'* of that behaviour and then *'translate the key components* . . . into the components of an experimental task' (Morley & Stephenson, 1977, p. 44). Limited definitions of negotiations, e.g. 'situations in which the ability of one participant to gain his ends is dependent to an important degree on the choices or decisions that the other participant will make' (Schelling, 1960, p. 25) tend to produce limited paradigms, as we shall see. In order to have a clear view of the aspects of negotiation explored by social psychologists, it is necessary to understand how they have set about their investigations.

Paradigm 1: Matrix Games. This is the simplest bargaining paradigm. In these games, two or more people each independently and simultaneously make one choice out of a set of alternatives. Each player's payoff is jointly determined by his or her choice, the other's choice and the corresponding values in the payoff matrix defining the conflict of interest.

As a paradigm for examining negotiations, matrix games have been very heavily criticized (see Chapter 5) and it has been argued that they do not simulate negotiations at all, in that no joint decision making is involved but merely a set of independent choices (Morley & Stephenson, 1977).

Paradigm 2: Acme – Bolt Trucking Game. This game for two players was invented by Deutsch and Krauss (1960). Each player pretends that he or she is in charge of a trucking company (Acme or Bolt), and they play the game by operating an electric control panel. They each have to get a lorryload of goods to its destination as fast as possible, and their winnings depend upon the speed with which they do it. Each person has a choice of two routes: (a) a short straight route of which one section is only wide enough for one lorry to go down, and to which both players have access from opposite directions; and (b) a long winding road to which they have exclusive access. The ability to threaten is usually built into this game, in that one or both players can control a 'gate'. They can use the gate to block the other's passage down the short route without restricting their own movement. The conflict of interest here is, of course, over the use of the short one-lane route. Players make simultaneous choices and usually play a number of 'trials'.

However, like matrix games, the trucking game is 'no longer . . . defined as relevant, since [it involves] a form of strategic decision making other than negotiation' (Morley, 1978a, p. 180). In particular, it typically omits one of the essential elements of negotiation: namely, that participants communicate verbally in an attempt to resolve together their conflict of interest.

Paradigm 3: Distribution Games (DG). These games do at least 'provide abstract formulations of negotiation tasks' (Morley & Stephenson, 1977, p. 49). There are typically two players. Each player is assigned a minimum number of points or amount of money (Minimum Necessary Share or MNS) which he or she must obtain, before going on to negotiate how a fixed amount is to be divided between them. They are paid according to the amount they gain over and above their MNS.

The problem with distribution games, according to Morley and Stephenson (1977), is that apart from the extremely heavy time pressures sometimes involved, communication is restricted in the sense that negotiators can only talk about outcomes. The game does not, therefore, simulate those far more common situations where participants can disagree over *inputs*.

Paradigm 4: Games of Economic Exchange (GEE). These games simulate negotiations between buyers and sellers. The most popular game of this type is called the 'Bilateral Monopoly' game (Siegel & Fouraker, 1960). Here one buyer negotiates with one seller over the price and quantity of goods which they wish to exchange. Each player is given a profit table, which shows the profit they will gain for each combination of price and quantity. They are paid according to the profit from the agreement reached. Communication usually consists only of an exchange of written bids and counterbids.

Again, as with distribution games, there can be very high time pressure and focus is upon outcomes only. This failure to simulate important aspects of negotiations can only limit the generality of the results obtained using such games (Morley & Stephenson, 1977).

Paradigm 5: Role-playing Debates (RPD). This paradigm was first introduced in a study by Campbell (1960). Participants play the roles of representatives of opposing groups. They are charged with attempting to negotiate an agreement concerning a disputed issue (or issues) by *unrestricted* verbal communication. They are also provided with background information about the dispute, and clearly they can negotiate over inputs as well as outcomes. This paradigm, then, provides a more appropriate way of studying negotiations than any of the preceding ones. It should fulfil the requirements implicit in the definition of negotiation set out at the beginning of this chapter, but of course it is limited in that it is simply a simulation. Participants *are* role-playing, they are not genuine representatives of parties with a genuine interest in the outcome; there are no personal consequences for them dependent upon the nature of the agreement reached (other than, perhaps, a small financial gain); they have no real-life party to go back to, to try and explain why they agreed to these terms and obtain their acceptance; the dispute is not set in a complex context with a history.

It is possible to overcome some of these objections by using a 'substitute debate' (Morley & Stephenson, 1977, p. 53). This method was first suggested by McGrath (1966). He laid down some fairly stringent criteria for a suitable paradigm for realistic experimental research into negotiation :

1. Subjects should be representatives of genuine parties.
2. The negotiation issues should be of importance to the parties and their representatives.
3. The conflict between the parties should occur independently of the experiment.
4. Full verbal communication must be allowed between the negotiators, and the issues should be sufficiently complex that a genuine interchange can take place.
5. The complexity of the issues should be such that subjects can set more than one goal and there is more than one dimension of 'payoff'.

Unfortunately, these criteria are very difficult to adhere to in practice. The role-playing debate paradigm does at least adhere to criteria four and five, and even greater realism can be obtained by allocating subjects to their roles according to their actual attitude on the negotiation issue. This paradigm, then, allows exploration of a number of important questions which have been neglected because of the popularity of more limited paradigms.

Overview. The matrix game held virtually undisputed sway as the paradigm for studying bargaining from the late 1950s to the late 1960s (more than 1000 studies have used it), when the use of the other four paradigms began to increase (particularly RPD). Studies using these four paradigms probably total about 100.

It must be emphasized at this point that the effects of the *paradigm itself* on negotiation behaviour and outcomes has not been a focus of attention. Klimoski (1978) has argued cogently that it needs to become so. It does not seem unreasonable to suppose that the type of methodology employed would affect negotiation processes. For example, while some games are 'zero-sum' — that is, what one gains the other must lose (see Chapter 5) — typically the conflict of interest is non-zero-sum. This means that although one can do better than the other, it is possible for both to do well or both to do badly. This is a 'major distinction between bargaining experiments' (Chertkoff & Esser, 1976, p. 465) and may have major effects.

The essential question asked by social psychologists using paradigms 1 – 4 has been : 'What effects do certain factors have upon the motivation to cooperate or compete?' Cooperation and competition are considered to be reflected by such dependent variables as final payoffs (paradigms 1 – 4), particularly participants' joint profit; plus cooperative and competitive choices (paradigm 1); and speed of reaching agreement and concession-making (paradigms 3 and 4).

As we shall see, the questions asked by RPD researchers in particular, have been more complex and have led gradually, it will be argued, to a shift in focus away from motivation and towards cognition (knowledge and thought).

The variables investigated (both independent and dependent) are, of course, limited by the paradigm used. By asking in this chapter what each paradigm *allows one to study*, the concerns of social psychologists in the study of negotiations will be revealed.

6.2 Negotiators as Individuals

6.2.1 Cooperative and Competitive Choices

Research using matrix games has tended primarily to concentrate on such things as the effects upon cooperative and competitive choices of the personal characteristics of the negotiators, the nature of their interpersonal relationship, characteristics of the task, bargaining orientation and the other's strategy. These independent variables are, of course, quite easily manipulatable within the confines of this simple paradigm. This research has been comprehensively reviewed elsewhere (see, e.g. Rubin & Brown, 1975; and Chapter 5 of this volume), and, as pointed out earlier, it has also been strongly argued that matrix games are in fact an inappropriate tool for the study of bargaining, so this body of research will not be examined here.

6.2.2 Threats

The Acme – Bolt trucking game was developed specifically to look at the effects of threat capability and use of threats (a competitive strategy) upon payoffs. However, control of a gate as an operationalization of threat capability has been criticized (Kelley, 1965; Morley & Stephenson, 1977). Kelley asserts that the gate does not constitute just a threat, in the sense of expressing an intent to damage another unless the other acts — or refrains from acting — in a certain way. It can be used, for example, as a punishment, in revenge, or as a trick. Morley and Stephenson have argued that use of the gate does not constitute a threat, but a sanction. Furthermore, this paradigm has suffered the same fate as matrix games and has been largely rejected as a bargaining paradigm.

Threats have, however, also been investigated using the DG and GEE paradigms (see Morley & Stephenson, 1977, pp. 105 – 109, for a review). Findings are not very clear. Deutsch and Krauss (1960, 1962), using their trucking game, found that if both people could threaten, a 'spiral of conflict', of threat and counterthreat, was set up. Subjects had initially been given an 'individualistic' orientation, that is, instructed to gain as much for themselves as they could. Deutsch and Krauss theorized that when people were threatened, their motivation would then become competitive — i.e. they would wish to do better than the other person — and they would threaten back. The use of the DG and GEE paradigms rather than the Acme – Bolt paradigm has, however, not provided evidence to support such a change in motivation, although it may sometimes occur if the threat is actually carried out. Indeed, it may be that using a threat will set up a 'spiral of conflict' only if the threatened person is offended by this (Tjosvold, 1974). Threats may not even always be seen as competitive and would, under such circumstances, not be expected to induce retaliation to save face (see Magenau & Pruitt, 1979). This may occur, for example, if the threat is seen as legitimate, a cry for help, or purely defensive. Furthermore, the damaging effects of threats on profits found by Deutsch and Krauss (mean joint profit was least if both people could threaten, more if only one could, and most if neither could) have not unequivocally been found using DG and GEE. It does seem to depend on circumstances, such as '(a) the magnitude and precision of the power available to subjects, and (b) the type of threat (compellence or deterrence) they choose to send' (Morley & Stephenson, 1977, p. 108). Compellence (or what Brams (1976) has called 'inducement') threats are designed to induce the other to do something; the purpose of deterrence threats is to *prevent* them from doing something (Schelling, 1966). Moreover, while Deutsch and Krauss found that a person who could threaten made more profit than an opponent who could not, a study by Fischer (1969) using a DG found that this need not be the case. In his low threat – high threat pairs, those with only a low threat potential tended to *win*. They achieved this by a relatively simple technique: lying (e.g. about their MNS). Thus although they did not have a threat based on the use of power — and outcomes do usually (but not always) tend to reflect the basic power distribution between the parties (Morley, 1979; and see, e.g. Rubin & Brown, 1975; Komorita, 1977; Magenau & Pruitt, 1979, re power in negotiations) — they could make use of 'informational tactics' (Morley & Stephenson, 1977, p. 109). I shall follow Morley and Stephenson in quoting extensively from Fischer:

> One immediate implication of this study is that experiments which narrow the behavioural alternatives of the subjects may create artifactual results. For instance, assuming a constant amount of competition in an average dyad, to restrict personal interaction to little more than mutual threats will channel competition through that means. A wider repertoire of possible behaviours, ranging in their subtleties, allows this competition to be expressed in various ways and degrees (p. 313).

In matrix games and the Acme – Bolt trucking game, choice is restricted to specific actions defined as cooperative and competitive which are directly, because of the structure of the game, linked to outcomes. When this is no longer the case, one begins to see that the way motivation finds its expression may be important.

6.2.3 Concession Making

Using threats is just one very narrow aspect of the negotiation process and of expressing one's desire to cooperate or compete. Examination of process becomes more subtle with the study of concession making using RPD and, more popularly, DG and GEE. Work has concentrated upon the following.

(a) Factors affecting concession making, e.g. concerns to save face (see, e.g. Brown, 1977); the presence of a solution that is prominent for both parties (see Magenau & Pruitt, 1979); and time pressure (*ibid.*). In particular, there has been considerable interest in the pattern of the other's concessions (see, e.g. Morley & Stephenson, 1977, pp. 85 – 101, for a review).

(b) The effects of certain patterns of concession making upon outcomes (see, e.g. Hamner & Yukl, 1977, for a review).

In this research the concept of 'toughness', which is implicitly considered to be a reflection of competitiveness, becomes the focus of attention. What is interesting for the argument of this chapter is that examination of concession making involves a move away from global concepts of cooperation and competition. Other questions begin to intrude. Motivation is defined as a drive towards a goal; but how will the drive be expressed and what form will the goal take in any particular circumstances? For example, what exactly do we mean by 'toughness'? According to Morley and Stephenson (1977), toughness comprises a number of dimensions: level of initial demand; mean level of demand; number of concessions; size of concessions; and level of minimum goal. An independent variable affecting one dimension in one way need not affect another in the same way (*ibid.*, p. 88). Again, why should the other's pattern of concessions affect one's own? It has been suggested, for example, that this occurs because that pattern conveys information about the other's preferences and intentions (and affects one's own 'level of aspiration' or goal – Siegel & Fouraker, 1960); it conveys information about their perceptions of one's own competence as an adversary (Rubin & Brown, 1975); it affects the negotiator's norms of equity, distributive justice or reciprocity (see Wall, 1977).

Mathematical models have been devised to explain concession making (e.g. Bartos, 1966; Druckman, 1978). Bartos' model predicts a negotiator's current demand on the basis of his or her previous demand and the opponent's previous offers. More recently, Bartos has moved away from such a mathematical approach and become interested in the importance of 'fairness' (Bartos, 1978). Druckman's model incorporates responses to the other's and one's own previous concessions and adjustment of expectations. However, while negotiation 'involves a great deal more than a process of bid and counterbid' (Morley, 1978a, p. 194), we can see that to come to grips with the question of what cooperation and competition really *means* in negotiations makes it necessary to ask different types of questions and to embrace more cognitive concepts.

The use of the most popular paradigms for studying concession making, DG and GEE, has been accompanied by an increase in the range of variables studied. These include, for example, the effects of time pressure (see, e.g. Hamner & Yukl, 1977) and the operation of equity and equality norms (see, e.g. Messé, 1971). Frequently, however, participants have represented only themselves, but it has been implicitly assumed that conclusions can be generalized to negotiations between groups. But does it make a difference to negotiations if participants are representing a group?

6.3 Negotiators as Representatives

6.3.1 Commitment

A number of writers have pointed out the importance of the negotiator's relationship with the group he or she represents for the negotiations themselves (e.g. Mack & Snyder, 1957; Schelling, 1960; Sherif, 1962; Turk & Lefcowitz, 1962; Walton & McKersie, 1965).

Negotiators are caught in a dilemma. On the one hand, their groups desire them to ensure that as many of their own aspirations as possible are incorporated into the final agreement. On the other hand, they are charged with the responsibility of reaching an agreement with a representative of another group with opposing aspirations. The more tightly the group binds the negotiator (in ways to be discussed later), the more committed he or she will be to the group's position.

It has been popularly assumed that commitment would always be deleterious for negotiations in certain ways. This was set out most clearly in McGrath's (1966) tri-forces model. McGrath considers that each negotiator is subjected to three forces:

1. Role: force towards the position of one's own group (R).
2. Agreement: force towards agreement with the other parties (A).
3. Community: force towards a creative, constructive solution from the point of view of the general community (C).

He sees the R and A forces as tugging in opposite directions, and the C force as orthogonal to them. Theoretically, then, the R force should, by opposing the A force, be detrimental to negotiating effectiveness. He assesses effectiveness according to the extent to which the outcome is acceptable to the negotiating parties and considered 'constructive' by the external system.

McGrath and others have shown that the role (R) forces can be detrimental to negotiating effectiveness (Vidmar & McGrath, 1965, 1970; Vidmar, 1971). The components which make up the R force include the negotiator's personal commitment to his or her group's position, his or her attraction towards the group, the clarity of the group's position, and so on. The implication of the model and related research findings is that reducing the strength of such a force will remove the constraints preventing negotiators reaching satisfactory and constructive agreements. This does not mean attempting to prevent negotiators wanting to obtain the best agreement they can for their own side, but encouraging them to do this with regard to the goals of the other side and to be open to possibilities of integrative bargaining (Walton & McKersie, 1965; Pruitt & Lewis, 1977). With integrative bargaining, all sides to the dispute gain from the settlement reached.

The latest model of the social psychology of bargaining contains the same central assumption, namely that forces towards one's bargaining position are directly opposed to forces towards reaching agreement with the other side (Magenau & Pruitt, 1979). Instead of R forces, Magenau and Pruitt have MD — 'a bargainer's motive to maintain his demands' (*ibid.*, p. 203). Replacing A forces, Magenau and Pruitt's term is MA — 'motive to reach agreement' (p. 203). The definitions are not identical, but the concepts are essentially similar. This model is one of strategic choice, in which the difference between MD and MA, in interaction with the level of 'trust in the other's cooperative intentions' (p. 204), determines whether the strategy chosen will be: (a) concession making, i.e. '[making] a new proposal that is worth less to the self than the prior proposal' (p. 182); (b) distributive behaviour, i.e. '[trying] to persuade the other to concede' (p. 182); or (c) coordinative behaviour, i.e. '[seeking] coordinated movement towards a mutually satisfactory outcome. Such an outcome may take the form of a compromise, in which the parties exchange concessions along some obvious dimension, or an integrative solution, which reconciles the needs of both parties' (p. 182). Integrative solutions, where they are available, are of two types: 'broadening the pie' and 'trading concessions on two or more issues where the bargainers have differing priorities' (p. 201). It must be pointed out that the first type of solution, where the available gains to be divided between the parties are increased, has no necessary implication for the division of that cake and 'it may mean that one party (the one that initiates the problem-solving activities) will get a very small slice' (Morley & Stephenson, 1977, p. 37). A popular measure of the integrativeness of a solution is, however, the size of the joint profit however it is split (see, e.g. Pruitt & Lewis, 1977).

For Magenau and Pruitt (1979), the fact that one is representing a group *can* be a source of MD (provided the negotiator believes that the group favours toughness rather than a 'soft' approach); for McGrath (1966), it *is*, by definition, the source of the R force. Thus the concept of the negotiator as representative is of different degrees of importance to the two models. But what sort of research has been done?

In the relatively recent research in which participants *have* acted as representatives of groups in dispute, mainly using the DG and RPD paradigms, the most common dependent variables have still been those considered to reflect cooperative and competitive motives. In particular, popular measures have been those thought to indicate difficulty in reaching agreement, particularly speed of reaching agreement, but also number of deadlocks, measures of compromise behaviour, number and size of concessions, competitiveness, satisfaction with outcomes, and joint profit. Negotiation 'effectiveness' (in all paradigms) has typically been construed in these terms.

It has been predicted, then, that commitment stemming from the fact that one is a group representative will impede negotiation effectiveness. There are at least three sources of commitment, which have not really been distinguished in the literature :

1. *Social commitment to one's group*, in terms of attraction to the group and group cohesiveness. To my knowledge, there is only one relevant experiment, and this did not show that increasing the cohesiveness of the group to which the negotiator belonged increased difficulty in reaching agreement (Klimoski, 1972).
2. *Personal belief in the group position*. Several studies have shown that such personal belief increased difficulty in reaching agreement (Hornstein & Johnson, 1966; Evan & MacDougall, 1967; Lamm, 1970; Vidmar & McGrath, 1970; Fischoff, 1972; Zechmeister & Druckman, 1973).

3. *Role obligations*, in terms of the scope of behaviour that negotiators think is permitted them within their role as representative of the group. This is affected by accountability, status, and social pressure from the group. They give rise to 'representational commitment' (Vidmar, 1971).

Role obligations *per se* have been shown to hinder effective negotiations by a number of experimenters who compared negotiations where the participants represented groups (sometimes as symbolized by a dependent constituent) or only themselves (Benton, 1972; Benton & Druckman, 1973, 1974). Effects of representation did, however, disappear if an obvious equal division of outcomes was possible (Benton & Druckman, 1973). Druckman *et al.* (1972) found such representation increased competitiveness without, however, affecting outcomes.

Davis & Triandis (1971) found indications that outcomes reflected pre-negotiation caucus positions, which negotiators were told to consider guiding but not binding, to a greater extent than they reflected individual personal opinions.

However, Druckman (1967) found no effects of representing the group *per se*, and Klimoski (1972) found effects of representation only when the representatives were highly attracted to their groups.

In the circumstances *of these experiments*, then, the necessity of representing a group appeared on the whole to have deleterious effects upon negotiating effectiveness, but with some exceptions.

But what of the factors affecting role obligations? Lamm (1973) defined accountability as 'the negotiator's expectation of punishment . . . or reward . . . from his group in response to the outcome of the negotiations' (p. 180). Studies of accountability have shown it to impede negotiations to some extent (Gruder, 1971; Gruder & Rosen, 1971; Benton, 1972; Klimoski, 1972; Breaugh & Klimoski, 1977; Pruitt *et al.*, 1978; Slusher, 1978). A prime effect of accountability appeared to be the extension of time taken to reach an agreement. According to Brown (1977), accountability to one's group does tend to result in pressure to maintain face in the negotiation, which could account (at least partially) for such a finding.

Another manipulation of factors thought to influence role obligations is that of status in the group which the negotiator represents (Hermann & Kogan, 1968; Lamm, 1970; Lamm & Kogan, 1970; Boyd, 1972; Kogan *et al.*, 1972; Cosentino, 1975; Haccoun & Klimoski, 1975), which has also been investigated in interaction with accountability (Klimoski & Ash, 1974; Haccoun & Klimoski, 1975) and considered to be mediated by accountability (Lamm, 1973). The findings were complex, but essentially it appeared that if role obligations, which vary according to the level and source of the negotiator's status, were not mitigated in some way, reaching agreement in negotiations was impeded by restriction of the negotiator's freedom to deviate from the group's position.

A number of studies concern the effects of social pressure from the group.

Representing a group with a cooperative orientation (Graeven, 1970; Gruder & Rosen, 1971; Rubin, 1971; Benton & Druckman, 1974; Wall, 1976); which trusts you (Frey & Adams, 1972; Wall, 1974, 1975a, b); which does not affirm your personal effectiveness during the negotiation (Tjosvold, 1977); and which is not present during the negotiations (Organ, 1971; Druckman *et al.*, 1976; Pruitt *et al.*, 1978; Carnevale *et al.*, 1979; although this may apply only to males – Benton, 1975) has been found to increase negotiating effectiveness. Rarely, findings were non-significant (Boyd, 1972 – cooperative orientation).

Supportive findings include those of Friedman and Jacka (1969), who found group disapproval of their negotiator's deviation from the group's position led to resumption of that position in the negotiations. They also found that, as implied by the above results, the negotiators did have some reason to fear sanctions from their group for deviation from its position (see also Blake & Mouton, 1961). Of course, this would only be expected to occur if negotiators are accountable to the group for their actions. Also, early concession making is likely to increase constituent dissatisfaction with the agreement reached (Klimoski & Breaugh, 1977).

In general, then, representative role obligations and other sources of commitment to the group position have been found to make it more difficult to reach agreement. However, 'most past experiments have employed unidimensional tasks that lack integrative potential' (Pruitt & Lewis, 1977, p. 182), where 'integrative potential' means the potential to satisfy both parties. It is certainly likely that commitment to the opposite poles of one dimension would slow negotiations up, as there is very little room for manoeuvre – what ground one gains the other must lose. Where there are several issues at stake or that could be introduced into the negotiation, then commitment may not necessarily impede reaching an agreement (Morley *et al.*, 1978); indeed, if there is pressure to do so, it may force participants to search for alternative solutions in order to reach agreement (Hoffman, 1961; Tysoe, 1979b).

The assumption underlying the models of McGrath and Magenau and Pruitt, then, that commitment to a group position always impedes reaching agreement in negotiations, may not be correct. It may be misleading to assume that group considerations (R forces) are 'grafted on' to an otherwise interpersonal exchange between negotiators and serve to distort it (Stephenson, 1978a). Rather, intergroup considerations should be seen as integral to, not an accessory of, the negotiation process. This becomes quite obvious when one thinks that without an intergroup dispute, there would *be* no negotiations between their representatives (*ibid.*). This is further supported by the recent work on group polarization in negotiations (see Morley, 1978b), the effects of size of the groups in conflict upon attitudes (Stephenson & Brotherton, 1975), and the discovery that there is no simple relationship between intergroup conflict and interpersonal bargaining relations between representatives – high conflict between groups can elicit strong personal relationships between the representatives (Stephenson, 1978a).

In this section, we have seen that initial conceptualizations of the effects of being a group representative were in terms of a tussle between forces to compete (and fight for one's group position) and forces to cooperate (to reach agreement with one's opponent), and that to represent a group (unless efforts were made to reduce its influence) enhanced competitive forces. But later work has suggested that such a 'tug-of-war' oversimplifies the processes involved. The relations between the forces, and the effects of being in an intergroup, rather than an interpersonal negotiation, may be much more complex. The R and A forces, for example, may possibly be orthogonal rather than opposing (see Tysoe, 1982).

It seems, then, that global concepts of cooperation and competition may be less useful in understanding the processes involved than an investigation of more specific aspects of what it means to be a representative. One way of grappling with this problem is to analyse the negotiation process itself, as we shall see in the next section.

6.3.2 Interpersonal and Interparty Levels of Exchange

In intergroup negotiations, negotiators have not only the fundamental problem of dealing with both the R and A forces, but also the need to represent their *parties* and, on the other hand, to manage a *personal* relationship with their opponent (Morley & Stephenson, 1977). Furthermore, 'good interpersonal relations may be regarded as a necessary but not sufficient condition for successful negotiation' (Morley, 1979, p. 213), and at certain stages of negotiation it is negotiators acting as *persons* in defence of their party position, rather than simply as party mouthpieces, which can facilitate the move towards agreement (cf. Douglas, 1957). R and A forces are not equivalent to these interpersonal and interparty levels of exchange on *a priori* grounds – for example, the party position may contain inbuilt pressure to reach agreement (A force) as well as being the subject of an R force, and the interpersonal level of exchange may be used in the service of maintaining the group's demands as well as contributing to the A force. Interpersonal and interparty aspects should not, therefore, be seen as equivalent to cooperative and competitive orientations.

The interpersonal and interparty 'climates' of negotiation, first identified by Douglas (1957), have implications for negotiation outcomes. If the number of available social cues (Morley & Stephenson, 1969; and see Rutter & Stephenson, 1979) is reduced, then this would be expected to enhance emphasis upon negotiators' role as party representatives and to reduce their concern to maintain or develop their personal relationship (Morley & Stephenson, 1977). When social cues are reduced, then, greater concentration on the negotiation issues and relevant arguments should lead to a more objective assessment of the contentious issues. And since reduced interpersonal considerations may also allow the stronger side to exploit its advantage and remove a tool from the weaker, this would be expected to lead to a settlement in favour of the side with the stronger case. Such settlements have, in fact, been found to occur when, using the RPD páradigm, social cues were reduced by conducting negotiations via a telephone system rather than face-to-face

(Morley & Stephenson, 1969, 1970a; Short, 1971; Morley, 1974). Face-to-face, the more common outcome was a compromise. Similar findings were obtained when two-person teams sat opposite each other to negotiate, thereby having greater visual access to the other side than when they were seated at equal intervals round the table, in such a way that each person had a member of the opposition on either side of him or her (Stephenson & Kniveton, 1978). The side with the stronger case was less likely to win in the 'opposite' condition.

Effects of altering the interpersonal and interparty levels of exchange, then, cannot be understood simply in terms of enhancing or reducing competitiveness.

6.3.3 *Negotiation Process*

Consideration of the interpersonal and interparty levels of exchange raises an important point about the RPD paradigm; it permits the study of *what people actually say* in negotiations. Content analyses of negotiations are still not very common, however (Morley & Stephenson, 1977), although the situation is improving: 'Social psychologists . . . are paying increasing attention to the *conduct* of negotiation' (Morley, 1979, p. 230; my italics). Examples of such work include analyses of experimental (Julian & McGrath, 1963; McGrath & Julian, 1963; Morley & Stephenson, 1977) and genuine (Landsberger, 1955a, b; Morley & Stephenson, 1977; Stephenson *et al.*, 1977) negotiations. In particular, emphasis has been upon the phases through which negotiations pass and comparisons of 'successful' and 'unsuccessful' negotiations (see Morley & Stephenson, 1977, for details). Morley and Stephenson have been critical of the category systems used in the early studies, and have devised a sophisticated content analysis (specifically for negotiations) called Conference Process Analysis (CPA), bearing in mind the distinction between interpersonal and interparty levels of exchange. Their analyses of stages in negotiations using CPA will be considered in a later section.

The importance of these new developments cannot be overestimated. In the past, with simple paradigms, the outcome of bargaining was considered to reflect directly the process by which it had been achieved, i.e. cooperative or competitive actions. But in paradigms where it is not *arranged* that way, it may not be possible to deduce process from outcome. It is, therefore, crucial to examine process directly.

6.3.4 *Implications: Studying Cooperative and Competitive Motives*

When the negotiation process is scrutinized, for example in terms of the interpersonal/interparty distinction and R and A forces, the notions of cooperation and competition become very blurred. As another example, Walton and McKersie (1965) distinguish four sub-processes of bargaining and their associated tactics: distributive bargaining; integrative bargaining; attitudinal structuring; and intra-organizational bargaining. 'Attitudinal structuring' refers to negotiators' attempts to improve the relationships between the parties, while 'intra-organizational bargaining' is negotiators' attempts to achieve a consensus of objectives and expectations within their party that is in line with their own. While Walton and McKersie's 'behavioural theory' has been criticized (see, e.g. Morley, 1979) and can be seen simply as 'an anecdotal description and analysis of negotiating behaviours and their functions placed in a conceptual framework, which gives rise to certain *a priori* propositions' (Tysoe, 1979a, p. 12), it has been of great theoretical influence (Warr, 1973; Morley, 1979). The notions of distributive and integrative bargaining, for example, have become key concepts. For Walton and McKersie, distributive bargaining refers to the activities that occur in response to a conflict which is zero-sum in nature, i.e. what one wins the other must lose. They take integrative bargaining, on the other hand, to be the type of bargaining that takes place in response to non-zero-sum tasks, where there is integrative potential. 'Integrative potential exists when the nature of a problem permits solutions which benefit both parties, or at least when the gains of one party do not represent equal sacrifices by the other' (Walton & McKersie, 1965, p. 5). However, Morley (1979) has argued that 'the distinction between distributive bargaining and integrative bargaining requires a distinction between certain kinds of *process* rather than certain kinds of task' (p. 215), and it is, indeed, in this sense that the terms are most commonly used (cf., e.g. Pruitt & Lewis, 1977).

At first sight, it might seem that the struggle to achieve one's party's goals in the face of opposition (distributive bargaining) is wholly competitive; while attempts to reach a *mutually* satisfactory agreement (integrative bargaining) are purely cooperative. Walton and McKersie 'assume that cooperative tactics are tied to integrative bargaining whereas competitive tactics are bound up with distributive bargaining' (Stephenson *et al.*, 1977, p. 239). But it has been argued that not only can distributive bargaining be served by both cooperative and competitive tactics (Stephenson *et al.*, 1977), and that integrative bargaining can be seen as essentially 'efficient' distributive bargaining in that it maximizes the joint profit (Morley, 1979), but also that cooperation and competition are in any case not alternatives but are closely interwoven (Druckman, 1977, p. 136). As pointed out earlier, negotiations are mixed-motive – motives to cooperate and compete do occur simultaneously. Indeed, once one escapes from pressing buttons and shutting gates, how easy is it to tell whether an action or a statement reflects a cooperative or a competitive orientation? Rather than continuing to focus upon nebulous concepts of cooperation and competition in negotiations, it becomes more illuminating to ask questions about how negotiators manage the task they have been set.

6.4 Negotiators as Decision Makers

The weakening interest in motivation to cooperate or compete *per se* as a dependent (or independent) variable is reflected in wider foci of attention.

6.4.1 Goals

Studies of the effects of goals on negotiation process and outcome have concentrated on two main areas: (a) the boundaries of the goal; and (b) whether or not the goal has an ideological component.

The goal which a negotiator wishes to achieve in relation to any particular issue is rarely a very specific demand from which he or she has no intention of moving. The goal of negotiators usually consists of an 'aspiration zone' (Walton & McKersie, 1965, p. 42) within which they would hope to settle (and which can, of course, alter during the negotiation). At one end they have a 'resistance point' (*ibid.*, p. 41), which marks the limit to what they are prepared to concede. They would rather break off negotiations than go further. At the other end they have their 'target point' (*ibid.*, p. 41), which marks what they would most like to achieve. The area between the parties' resistance points is called the 'settlement range' (*ibid.*, p. 42). Settlement ranges can be positive, in that the aspiration zones of the parties overlap, or negative, where there is no such overlap. If the settlement range is negative and resistance points are incompatible in that 'there is no settlement which would be minimally acceptable to both parties' (*ibid.*, p. 43), no agreement is possible unless the resistance points are moved (Pruitt, 1969). The target and resistance points may, of course, involve a range of possibilities rather than just one settlement point (see Morley & Stephenson, 1970b, p. 20).

It is more common to refer to target points as 'levels of aspiration' (LOA), and to resistance points as 'limits'. Research has examined such issues as the determinants of the location of LOAs and limits, e.g. the presence of prominent alternatives, such as a 10% wage rise rather than, say, a 9% or an 11% rise (Schelling, 1960); the effects of LOAs and limits on the bargainer's level of demand in the negotiation, and upon concession making and final outcomes (see Magenau & Pruitt, 1979, for a review).

Conflicts are rarely pure conflicts of interest, however, with no ideological disagreement involved (Druckman *et al.*, 1977). Druckman and Zechmeister have conducted a number of experiments using the RPD paradigm to examine two perspectives on conflicts of interest and value dissensus (see Druckman *et al.*, 1977, for a review). The first perspective assumes that negotiators *balance* interests in the outcome (motives) against values (taken to be cognitive factors) in the course of their decision making, and asks which are assigned the greater weight. Experimental findings indicate, unsurprisingly, that this varies with the negotiation context. The second perspective assumes that the two are inextricably entangled in a circle of cause and effect. Findings indicate that the more explicit the link between the conflict of interest and of values, the more difficult it will be to resolve the conflict through negotiation.

Work on the effects of goal boundaries and ideological linkages, then, does emphasize the cognitive, rather than purely the motivational, aspects of the negotiation process.

6.4.2 *Preparations*

There is a considerable body of evidence, primarily using the RPD paradigm, that negotiators' cognitive preparations affect the negotiations themselves.

It was recognized early on, in an anecdotal fashion, that pre-negotiation caucus sessions with one's group, in which the group discusses its position, might affect behaviour in the negotiation (Garfield & Whyte, 1950, part 1). Participation in such sessions *per se* has been shown in three experiments to impede negotiations by enhancing negotiator commitment (Kohls, 1970; Fischoff, 1972; Louche, 1975).

However, in these experiments subjects who did not participate in the caucus session were not exposed to the discussion either. Thus participation was confounded with the acquisition of information. Stephenson *et al.* (1976) have since shown that actual participation may not influence negotiation behaviour and attitudes over and above sympathy with the group's position and, through observation, knowledge of its discussions. But perhaps the nature of the group position and its method of formulation is also important?

Lamm and Kogan (1970) and Kogan *et al.* (1972) compared 'fixed' initial positions (positions decided upon by the group) with 'open' (undiscussed by the group) positions and found the former to impede negotiations. Rather similarly, Zechmeister and Druckman (1973) varied negotiators' degree of decision latitude by comparing the effects of formally assigned with self-formulated positions, and found that negotiations lasted longer in the former condition.

The way in which participants prepare for negotiations has also been examined in a number of studies, comparing the planning of specific strategies with a general study of the issues involved in order to gain some understanding of them. It was expected that strategy planning would hinder negotiations by increasing negotiators' commitment to their group positions, but findings have been complex and have not unequivocally shown difficulties in reaching agreement (see Morley & Stephenson, 1977, pp. 74 – 78; Tysoe, 1979a, pp. 79 – 84, for reviews; and cf. earlier discussion of commitment).

Although the dependent variables in these studies (primarily using the RPD paradigm) have included those traditionally thought to reflect cooperation and competition, such as time to reach agreement and number of deadlocks, in some of them indices of negotiation effectiveness have been widened in scope. For example, it has been recognized that ease of negotiation has no necessary implications for the nature of the agreement reached (Morley & Stephenson, 1977, p. 75) — and, as already pointed out, measures of outcome cannot be taken as indicators of the negotiation process. Moreover, the concepts invoked to understand the processes involved include cognitive notions such as information and decision latitude. Indeed, Morley *et al.* (1978), when referring to strategy and study preparation, have pointed out that 'ultimately, to understand what is going on we shall have to explore the nature of the study and of the strategic choices in much more detail' (p. 11) and, furthermore, that 'to understand the process of negotiation we need to explore the ways in which negotiators formulate and define the problems they are likely to face . . . preparation and process are linked by virtue of the fact that they are *the intra-group and inter-group phases of a complex decision making task*' (Morley, 1978b, p. 23).

6.4.3 Issues

In the paradigms used by social psychologists to study negotiations, Morley and Stephenson (1977) have identified at least three types of experimental task classified according to the structure of the disputed issues:

1. Tasks of Type 1, in which subjects negotiate a single (complex) issue requiring agreement on two dimensions, such as price and quantity . . .
2. Tasks of Type 2, in which subjects negotiate a single (one-dimensional) issue involving either the exchange of a single item . . . or the division of a single sum of money . . .
3. Tasks of Type 3, in which subjects negotiate a number of issues, each involving the exchange of a single item or the division of a single sum of money . . . (p. 54).

Results of experiments using one type of task may not generalize to other tasks – for example, Type 2 is a very simple negotiation where it is not possible to formulate package deals or devise new solutions, thus restricting the generality of results obtained using it (*ibid*., pp. 54 – 56).

Experimental work on the effects of issue structure has tended to concentrate on tasks of Type 3. In particular, one can cite the research on the effects of negotiating several issues all together or one at a time (using primarily the DG and RPD paradigms), and also of differing issue emphases. There is evidence that arguing over several issues simultaneously, which permits package deals and trading concessions on the various issues, leads to faster negotiations than trying to negotiate a compromise on one issue at a time without reference to the others (see, e.g. Froman & Cohen, 1970; Shapira & Bass, 1975; Schulz, 1976) as well as higher joint profits (Froman & Cohen, 1970; Schulz, 1976; Yukl *et al*., 1976). Kelley (1966) found his subjects to prefer to negotiate their five issues all together, rather than one at a time or in subsets. Kelley suggests that this occurred because to agree on one issue or a subset of issues effectively restricted the possible trade-offs which one could make on the remainder. It may also be that negotiating issues all at once gave subjects the opportunity to discover it was worthwhile to 'explore various contracts at a given level of profit before moving on to contracts at a lower level' (Morley & Stephenson, 1977, p. 91). The effects of attending to subsets rather than to all the issues at once have not been investigated experimentally, although it may be that the differences between these two styles would become important if there were a very large number of issues. In such a case, it might be impossible to manage them effectively all at once (Rubin & Brown, 1975), presumably because of an information overload. Again, it has been suggested that under certain circumstances it may be better to divide large issues 'into smaller, more workable ones, in order to alleviate the negative effects of excessive commitment that are often associated with attempting to resolve large or all-encompassing issues' (*ibid.*, p. 148). The effects of 'compromise' (negotiating one issue at a time) v. 'logrolling' (trading a concession on one or more issues in return for concessions from the opponent on other issues) clearly varies according to the circumstances, in ways that are yet to be determined (Morley & Stephenson, 1977). It seems from the terms in which the above speculations are cast that it is the cognitive aspects of those circumstances that are likely to be important.

Similarly, the role played by cognitive concepts in explaining findings is illustrated by the limited amount of work on differences in issue emphasis. Bonham (1971) used the RPD paradigm to simulate a series of international disarmament negotiations. He found that giving the parties differing priorities concerning the importance of the various issues can lead to either reduced interaction to avoid the problem, or increased interaction involving hostility and a reduced likelihood that concessions would be reciprocated. Again cognitive difficulties have been suggested to underlie these findings, particularly misunderstandings (see Morley & Stephenson, 1977; Morley, 1978b; for more detailed discussion of this study).

6.4.4 Phases

Another example of cognitive aspects of the negotiation task is the way in which negotiators reconcile the interparty and interpersonal levels of exchange, referred to earlier. Douglas (1957, 1962), in her case studies of industrial negotiations where a mediator had been introduced to break a deadlock, found that negotiations which ended in agreement passed through three distinct phases. The first phase, which she termed 'establishing the bargaining range' (Douglas, 1957, p. 72), consisted of protracted statement of cases from both parties and attacks on that of the opponent, 'with all the outward signs of deep and irreconcilable cleavage between the parties' (*ibid.*, p. 72). It was important, though, that the hostility was at a party, *not* a personal, level. The second phase, 'reconnoitering the range' (p. 75), involved exploration of the possibilities and jockeying for position within the range established by the initial battle. The third and final phase, 'precipitating the decision-making crisis' (p. 80), marked negotiators' closing off of the other's options and forcing each other towards a settlement. Douglas noted that in the second phase the exploration of alternatives was carried out more as persons than as party representatives, under cover of continuing 'breast-beating' which was superficially similar to that in Phase 1.

> In general, by the time this stage has been reached, the properties of organizational action have become too limited to meet the demands of the bargaining situation, which now calls on negotiators to put at the disposal of their respective parties their individual capacities to assay the rapid conversions going on in the environment and to improvise adaptive behaviours on the spot (p. 77).

Party roles again take over when the decision-making crisis is reached.

Morley and Stephenson have also examined phase movement, using (a) their content analysis, Conference Process Analysis, and (b) judges' identification, from unlabelled transcripts, of which party representative was responsible for each speech ('role identifiability') (see Morley & Stephenson, 1977; Stephenson *et al.*, 1977; Stephenson, 1978b, for details of their complex findings). Their analyses of a number of genuine industrial negotiations have provided some empirical support for Douglas' sequence of phases, but with some interpersonal emphasis continuing into Phase 3. They also aver that Phase 1 is used to determine: (a) the balance of power to inflict damage on the other if there is deadlock; and (b) the relative strengths of the cases (Morley & Stephenson, 1977). In addition, if a negotiation is composed of a number of different sessions, their findings indicate that the phase sequence may be different within different sessions, giving rise to an overall fluctuation between phases. More recent evidence (see Stephenson, 1978a) suggests that, indeed, with successfully negotiated issues 'the precise pattern of alternation between [partisanship and integration] will vary according to how the issue originated, by whom and with what degree of preparation' (*ibid.*, p. 11).

It seems that the 'separation of interparty and interpersonal roles in time may account for the ability of practised negotiators to compete agreeably' (Stephenson *et al.*, 1977, p. 240). The two levels of exchange, then, are reconciled by their relative prominence at *different stages* of the negotiation, and the emerging emphasis on the interpersonal level appeared to facilitate the movement towards agreement after the strong defence of the party demands.

A final point worth making is that the notion of an interpersonal level of exchange has two facets. First, it incorporates the idea of a negotiator operating as a person in the negotiation. This does not mean that he or she is not acting with his or her party interests in mind, but rather that the negotiator is acting as he or she personally thinks fit in the defence of those interests (cf. Douglas, 1957), while at the same time being aware of the other negotiator as a person and not simply as a party representative (Stephenson, 1980, personal communication). The other facet of the interpersonal level of exchange involves negotiators' attempts to develop or maintain a *good* personal relationship with opponents (cf. Stephenson *et al.*, 1977). These two facets have generally been confused in the literature, and both the distinction between them and the relationship between them remain to be clarified.

6.4.5 Approaches

Finally, I shall mention three approaches to negotiation processes emphasizing the cognitive, rather than purely the motivational, aspects of negotiating. None of these approaches has been well developed as yet.

The first approach of interest is the research on the effects of 'bilateral focus' techniques (see Walcott *et al.*, 1977) in negotiations. Bilateral focus refers to focus on the positions of *both* parties. Such a focus has been expected by some primarily to reduce commitment to party positions, and others have been more interested in these techniques as a means of increasing understanding of the other side's position (see Tysoe, 1979a).

A serious problem with this area of research is that bilateral focus has been operationalized in a variety of ways that are not really comparable. Examples include restating the opponent's position to his or her satisfaction (e.g. Johnson, 1967); conducting the entire negotiation in the role of the other by all (e.g. Stephenson *et al.*, 1976; and cf. Brenenstuhl & Blalack, 1978) or half (e.g. Vidmar & McGrath, 1965) the participants; studying the positions of both sides before the negotiation (referred to earlier); studying the issues before the negotiation with members of the opposing party (e.g. Druckman, 1968); discussion in reversed roles before proceeding to negotiate in own roles (e.g. Muney & Deutsch, 1968); and exchanging members of the negotiating teams for part of the negotiation (e.g. Stern *et al.*, 1975). Findings are complex, and the reader is referred to Walcott *et al.* (1977) and Tysoe (1979a) for detailed reviews of the relevant research, which has primarily used the RPD paradigm. It does seem that, depending on the circumstances, the various techniques can have cognitive effects (such as increased understanding of the other's position) as well as effects on attitudes and outcomes. It may well be that pursuing research into such techniques will help us to understand the ways in which negotiators do come to grips with the complexities and subtleties of the opponent's cognitions (ideas, views, knowledge) relevant to the negotiation.

A second approach highlighting the cognitive elements of negotiation is Pruitt and Lewis's (1977) 'flexible rigidity' model. Here Pruitt and Lewis distinguish between the flexibility of a negotiator's ends (FE), i.e. the extent to which high goals are set and maintained; and the flexibility of means (FM), i.e. bargainers' willingness 'to explore many options in a search for mutually acceptable alternatives' (p. 183). Pruitt and Lewis suggest (p. 184) that High FE/ High FM will lead to premature concessions, 'before the boundaries of the situation are fully explored'; High FE/ Low FM will lead to compromise, probably 'based on norms or existing precedents'; Low FE/ Low FM will lead to distributive bargaining where 'each side attempts to persuade the other to accept his position'; while Low FE/ High FM will lead to integrative bargaining that reconciles bargainers' different needs and values and may involve the creation of new alternatives. Pruitt and Lewis call the last combination *flexible rigidity*, where negotiators are rigid with respect to ends but flexible with regard to means, searching for an option satisfactory to both. They suggest that there are two ways of achieving flexibility of means : either information exchange or heuristic trial and error. Magenau & Pruitt (1979, pp. 202 – 203) have pointed out that only the former is actually cooperative, in the sense of involving 'a joint enterprise with the other party' , as opposed to being 'sophisticated versions of individualistic activity'. Heuristic trial and error refers to four tactics that 'lead to integrative agreements by 'trial and error', in the sense of emerging from a series of proposals rather than from insight into how to satisfy both parties' needs'. The tactics are:

(1) frequently change one's proposal, (2) seek the other party's reaction to these proposals, (3) make concessions on low-priority issues while holding firm on high-priority issues, (4) explore all possible options at one level of value to the self before proceeding to a lower level (*ibid.*, p. 202).

Information exchange, on the other hand, refers to exchange, either direct or indirect, of information about negotiators' 'needs and values and their priorities among the issues' (Pruitt & Lewis, 1977, p. 171).

This model was derived from Pruitt and Lewis's own research, and has yet to be subjected to experimental test *as* a model (but see Kimmel *et al.*, 1980, for a relevant experiment). Nevertheless, the distinction between flexibility of means and of ends may prove a fruitful one.

The third approach I should like to identify is, as yet, hardly an approach at all; namely, consideration of the role of information in negotiations. What factors affect negotiators' search for information from the other side? What affects the disclosure of information by negotiators? What are the effects of obtaining or withholding certain types of information on negotiation processes and outcomes? The importance of information in negotiations has been frequently discussed, but studies have revolved almost solely around the question of whether or not a negotiator has knowledge of the *other's* payoffs for each of the various alternative outcomes, as well as his or her own (e.g. Lamm, 1976; Yukl, 1976). In Pruitt and Lewis's work (see above) using the RPD paradigm, for example, 'information exchange' was manipulated simply by allowing negotiators access to each other's profit schedules. But *many* types of information may be relevant to a negotiation, and it may be that 'it is . . . exchange of information, the attributions to which it leads, and the ways in which it is shaped for the purposes of mutual social influence, that represents the fundamental strategic issue in bargaining' (Rubin & Brown, 1975, p. 260). Perhaps less strongly, it has been pointed out that 'a general theory of negotiation requires *some* account of the ways in which people search for information and choose between alternatives on the basis of the information they obtain' (Morley, 1978b, p. 24). Any research undertaken on the part which information plays in negotiations may be productive indeed.

The five areas of interest outlined in this section on 'negotiators as decision makers' have in common an underlying concern not primarily with *motivational* processes, but with *cognitive* processes. There is, of course, a link in that cooperative and competitive motives are served by cognitive strategies. Motivation is the drive towards a goal – but decisions have to be made as to how the drive is to be expressed and the goal formulated and changed in the light of circumstances. Motivation can become indistinguishable from cognitive strategies, and more than one motive may be satisfied by a particular action (McClintock, 1977). It may even be that cognition and motivation 'are inextricably intertwined, with preferences deriving from conceptualizations, and vice versa' (Druckman, 1977, p. 24).

Studying the decisions that negotiators have to make to cope with the 'cognitive demands of the task' (Morley, 1979, p. 230) may enhance our understanding of negotiation processes more than simply appealing to entangled cooperative and competitive motives as the sources of behaviour. Negotiation cannot be understood solely in terms of motivational processes.

6.5 The Way Forward

6.5.1 Cognitive Processes

It has become increasingly clear that we need to understand how negotiators think and how they link their thought processes with those of the opponent. The importance of cognitive *as well as* motivational factors has been taken up by Druckman (1977), who identifies the question of their relative importance in different negotiation settings as one of the critical issues for future research. As he says, 'In any particular negotiation, both motivational and cognitive processes operate. Or, put another way, negotiating behaviour is *driven* by preferences and *directed* by a plan' (p. 23).

The importance of cognitive factors in conflict *is* now being stressed by, for example, Brehmer and Hammond (1977). The research into 'cognitive conflict' of Hammond and his colleagues has, however, concentrated exclusively on judgement policies, using mathematical modelling. By 'cognitive conflict', where conflict is caused by cognitive not motivational factors, Hammond means:

> interpersonal conflicts (quarrels) which arise when two persons must exercise their judgements under conditions of uncertainty. Such quarrels are studied in settings in which two or more individuals who have learned to utilize probabilistic cues in quite different ways . . . are required to reach joint agreement in multiple-cue probability learning tasks (Hammond & Summers, 1972, p. 63).

These ideas have since been extended from interpersonal to intergroup (e.g. union – management) negotiations (see Brehmer & Hammond, 1977; Morley, 1979, pp. 227 – 228).

Reinforcing the importance of cognitive processes, Morley (1978b) has pointed out that the separation between studies of negotiation and of decision making has been detrimental to both, and argues strongly for the need to develop a theory of decision making that will cast some light upon the study of negotiations (cf. Snyder & Diesing, 1977; Morley, in press). As Morley has said, 'Negotiation is an example of decision-making under uncertainty in which values, interests, and power relations have to be worked out as arguments are exchanged and moves are made' (p. 13). Again, 'The art [of negotiation] is working through the core processes of information interpretation, influence, and decision-making which are involved' (*ibid.*, p. 37).

This change in perspective on negotiators from 'driven' to 'thinking' perhaps reflects the shift in social psychology's models of humankind that has already taken place (e.g. with the arrival of Kelly's theory of personal constructs and his model of people as scientists – see, e.g. Kelly, 1963). It has been argued that an understanding of cognition is an important step towards the understanding of social processes (see, e.g. Brandstätter & Schuler, 1978), and there is an increasing amalgamation of cognitive and social psychology (see, e.g. Eiser, 1980). So far, however, it has been mainly individualistic, in terms of how an individual sees the social world and the consequences for social behaviour. Work has concentrated on the effects of an individual's cognitive processes upon the individual's social behaviour: towards another individual (e.g. bystander intervention; see, e.g. Latané & Darley, 1970); within a group (e.g. conformity; see, e.g. Eiser, 1980); towards another group (e.g. stereotyping; see, e.g. Tajfel, 1978); and as a group member with another group (e.g. the social identity theory of intergroup relations; see Chapter 8 of this volume). Perhaps the next step in cognitive social psychology will be from the study of individual cognition to the study of 'interactive' cognition, in terms of how individuals *deal with each other's* cognitive processes. As well as understanding processes of *individual* decision making in negotiations (Morley, 1978b), the interactive nature of negotiations, where participants are dependent on each other for their outcomes which they must decide upon together, surely makes it necessary to study *interactive* cognition (cf. the work on cognitive conflict; and on group polarization, see, e.g. Myers & Lamm, 1976) also. It is in these directions that research on negotiation appears gradually to be moving.

6.5.2 Theory and Method

The move towards a more cognitive perspective on negotiations, and the relatively recent recognition of the need to come to terms with the dimension of complexity in negotiations and the ways in which it influences cognitive processes (see, e.g. Midgaard & Underdal, 1977; Winham, 1977; Morley, 1978b; Steinbruner, 1974), can only add weight to pleas for theoretical and methodological development. The need for a predictive and integrative social psychological theory of negotiation has been indicated by, for example, Rubin and Brown (1975) and Druckman (1977). These authors, while they did not attempt such a formulation themselves on the basis of extensive reviews of the literature, did at least identify a range of issues which such a theory would need to encompass. Magenau and Pruitt's (1979) strategic choice model could perhaps be a starting point.

Pleas for further methodological development have also been lodged. First, in terms of ascertaining: (a) the reliability of research findings by replication; and (b) their generality across different experimental procedures, tasks and subject populations (see Morley & Stephenson, 1977, pp. 121 – 122). Second, in terms of 'attempt[ing] to build some of the complexities identified by Winham [1977] and Steinbruner [1974] into laboratory simulations of negotiation groups' (Morley, 1978b, p. 25), and moving away from the almost exclusive emphasis on dyads (Morley, 1978a; Stephenson, 1978a). There is also a need for more research in the field as well as the laboratory (see, e.g. Druckman, 1977), and of derivation of hypotheses from the field and not simply from other laboratory research (Morley, 1978a). The arrival of a coherent and precise theory will, perhaps, be facilitated by such methodological developments.

6.6 Conclusions

I have attempted in this chapter to give the flavour of social psychological research into negotiation, and to indicate how it has progressed from simple to more complex paradigms. But, more importantly, we have seen how the motivation to cooperate or compete *per se* has lost its place at the centre of the stage. Rather, it is clear that without shifting the spotlight of attention much more towards the role played by cognition, we cannot hope to advance significantly our understanding of negotiation processes.

References

BARTOS, O.J. (1966). Concession-making in experimental negotiations. In J. BERGER, M. ZELDITCH, Jr. and B. ANDERSON (Eds.), *Sociological Theories in Progress*, Vol. 1. Boston: Houghton-Mifflin.

BARTOS, O.J. (1978). Simple model of negotiation: A sociological point of view. In I.W. Zartman (Ed.), *The Negotiation Process: Theories and Applications*. Beverly Hills: Sage.

BENTON, A.A. (1972). Accountability and negotiations between group representatives. *Proceedings of the 80th Annual Convention of the American Psychological Association*, 227 – 228.

BENTON, A.A. (1975). Bargaining visibility and the attitudes and negotiation behaviour of male and female group representatives. *Journal of Personality*, **43**, 661 – 677.

BENTON, A.A. and DRUCKMAN, D. (1973). Salient solutions and the bargaining behaviour of representatives and non-representatives. *International Journal of Group Tensions*, **3**, 28 – 39.

BENTON, A.A. and DRUCKMAN, D. (1974). Constituent's bargaining orientation and intergroup negotiations. *Journal of Applied Social Psychology*, **4**, 141 – 150.

BLAKE, R.R. and MOUTON, J.S. (1961). Heroes and traitors: two patterns of representing groups in a competitive relation. Unpublished paper cited in BLAKE, R.R. and MOUTON, J.S. (1961). Competition, communication and conformity. In I.A. BERG and B.M. BASS (Eds.), *Conformity and Deviation*. New York: Harper.

BONHAM, M.G. (1971). Simulating international disarmament negotiations. *Journal of Conflict Resolution*, **15**, 299 – 315.

BOYD, N.K. (1972). Negotiation behaviour by elected and appointed representatives serving as group leaders or spokesmen under different cooperative group expectations. *Dissertation Abstracts International*, **33** (5 – A), 2492 – 2493.

BRAMS, S.J. (1976). *Paradoxes in Politics: An Introduction to the Nonobvious in Political Science*. New York: Free Press.

BRANDSTÄTTER, H. and SCHULER, H. (1978). Social decision situations: integration and application. In H. BRANDSTÄTTER, J.H. DAVIS and H. SCHULER (Eds.), *Dynamics of Group Decisions*. London: Sage.

BREAUGH, J.A. and KLIMOSKI, R.J. (1977). The choice of a group spokesman in bargaining: member or outsider? *Organizational Behavior and Human Performance*, **19**, 325 – 336.

BREHMER, B. and HAMMOND, K.R. (1977). Cognitive factors in interpersonal conflict. In D. DRUCKMAN (Ed.), *Negotiations: Social-Psychological Perspectives*. Beverly Hills: Sage.

BRENENSTUHL, D.C. and BLALACK, R.O. (1978). Role preference and vested interest in a bargaining environment. *Simulation & Games*, **9**, 53 – 65.

BROWN, B.R. (1977). Face-saving and face-restoration in negotiation. In D. DRUCKMAN (Ed.), *Negotiations: Social-Psychological Perspectives*. Beverly Hills: Sage.

CAMPBELL, R.J. (1960). Originality in group productivity III. Partisan commitment and productive independence in a collective bargaining situation. Columbus, Ohio: Ohio State University Research Foundation. Conducted under contract with Office of Naval Research, Nonr – 495 (15) (NR 170 – 396).

CARNEVALE, P.J.D., PRUITT, D.G. and BRITTON, S.D. (1979). Looking tough: the negotiator under constituent surveillance. *Personality and Social Psychology Bulletin*, **5**, 118 – 121.

CHERTKOFF, J.M. and ESSER, J.K. (1976). A review of experiments in explicit bargaining. *Journal of Experimental Social Psychology*, **12**, 464 – 486.

COSENTINO, C.J. (1975). The independence of group representatives as a function of their source of formal authority, perceived competence and expected future interactions. *Dissertation Abstracts International*, **36**(3 – B), 1501.

DAVIS, E.E. and TRIANDIS, H.C. (1971). An experimental study of black – white negotiations. *Journal of Applied Social Psychology*, **1**, 240 – 262.

DEUTSCH, M. and KRAUSS, R.M. (1960). The effect of threat upon interpersonal bargaining. *Journal of Abnormal and Social Psychology*, **61**, 181 – 189.

DEUTSCH, M. and KRAUSS, R.M. (1962). Studies of interpersonal bargaining. *Journal of Conflict Resolution*, **6**, 57 – 76.

DOUGLAS, A. (1957). The peaceful settlement of industrial and intergroup disputes. *Journal of Conflict Resolution*, **1**, 69 – 81.

DOUGLAS, A. (1962). *Industrial Peacemaking*. New York: Columbia University Press.

DRUCKMAN, D. (1967). Dogmatism, prenegotiation experience and simulated group representation as determinants of dyadic behaviour in a bargaining situation. *Journal of Personality and Social Psychology*, **6**, 279 – 290.

DRUCKMAN, D. (1968). Prenegotiation experience and dyadic conflict resolution in a bargaining situation. *Journal of Experimental Social Psychology*, **4**, 367 – 383.

DRUCKMAN, D. (1971). The influence of the situation in interparty conflict. *Journal of Conflict Resolution*, **15**, 523 – 554.

DRUCKMAN, D. (Ed.) (1977). *Negotiations: Social-Psychological Perspectives*. Beverly Hills: Sage.

DRUCKMAN, D. (1978). Boundary role conflict: negotiation as dual responsiveness. In I.W. ZARTMAN (Ed.), *The Negotiation Process: Theories and Applications*. Beverly Hills: Sage.

DRUCKMAN, D., BENTON, A.A., ALI, F. and BAGUR, J.S. (1976). Cultural differences in bargaining behaviour: India, Argentina, and the United States. *Journal of Conflict Resolution*, **20**, 413 – 452.

DRUCKMAN, D., ROZELLE, R. and ZECHMEISTER, K. (1977). Conflict of interest and value dissensus: two perspectives. In D. DRUCKMAN (Ed.), *Negotiations: Social-Psychological Perspectives*. Beverly Hills: Sage.

DRUCKMAN, D., SOLOMON, D. and ZECHMEISTER, K. (1972). Effects of representational role obligations on the process of children's distribution of resources. *Sociometry*, **35**, 387 – 410.

DULANY, D.E. (1974). On the support of cognitive theory in opposition to behaviour theory: a methodological problem. In W.B. WEIMER and D.S. PALERMO (Eds.), *Cognition and the Symbolic Processes*. Hillsdale, NJ: Lawrence Erlbaum.

EISER, J.R. (1980). *Cognitive Social Psychology: A Guidebook to Theory and Research*. London: McGraw-Hill.

EVAN, W.M. and MACDOUGALL, J.A. (1967). Interorganizational conflict: a labor – management bargaining experiment. *Journal of Conflict Resolution*, **11**, 398 – 413.

FISCHER, C.S. (1969). The effect of threats in an incomplete information game. *Sociometry*, **32**, 301 – 314.

FISCHOFF, S.P. (1972). The effects of ego-involvement, pre-negotiation experience and reference group influence on outcomes in an experimental simulation of inter-group negotiation. *Dissertation Abstracts International*, **33** (5 – A), 2494.

FREY, R.L., Jr. and ADAMS, J.S. (1972). The negotiator's dilemma: simultaneous in-group and out-group conflict. *Journal of Experimental Social Psychology*, **8**, 331 – 346.

FRIEDMAN, M.I. and JACKA, M.E. (1969). The negative effect of group cohesiveness on intergroup negotiation. *Journal of Social Issues*, **25**, 181 – 194.

FROMAN, L.A. Jr. and COHEN, M.D. (1970). Compromise and logroll: comparing the efficiency of two bargaining processes. *Behavioral Science*, **15**, 180 – 183.

GARFIELD, S. and WHYTE, W.F. (1950). The collective bargaining process: a human relations analysis. Part 1. *Human Organisation*, **9**, 5 – 10.

GRAEVEN, D.B. (1970). Intergroup conflict and the group representative: the effects of power and the legiti macy of the power relation on negotiations in an experimental setting. *Dissertation Abstracts International*, **31** (6 – A), 3037.

GRUDER, C.L. (1971). Relationships with opponent and partner in mixed-motive bargaining. *Journal of Conflict Resolution*, **15**, 403 – 416.

GRUDER, C.L. and ROSEN, N.A. (1971). Effects of intragroup relations on intergroup bargaining. *International Journal of Group Tensions*, **1**, 301 – 317.

HACCOUN, R.R. and KLIMOSKI, R.J. (1975). Negotiator status and accountability source: a study of negotiator behaviour. *Organizational Behavior and Human Performance*, **14**, 342 – 359.

HAMMOND, K.R. and SUMMERS, D.A. (1972). Cognitive control. *Psychological Review*, **79**, 58 – 67.

HAMNER, W.C. and YUKL, G.A. (1977). The effectiveness of different offer strategies in bargaining. In D. DRUCKMAN (Ed.), *Negotiations: Social-Psychological Perspectives*. Beverly Hills: Sage.

HERMANN, M.G. and KOGAN, N. (1968). Negotiation in leader and delegate groups. *Journal of Conflict Resolution*, **12**, 332 – 344.

HOFFMAN, L.R. (1961). Conditions for creative problem-solving. *Journal of Psychology*, **52**, 429 – 444.

HORNSTEIN, H. and JOHNSON, D. (1966). The effects of process analysis and ties to his group upon the negotiator's attitudes toward the outcomes of negotiations. *Journal of Applied Behavioral Science*, **2**, 449 – 463.

IKLÉ, F.C (1964). *How Nations Negotiate*. New York: Harper & Row.

JOHNSON, D.W. (1967). Use of role reversal in intergroup competition. *Journal of Personality and Social Psychology*, **7**, 135 – 141.

JULIAN, J.W. and MCGRATH, J.E. (1963). The influence of leader and member behaviour on the adjustment and task effectiveness of negotiation groups. Technical Report No. 17, Office of the Surgeon General Contract DA – 49 – 193 – MD – 2060. Urbana, Illinois: Group Effectiveness Research Laboratory, University of Illinois.

KELLEY, H.H. (1965). Experimental studies of threats in interpersonal negotiations. *Journal of Conflict Resolution*, **9**, 79 – 105.

KELLEY, H.H. (1966). A classroom study of the dilemmas in interpersonal negotiations. In K. ARCHIBALD (Ed.), *Strategic Interaction and Conflict: Original Papers and Discussion*. Berkeley, California: Institute of International Studies.

KELLY, G.A. (1963). *A Theory of Personality: The Psychology of Personal Constructs*. New York: W.W. Norton.

KERR, C. (1954). Industrial conflict and its mediation. *American Journal of Sociology*, **60**, 230 – 245.

KIMMEL, M.J., PRUITT, D.G., MAGENAU, J.M., KONAR-GOLDBAND, E. and CARNEVALE, P.J.D. (1980). Effects of trust, aspiration and gender on negotiation tactics. *Journal of Personality and Social Psychology*, **38**, 9 – 22.

KLIMOSKI, R.J. (1972). The effects of intragroup forces on intergroup conflict resolution. *Organizational Behavior and Human Performance*, **8**, 363 – 383.

KLIMOSKI, R.J. (1978). Simulation methodologies in experimental research on negotiations by representatives. *Journal of Conflict Resolution*, **22**, 61 – 77.

KLIMOSKI, R.J. and ASH, R.A. (1974). Accountability and negotiator behaviour. *Organizational Behavior and Human Performance*, **11**, 409 – 425.

KLIMOSKI, R.J. and BREAUGH, J.A. (1977). When performance doesn't count: a constituency looks at its spokesman. *Organizational Behavior and Human Performance*, **20**, 301 – 311.

KNIVETON, B.H. (1974). Industrial negotiating: some training implications. *Industrial Relations Journal*, **5**, 27 – 37.

KOGAN, N., LAMM, H. and TROMMSDORFF, G. (1972). Negotiation constraints in the risk-taking domain: effects of being observed by partners of higher or lower status. *Journal of Personality and Social Psychology*, **23**, 143 – 156.

KOHLS, J.W. (1970). Bargaining behaviour and outcomes. *Dissertation Abstracts International*, **31** (6 – B), 3744.

KOMORITA, S.S. (1977). Negotiation from strength and the concept of bargaining strength. *Journal for the Theory of Social Behaviour*, **7**, 65 – 79.

LALL, A. (1966). *Modern International Negotiation: Principles and Practice*. New York: Columbia University Press.

LAMM, H. (1970). Soziale und Persönlichkeits-Einflüsse auf das Verhandeln. *Zeitschrift für Sozialpsychologie*, **1**, 167 – 181.

LAMM, H. (1973). Intragroup effects on intergroup negotiation. *European Journal of Social Psychology*, **3**, 179 – 192.

LAMM, H. (1976). Dyadic negotiations under asymmetric conditions: comparing the performance of the uniformed and of the informed party. *European Journal of Social Psychology*, **6**, 255 – 259.

LAMM, H. and KOGAN, N. (1970). Risk taking in the context of intergroup negotiations. *Journal of Experimental Social Psychology*, **6**, 351 – 363.

LANDSBERGER, H.A. (1955a). Interaction process analysis of mediation of labour – management disputes. *Journal of Abnormal and Social Psychology*, **57**, 552 – 558.

LANDSBERGER, H.A. (1955b). Interaction process analysis of professional behaviour: a study of labour mediators in twelve labour – management disputes. *American Sociological Review*, **20**, 566 – 575.

LATANÉ, B. and DARLEY, J.M. (1970). *The Unresponsive Bystander: Why Doesn't He Help?* Appleton Century Crofts.

LOUCHE, C. (1975) [The preparation of a group negotiation and its effects on the behaviour of the negotiators and their attitudes.] (Fren.) *Bulletin de Psychologie*, **28**, 113 – 117.

MACK, R.W. and SNYDER, R.C. (1957). The analysis of social conflict — toward an overview and synthesis. *Journal of Conflict Resolution*, **1**, 212 – 248.

MAGENAU, J.M. and PRUITT, D.G. (1979). The social psychology of bargaining. In G.M. STEPHENSON and C.J. BROTHERTON (Eds.), *Industrial Relations: A Social Psychological Approach*. Chichester: John Wiley & Sons.

MCCLINTOCK, C.G. (1977). Social motivation in settings of outcome interdependence. In D. DRUCKMAN (Ed.), *Negotiations: Social-Psychological Perspectives*. Beverly Hills: Sage.

MCGRATH, J.E. (1966). A social psychological approach to the study of negotiation. In R.V. BOWERS (Ed.), *Studies on Behaviour in Organizations: A Research Symposium*. Athens, Georgia: University of Georgia Press.

MCGRATH, J.E. and JULIAN, J.W. (1963). Interaction process and task outcomes in experimentally created negotiation groups. *Journal of Psychological Studies*, **14**, 117 – 138.

MESSÉ, L.A. (1971). Equity in bilateral bargaining. *Journal of Personality and Social Psychology*, **17**, 287 – 291.

MIDGAARD, K. and UNDERDAL, A. (1977). Multiparty conferences. In D. DRUCKMAN (Ed.), *Negotiations: Social-Psychological Perspectives*. Beverly Hills: Sage.

MORLEY, I.E. (1974). Social interaction in experimental negotiations. Unpublished Ph.D. thesis, University of Nottingham.

MORLEY, I.E. (1978a). Bargaining and negotiation: the character of experimental studies. In H. BRANDSTÄTTER, J.H. DAVIS and H. SCHULER (Eds.), *Dynamics of Group Decisions*. London: Sage.

MORLEY, I.E. (1978b). Preparation for negotiation: conflict, commitment and choice. Revised version of paper presented at the 3rd Symposium of the European Association of Experimental Social Psychology, 'A Symposium on Group Decision Making', Castle Reisensburg, Fed. Rep. of Germany (see BRANDSTÄTTER, M., DAVIS, J.H. and STOCKER-KREICHGAUER, G. (Eds.) (1982). *Group Decision Making*. Academic Press).

MORLEY, I.E. (1979). Behavioural studies of industrial bargaining. In G.M. STEPHENSON and C.J. BROTHERTON (Eds.), *Industrial Relations: A Social Psychological Approach*. Chichester: John Wiley & Sons.

MORLEY, I.E. (in press). Negotiation and bargaining. In M. ARGYLE (Ed.), *Social Skills and Work*. London: Methuen. (Pre-publication copy.)

MORLEY, I.E. and STEPHENSON, G.M. (1969). Interpersonal and inter-party exchange: a laboratory simulation of an industrial negotiation at the plant level. *British Journal of Psychology*, **60**, 543 – 545.

MORLEY, I.E. and STEPHENSON, G.M. (1970a). Formality in experimental negotiations: a validation study. *British Journal of Psychology*, **61**, 383 – 384.

MORLEY, I.E. and STEPHENSON, G.M. (1970b). Strength of case, communication systems and outcomes of simulated negotiations: some social psychological aspects of bargaining. *Industrial Relations Journal*, **1**, 19 – 29.

MORLEY, I.E. and STEPHENSON, G.M. (1977). *The Social Psychology of Bargaining*. London: George Allen & Unwin.

MORLEY, I.E., TYSOE, M. and STEPHENSON, G.M. (1978). Role reversal and preparation for negotiation in management training groups. Paper presented at the London Conference of the British Psychological Society, University College London, December.

MUNEY, B.F. and DEUTSCH, M. (1968). The effects of role-reversal during the discussion of opposing viewpoints. *Journal of Conflict Resolution*, **12**, 345 – 360.

MURNIGHAN, J.K. (1978). Models of coalition behaviour: game theoretic, social psychological, and political perspectives. *Psychological Bulletin*, **85**, 1130 – 1153.

MYERS, D.G. and LAMM, H. (1976). The group polarization phenomenon. *Psychological Bulletin*, **83**, 602 – 627.

NEUMANN, J. VON, and MORGENSTERN, O. (1944). *Theory of Games and Economic Behaviour*. Princeton, New Jersey: Princeton University Press.

NOGEE, J. (1960). The diplomacy of disarmament. *International Conciliation*, 526, Carnegie Endowment for International Peace.

ORGAN, D.W. (1971). Some variables affecting boundary role behaviour. *Sociometry*, **34**, 524 – 537.

PRUITT, D.G. (1969). Indirect communication in the search for agreement in negotiation. In *Indirect Communication in Negotiation Project*, Working Paper II 1. Buffalo, NY: Centre for International Conflict Studies, State University of New York.

PRUITT, D.G., KIMMEL, M.J., BRITTON, S., CARNEVALE, P.J.D., MAGENAU, J.M., PERAGALLO, J. and ENGRAM, P. (1978). The effect of accountability and surveillance on integrative bargaining. In H. SAUERMANN (Ed.), *Contributions to Experimental Economics*, Vol. 7. Tübingen: Mohr.

PRUITT, D.G. and LEWIS, S.A. (1977). The psychology of integrative bargaining. In D. DRUCKMAN (Ed.), *Negotiations: Social-Psychological Perspectives*. Beverly Hills: Sage.

RUBIN, J.Z. (1971). The nature and success of influence attempts in a four-party bargaining relationship. *Journal of Experimental Social Psychology*, **7**, 17 – 35.

RUBIN, J.Z. (1980). Experimental research on third-party intervention in conflict: toward some generalizations. *Psychological Bulletin*, **87**, 379 – 391.

RUBIN, J.Z. and BROWN, B.R. (1975). *The Social Psychology of Bargaining and Negotiation*. Academic Press.

RUTTER, D.R. and STEPHENSON, G.M. (1979). The role of visual communication in social interaction. *Current Anthropology*, **20**, 124 – 125.

SAWYER, J. and GUETZKOW, H. (1965). Bargaining and negotiation in international relations. In H.C. KELMAN (Ed.), *International Behaviour and Social Psychological Analysis*. New York: Holt, Reinhart & Winston.

SCHELLING, T.C. (1960). *The Strategy of Conflict*. Cambridge, Mass.: Harvard University Press.

SCHELLING, T.C. (1966). *Arms and Influence*. New Haven, Conn.: Yale University Press.

SCHULZ, J.W. (1976). Integrative bargaining in couples: the effects of normative structure. *Dissertation Abstracts International*, **37**(5 – B), 2578 – 2579.

SHAPIRA, Z. and BASS, B.M. (1975). Settling strikes in real life and simulations in North America and different regions of Europe. *Journal of Applied Psychology*, **60**, 466 – 471.

SHERIF, M. (Ed.) (1962). *Intergroup Relations and Leadership*. New York: John Wiley & Sons.

SHORT, J. (1971). Bargaining and negotiation — an exploratory study: a partial replication of Morley & Stephenson (1969). In Communications Studies Group Bulletin, Vol. 4, University College London. Ref: E/71065/SH.

SIEGEL, S. and FOURAKER, L.E. (1960). *Bargaining and Group Decision Making*. New York: McGraw-Hill.

SLUSHER, E.A. (1978). Counterpart strategy, prior relations, and constituent pressure in a bargaining simulation. *Behavioral Science*, **23**, 470 – 477.

SNYDER, G.H. and DIESING, P. (1977). *Conflict Among Nations: Bargaining, Decision Making, and System Structure in International Crises*. Princeton, New Jersey: Princeton University Press.

STEINBRUNER, J.D. (1974). *The Cybernetic Theory of Decision*. Princeton, New Jersey: Princeton University Press.

STEPHENSON, G.M. (1971). Intergroup relations and negotiating behaviour. In P. WARR (Ed.), *Psychology at Work*, 1st edn. Harmondsworth: Penguin Books.

STEPHENSON, G.M. (1978a). Intergroup bargaining and negotiation. Paper presented at the British Psychological Society Social Psychology Section One Day Conference on 'The Social Psychology of Intergroup Behaviour', University of Bristol, November. Obtainable from the Social Psychology Research Unit, University of Kent at Canterbury.

STEPHENSON, G.M. (1978b). Interparty and interpersonal exchange in negotiation groups. In H. BRANDSTÄTTER, J.H. DAVIS and H. SCHULER (Eds.), *Dynamics of Group Decisions*. London: Sage.

STEPHENSON, G.M. and BROTHERTON, C.J. (1975). Social progression and polarization: a study of discussion and negotiation in groups of mining supervisors. *British Journal of Social and Clinical Psychology*, **14**, 241 – 252.

STEPHENSON, G.M. and KNIVETON, B.H. (1978). Interpersonal and interparty exchange: an experimental study of the effect of seating position on the outcome of negotiations between teams representing parties in dispute. *Human Relations*, **31**, 555 – 566.

STEPHENSON, G.M., KNIVETON, B.H. and MORLEY, I.E. (1977). Interaction analysis of an industrial wage negotiation. *Journal of Occupational Psychology*, **50**, 231 – 241.

STEPHENSON, G.M., SKINNER, M. and BROTHERTON, C.J. (1976). Group participation and intergroup relations: an experimental study of negotiation groups. *European Journal of Social Psychology*, **6**, 51 – 70.

STERN, L.W., STERNTHAL, B. and CRAIG, C.S. (1975). Strategies for managing interorganizational conflict: a laboratory paradigm. *Journal of Applied Psychology*, **60**, 472 – 482.

STEVENS, C.M. (1963). *Strategy and Collective Bargaining Negotiation*. New York: McGraw-Hill.

TAJFEL, H. (1978). Intergroup behaviour: II Group perspectives. In H. TAJFEL and C. FRASER (Eds.), *Introducing Social Psychology*. Harmondsworth: Penguin Books.

TJOSVOLD, D. (1974). Threat as a low power person's strategy in bargaining: social face and tangible outcomes. *International Journal of Group Tensions*, **4**, 494 – 510.

TJOSVOLD, D. (1977). The effect of the constituent's affirmation and the opposing negotiator's self-presentation in bargaining between unequal status groups. *Organizational Behavior and Human Performance*, **18**, 146 – 157.

TURK, H. and LEFCOWITZ, M. (1962). Toward a theory of representation between groups. *Social Forces*, **40**, 337 – 341.

TYSOE, M. (1979a). An experimental investigation of the efficacy of some procedural role requirements in simulated negotiations. Unpublished Ph.D. thesis, University of Nottingham.

TYSOE, M. (1979b). Sex of negotiators: does it make a difference? Paper presented at the British Psychological Society Social Psychology Section Annual Conference, University of Surrey, September.

TYSOE, M. (1982). Social psychology and training techniques for industrial negotiators. *Industrial Relations Journal*, **13**, 64 – 75.

VIDMAR, N. (1971). Effects of representational roles and mediators on negotiation effectiveness. *Journal of Personality and Social Psychology*, **17**, 48 – 58.

VIDMAR, N. and MCGRATH, J.E. (1965). Role assignment and attitudinal commitment as factors in negotiation. Technical Report Number 3, Urbana, Illinois: AFOSR

Contract AF49 (638) – 1291, Department of Psychology, University of Illinois.

VIDMAR, N. and MCGRATH, J.E. (1970). Forces affecting success in negotiation groups. *Behavioral Science*, **15**, 154 – 163.

WALCOTT, C., HOPMANN, P.T. and KING, T.D. (1977). The role of debate in negotiation. In D. DRUCKMAN (Ed.), *Negotiations: Social-Psychological Perspectives*. Beverly Hills: Sage.

WALL, J.A. (1974). Intergroup bargaining studied as a dynamic process: the effects of constituent trust and representative bargaining visibility. *Personality and Social Psychology Bulletin*, **1**, 225 – 227.

WALL, J.A. (1975a). Effects of constituent trust and representative bargaining orientation on intergroup bargaining. *Journal of Personality and Social Psychology*, **31**, 1004 – 1012.

WALL, J.A. (1975b). The effects of constituent trust and representative bargaining visibility on intergroup bargaining. *Organizational Behavior and Human Performance*, **14**, 244 – 256.

WALL, J.A. (1976). Effects of sex and opposing representative's bargaining orientation on intergroup bargaining. *Journal of Personality and Social Psychology*, **33**, 55 – 61.

WALL, J.A. (1977). Intergroup bargaining: effects of opposing constituent stances, opposing representative's bargaining, and representative's locus of control. *Journal of Conflict Resolution*, **21**, 459 – 474.

WALTON, R.E. and MCKERSIE, R.B. (1965). *A Behavioural Theory of Labour Negotiations*. New York: McGraw-Hill.

WARR, P.B. (1973). *Psychology and Collective Bargaining*. London: Hutchinson.

WEBB, J. (1979). Behavioural studies of third-party intervention. In G.M. STEPHENSON and C.J. BROTHERTON (Eds.), *Industrial Relations: A Social Psychological Approach*. Chichester: John Wiley & Sons.

WINHAM, G.R. (1977). Complexity in international negotiation. In D. DRUCKMAN (Ed.), *Negotiations: Social-Psychological Perspectives*. Beverly Hills: Sage.

YOUNG, O.R. (Ed.) (1975). *Bargaining: Formal Theories of Negotiation*. University of Chicago Press.

YUKL, G.A. (1976). Effects of information, payoff magnitude, and favourability of alternative settlement on bargaining outcomes. *Journal of Social Psychology*, **98**, 269 – 282.

YUKL, G.A., MALONE, M.P., HAYSLIP, B. and PAMIN, T.A. (1976). The effects of time pressure and issue settlement order on integrative bargaining. *Sociometry*, **39**, 277 – 281.

ZECHMEISTER, K. and DRUCKMAN, D. (1973). Determinants of resolving a conflict of interest: a simulation of political decision-making. *Journal of Conflict Resolution*, **17**, 63 – 88.

CHAPTER 7

Naturalistic Experiments on Helping Behaviour

David P. Farrington

7.1 Introduction

Helping behaviour is the first area of social psychology which has been studied in large numbers of naturalistic field experiments, as opposed to experiments carried out with college students in campus locations. Research on helping has increased dramatically since the publication of two important books in 1970 (Latané & Darley, 1970; Macaulay & Berkowitz, 1970) and of important papers in the late 1960s, notably the naturalistic experiments of Bryan and Test (1967) and Piliavin *et al.* (1969), and the research on children by Rosenhan and White (1967).

This chapter focuses on the determinants of helping behaviour, studied as a dependent variable in naturalistic (real life) experiments. It does not attempt to review research in which helping is investigated as an independent variable. Excluded are studies of the evaluation of helping (e.g. Peterson *et al.*, 1977; Leahy, 1979; Wispé & Kiecolt, 1980), of the effects of helping on helpers (e.g. Harris, 1977) and recipients (e.g. Nadler *et al.*, 1976), and of help seeking (e.g. Tessler & Schwartz, 1972; Morris & Rosen, 1973). The chapter only attempts to review studies published in the English language. Most of these have been carried out in the United Sates, with smaller numbers in Canada, Great Britain, Australia and a few other countries.

7.1.1 *Defining Helping*

Psychologists rarely discuss the problems involved in specifying whether an act is helpful or not. Helping is often relative, and defining an act as helpful may involve a value judgement. Whether an act is judged helpful may depend on who is doing the judging. The same act may be helpful to one person and unhelpful to another. For example, intervening to prevent a crime may be helpful to the victim but not to the offender. It is difficult to classify acts objectively as helpful or unhelpful, or to score them on some scale of helpfulness.

There are many subjective aspects of helping. In order to help someone, it is desirable to know what the other person wants or needs. There may be a difference between intentions and consequences. Problems of definition can arise with behaviour which is intended to help but which does not, and with behaviour which is helpful but which was not intended to be. It is very difficult to establish someone's intentions. Since helping is generally considered to be socially desirable behaviour, people may deliberately present a false picture of themselves to an interviewer, to induce him to believe that they are trying to help. What people say cannot be relied on as a true reflection of their mental processes (see Nisbett & Wilson, 1977, and Section 7.1.4 of this chapter).

There are also problems in classifying different kinds of helpful behaviour. Quite a lot of research has been aimed at studying altruism, often defined as helping with no obvious benefit to the helper (e.g. Cohen, 1978). However, it is difficult to know what are the costs and benefits of helping in any situation. Even if the helper does not receive any material reward and is unlikely to see the recipient again, he may still benefit from social approval, self-esteem, an empathic appreciation of the happiness felt by the recipient, or a reduction of the empathic distress he felt at seeing the recipient in need. The idea of altruism was originally thought to pose problems for traditional hedonistic theories of psychology, which suggested that behaviour was governed by rewards and punishments, but it may just be that the rewards of altruistic behaviour are less obvious than other rewards. This chapter adopts a very wide definition of helping, reflecting the operational definitions used in experiments (see Section 7.1.2), and is not restricted to any sub-category of helping such as altruism.

There are many possible ways of classifying helping, for example in relation to the costs and benefits to the helper, the relationship between the helper and the recipient, characteristics of the helper and the recipient, or the kinds of helping behaviour involved. No classification scheme has been widely accepted. Certain people are required to help in the process of carrying out their jobs, and there have been some studies of helping by such groups as clergymen (e.g. McKenna, 1976) and policemen (e.g. Brenner & Levin, 1973). The relationships between different kinds of helping behaviour studied in experiments are discussed in Section 7.1.5.

7.1.2 Operational Definitions in Experiments

Many different kinds of helping have been studied in experiments. Several operational definitions of helping were inspired by the work of Latané and Darley (1970). They had researchers approach members of the public on the streets and in other public places, to ask for directions, for the time, for change, for money, or for their names. In the subway, they engineered a situation where one confederate asked for directions and was given incorrect information by another confederate, to see if a bystander would help by giving the correct information. In a railway station, they had two girls throw a frisbee to a member of the public, to see if he would throw it back. They also faked a theft from a store, to see if members of the public would report it to the cashier. They also had a man on crutches trip in front of people at an airport and a railway station, to see if he would be helped. Latané and Darley (1970) also carried out experiments on campus, in which students heard sounds of a lady falling off a chair, or of an epileptic seizure, or of one child beating up another, again to see if they would try to help in any way. These methods have been used by many subsequent researchers.

Helping experiments have also been carried out on highways. Bryan and Test (1967) stood a person next to a car with a flat tyre, to see if passing motorists would stop to help, and West *et al.* (1975) investigated if passing motorists would stop to help someone whose car had broken down. Several researchers (e.g. Pomazal & Clore, 1973; Forsyth, 1978) have studied motorists' willingness to pick up hitch-hikers, and Clark *et al.* (1976) investigated if people would turn off the headlights of a car parked with them on. The method of Gaertner and Bickman (1971), based on people's willingness to telephone a garage to get help for a motorist who had broken down, has proved especially popular. The final sample of subjects in this kind of telephone research is often considerably less than the initial one. For example, Gruder *et al.* (1978) called 291 telephone numbers selected at random; 96 were out of service or not answered, 12 subjects did not understand English, 22 hung up, and 12 were lost through experimenter error. This left 149 subjects in the experiment, of whom more than two-thirds were females, because women were more likely to be at home in the afternoons when the calls were made.

Shops have also proved a favourite site for naturalistic helping experiments. Wispé and Freshley (1971) investigated people's willingness to pick up dropped groceries, and others (e.g. Ellsworth & Langer, 1976; Murray & Vincenzo, 1976) have studied people's willingness to help search for a lost contact lens. Many experiments have been carried out on the willingness of shoppers to report shoplifting (e.g. Steffensmeier & Steffensmeier, 1977; Bickman & Helwig, 1979). Other researchers have collected for charity in stores (e.g. Bryan & Test, 1967) or asked shoppers for money towards the purchase of items (e.g. Bickman & Kamzan, 1973). Store employees, as well as customers have served as subjects. For example, Dorris (1972) investigated how much money employees offered for rare coins, Schaps (1972) studied how many pairs of shoes a salesman was willing to show a customer, and Brigham and Richardson (1979) attempted to purchase items costing more than the money they possessed. Employees have also served as experimenters, as in research where helping was measured by the amount of tips given to waitresses (e.g. Tidd & Lockard, 1978; Cunningham, 1979).

Quite a number of researchers have used a non-reactive method, the lost letter technique. In this, members of the public find in a public place a letter which has apparently been lost. They can then choose whether or not to help by posting the letter. This method has been used both to study helping (e.g. Hornstein *et al.*, 1968; Gross, 1975) and dishonest behaviour (e.g. Merritt & Fowler, 1948; Farrington & Knight, 1979). If the lost letter contains money, posting it is helpful, while keeping the money is dishonest. In the research of Penner *et al.* (1976), in which students found a lost dollar, they were able to return it, keep it or ignore it, thereby making it more possible to separate helping and dishonesty. There are several variants of the lost letter technique, for example using a lost postcard (e.g. Huey & Jacobs, 1978) or a lost key (e.g. Forbes *et al.*, 1972). The lost letter technique has been used to investigate political and social attitudes (e.g. Milgram *et al.*, 1965; Georgoff *et al.*, 1972), but its validity for this purpose is not clear (e.g. Wicker, 1969; Shotland *et al.*, 1970; Jacoby & Aranoff, 1971; Baskett *et al.*, 1973; Bolton, 1974; Cherulnik, 1975; Zelnio & Gagnon, 1977).

Many other methods have been used to study helping in naturalistic experiments. Piliavin *et al.* (1969) investigated helping in the subway by having a confederate collapse in a carriage, and Staub and Baer (1974) had confederates collapse in the street. In the research of Borges and Penta (1977), members of the public passed someone lying on the ground moaning. Several researchers have collected door to door for charity (e.g. Catt & Benson, 1977) or asked people to answer questions (e.g. Snyder & Cunningham, 1975; Baer & Goldman, 1978). Others have given people opportunities to help pick up dropped objects in the street (e.g. Konecni *et al.*, 1975) or in lifts (e.g. Latane & Dabbs, 1975), or have asked members of the public to allow them into their houses to make telephone calls (e.g. Milgram, 1970; Feinman, 1978), or have investigated people's willingness to answer a ringing public telephone (Feldman & Rezmovic, 1979). One of the most ingenious methods was used by Thayer (1973), who had an apparently deaf confederate approach members of the public with a written message asking them to make a telephone call on his behalf. Helping has also been studied in relation to looking after belongings on beaches (e.g. Moriarty, 1975).

The above experiments concern helping by adults, and the helping rates have varied from 97 – 100% for helping a person on crutches who drops something (Schneider, 1973) to less than 1% for intervening to prevent a staged murder (Schreiber, 1979). Many experiments have also been carried out with children. Following Rosenhan and White (1967), it has been common to arrange for children to win something in a game and then to investigate whether they will give some of their winnings to other children or to a good cause (e.g. Isen *et al.*, 1973; Grusec *et al.*, 1978a). It has been rare for the helper to meet the recipient, although this happened in the research of Staub and Sherk (1970). A more naturalistic measure of helping was used by Yarrow *et al.* (1973), who carried out their research in a house (rather than a mobile laboratory containing a one-way mirror) and studied how far children would help pick up toys for a baby.

Many other tasks have been used in research carried out on campuses. An example of an extreme campus-specific method which has a long history is to investigate whether students will agree to participate in research (e.g. Rosenbaum & Blake, 1955; Schopler & Bateson, 1965). Another favourite method has been for a confederate to drop a stack of computer cards, to see if the subject will help pick them up (e.g. Wegner & Crano, 1975; Kidd & Berkowitz, 1976). Other researchers have built on existing social psychological methods, for example investigating how far students would help learners in electric shock experiments (e.g. Tilker, 1970; Midlarsky, 1971; Tipton & Jenkins, 1974). Carlsmith and Gross (1969) studied students' expressed willingness to make telephone calls to try to save California redwood trees; Aderman and Berkowitz (1970) investigated students' willingness to score tests for an experimenter; and Kazdin and Bryan (1971) enquired about their willingness to donate blood. In an attempt to obtain an intervally scaled dependent variable, desirable for the preferred method of analysis of variance, social psychologists have sometimes made rather implausible requests. For example, Schopler and Thompson (1968) asked female students how many times they were willing to wash a blouse (on a scale from 1 to 50).

7.1.3 *Internal and External Validity*

Ideally, research should be high on both internal and external validity (see, e.g. Campbell & Stanley, 1966). It should be able to demonstrate unambiguously, by isolating and manipulating the variables of interest and controlling others, that changes in one variable produce changes in another. This (internal validity) is best achieved in random allocation experiments. Results obtained in one research setting, with certain subjects and certain operational definitions of variables, should be generalizable to other settings, and especially to real life. This (external validity) is best achieved by carrying out research with members of the public who do not realize that they are being studied. It follows that naturalistic field experiments on helping are likely to have the highest internal and external validity, and this is why this chapter concentrates on them (see also Farrington, 1979b; Farrington, 1980).

Much of the early research on helping carried out in the 1960s used students (often introductory psychology students participating as a course requirement) as subjects and was conducted in campus locations. Huston and Korte (1976) estimated that 80% of bystander intervention research had been carried out in college laboratories. Since their paper was published (during the period 1977 – 80 inclusive), the proportion of helping experiments in campus locations has been around 50%, excluding studies of children or adolescents. Of a sample of 30 papers in the *Journal of Social Psychology* during this period, 15 (50%) were based on campus locations. Of 20 papers in the *Journal of Personality and Social Psychology* during this period, 17 (85%) were wholly in campus locations and a further 1 (5%) was partly so. Of 44 papers in all other journals during this period, 14 (32%) were based on campus locations. Thus, of 94 papers published in 1977 – 80, 47 were based wholly or partly on campus locations (50%), and the remainder were conducted in naturalistic settings. I cannot claim to have read all papers on helping published in 1977 – 80, but I can claim to have read the majority. (This analysis is restricted to studies which appeared to have random allocation of subjects to conditions and helping as a dependent variable).

The reason why the *Journal of Personality and Social Psychology* overwhelmingly publishes campus-based research is easy to see. This journal requires methodological controls and manipulation checks which are easy to carry out with docile introductory psychology students but very hard to carry out with members of the public unwittingly participating in an experiment. In its quest for high internal validity, the journal underemphasizes external validity. Both should be taken into account in evaluating research, and indeed this has been stated by the editors of another journal (Wyer *et al.*, 1978). In any case, the manipulation checks and other controls usually depend on verbal statements made by subjects, and it will be argued in Section 7.1.4 that these cannot be relied on. No one could deny that many of the naturalistic experiments published in the *Journal of Social Psychology* are low in internal validity, but they are not necessarily worse than the campus experiments published in the *Journal of Personality and Social Psychology* which are likely to be low in external validity.

The difficulties of campus research are well known, as evidenced by the edited book of Miller (1972). Latané and Darley (1970, pp. 7 – 8) drew attention to some of the problems of campus research on helping:

> A major difficulty with laboratory studies of helping is that they are hard to relate to real-life situations. On the one hand, subjects are under unusual pressures in the laboratory. They are known by name to the experimenter and sometimes to other subjects and they may be eager to gain favorable evaluations from them. They have been pulled out of their daily routine and are shorn of many of their usual defences. They cannot easily leave the situation and they may find it hard simply to ignore a request. These heightened pressures and lowered defences may make the laboratory subject much more vulnerable to a request for help than the man on the street.
> Furthermore, laboratory experiments often have an 'as if' quality about them. If subjects know that they are participating in an experiment, they may react not to what they see, but to what they think the experiment is about. Anxious to make a favorable impression, they may be willing to act quite unnaturally in order to appear normal. They are likely to play-act. These forces may be especially strong in situations where norms are involved. Self-conscious and apprehensive about being evaluated, laboratory subjects may make an unusual attempt to behave normatively.
> A third dissimilarity between laboratory helping situations and life is that in order to make a request for help believable in its laboratory context and in order to increase the measurement utility of the response, subjects may be faced with rather unusual demands. 'How many hours are you willing to spend in sensory deprivation?' 'Will you help stack these papers?' 'How many letters will you address for "Save the Redwoods"?' Although laboratory experiments constitute an invaluable technique for testing theoretical derivations, they may not tell us much about the determinants of helping in everyday situations.

External validity is essentially an empirical question which can be investigated by repeating experiments with different operational definitions of variables in different settings. Little of this kind of research has been done. When the same experiment has been carried out both on campus and in a naturalistic context, different results have often been obtained. For example, West *et al.* (1975) investigated the willingness of motorists to help people in broken-down cars in college and non-college neighbourhoods. In the non-college areas, black recipients were helped faster in black neighbourhoods, and white recipients were helped faster in white neighbourhoods. In the college areas, black recipients were helped faster in white neighbourhoods and white recipients in black neighbourhoods. Bickman (1976) carried out two experiments to investigate the effect of a prior pleasant or unpleasant interaction with a sales clerk on the reporting of shoplifting. In the real-life experiment with customers in a department store, fewer reported after the unpleasant interaction. In a second experiment with student subjects, the pleasant – unpleasant manipulation had no effect on reporting. More research of this kind could be carried out to investigate the external validity of campus research, but it might be better merely to carry out real-life experiments where these are possible.

As already stated, this chapter will concentrate on naturalistic field experiments to the neglect of campus research. Studies carried out in other artificial environments, such as prisons (e.g. Sechrest & Flores, 1974), or with other unusual populations, such as navy enlisted men (e.g. Wagner & Wheeler, 1969), will also be neglected. Experiments with children will be given some prominence, although they rarely involve naturalistic settings. It seems unlikely that the results of studies in which children know that they are participating in an experiment, which are carried out in the artificial surroundings of a mobile testing unit, and in which opportunities for helping come essentially as part of a game, can be generalized with confidence to real-life helping. In a review of research on the effects of prosocial television programmes on helping behaviour of children, Rushton (1979) concluded that the effects found in the laboratory were stronger than effects obtained in more naturalistic settings. Because of low internal validity, correlational research on helping will be neglected, except in Section 7.1.5 devoted to correlational research with special relevance to experiments.

Despite their high internal and external validity, naturalistic experiments have limitations. As Mussen and Eisenberg-Berg (1977, p. 162) pointed out, 'the horror story of Kitty Genovese's murder, in full view of many witnesses [who did nothing to help], probably set into motion more research on helping and altruism than any theory'. However, just as it seems far-fetched to generalize from the research of Milgram (1974) to the incineration of Jews by Nazis, it is overoptimistic to think that field experiments on helping can throw much light on reasons for not trying to help prevent violent murders. The gap between the experiment and real life with this kind of event is very great. Similarly, in investigating why people risk their lives in conditions of great danger to help other people, interview studies such as those of London (1970) and Huston *et al.* (1981) are likely to provide more valid information than a field experiment.

Naturalistic experiments are especially useful in studying short-term or situational determinants of helping. They are less useful in investigating long-term or historical determinants, such as methods of child-rearing used by parents (cf. Bar-Tal *et al.*, 1980a). Most of the experiments involve a special kind of helping, between persons who have never met before and are unlikely to meet again. The results may not generalize to helping between relations, friends or acquaintances. There are undoubtedly problems of control in naturalistic experiments. For example, imagine the situation in which a researcher approaches a member of the public and asks for change. Has the member of the public really been chosen at random, or was he selected in some way? If he fails to give change, is he being unhelpful, or is it just that he does not have sufficient change on him? If the experimental manipulation is the dress of the researcher, there is a problem in ensuring that only dress varies between the conditions, and that other variables (such as the behaviour of the researcher or the selection of subjects) are not confounded with dress. There is inevitably a trade-off between internal and external validity, so that the move out of the laboratory into real life involves some loss of experimental control.

Laboratory experiments and correlational research can both be useful in advancing our knowledge about helping. Just as it is easier in correlational research to investigate long-term historical influences on helping, it is easier in the laboratory to study internal processes which might underly helping (such as physiological arousal), unusual variables such as de-individuation (e.g. Becker-Haven & Lindskold, 1978), or to obtain detailed information about the subject going beyond that which is readily observable, such as sex, estimated age, and dress. The argument here is not that such methods should not be used but that, because of relatively high internal and external validity, naturalistic experimentation should be the more usual and preferred procedure.

7.1.4 Words and Deeds

The emphasis is this chapter is on observable helping behaviour. In many campus experiments (e.g. Duval *et al.*, 1979), the student subjects have to say whether they would help, but do not actually have to perform the helping act. In other researches (e.g. Black *et al.*, 1980), subjects are asked to guess how people would behave in hypothetical situations where helping is possible. The problem is that what people say they or others will do often differs from what actually happens, with the deeds usually being less praiseworthy that the words.

Perhaps the most extensive comparison of helping words and deeds can be found in the blood donation experiments, where students are asked whether they are willing to donate blood and later given an opportunity to do it. In every one of five studies, less than half of those who said that they would give blood actually did so (Kazdin & Bryan, 1971; Bloom & Clark, 1976; Cialdini & Ascani, 1976; Pomazal & Jaccard, 1976; Rushton & Campbell, 1977). West and Brown (1975) found that the actual amount of money donated to help a student in an experiment was considerably less than the amount predicted by students when the experiment was described to them. Shaffer *et al.* (1975) reported that 85% of students said that they would intervene to prevent a theft in a college library, but only 40% actually did so in an experiment. When the lost dollar experiment of Penner *et al.* (1976) was described to students as a hypothetical situation, the returning rate was overestimated in comparison with the actual results (see Penner *et al.*, 1979). Farrington *et al.* (1980) also found considerable differences between the actual non-return rates in lost letter experiments and the estimated non-return rates given by people to whom the experiments were described, and differences between words and deeds were also discovered in the helping experiment of Bickman (1974) and in the crime reporting studies of Bickman (1975) and Bickman and Helwig (1979). Such discrepancies have also been found in research with children. For example, Green and Schneider (1974) reported that helping behaviour and sharing behaviour increased from age 5 to age 14, but that there was no change with age in the verbal measure of volunteering to work for needy children.

Students not only give socially desirable responses to experimenters but also tell lies. This has been demonstrated most clearly in research on the effect of transgression on helping. For example, McMillen (1971) carried out an experiment in which students were told the answers to a test by a confederate in advance. When asked by the experimenter if they had heard anything about the test, every student told a lie and denied this. (This was the transgression manipulation.) Similar results were obtained by Freedman *et al.* (1967), McMillen and Austin (1971), McMillen *et al.* (1974) and Silverman *et al.* (1979). This series of studies suggests that, in post-experimental questionnaires, students may be unwilling to tell researchers that they saw through the experimental manipulation. Even so, substantial percentages of students in some experiments have reported that they thought an incident was faked. In Latané and Darley's (1970) research, 75% of students thought that the fight between two children was faked, and 31% thought this about the epileptic attack. In Shotland and Straw's (1976) work, 40% of students thought that a fight was faked.

Staged incidents are so common on some American campuses that even real incidents may be perceived as faked. Diener and Crandall (1978) reported that one student shot another on the campus of the University of Washington in Seattle in 1973. Students on their way to class did not stop to aid the victim, and neither did anyone follow the offender. When the campus reporters asked some students about their lack of concern over the murder, the students said that they thought it was a psychology experiment.

The extent and meaning of relationships between behavioural measures of helping and other verbal measures are also unclear. The most usual verbal measures studied are of moral judgement (e.g. Rubin & Schneider, 1973; Emler & Rushton, 1974; Eisenberg-Berg, 1979; Peterson, 1980), but perspective-taking has also been investigated (e.g. Waxler *et al.*, 1977). Much of the moral judgement research has been reviewed by Burton (1976, p. 177), who concluded that 'the small magnitude of overlap . . . suggests that the primary determinants of verbal responses to moral dilemmas may well be different from the major determinants of overt behaviour in specific situations'. On the other hand, Rushton (1981, p. 262) concluded that 'individuals with high scores on paper-and-pencil or verbal measures of social responsibility, other-oriented values, or moral reasoning tasks were more likely to engage in prosocial behaviour than those with lower scores on the same tests'. While not denying that unobservable, internal hypothetical constructs may underly or mediate helping, the focus of interest in this chapter will be on helping behaviour.

7.1.5 Correlational Research Relevant to Experiments

Experimental research is designed to test hypotheses about the effect of changes in an independent variable on a dependent variable. It is often desirable to precede hypothesis-testing research with hypothesis-generating research, but this rarely seems to have happened in the field of helping. Before embarking on an experiment, it would be desirable to carry out correlational, observational research such as that done by Jiobu and Knowles (1974) or Lincoln (1977). It seems that many social psychologists prefer to test hypotheses derived from existing theories or from the armchair rather than to carry out empirical hypothesis-generating research.

Correlational research is necessary to validate the operational definitions of helping used in experiments against external criteria of helping, and hence to establish which of the measures described in Section 7.1.2 have the highest external validity. It is also necessary to investigate the relationships among different kinds of helping, the extent of generality as opposed to specificity in helping, and the number of different theoretical concepts being measured by the empirical variables. It is also necessary to establish the longitudinal and situational consistency of individuals in helping, and hence the extent to which it might be meaningful to postulate a stable personality trait of helpfulness. Little of this kind of correlational research has been done with helping, in comparison with aggression for example (cf. Shemberg *et al.*, 1968; Olweus, 1979), although it was called for by Bryan (1972).

Existing results, mostly obtained with children, indicate that the measures of helping used in experiments do not all reflect the same theoretical concept. Yarrow and Waxler (1976) found that helping was not significantly correlated with sharing either in an experimental or a naturalistic (free play) situation. Sharing in the experiment was correlated with sharing in free play, but this was not true of helping. Rubin and Schneider (1973) and O'Bryant and Brophy (1976) both reported no significant correlation between helping and donating. Rushton and Wheelwright (1980) found that sharing and donating were related, but also discovered that, whereas donating increased significantly with age, sharing did not. Another discrepant result was obtained by Grusec *et al.* (1978b), in finding that a donating model increased children's donating but decreased their helping. In Payne's (1980) research, helping was not correlated with donating or sharing, and sharing and donating were not related. However, donating has been associated with teacher or peer ratings of generosity or unselfishness in several studies (Rutherford & Mussen, 1968; Dlugolinski & Firestone, 1973; Rushton and Wheelwright, 1980; see also Rushton, 1980). In a rare study with adults, Harris and Samerotte (1975) reported that giving money and agreeing to answer questions for a survey were correlated. What is needed is a method of classifying different activities labelled as helpful, based on correlations between them.

Experimental research typically establishes whether a few factors have independent effects on helping, while correlational research, within the limitations of its low internal validity, can show the relative importance of a large number of factors and the ways in which they interact. One limitation of current tests of statistical significance is that a given level of significance can indicate a large effect in a small sample or a small effect in a large sample. More notice should be taken of the strength of effects. In the area of helping, experimental manipulations can have a dramatic effect on the percentage of people who help, suggesting that helping is greatly affected by situational factors. For example, in Isen and Levin's (1972) research, 87% of those who found a dime in a telephone booth helped a female confederate pick up folders, in comparison with only 4% who did not. Tipton and Browning (1972b) discovered that the rate of helping to pick up dropped groceries increased from 0% to 71% as the recipient changed from young and slim to old and fat. Valentine (1980) showed that the rate of helping to pick up dropped coins at a bus stop varied from 11% to 82%, depending whether the helper was alone and whether the recipient gazed at him. In their lost letter experiments, Farrington and Knight (1979) found that the non-return rate varied from 6% to 78%, depending on the form of the money and the apparent recipient. Large effects have also been found in other helping experiments (e.g. Regan *et al.*, 1972; Moriarty, 1975; Miller & Suls, 1977). In contrast, the significant results in the 'wrong number' telephoning technique of Gaertner and Bickman (1971) reflected small effects in a very large (over 1100) sample.

Correlational research can also demonstrate the relationships between helping and other kinds of behaviour, and hence the extent to which the determinants (and theories) of helping are similar to those of other behaviour. Of particular interest is the extent to which helping is at the other end of the spectrum from antisocial behaviour, in view of the much greater volume of research and theorizing about different kinds of antisocial behaviour. As already mentioned, the design of some experiments forces the subject to choose between helping and antisocial behaviour (e.g. Farrington and Knight, 1979). In a study which attempted to separate helping and dishonesty, Newman (1979) concluded that they were not opposite extremes of the same theoretical variable, since results with helping were different from those with dishonesty. Wener and Pisano (1977) reported a significant negative correlation between aggression and helping among students, but Harris and Siebel (1975) and Barrett (1979) found no significant relationship between aggression and sharing by children. More research of this kind is needed.

7.1.6 Ethical Issues

It is doubtful that the ethical issues arising in helping experiments are very different in degree or in kind from those arising in other areas of social psychology. Many helping experiments are discussed in the book on ethics by Diener and Crandall (1978), but this is probably because of the large number of naturalistic experiments in this area, which are thought to raise more ethical problems than laboratory experiments with students. This is arguable, in view of the frequent blackmailing of undergraduates into serving as subjects as a course requirement, and the exploitation of the graduate students who usually act as experimenters.

Diener and Crandall (1978) pointed out that one approach frequently used in evaluating whether a project is ethical is whether its likely benefits (usually consisting of, or consequent upon, advancement of knowledge) outweigh its likely costs (e.g. in terms of deception, invasion of privacy of, or harm caused to, subjects). By this criterion, most experiments on helping fare quite well. For example, Diener and Crandall considered that the lost letter technique was not risky, did not invade subjects' rights, was a minor deception, and did not require informed consent. It would be easier to justify experiments on helping if it could be claimed that the knowledge emerging from them would help to prevent crimes such as that committed against Kitty Genovese or would help to increase human helpfulness generally.

The only harm which usually befalls subjects in helping experiments is that they are placed in a moral dilemma, but most such dilemmas are not unusual in everyday life. There are some ethical problems involved in persuading people to give money, but the money is usually collected for charity. When motorists stop to help a broken down car and are then told that it was all part of an experiment (e.g. Hurley & Allen, 1974; Skolnick, 1977), there is the danger that they will become less likely to stop to help in the future. Similar comments apply to motorists who stop for a hitch-hiker who declines a ride (e.g. Morgan *et al.*, 1975). It is often unclear in naturalistic experiments on helping whether the subjects were debriefed, but it can be argued that it is more ethical not to debrief them, since most naturalistic experiments without debriefing are likely to have a negligible impact on people's lives (see Farrington & Kidd, 1977).

Some experiments raise idiosyncratic ethical issues. For example, Brigham and Richardson (1979) had confederates try to purchase items marked between $1.15 and $1.50 in grocery stores for $1.00, which they said was all the money they had on them. The majority (55%) of confederates succeeded. Is it implausible to suggest that, if this result became widely publicized, dishonesty in grocery stores would increase? Ethical issues raised in research with children are perhaps the most worrying. In one series of experiments, children were asked to think about sad experiences. Attempts were made to limit the sadness, for example by telling them not to think about the death of a parent (e.g. Moore *et al.*, 1973), or to neutralize it at the end of the experiment by having them think about happy experiences (e.g. Kenrick *et al.*, 1979). However, this research clearly has costs, in terms of sadness experienced by children, and therefore needs special justification.

In keeping with their commitment to empirical research, social psychologists have investigated the opinions of actual and potential subjects about helping experiments. Wilson and Donnerstein (1976) described several naturalistic experiments to members of the public selected randomly in field locations, including several studies of helping : the lost letter technique, asking for money, asking to enter a house and use the telephone, the 'foot of the door' technique of Freedman and Fraser (1966) in which a large request followed a smaller one, the subway emergency of Piliavin and Piliavin (1972), and the study with shoe salesmen of Schaps (1972). In none of these cases did the majority of people say that the research was unethical or that it would invade their privacy. The most objectionable of these techniques seemed to be asking for money, since 43% thought it was unethical, 43% said that it was an invasion of privacy, 54% said that they would mind being a subject, and 54% said that psychologists should not be doing it. In contrast, the corresponding figures for the lost letter technique were 24%, 11%, 38% and 34%.

When researchers have asked student subjects for their opinions about helping experiments in which they have participated, critical comments have been rare. For example, Clark and Word (1974) exposed students to an emergency in which a technician was knocked unconscious by a high-voltage electric shock. The majority of subjects (68%) claimed to be upset at the time of the emergency, but they reported few negative after-effects in follow-up interviews three to six months later. Schwartz and Gottlieb (1976) exposed students to a violent theft, and found that only one considered the experiment unethical, none regretted participating or said that the experience would decrease their likelihood of helping a real victim in the future, and several said it would increase their helping in the future. In similar research published four years later, Schwartz and Gottlieb (1980) reported that 98% of students thought that their experiments should be allowed to continue, 97% did not regret participating, 95% thought the experiment ethically justified, and only 2% resented the deception. Whether members of the public would have similar opinions of this kind of research is unknown.

7.2 Major Theoretical Approaches

Section 7.2 will provide brief outlines of some of the major theories put forward to explain helping in experiments. Usually, these are adaptations of theories proposed to explain other kinds of social behaviour, and are not specific to helping. Also, they are not mutually exclusive. More general theories have been put forward which combine elements of several of the theories outlined here.

7.2.1 Cost-Benefit Theories

One of the most popular theories suggests that individuals will help if the benefits of helping outweigh its costs. For example, Piliavin *et al.* (1969) mentioned costs of helping (e.g. effort, embarrassment, possible disgusting experiences, possible physical harm), costs of not helping (e.g. self-blame and perceived censure from others), benefits of helping (e.g. praise from self, victim and others) and benefits of not helping (e.g. continuation of other activities). According to this theory, helping is a rational, hedonistic or selfish act rather than an altruistic one. The major problem in testing this kind of a theory is to operationalize and measure costs and benefits.

An obvious extension of the general cost – benefit idea is to apply the subjectively expected utility (SEU) theory of risky decision making to explain helping, as Lynch and Cohen (1978) tried to do. The SEU of an event or outcome is the product of the subjective probability of its occurrence and its utility, or subjective value, attractiveness, benefit or cost. In a risky decision, each alternative course of action has a certain SEU, which is the sum of the SEUs associated with each outcome. According to this theory, a person will help if the SEU of helping exceeds the SEUs of alternative courses of action. This theory has also been applied to explain dishonesty (e.g. Farrington, 1979b; Farrington & Knight, 1980a).

A variant of the cost – benefit theory is social learning theory, which suggests that helping depends on an individual's past experience of costs and benefits (or rewards and punishments) of helping. For an exposition of this, see Aronfreed (1976). Another variant is exchange theory (e.g. Homans, 1961), which suggests that individuals act to maximize their profits (benefits minus costs) in interaction with others. Since each person attempts to maximize his own profit, interactions stabilize when everyone is gaining some profit from the interaction. It is argued that it is of mutual advantage to arrive at a relationship based on the exchange of benefits, and once such a relationship develops it comes to be guided by norms and expectations.

7.2.2 Reciprocity, Equity and the Just World

The ideas of reciprocity, equity and justice are quite closely related to the cost – benefit theories mentioned in Section 7.2.1. Berkowitz (1972) has argued that a social or moral norm of reciprocity underlies many helping acts. A person who has been helped is obliged to repay this help in some way, and people are less willing to help in circumstances where there is no possibility of reciprocation. Equity theory (e.g. Hatfield *et al.*, 1978) suggests that individuals will act so as to maintain equity in relationships, that is a proper balance between a person's benefits and the efforts he puts in. If people are in inequitable relationships, they will attempt to make them equitable, and this may involve helping. The 'just world' theory (e.g. Lerner, 1970) assumes that people want to believe in a world characterized by justice, where people deserve what they get and get what they deserve. If people are faced with injustice (e.g. undeserved suffering), they will attempt to re-establish justice, either by helping the victim or in some other way (e.g. persauding themselves that for some reason the victim deserved to suffer).

7.2.3 Moral Standards

One of the most famous theories of moral development is that put forward by Kohlberg (1976), and this has been applied explicitly to helping by Krebs (1978). This theory suggests that children pass through a series of stages of moral development. In the first stage, children help in order to obtain rewards or avoid punishments or when they are told to by parents. In the second, the emphasis is on reciprocity, on helping those who help you. In the third, children behave towards others as they would like the others to behave towards them. In the fourth, helping falls within larger concerns, such as the welfare of society, which may override the welfare of friends for example. In the fifth stage, helping might depend on fostering the greatest good for the greatest number, while in the sixth and final stage helping would depend on universal principles of justice or human rights.

A similar developmental theory has been proposed by Bar-Tal *et al.* (1980b). According to this, motives for helping change with age, and children pass through six stages. In the first, they help in order to gain concrete rewards or avoid punishments, while in the second they help in order to comply with the commands of those in authority. In the third stage, helping is in response to other people's needs, while the motivation in the fourth stage is normative, to gain social approval. The main consideration in the fifth stage is generalized reciprocity, or helping others in the hope that they or others may help you. In the sixth and final stage, helping is altruistic, with no expectation of extrinsic reward, and altruism is said to be a developmental achievement.

Other researchers have also related helping to moral standards. For example, Schwartz (1977) has outlined a theory of helping in which the key concept is moral obligation. There are four steps in this theory. The activation step involves the perception of need and responsibility, the obligation step involves the generation of feelings of moral obligation, the defensive step involves the assessment and evaluation of potential responses, and the final step is action or inaction.

7.2.4 Empathy, Arousal and Tension

These theories all assume that people help in order to reduce or eliminate an unpleasant internal state. As with other theories, a key problem is to measure the internal state. It is often treated as a hypothetical construct. The empathy theory suggests that a person who observes someone in need vicariously experiences the other's distress, which is unpleasant (e.g. Aronfreed, 1970). One way of reducing the unpleasant internal state is to eliminate the other's need by helping. The arousal theory is similar, except that the key construct is arousal rather than empathy (e.g. Piliavin *et al.*, 1975). According to this, a person who observes someone in need has an increased arousal level, which is unpleasant, and which can be reduced by helping. The tension idea, popularized by Hornstein *et al.* (1971), suggests that the existence of an unfulfilled goal gives rise to tension, which in turn produces activity leading to the achievement of the goal (such as helping) and hence to a reduction in tension.

Not all theories suggest that an unpleasant internal state generated by someone else's need is conducive to helping. For example, Berkowitz (1973) argued that reactance might be aroused when a person found that someone else depended on him for help, because the other's dependence was a threat to the first person's independence. This reactance could lead to a decreased willingness to help.

In recent years, the concept of attribution has been added to the internal state theory of helping. For example, Weiner (1980) outlined a theory in which the perception of a person in need gave rise to a search for the cause of this event. Depending on the attributed cause, the potential helper might attribute his internal state to different emotions (e.g. sympathy or disgust), and would be much more likely to help if he felt sympathy.

7.2.5 Sequential Theories and Combinations

Several researchers other than Schwartz (1977) have proposed sequential theories of helping, in which the helping process is broken down into a sequence of decision stages. For example, Latané and Darley (1970) proposed a five-stage process for bystander intervention. The bystander has to notice that something is happening, has to interpret it as an emergency, has to decide that it is his personal responsibility to act, has to decide what form of help to give, and has to actually help.

Some combination of the above theories seems most plausible at the present time. At a minimum, it seems necessary to break down the helping process into perception and decision stages. It seems desirable to include some idea of empathy, arousal or tension in the perception stage, possibly in conjunction with some attribution ideas. It also seems desirable to include some cost – benefit ideas in the decision stage. However, this theory of the immediate, situational determinants of helping needs filling out with a great deal of empirical research, and work is especially needed on the operational definition of key concepts.

7.3 Major Independent Variables

7.3.1 Demographic Factors

This section will discuss what is known about helping in relation to the sex, race, nationality and age of the helper and recipient, and in relation to the area of residence (especially urban versus rural) and physical situation (such as weather and time of day). Some of these variables cannot be manipulated experimentally, and in these cases it is difficult to establish their influence on helping unambiguously. It is hard to disentangle them from uncontrolled factors confounded with them. However, they are sufficiently important and well researched to deserve some consideration.

Sex. The results in relation to sex depend a great deal on the kind of helping. In motoring contexts, females are helped more, whether in broken-down cars (Penner *et al*., 1973; West *et al*., 1975; Simon, 1976; Ahmed, 1979) or as hitch-hikers (Pomazal & Clore, 1973; Snyder *et al.*, 1974; Morgan *et al.*, 1975). Conversely, male drivers help more (Pomazal & Clore, 1973; West *et al.*, 1975), possibly reflecting their greater competence or familiarity with car-related activities. When males and females are equally able to help in a motoring context, they do help equally. For example, Clark *et al.* (1976) found that males and females were equally likely to turn off the headlights of a car left with them on. The most surprising result is that reported by Skolnick (1977), namely that, while males and females in broken-down cars were helped equally, females on a lonely road at night were the least likely to be helped of all conditions. Skolnick speculated that drivers might have suspected a trap in these cases.

In experiments in which the help is given by telephone, females tend to be helped more (Simon, 1971; Thayer, 1973; Clark, 1974; Rotton, 1977), although Franklin (1974) found no difference. There is no consistent tendency for males to help more than females, although Gaertner and Bickman (1971) reported more helping by males and Wunderlich and Willis (1977) more helping by females. It may be significant in the latter study that the recipient was a child. In the non-reactive lost letter technique, females also tend to be helped more (Farrington & Knight, 1979; Farrington & Knight, 1980b), although Benson *et al.* (1976) found no sex difference. Males and females were equally likely to help in these three studies, and also in the lost letter research of Knox and McTiernan (1973). Bihm *et al.* (1979) reported an interesting interaction effect, with females especially helping females and males especially helping males.

The findings are less consistent in research in which people can help by picking up dropped groceries or other objects. All three possibilities of females being helped more (Latané & Dabbs, 1975; Murray & Vincenzo, 1976), males being helped more (Valentine & Ehrlichman, 1979) and no sex difference (Karabenick *et al.*, 1973) have been reported. Similarly, all three possibilities of females helping more (Lerner & Frank, 1974), males helping more (Latané & Dabbs, 1975; Samerotte & Harris, 1976) and no sex difference in helping (Karabenick *et al.*, 1973; Edwards, 1975; Murray & Vincenzo, 1976) have been reported. In complying with small requests such as for directions or change, females tend to be helped more (Pearce, 1980; Sissons, 1981), although again some researchers have found no sex difference (Feinman, 1978; Rushton, 1978). The sex of the helper usually has no effect (Harris, 1972; Harris *et al.*, 1973a; Harris & Samerotte, 1975; Rushton, 1978; Sissons, 1981), although males helped more in the research of Kleinke (1977a, 1977b) and Feinman (1978).

In experiments on donating by children, males and females usually give equally (Dlugolinski & Firestone, 1973; Rubin & Schneider, 1973; Rushton & Owen, 1975; Yarrow & Waxler, 1976; Grusec *et al.*, 1978b; Grusec *et al.*, 1979). O'Bryant and Brophy (1976) found that, while there was no sex difference in donating, females helped a younger child more, and Harris and Siebel (1975) reported that females shared more.

Attempting to summarize the results of these experiments, females are helped more than males in many situations. There are few consistent sex differences in helping, although males tend to help more than females in motoring contexts and females may help more than males if the recipient is a child.

Race. Most of the racial comparisons have been between blacks and whites in the United States. In regard to the race of the helper, Shaffer and Graziano (1980) in telephoning, Benson and Catt (1978) in donating to charity, and Doland and Adelberg (1967) in children's sharing, all showed that whites helped more than blacks. On the other hand, Wispé and Freshley (1971) in picking up dropped groceries, and Lerner *et al*. (1971) in giving directions and money, reported no race differences. In their subway research, Piliavin *et al*. (1969) found that whites and blacks helped equally if the victim's distress was due to natural causes, but whites tended to help whites and blacks tended to help blacks when the victim appeared to be drunk.

Moving on to the race of the recipient, the most usual results are for whites to be helped more or for whites and blacks to be helped equally. Whites were helped more in the lost letter research of Benson *et al*. (1976), in the telephoning research of Thayer (1973), Clark (1974) and Franklin (1974), and in the donating research of Bryan and Test (1967). On the other hand, Wunderlich and Willis (1977) and Shaffer and Graziano (1980) in telephoning, Wispé and Freshley (1971) in picking up groceries, and Bickman and Kamzan (1973) in giving money, found that blacks and whites were helped equally. In telephoning, Gaertner and Bickman (1971) reported that whites helped whites more than they helped blacks, but blacks helped whites and blacks equally. Katz *et al*. (1975) obtained some interesting results, namely that members of the public were more willing to answer questions for a black interviewer than for a white one, although they were more likely to give change to a white man than to a black. Finally, the campus experiment of Dutton and Lake (1973) is worth mentioning, since they found that whites gave more to whites than to blacks if they received false physiological feedback suggesting that they were prejudiced.

Attempting to summarize these results, there are either no racial differences in helping or a tendency for whites to help and to be helped more.

Nationality. Generally, people help compatriots more than foreigners, or nationality is not related to helping. In two lost letter studies, Howitt *et al*. (1977) and Howitt and McCabe (1978) found that English people helped the English more than Asians or Irish, although Asians helped English and Asians equally. Sissons (1981) also reported that English people helped the English more than they helped Asians in giving change, especially in same-sex encounters. In another experiment on giving change carried out in the United States, Harris and Baudin (1973) discovered that Spanish-Americans helped a Spanish-American more than they helped an Anglo-American. However, Karpienia and Zippel (1974) found no tendency for Irish or Italian people to help their own compatriots more by answering questions, and Pearce (1980) reported that Americans helped Australians and Americans equally in complying with small requests.

Age. In research with children, donating usually increases from about age 7 to about age 13 (Barnett & Bryan, 1974; Emler & Rushton, 1974; Green & Schneider, 1974; White & Burnam, 1975; Underwood *et al.*, 1977; Raviv *et al.*, 1980). Green and Schneider (1974) also showed that helping and sharing increased with age, from about 5 to 14. However, Yarrow and Waxler (1976) found no change in helping and sharing between 3 and 7, and Dlugolinski and Firestone (1973) reported no change in donating between 10 and 13.

With adults, findings are less consistent. Older people help more in returning lost letters (Lowe & Ritchey, 1973; Farrington & Knight, 1979; Farrington & Knight, 1980b), but younger people help more in answering questions (Katz *et al.*, 1975). Age was not related to giving change in the research of Raymond and Unger (1972), nor to lending money in the experiment of Kleinke (1977a), nor to helping to pick up election material in the work of Karabenick *et al.* (1973). There have been few studies which attempted to vary the age of the recipient, but Tipton and Browning (1972b) discovered that older people were helped more in picking up groceries.

Area. There have been very few cross-national studies of helping, but these suggest that helping in the United States is less likely than in some other countries. For example, Luck (1978) reported German replications of some classic studies of helping (Merritt & Fowler, 1948; Gaertner & Bickman, 1971; Latané & Darley, 1970), and found higher helping rates in West Germany than in the United States. Innes (1974) and Innes and Gilroy (1980) replicated Langer and Abelson's (1972) research, on asking people to post a bulky parcel, in Scotland and Australia, and again reported higher helping rates than in the original American study. Huang and Harris (1973) also found higher helping rates in Taiwan than in the United States. However, Feldman (1968) discovered no tendency for helping to be less in Boston than in Paris or Athens. His major interest was in the treatment of compatriots as opposed to foreigners, and he showed that compatriots were helped more in Boston and Paris but less in Athens. The number of uncontrolled variables is so large in these cross-national studies that it is difficult to draw definite conclusions.

Helping is usually greater in rural areas or small towns than in cities. This has been shown using the lost letter technique (Korte & Kerr, 1975; Hansson & Slade, 1977), in complying with a variety of small requests (Milgram, 1970; Merrens, 1973; Rushton, 1978), in telephoning for help (McKenna, 1976), and in answering questions (House & Wolf, 1978). However, Forbes and Gromoll (1971) found no difference in lost letter return rates between large, medium and small towns, and Korte *et al*. (1975) reported no city – town differences in helping in Holland. Some researchers (Lowe & Ritchey, 1973; Knox & McTiernan, 1973) have discovered more helping in wealthier areas, but Farrington and Knight (1979, 1980b) reported that lost letter return rates were not related to the social class or type (e.g. shopping, offices, residential) of area.

Physical Factors. Generally, helping is greater in sunny weather (Ahmed, 1979; Cunningham, 1979), although other researchers have found no relationship between helping and time of day (Skolnick, 1977; Farrington & Knight, 1979; Farrington & Knight, 1980b). In motoring experiments, helping is more likely, although slower, on lonely roads (Hurley & Allen, 1974; Mason & Allen, 1976; Skolnick, 1977; Ahmed, 1979). Again, because of the confounded variables, these results will not be discussed further.

7.3.2 *Recipient Characteristics and Behaviour*

This section will discuss what is known about helping in relation to characteristics of the recipient, notably appearance, the presence or absence of some kind of handicap, attractiveness, need, political affiliation, and similarity to the helper. It will also discuss the effects of the behaviour of the recipient, especially in terms of asking for help, gazing at the helper, and behaving pleasantly or unpleasantly to the helper.

Appearance. Generally, persons dressed smartly are helped more than those dressed untidily, for example as hippies. This has been shown in giving change (Raymond & Unger, 1972; Harris & Baudin, 1973), giving money (Bickman, 1971; Kleinke, 1977b), signing petitions (Keasey & Tomlinson-Keasey, 1973; Chaikin *et al*., 1974), answering questions (Walker *et al*., 1980), giving directions (Schiavo *et al*., 1974) and allowing someone into a house to make a telephone call (Feinman, 1978). Conversely, hippies are more likely to be reported for shoplifting (Steffensmeier & Terry, 1973; Steffensmeier & Steffensmeier, 1977), although Gelfand *et al*. (1973) did not find this. Dress seems to have less effect on employees than on members of the public, since Kroll and Moren (1977) reported that dress did not influence helping by librarians, and Brigham and Richardson (1979) discovered that dress did not influence helping by shop employees. Green and Giles (1973) found that men entering a Conservative club were more likely to answer questions if the researcher wore a tie, whereas wearing a tie did not influence the helpfulness of men entering a transport café.

Aspects of appearance other than dress can also influence helping. For example, Graf and Riddell (1972) showed that white males with short hair were helped in a motoring context more than white males with long hair. Similarly, the appearance of a person's car can influence helping, although findings on this tend to be contradictory. Clark *et al*. (1976) found that people were more likely to turn off lights on a low price car than on a high price car, but Solomon and Herman (1977) reported that people were more likely to help someone pick up groceries being loaded into a new, shiny car rather than an old, dirty one.

Handicap. It has often been found that people with some kind of physical handicap are helped more than those without any handicap. For example, Levitt and Kornhaber (1977) reported that people with a leg brace or on crutches were given more money, and Ungar (1979) discovered that someone wearing an eyepatch was given directions more, providing he stayed close to the helper. Doob and Ecker (1970) showed that housewives were more likely to complete a questionnaire if the requester had an eyepatch, and Cairns and Bochner (1974) found that lost letters were returned more if they were addressed to a handicapped children's aid group. Somerotte and Harris (1976) obtained more help in picking up envelopes if the recipient was bandaged than if he was wearing an eyepatch or not handicapped. On the other hand, Walker *et al.* (1980) reported that people were no more likely to answer questions if the requester had an arm in a sling, and Pomazal and Clore (1973) found that a hitch-hiker with a knee brace and a sling was less likely to be picked up.

Other kinds of physical difficulties do not lead to consistent increases in helping. For example, Piliavin and Piliavin (1972) discovered that persons who collapsed in the subway were less likely to be helped if they had blood trickling from the mouth. In their earlier subway experiments, Piliavin *et al.* (1969) showed that a person who collapsed was less likely to be helped if he appeared to be drunk than if he appeared to be ill. Staub and Baer (1974) studied helping of someone who collapsed on the street either holding his knee or with his hand on his heart, but obtained contradictory results in two experiments.

It could be that there are two effects acting in opposite directions in these experiments (cf. Staub, 1978, p. 239). Handicapped people are more in need, and increased need might lead to increased helping. On the other hand, the potential costs and inconvenience of helping are likely to increase with the severity of the handicap, and therefore increased handicap might lead to decreased helping. Whether physical handicap produces increased helping in any given situation may depend on the degree and kind of handicap and the degree and kind of helping.

Attractiveness. Physically attractive people tend to be helped more than others. For example, Sroufe *et al.* (1977) reported that people who found a coin in a telephone booth were more likely to return it if the recipient was attractive, and Benson *et al.* (1976) found that they were more likely to post a lost letter if the beneficiary was attractive. In the subway research of Piliavin *et al.* (1975), recipients who were facially disfigured by a red birthmark were helped less, and Soble and Strickland (1974) discovered that housewives were unwilling to answer questions if the interviewer was a hunchback. In the hitch-hiking research of Morgan *et al.* (1975), a female with an augmented bust was more likely to be picked up, although this tendency did not reach statistical significance. However, Bull and Stevens (1980) found that people were no less willing to be interviewed by someone with unsightly teeth, and Tipton and Browning (1972b) reported that fat people were helped more in picking up groceries. In the latter case, it could be that any effect of unattractiveness was outweighed by the perceived need.

Need. Children tend to share with and donate to deserving recipients more than less deserving ones. For example, Zinser *et al.* (1975) found that they donated more to poor recipients, Krantz and Andrews (1979) showed that they shared more with under-rewarded people, and Barnett (1975) and Miller and

Smith (1977) reported that they donated more to children who were unable to play than to those who had played and lost. However, Emler and Rushton (1974) could detect no effect of the poverty of the recipient on children's donating.

There has been less research on this topic with adults, apart from campus experiments such as that of Harrell and Goltz (1980), who showed that students were more likely to intervene to prevent a theft if the victim had money problems. However, Benson and Catt (1978) found that people donated to charity more if the recipients were not responsible for their plight. Also, Harris and Meyer (1973) and Lesk and Zippel (1975) reported that people helped more in giving signatures if the recipients needed the help more (to avoid failing a course).

Political Affiliation and Similarity. Lost letter experiments have shown dramatic differences in helping rates according to the political affiliation of the recipient. For example, Cahill and Sherrets (1979) found a return rate of 84% for letters addressed to 'Medical Research Associates', as opposed to 62% for a control condition (Mr Carnap) and only 36% for 'Friends of the Nazi Party'. Hansson and Slade (1977) reported a 13% return rate for letters addressed to the Communist Party, in comparison with 46% for a control address. In telephone research, Shaffer and Graziano (1980) showed that recipients associated with more reputable or traditional associations were helped more.

Generally, people help those who are similar in attitudes or political preferences more than others. Three lost letter studies (Hornstein *et al.*, 1971; Sole *et al.*, 1975; Tucker *et al.*, 1977), mostly concerned with attitudes to Arabs in Jewish neighbourhoods, consistently indicated more helping of those with similar opinions. Karabenick *et al.* (1973) reported that people were more likely to help pick up election literature if it was congruent with their own political preference, although the similarity effect was not seen in helping to pick up literature which was for or against capital punishment (Karabenick *et al.*, 1975).

Asking for Help. Several experiments with students (e.g. Yakimovich & Saltz, 1971; Clark & Word, 1972) indicate more helping if the recipient cried out for help. This has rarely been investigated in naturalistic settings. Murray and Vincenzo (1976) reported more helping to find a contact lens if the recipient asked for help, but Samerotte and Harris (1976) did not find that this resulted in more helping to pick up envelopes. Moriarty (1975) showed that people were more likely to intervene to prevent a theft on a beach if the recipient asked them to look after his belongings, and this has also been found in campus research (e.g. Shaffer *et al.*, 1975).

Eye Contact. In hitch-hiking research, helping is more likely if the recipient gazes or stares at the driver (Snyder *et al.*, 1974; Morgan *et al.*, 1975). However, Ellsworth and Langer (1976) reported that staring had no effect on being helped in a store. Valentine and Ehrlichman (1979) found that, although there was no main effect of gaze on helping to pick up coins, females helped females more and males helped males less. They suggested that a male – male gaze was interpreted as hostile, while a female – female gaze was seen as friendly. The result with females was replicated by Valentine (1980). Kleinke (1977a) showed that people were more likely to return or lend money when they were gazed at and touched by the recipient, but Konecni *et al.* (1975) reported that helping to pick things up was less likely if the recipient had previously stood close to the helper. This latter result seems to conflict with some student findings (Baron & Bell, 1976).

Previous Behaviour of the Recipient. Generally, recipients are helped more if they have previously been pleasant rather than unpleasant to the helper. Allen (1972) found in subway research that confederates were helped less if they had previously been threatening or sarcastic, and Katz *et al.* (1975) and Kriss *et al.* (1974) showed that a politer and more pleasant appeal was more successful in eliciting helping on the telephone. In the research of Tidd and Lockard (1978), a cocktail waitress received more tips if she approached customers with a wider smile. Bickman and Green (1975) found that people were particularly likely to be unhelpful to a shoplifter (by intervening or reporting him) if he had previously been rude to them. In a study with children, Staub and Sherk (1970) reported that they shared more if the recipient had previously shared with them. All these results suggest some reciprocity in helping.

Mere familiarity can also influence helping. For example, Pearce (1980) discovered that familiar strangers (fellow bus travellers) helped more in answering small requests than unfamiliar strangers. This has also been found in campus research. For example, Howard & Crano (1974) showed that students were more likely to intervene to prevent a theft if they had previously had a conversation with the victim.

7.3.3 Mood and Motive

This section will discuss what is known about helping in relation to the mood of the helper, including such concepts as guilt, arousal and attribution. It will also discuss helping in relation to the motive or reason for help, including the costs or benefits of helping. Much of the research carried out with students in recent years has been concerned with these topics. As always, priority will be given to naturalistic experiments, but mention will be made of some of the campus studies.

Mood. Research with students in the 1960s suggested that helping was greater after they had administered electric shock (Carlsmith & Gross, 1969) or upset a stack of computer cards (Freedman *et al.*, 1967). In naturalistic experiments, Konecni (1972) and Samerotte and Harris (1976) also found more help to pick up dropped objects after members of the public believed that they had caused some objects to drop. In the research of Regan *et al.* (1972) and Cunningham *et al.* (1980), people who were led to believe that they were responsible for the malfunctioning of a camera were more likely to help pick up dropped groceries. One possible explanation for these results is to suggest that transgression produces guilt, which in turn is alleviated by helping. Following this argument, people will help less if their guilt is reduced. In agreement with this and with the assumption that confessing in the Roman Catholic church decreases guilt, Harris *et al.* (1975) reported that people entering a church during confessional hours were more likely to donate to charity than others who were leaving.

Generally, people who are in a good mood are more likely to help. If someone finds a coin in the slot of a telephone booth, he is more likely to help in picking up papers (Isen & Levin, 1972; Cunningham *et al.*, 1980) or returning lost keys (Forbes & TeVault, 1975). Blevins and Murphy (1974) failed to detect any effect on helping of finding a coin, but their research involved very small numbers. Isen *et al.* (1976) discovered that people who were given free packets of stationery helped more in telephoning, and Harris *et al.* (1973b) reported more helping after people were given free cookies. The results of Isen and Noonberg (1979), showing less donation to charity when people were shown a picture of a handicapped child than when they were merely shown a simple logo, might be explained on the basis of a negative mood decreasing helping.

Several studies (Moore *et al.*, 1973; Rosenhan *et al.*, 1974; Underwood *et al.*, 1977) indicate that children will donate more if they are asked to reminisce about happy experiences and less if they are asked to reminisce about sad ones. However, Cialdini and Kenrick (1976) and Kenrick *et al.* (1979) found that children donated more after sad reminiscences than after neutral ones, and Harris and Siebel (1975) reported no effect on sharing of thinking happy or sad thoughts. Children who have been successful in a game (Isen *et al.*, 1973; Barnett & Bryan, 1974) or who have been overpaid (Long & Lerner, 1974; Miller & Smith, 1977) also tend to donate more, although McGuire and Thomas (1975) found that only males shared less after failure. Another result which might be mentioned is the demonstration by Grusec *et al.* (1978a) that children who were complimented by being told 'you're the kind of person who likes to help' tended to donate and share more. This might be explained either on the basis of a good mood or on self-attribution.

Recent research with students has tended to concentrate on arousal and attribution rather than mood, although Fried and Berkowitz (1979) reported more helping after soothing music. Harris and Huang (1973) found that students helped less if they could attribute arousal symptoms to a noise, and Gaertner and Dovidio (1977) and Coke *et al.* (1978) obtained slower helping if students could attribute arousal to a drug. In agreement with the hypothesis that arousal mediates helping, Gaertner and Dovidio discovered a significant correlation (0.61) between increased heart rate and relatively fast intervention in an emergency. On the other hand, Caldwell and Harris (1979) did not find any effect of noise on the likelihood of intervening to prevent a theft. One study with students which is worth quoting because of its ingenuity is Darley and Batson's (1973), showing that seminary students on their way to give a talk on the parable of the good samaritan were no more likely to stop to help someone lying by the side of the road than were others. (Their conclusion has been questioned by Greenwald, 1975.)

Motive. Generally, helping is more likely when the reason for helping is more legitimate. For example, members of the public are more likely to help post a package if the recipient is late for a train than if she merely wishes to go shopping (Langer & Abelson, 1972; Innes, 1974; Kleinke *et al*., 1978; Innes & Gilroy, 1980). Similarly, people will give more money for a sandwich than for cake (Harris & Samerotte, 1976) and more for milk than for cookie dough (Bickman & Kamzan, 1973).

Helping is also more likely if people are told that it will make them feel good rather than if they are told that it is their social responsibility (Benson & Catt, 1978), and there is a good deal of research suggesting that people are responsive to costs and benefits when deciding whether to help. For example, people help less when it involves more effort in the way of questions to answer (Baer & Goldman, 1978), or when it might have negative consequences in the future, as when someone is asked to give his telephone number (Harris & Meyer, 1973; Lesk & Zippel, 1975). People help more when it is more important (Deaux, 1973; Barefoot & Strickland, 1977), and less when it is more embarrassing, as when a person can help by picking up a dropped packet of Tampax (Edwards, 1975). There is also a tendency for members of the public to help more when escape is more difficult, as when a person collapses nearby (Staub & Baer, 1974). Helping also decreases with increasing cost, whether in terms of money (Simon & Gillen, 1971; Knox & McTiernan, 1973; Farrington & Knight, 1979) or in potential loss of sales to customers (Schaps, 1972). Research with students also suggests that helping depends on costs and benefits (e.g. Wilson & Kahn, 1975; Weyant, 1978). However, in the research of Bickman & Helwig (1979) it was surprising that the likelihood of reporting shoplifting was not affected by the rewards offered by the shop or by the likelihood of publicity.

7.3.4 Models and Bystanders

Models. People are more likely to help if they observe someone else (a model) helping. The importance of models was demonstrated in some early campus experiments on volunteering to participate in research (Rosenbaum & Blake, 1955) and on signing a petition (Helson *et al*., 1958). Bryan and Test (1967) showed a significant effect of a model on stopping to help someone in a broken-down car and on donating to charity, and Macaulay (1970) confirmed the latter result. Solomon and Grota (1976) found a modelling effect in picking up a folder in a mild emergency, and Catt and Benson (1977) discovered that people's contributions to charity were influenced by the proportion of others they thought had contributed. In a rare study using different kinds of helping, Harris *et al*. (1973a) showed an effect on giving money of observing someone help pick up cards. In lost letter research, Hornstein *et al*. (1968) found that a modelling effect was especially likely if the model was similar to the helper,

Hornstein (1970) reported a modelling effect particularly when the model was responding to recipient need rather than social pressure or reciprocity, and Gross (1975) obtained imitation especially of a generous model.

More research on modelling has been carried out with children than with adults. Children who see a model donate are more likely to donate themselves, but this is not true, or much less true, of children who see a model advocate donating (Rosenhan & White, 1967; Bryan & Walbek, 1970; Grusec & Skubiski, 1970; Grusec, 1972; White & Burnam, 1975; Dressel & Midlarsky, 1978). The results of Poulos and Liebert (1972), Rushton (1975) and Rice and Grusec (1975) are unusual in showing that both the words and deeds of the model had an effect. Additionally, Rushton (1975) and Rice and Grusec (1975) found that the effects persisted over several months, whereas others (Rushton & Owen, 1975; Grusec *et al.*, 1978b) reported that the effects of a model's behaviour disappeared within three weeks. Rushton and Littlefield (1979) showed that a donating model had no effect on children's sharing, and Grusec *et al.* (1978b) discovered that children were less likely to help by picking things up after seeing a donating model. Therefore, the evidence for the durability and generalizability of modelling effects is not conclusive.

Characteristics of the model, and the consequences of helping, also affect children's imitation. Grusec and Skubiski (1970) found that a highly nurturant model was likely to be imitated, Presbie and Coiteux (1971) demonstrated that a praised model was likely to produce sharing, and conversely Morris *et al.* (1973) showed that a punished non-sharing model resulted in an increase in children's sharing. It might be expected that television programmes could encourage helpfulness, and indeed Sprafkin *et al.* (1975) reported that children who had watched a programme about a boy helping a dog were more likely to help a dog themselves when given an opportunity to do so. However, in more naturalistic research, Friedrich and Stein (1975) and Friedrich-Cofer *et al.* (1979) found little effect of prosocial television programmes on helping.

Bystanders. Latané and Darley (1970) showed that helping in several different settings was more likely if the helper was alone than if he was in the presence of one or more bystanders. These results have since been replicated, for example by Konecni and Ebbesen (1975) in helping a collapsed person and by Latané and Dabbs (1975) in picking up dropped objects. However, Harris *et al.* (1975) found more donating by persons accompanied by females than by those alone, Lerner *et al.* (1971) reported no decrease in giving directions with group size, and Bihm *et al.* (1979) and Farrington and Knight (1979) demonstrated that lost letter return rates were not significantly affected by the presence of others.

Bystanders who suggest that helping is appropriate have a big effect, on assisting a collapsed person (Borges & Penta, 1977) and on reporting shoplifting (Bickman & Rosenbaum, 1977; Bickman, 1979). Authoritative-looking bystanders who order helping are similarly effective (Bickman, 1974). Research with children has compared donating in public and in private, but the results are inconsistent. Long and Lerner (1974) found no difference between these conditions, but Kenrick *et al*. (1979) reported more donating in public, in agreement with some campus research (Satow, 1975).

7.3.5 Effects of Prior Helping Experiences

The Foot in the Door. Generally, agreeing to an initial small request increases the probability of agreeing to a subsequent larger one. This was called the 'foot in the door' phenomenon by Freedman and Fraser (1966). They showed that housewives who were initially asked to answer a few questions were more likely to allow a survey team into their homes later. These results were essentially replicated by Baer and Goldman (1978). Harris (1972) found that people were more likely to give money after giving directions, and Pliner *et al*. (1974) reported that people donated to charity more after agreeing to wear a lapel pin.

Whether members of the public who are initially asked to agree to a large request are subsequently more likely to agree to a smaller one is uncertain. Miller and Suls (1977) demonstrated that helping to pick up groceries was greater after a small request and less after a large one, in comparison with no request (for directions). Similar results were obtained by Snyder and Cunningham (1975) in relation to answering small or large numbers of questions. However, Cann *et al*. (1975) showed that helping to give out pamphlets was greater one week after a large request than after a smaller one. In these kinds of studies, the majority of people tend to refuse the initial large request. For example, in a campus experiment (Cialdini *et al*., 1975) everyone refused a request to counsel juvenile delinquents for two years.

Learning to Help. It might be expected that, if a person helps and is rewarded for it, this will increase his likelihood of helping on a second occasion. Conversely, if a person helps and is punished for it, this might decrease his likelihood of helping subsequently. Moss and Page (1972) carried out an experiment in which people were first asked for directions by a confederate, who reacted positively or negatively, and then had the opportunity to help pick up dropped groceries. They found decreased helping after a negative reaction, but no increase after a positive reaction. Tipton and Browning (1972a) had picking up dropped packages as the first helping act and helping to push someone in a wheelchair up a kerb as the second. Those who helped in the first case were less likely to help in the second, whether they were rewarded or punished, in comparison with a control group not exposed to the first helping opportunity. However, in research with children, Gelfand *et al*. (1975) showed that donating was increased by praising, and Hartmann *et al*. (1976) reported that it was increased by fines for not donating. Barton and Ascione (1979) also demonstrated that children could be taught to share by praising, and that the effect persisted over four weeks. Why findings with adults seem to differ from those with children is not clear.

Labelling after helping can affect subsequent helping by adults and children. Kraut (1973) and Swinyard and Ray (1979) showed that positive labelling of people as generous or interested in others increased subsequent donations to charity, while Steele (1975) found increased helping even after negative labelling as not interested in others. With children, Grusec and Redler (1980) reported increased donating by those who were told that they were helpful. The results of Uranowitz (1975), in which people were asked to look after packages and later had an opportunity to help by picking up a package, might be interpreted as showing that those who labelled themselves as helpful in the first situation were more likely to help in the second.

7.4 Conclusions

7.4.1 What is Known about Helping?

This section will attempt to summarize what has been learned about helping in naturalistic experiments. Beginning with sex, females are helped more than males in many settings. There are few consistent sex differences in helping, although males tend to help more in motoring contexts and females may help more if the recipient is a child. In comparisons between whites and blacks in the United States, there are either no racial differences in helping or a tendency for whites to help and to be helped more. People tend to help compatriots more than foreigners, or sometimes nationality is unrelated to helping. In research with children, helping often increases with age, but results with adults are inconsistent. Helping may be less in the United States than in some other countries, and it is usually greater in rural areas or small towns than in cities. It is also greater in sunny weather and on lonely roads.

Persons dressed smartly are helped more than those dressed untidily or deviantly, and those with physical handicaps are often helped more. Physically attractive and more deserving people also tend to be helped more, as do persons who are similar in attitudes or political preferences to the helper. Helping is more likely if the recipient gazes at the helper or if the recipient has previously been pleasant to him. People who feel guilty, and those who are in a good mood, are more likely to help. Helping is more likely when the reason for help is more legitimate, when the costs are low and when the benefits are great.

People are more likely to help if they observe someone else helping. It is not certain if people help more when they are alone or with others, but bystanders who suggest helping can have a large effect on it. Generally, agreeing to an initial small request increases the probability of agreeing to a subsequent larger one. Children's helping can be increased by the use of rewards and punishments, and labelling can also increase helping.

7.4.2 How can Helping be Explained?

No existing theory is sufficiently wide-ranging to explain all the results summarized in Section 7.4.1. At a minimum, it seems necessary to break down the helping process into perception and decision stages, and to consider the interaction between the type of individual and the type of situation. It seems desirable to include some idea of mood or arousal in the perception stage, possibly in conjunction with attribution. It also seems desirable to include some cost – benefit ideas in the decision stage. Any theory needs to be dynamic as well as static, considering how helping is learned and including the importance of models. Theories arising from experiments stress immediate, situational factors, and these need to be combined with the historical or individual factors arising from other research methods. The operational definition of theoretical concepts is always a problem.

7.4.3 *How can Helping be Increased?*

Assuming that helping in certain kinds of situations is socially desirable, how can it be increased? One possibility would be to require helping in the law (see, e.g. Huston & Korte, 1976; Kaplan, 1978). With rare exceptions, Anglo – American law does not oblige people to help others. In English common law, if a policeman is concerned with a breach of the peace and calls for assistance from a member of the public, that person is required to help and is committing an offence if he does not. Some American states have passed 'Good Samaritan' laws which shield doctors (and sometimes others) from liability if they stop voluntarily to help at roadside emergencies. However, only Vermont has followed the example of France and some other European countries in requiring people by law to give assistance to those in danger.

Whether helping could be increased by a change in the law is uncertain. Berkowitz and Walker (1967) and Walker and Argyle (1964) found little evidence that changes in the law affected attitudes or moral judgements. It seems more likely that helping could be increased by the systematic application of rewards for helping and punishments for not helping, together with the judicious use of models. Much research has been carried out on the modification of delinquent behaviour (see, e.g. Farrington, 1979a), and more is needed on the modification of helping behaviour.

7.4.4 *Helping Research in the 1980s*

Researchers on helping in the 1980s should be especially concerned with internal and external validity. In order to maximize both, the preferred method should be naturalistic experimentation, concentrating on helping behaviour rather than words. Researchers should seek better methods of controlling independent and extraneous variables in naturalistic settings.

Researchers should also carry out correlational, observational studies to generate hypotheses. Correlational research should also be used to validate operational definitions of helping used in experiments against external criteria of helping. It should also be used to develop a classification system for helping behaviour, to investigate the relationships among different kinds of helping, the extent of generality as opposed to specificity, and the number of different theoretical concepts being measured by the empirical variables. Before carrying out experiments, more information is needed about the dependent variable of helping. Correlational research is also desirable to establish the longitudinal and situational consistency of individuals in helping, and hence the extent to which it might be meaningful to postulate a stable personality trait of helpfulness. Correlational research is also useful in showing the relative importance of a large number of independent variables and the ways in which they interact, and also the relationships between helping and other kinds of behaviour.

Because of the large number of naturalistic experiments, it is no exaggeration to suggest that more is known about real-life helping than about any other real-life social behaviour. It is to be hoped that future social psychology research will build on this solid foundation and not be diverted by the vagaries of fashion.

References

ADERMAN, D. and BERKOWITZ, L. (1970). Observational set, empathy, and helping. *Journal of Personality & Social Psychology*, **14**, 141 – 148.

AHMED, S.S. (1979). Helping behaviour as predicted by diffusion of responsibility, exchange theory, and traditional sex norm. *Journal of Social Psychology*, **109**, 153 – 154.

ALLEN, H. (1972). Bystander intervention and helping on the subway. In L. BICKMAN and T. HENCHY (Eds.), *Beyond the Laboratory: Field Research in Social Psychology*. New York: McGraw-Hill.

ARONFREED, J. (1970). The socialization of altruistic and sympathetic behaviour: some theoretical and experimental analyses. In J. MACAULAY and L. BERKOWITZ (Eds.), *Altruism and Helping Behaviour*. New York: Academic Press.

ARONFREED, J. (1976). Moral development from the standpoint of a general psychological theory. In T. LICKONA (Ed.), *Moral Development and Behaviour*. New York: Holt, Rinehart & Winston.

BAER, R. and GOLDMAN, M. (1978). Compliance as a function of prior compliance, familiarization, effort and benefits: the foot-in-the-door technique extended. *Psychological Reports*, **43**, 887 – 893.

BAREFOOT, J.C. and STRICKLAND, L.H. (1977). The confidentiality of 'confidential' lost letters. *Journal of Social Psychology*, **101**, 123 – 126.

BARNETT, M.A. (1975). Effects of competition and relative deservedness of the other's fate on children's generosity. *Developmental Psychology*, **11**, 665 – 666.

BARNETT, M.A. and BRYAN, J.H. (1974). Effects of competition with outcome feedback on children's helping behaviour. *Developmental Psychology*, **10**, 838 – 842.

BARON, R.A. and BELL, P.A. (1976). Physical distance and helping: some unexpected benefits of 'crowding in' on others. *Journal of Applied Social Psychology*, **6**, 95 – 104.

BARRETT, D.E (1979). Relations between aggressive and prosocial behaviours in children. *Journal of Genetic Psychology*, **134**, 317 – 318.

BAR-TAL, D., NADLER, A. and BLECHMAN, N. (1980a). The relationship between Israeli children's helping behaviour and their perception of parents' socialization practices. *Journal of Social Psychology*, **111**, 159 – 167.

BAR-TAL D., RAVIV, A. and LEISER, T. (1980b). The development of altruistic

behaviour: further evidence. *Developmental Psychology*, **16**, 516 – 524.
BARTON, E.J. and ASCIONE, F.R. (1979). Sharing in preschool children: facilitation, stimulus generalization, response generalization, and maintenance. *Journal of Applied Behaviour Analysis*, **12**, 417 – 430.
BASKETT, G.D., PEET, J.G., BRADFORD, D. and MULAIK, S.A. (1973). An examination of the lost-letter technique. *Journal of Applied Social Psychology*, **3**, 165 – 173.
BECKER-HAVEN, J.F. and LINDSKOLD, S. (1978). Deindividuation manipulations, self-consciousness, and bystander intervention. *Journal of Social Psychology*, **105**, 113 – 121.
BENSON, P.L. and CATT, V.L.(1978). Soliciting charity contributions: the parlance of asking for money. *Journal of Applied Social Psychology*, **8**, 84 – 95.
BENSON, P.L., KARABENICK, S.A. and LERNER, R.M. (1976). Pretty pleases: the effects of physical attractiveness, race, and sex on receiving help. *Journal of Experimental Social Psychology*, **12**, 409 – 415.
BERKOWITZ, L. (1972). Social norms, feelings, and other factors affecting helping and altruism. In L. BERKOWITZ (Ed.), *Advances in Experimental Social Psychology*, Vol. 6. New York: Academic Press.
BERKOWITZ, L. (1973). Reactance and the unwillingness to help others. *Psychological Bulletin*, **79**, 310 – 317.
BERKOWITZ, L. and WALKER N. (1967). Laws and moral judgments. *Sociometry*, **30**, 410 – 422.
BICKMAN, L. (1971). The effect of social status on the honesty of others. *Journal of Social Psychology*, **85**, 87 – 92.
BICKMAN, L. (1974). The social power of a uniform. *Journal of Applied Social Psychology*, **4**, 47 – 61.
BICKMAN, L. (1975). Bystander intervention in a crime: the effect of a mass-media campaign. *Journal of Applied Social Psychology*, **5**, 296 – 302.
BICKMAN, L. (1976). Attitude toward an authority and the reporting of a crime. *Sociometry*, **39**, 76 – 82.
BICKMAN, L. (1979). Interpersonal influence and the reporting of a crime. *Personality & Social Psychology Bulletin*, **5**, 32 – 35.
BICKMAN, L. and GREEN, S. (1975). Is revenge sweet? The effect of attitude toward a thief on crime reporting. *Criminal Justice & Behaviour*, **2**, 101 – 112.
BICKMAN, L. and HELWIG, H. (1979). Bystander reporting of a crime: The impact of incentives. *Criminology*, **17**, 283 – 300.
BICKMAN, L. and KAMZAN, M. (1973). The effect of race and need on helping behaviour. *Journal of Social Psychology*, **89**, 73 – 77.
BICKMAN, L. and ROSENBAUM, D.P. (1977). Crime reporting as a function of bystander encouragement, surveillance, and credibility. *Journal of Personality & Social Psychology*, **35**, 577 – 586.
BIHM, E., GAUDET, I. and SALE, O. (1979). Altruistic responses under conditions of anonymity. *Journal of Social Psychology*, **109**, 25 – 30.
BLACK, C.R., WEINSTEIN, E.A. and TANUR, J.M. (1980). Development of expectations of altruism versus self-interest. *Journal of Social Psychology*, **111**, 105 – 112.
BLEVINS, G.A. and MURPHY, T. (1974). Feeling good and helping: Further phone-booth findings. *Psychological Reports*, **34**, 326.
BLOOM, L.M. and CLARK, R.D. (1976). The cost – reward model of helping behaviour: a nonconfirmation. *Journal of Applied Social Psychology*, **6**, 76 – 84.
BOLTON, G.M. (1974). The lost letter technique as a measure of community attitudes toward a major social issue. *Sociological Quarterly*, **15**, 567 – 570.
BORGES, M.A. and PENTA, J.M. (1977). Effects of third party intercession on bystander

intervention. *Journal of Social Psychology*, **103**, 27 – 32.
BRENNER, A.R. and LEVIN, J.M. (1973). Off-duty policemen and bystander 'apathy'. *Journal of Police Science & Administration*, **1**, 61 – 64.
BRIGHAM, J.C. and RICHARDSON, C.B. (1979). Race, sex, and helping in the marketplace. *Journal of Applied Social Psychology*, **9**, 314 – 322.
BRYAN, J.H. (1972). Why children help: a review. *Journal of Social Issues*, **28** (3), 87 – 104.
BRYAN, J.H. and TEST, M.A. (1967). Models and helping: naturalistic studies in aiding behaviour. *Journal of Personality & Social Psychology*, **6**, 400 – 407.
BRYAN, J.H. and WALBEK, N.H. (1970). Preaching and practising generosity: children's actions and reactions. *Child Development*, **41**, 329 – 353.
BULL, R. and STEVENS, J. (1980). Effect of unsightly teeth on helping behaviour. *Perceptual & Motor Skills*, **51**, 438.
BURTON, R.V. (1976). Honesty and dishonesty. In T. LICKONA (Ed.), *Moral Development and Behaviour*. New York: Holt, Rinehart & Winston.
CAHILL, N. and SHERRETS, S. (1979). The lost-letter technique: a measure of social and political attitudes in three socio-economic groups. *Psychological Reports*, **45**, 144 – 146.
CAIRNS, L.G. and BOCHNER, S. (1974). Measuring sympathy toward handicapped children with the 'lost letter' technique. *Australian Journal of Psychology*, **26**, 89 – 91.
CALDWELL, J.A. and HARRIS, M.B. (1979). The effect of mood and arousal on confronting a thief. *Journal of Psychology*, **103**, 231 – 239.
CAMPBELL D.T. and STANLEY, J.C. (1966) *Experimental and Quasi-Experimental Designs for Research*. Chicago: Rand-McNally.
CANN, A., SHERMAN, S.J. and ELKES, R. (1975). Effects of initial request size and timing of a second request on compliance: the foot in the door and the door in the face. *Journal of Personality & Social Psychology*, **32**, 774 – 782.
CARLSMITH, J.M. and GROSS, A.E. (1969). Some effects of guilt on compliance. *Journal of Personality & Social Psychology*, **11**, 232 – 239.
CATT, V. and BENSON, P.L. (1977). Effect of verbal modelling on contributions to charity. *Journal of Applied Psychology*, **62**, 81 – 85.
CHAIKIN, A.L., DERLEGA, V.J., YODER, J. and PHILLIPS, D. (1974). The effects of appearance on compliance. *Journal of Social Psychology*, **92**, 199 – 200.
CHERULNIK, P.D. (1975). An independent validation of the lost-letter technique. *Journal of Social Psychology*, **96**, 299 – 300.
CIALDINI, R.B. and ASCANI, K. (1976). Test of a concession procedure for inducing verbal, behavioural, and further compliance with a request to give blood. *Journal of Applied Psychology*, **61**, 295 – 300.
CIALDINI, R.B. and KENRICK, D.T. (1976). Altruism as hedonism: a social development perspective on the relationship of negative mood state and helping. *Journal of Personality & Social Psychology*, **34**, 907 – 914.
CIALDINI, R.B., VINCENT, J.E., LEWIS, S.K., CATALAN, J., WHEELER, D. and DARBY, B.L. (1975). Reciprocal concessions procedure for inducing compliance: the door-in-the-face technique. *Journal of Personality & Social Psychology*, **31**, 206 – 215.
CLARK, R.D. (1974). Effects of sex and race on helping behaviour in a non-reactive setting. *Representative Research in Social Psychology*, **5**, 1 – 6.
CLARK, R.D., MATHERON, M.M. & MATHERON, M.J. (1976). Affluence of victim in helping behaviour. *Psychological Reports*, **38**, 494.
CLARK, R.D. and WORD, L.E. (1972). Why don't bystanders help? Because of ambiguity? *Journal of Personality & Social Psychology*, **24**, 392 – 400.

CLARK, R.D. and WORD, L.E. (1974). Where is the apathetic bystander? Situational characteristics of the emergency. *Journal of Personality & Social Psychology*, **29**, 279 – 287.

COHEN, R. (1978). Altruism: human, cultural, or what? In L. WISPÉ (Ed.), *Altruism, Sympathy, and Helping*. New York: Academic Press.

COKE, J.S., BATSON, C.D. and MCDAVIS, K. (1978). Empathic mediation of helping: a two-stage model. *Journal of Personality & Social Psychology*, **36**, 752 – 766.

CUNNINGHAM, M.R. (1979). Weather, mood, and helping behaviour: quasi-experiments with the sunshine samaritan. *Journal of Personality & Social Psychology*, **37**, 1947 – 1956.

CUNNINGHAM, M.R., STEINBERG, J. and GREV, R. (1980). Wanting to and having to help: separate motivations for positive mood and guilt-induced helping. *Journal of Personality & Social Psychology*, **38**, 181 – 192.

DARLEY, J.M. and BATSON, C.D. (1973). 'From Jerusalem to Jericho': a study of situational and dispositional variables in helping behaviour. *Journal of Personality & Social Psychology*, **27**, 100 – 108.

DEAUX, K. (1973). Anonymous altruism: extending the lost letter technique. *Journal of Social Psychology*, **92**, 61 – 66.

DIENER, E. and CRANDALL, R. (1978). *Ethics in Social and Behavioural Research*. Chicago: University of Chicago Press.

DLUGOLINSKI, E. and FIRESTONE, I.J. (1973). Congruence among four methods of measuring other-centredness. *Child Development*, **44**, 304 – 308.

DOLAND, D.J and ADELBERG, K. (1967). The learning of sharing behaviour. *Child Development*, **38**, 695 – 700.

DOOB, A.N. and ECKER, B.P. (1970). Stigma and compliance. *Journal of Personality & Social Psychology*, **14**, 302 – 304.

DORRIS, J.W. (1972). Reactions to unconditional cooperation: a field study emphasising variables neglected in laboratory research. *Journal of Personality & Social Psychology*, **22**, 387 – 397.

DRESSEL, S. and MIDLARSKY, E. (1978). The effects of model's exhortations, demands and practices on children's donation behaviour. *Journal of Genetic Psychology*, **132**, 211 – 223.

DUTTON, D.G. and LAKE, R.A. (1973). Threat of own prejudice and reverse discrimination in interracial situations. *Journal of Personality & Social Psychology*, **28**, 94 – 100.

DUVAL, S., DUVAL, V.H. and NEELY, R. (1979). Self-focus, felt responsibility, and helping behaviour. *Journal of Personality & Social Psychology*, **37**, 1769 – 1778.

EDWARDS, D.J.A. (1975). Returning a dropped object: effect of response cost and number of potential helpers. *Journal of Social Psychology*, **97**, 169 – 171.

EISENBERG-BERG, N. (1979). Relationship of prosocial moral reasoning to altruism, political liberalism, and intelligence. *Developmental Psychology*, **15**, 87 – 89.

ELLSWORTH, P.C. and LANGER, E.J. (1976). Staring and approach: an interpretation of the stare as a non-specific activator. *Journal of Personality & Social Psychology*, **33**, 117 – 122.

EMLER, N.P. and RUSHTON, J.P. (1974). Cognitive-developmental factors in children's generosity. *British Journal of Social & Clinical Psychology*, **13**, 277 – 281.

FARRINGTON, D.P. (1979a). Delinquent behaviour modification in the natural environment. *British Journal of Criminology*, **19**, 353 – 372.

FARRINGTON, D.P. (1979b). Experiments on deviance with special reference to dishonesty. In L. BERKOWITZ (Ed.), *Advances in Experimental Social Psychology*, Vol. 12 New York: Academic Press.

FARRINGTON, D.P. (1980). External validity: a problem for social psychology. In R.F. KIDD and M.J. SAKS (Eds.), *Advances in Applied Social Psychology*, Vol. 1. Hillsdale: Lawrence Erlbaum.

FARRINGTON, D.P. and KIDD, R.F. (1977). Is financial dishonesty a rational decision? *British Journal of Social & Clinical Psychology*, **16**, 139 – 146.

FARRINGTON, D.P., KNAPP, W.S., ERICKSON, B.E. and KNIGHT, B.J. (1980). Words and deeds in the study of stealing. *Journal of Adolescence*, **3**, 35 – 49.

FARRINGTON, D.P. and KNIGHT, B.J. (1979). Two non-reactive field experiments on stealing from a 'lost' letter. *British Journal of Social and Clinical Psychology*, **18**, 277 – 284.

FARRINGTON, D.P. and KNIGHT, B.J. (1980a). Four studies of stealing as a risky decision. In P.D. LIPSITT and B.D. SALES (Eds.), *New Directions in Psycholegal Research*. New York: Van Nostrand Reinhold.

FARRINGTON, D.P. and KNIGHT, B.J. (1980b). Stealing from a 'lost' letter: effects of victim characteristics. *Criminal Justice & Behaviour*, **7**, 423 – 436.

FEINMAN, S. (1978). When does sex affect altruistic response? *Psychological Reports*, **43**, 1218.

FELDMAN, R.E. (1968). Response to compatriot and foreigner who seek assistance. *Journal of Personality & Social Psychology*, **10**, 202 – 214.

FELDMAN, R.H.L. and REZMOVIC, V. (1979). A field study of the relationship of environmental factors to helping behaviour. *Journal of Social Psychology*, **108**, 283 – 284.

FORBES, G.B. and GROMOLL, H.F. (1971). The lost letter technique as a measure of social variables. *Social Forces*, **50**, 113 – 115.

FORBES, G.B. and TEVAULT, R.K. (1975). The facilitation of anonymous helpfulness by a fortuitous pleasant event. *Journal of Social Psychology*, **97**, 299 – 300.

FORBES, G.B., TEVAULT, R.K. and GROMOLL, H.F. (1972). Regional differences in willingness to help strangers: a field experiment with a new unobtrusive measure. *Social Science Research*, **1**, 415 – 419.

FORSYTH, S.J. (1978). Predicting motorists' altruism. *Psychological Reports*, **43**, 567 – 572.

FRANKLIN, B.J. (1974). Victim characteristics and helping behaviour in a rural Southern setting. *Journal of Social Psychology*, **93**, 93 – 100.

FREEDMAN, J.L. and FRASER, S.C. (1966). Compliance without pressure: The foot-in-the-door technique. *Journal of Personality & Social Psychology*, **4**, 195 – 202.

FREEDMAN, J.L., WALLINGTON, S.A. and BLESS, E. (1967). Compliance without pressure: The effect of guilt. *Journal of Personality & Social Psychology*, **7**, 117 – 124.

FRIED, R. and BERKOWITZ, L. (1979). Music hath charms — and can influence helpfulness. *Journal of Applied Social Psychology*, **9**, 199 – 208.

FRIEDRICH, L.K. and STEIN, A.H. (1975). Prosocial television and young children: the effects of verbal labelling and role playing on learning and behaviour. *Child Development*, **46**, 27 – 38.

FRIEDRICH-COFER, L.K., STEIN, A.H., KIPNIS, D.M., SUSMAN, E.J. and CLEWETT, A.S. (1979). Environmental enhancement of prosocial television content: effects on interpersonal behaviour, imaginative play, and self-regulation in a natural setting. *Developmental Psychology*, **15**, 637 – 646.

GAERTNER, S. and BICKMAN, L. (1971). Effects of race on the elicitation of helping behaviour: the wrong number technique. *Journal of Personality & Social Psychology*, **20**, 218 – 222.

GAERTNER, S.L. and DOVIDIO, J.F. (1977). The subtlety of white racism, arousal, and helping behaviour. *Journal of Personality & Social Psychology*, **35**, 691 – 707.

GELFAND, D.M., HARTMANN, D.P., CROMER, C.C., SMITH, C.L. and PAGE, B.C. (1975). The effects of instructional prompts and praise on children's donation rates. *Child Development*, **46**, 980 – 983.

GELFAND, D.M., HARTMANN, D.P., WALDER, P. and PAGE, P. (1973). Who reports shoplifters? A field-experimental study. *Journal of Personality & Social Psychology*, **25**, 276 – 285.

GEORGOFF, D.M., HERSKER, B.J. and MURDICK, R.G. (1972). The lost-letter technique: a scaling experiment. *Public Opinion Quarterly*, **36**, 114 – 119.

GRAF, R.G. and RIDDELL, J.C. (1972). Helping behaviour as a function of interpersonal perception. *Journal of Social Psychology*, **86**, 227 – 231.

GREEN, F.P. and SCHNEIDER, F.W. (1974). Age differences in the behaviour of boys on three measures of altruism. *Child Development*, **45**, 248 – 251.

GREEN, W.P. and GILES, H. (1973). Reactions to a stranger as a function of dress style: the tie. *Perceptual & Motor Skills*, **37**, 676.

GREENWALD, A.G. (1975). Does the Good Samaritan parable increase helping? A comment on Darley and Batson's no-effect conclusion. *Journal of Personality & Social Psychology*, **32**, 578 – 583.

GROSS, A.E (1975). Generosity and legitimacy of a model as determinants of helpful behaviour. *Representative Research in Social Psychology*, **6**, 45 – 50.

GRUDER, C.L., ROMER, D. and KORTH, B. (1978). Dependency and fault as determinants of helping. *Journal of Experimental Social Psychology*, **14**, 227 – 235.

GRUSEC, J.E. (1972). Demand characteristics of the modelling experiment: altruism as a function of age and aggression. *Journal of Personality & Social Psychology*, **22**, 139 – 148.

GRUSEC, J.E., KUCZYNSKI, L., RUSHTON, J.P. and SIMUTIS, Z.M. (1978a). Modelling, direct instruction, and attributions: effects on altruism. *Developmental Psychology*, **14**, 51 – 57.

GRUSEC, J.E., KUCZYNSKI, L., RUSHTON, J.P. and SIMUTIS, Z.M. (1979). Learning resistance to temptation through observation. *Developmental Psychology*, **15**, 233 – 240.

GRUSEC, J.E. and REDLER, E. (1980). Attribution, reinforcement, and altruism: a developmental analysis. *Developmental Psychology*, **16**, 525 – 534.

GRUSEC, J.E., SAAS-KORTSAAK, P. and SIMUTIS, Z.M. (1978b). The role of example and moral exhortation in the training of altruism. *Child Development*, **49**, 920 – 923.

GRUSEC, J.E. and SKUBISKI, S.L. (1970). Model nurturance, demand characteristics of the modelling experiment, and altruism. *Journal of Personality & Social Psychology*, **14**, 352 – 359.

HANSSON, R.O. and SLADE, K.M. (1977). Altruism toward a deviant in city and small town. *Journal of Applied Social Psychology*, **7**, 272 – 279.

HARRELL, W.A. and GOLTZ, J.W. (1980). Effect of victim's need and previous accusation of theft upon bystander's reaction to theft. *Journal of Social Psychology*, **112**, 41 – 49.

HARRIS, M.B. (1972). The effects of performing one altruistic act on the likelihood of performing another. *Journal of Social Psychology*, **88**, 65 – 73.

HARRIS, M.B. (1977). Effect of altruism on mood. *Journal of Social Psychology*, **102**, 197 – 208.

HARRIS, M.B. and BAUDIN, H. (1973). The language of altruism: The effects of language, dress, and ethnic group. *Journal of Social Psychology*, **91**, 37 – 41.

HARRIS, M.B., BENSON, S.M. and HALL, C.L. (1975). The effects of confession on altruism. *Journal of Social Psychology*, **96**, 187 – 192.

HARRIS, M.B. and HUANG, L.C. (1973). Helping and the attribution process. *Journal of Social Psychology*, **90**, 291 – 297.
HARRIS, M.B., LIGUORI, R. and JONIAK, A. (1973a). Aggression, altruism, and models. *Journal of Social Psychology*, **91**, 343 – 344.
HARRIS, M.B. LIGUORI, R.A. and STACK, C. (1973b). Favours, bribes, and altruism. *Journal of Social Psychology*, **89**, 47 – 54.
HARRIS, M.B. and MEYER, F.W. (1973). Dependency, threat, and helping, *Journal of Social Psychology*, **90**, 239 – 242.
HARRIS, M.B. and SAMEROTTE, G. (1975). The effects of aggressive and altruistic modelling on subsequent behaviour. *Journal of Social Psychology*, **95**, 173 – 182.
HARRIS, M.B. and SAMEROTTE, G.C. (1976). The effects of actual and attempted theft, need, and a previous favour on altruism. *Journal of Social Psychology*, **99**, 193 – 202.
HARRIS, M.B. and SIEBEL, C.E. (1975). Affect, aggression, and altruism. *Developmental Psychology*, **11**, 623 – 627.
HARTMANN, D.P., GELFAND, D.M., SMITH, C.L., PAUL, S.C., CROMER, C.C., PAGE, B.C. and LEBENTA, D.V. (1976). Factors affecting the acquisition and elimination of children's donating behaviour. *Journal of Experimental Child Psychology*, **21**, 328 – 338.
HATFIELD, E., WALSTER, G.W. and PILIAVIN, J.A. (1978). Equity theory and helping relationships. In L. WISPÉ (Ed.), *Altruism, Sympathy, and Helping*. New York: Academic Press.
HELSON, H., BLAKE, R.R. and MOUTON, J.S. (1958). Petition-signing as adjustment to situational and personal factors. *Journal of Social Psychology*, **48**, 3 – 10.
HOMANS, G.C. (1961). *Social Behaviour: Its Elementary Forms*. London: Routledge & Kegan Paul.
HORNSTEIN, H.A (1970). The influence of social models on helping. In J. MACAULAY and L. BERKOWITZ (Eds.), *Altruism and Helping Behaviour*. New York: Academic Press.
HORNSTEIN, H.A., FISCH, E. and HOLMES, M. (1968). Influence of a model's feeling about his behaviour and his relevance as a comparison other on observer's helping behaviour. *Journal of Personality & Social Psychology*, **10**, 222 – 226.
HORNSTEIN, H.A., MASOR, H.N., SOLE, K. and HEILMAN, M. (1971). Effects of sentiment and completion of a helping act on observer helping: a case for socially mediated Zeigarnik effects. *Journal of Personality & Social Psychology*, **17**, 107 – 112.
HOUSE, J.S. and WOLF, S. (1978). Effects of urban residence on interpersonal trust and helping behaviour. *Journal of Personality & Social Psychology*, **36**, 1029 – 1043.
HOWARD, W. and CRANO, W.D. (1974). Effects of sex, conversation, location, and size of observer group on bystander intervention in a high risk situation. *Sociometry*, **37**, 491 – 507.
HOWITT, D., CRAVEN, G., IVESON, C., KREMER, J., MCCABE, J. and ROLPH, T. (1977). The misdirected letter. *British Journal of Social & Clinical Psychology*, **16**, 285 – 286.
HOWITT, D. and MCCABE, J. (1978). Attitudes do predict behaviour — in mails at least. *British Journal of Social & Clinical Psychology*, **17**, 285 – 286.
HUANG, L.C. and HARRIS, M.B. (1973). Conformity in Chinese and Americans. *Journal of Cross-Cultural Psychology*, **4**, 427 – 434.
HUEY, L.B. and JACOBS, K.W. (1978). The 'lost postcard' technique: a non-replication of the lost letter technique. *Psychological Reports*, **43**, 610.
HURLEY, D. and Allen, B.P. (1974). The effect of the number of people present in a non-emergency situation. *Journal of Social Psychology*, **92**, 27 – 29.
HUSTON, T.L. and KORTE, C. (1976). The responsive bystander: why he helps. In T.

LICKONA (Ed.), *Moral Development and Behaviour.* New York: Holt, Rinehart & Winston.

HUSTON, T.L., RUGGIERO, M., CONNER, R. and GEIS, G. (1981). Bystander intervention into crime: a study based on naturally-occurring episodes. *Social Psychology Quarterly*, **44**, 14 – 23.

INNES, J.M. (1974). The semantics of asking a favour: an attempt to replicate cross-culturally. *International Journal of Psychology*, **9**, 57 – 61.

INNES, J.M. and GILROY, S. (1980). The semantics of asking a favour: asking for help in three countries. *Journal of Social Psychology*, **110**, 3 – 7.

ISEN, A.M., CLARK, M. and SCHWARTZ, M. (1976). Duration of the effect of good mood on helping: 'Footprints on the sands of time'. *Journal of Personality & Social Psychology*, **34**, 385 – 393.

ISEN, A.M., HORN, N. and ROSENHAN, D.L. (1973). Effects of success and failure on children's generosity. *Journal of Personality & Social Psychology*, **27**, 239 – 247.

ISEN, A.M. and LEVIN, P.F. (1972). Effect of feeling good on helping: cookies and kindness. *Journal of Personality & Social Psychology*, **21**, 384 – 388.

ISEN, A.M. and NOONBERG, A. (1979). The effect of photographs of the handicapped on donation to charity: when a thousand words may be too much. *Journal of Applied Social Psychology*, **9**, 426 – 431.

JACOBY, J. and ARANOFF, D. (1971). Political polling and the lost-letter technique. *Journal of Social Psychology*, **83**, 209 – 212.

JIOBU, R.M. and KNOWLES, E.S. (1974). Norm strength and alms giving: an observational study. *Journal of Social Psychology* **94**, 205 – 211.

KAPLAN, J. (1978). A legal look at prosocial behaviour: what can happen if one tries to help or fails to help another. In L. WISPÉ (Ed.), *Altruism, Sympathy, and Helping*. New York: Academic Press.

KARABENICK, S.A., LERNER, R.M. and BEECHER, M.D. (1973). Relation of political affiliation to helping behaviour on election day, November 7, 1972. *Journal of Social Psychology*, **91**, 223 – 227.

KARABENICK, S.A., LERNER, R.M. and BEECHER, M.D. (1975). Helping behaviour and attitude congruence toward capital punishment. *Journal of Social Psychology*, **96**, 295 – 296.

KARPIENIA, J. and ZIPPEL, B. (1974). Ethnicity and helping behaviour. *Journal of Social Psychology*, **94**, 31 – 32.

KATZ, I., COHEN, S. and GLASS, D. (1975). Some determinants of cross-racial helping behaviour. *Journal of Personality & Social Psychology*, **32**, 964 – 970.

KAZDIN, A.E. and BRYAN, J.H. (1971). Competence and volunteering. *Journal of Experimental Social Psychology*, **7**, 87 – 97.

KEASEY, C.B. and TOMLINSON-KEASEY, C. (1973). Petition signing in a naturalistic setting. *Journal of Social Psychology*, **89**, 313 – 314.

KENRICK, D.T., BAUMANN, D.J. and CIALDINI, R.B. (1979). A step in the socialization of altruism as hedonism: effects of negative mood on children's generosity under public and private conditions. *Journal of Personality & Social Psychology*, **37**, 747 – 755.

KIDD, R.F. and BERKOWITZ, L. (1976). Effect of dissonance arousal on helpfulness. *Journal of Personality & Social Psychology*, **33**, 613 – 622.

KLEINKE, C.L. (1977a). Compliance to requests made by gazing and touching experimenters in field settings. *Journal of Experimental Social Psychology*, **13**, 218 – 223.

KLEINKE, C.L. (1977b). Effects of dress on compliance to requests in a field setting. *Journal of Social Psychology*, **101**, 223 – 224.

KLEINKE, C.L., MACINTYRE, S.C. and RIDDLE, D.M. (1978). Sex differences in compliance with legitimate and illegitimate requests. *Journal of Social Psychology*, **105**, 153 – 154.

KNOX, R.E. and MCTIERNAN, T.J. (1973). Lost letters and social responsibility in Dublin. *Social Studies*, **2**, 511 – 518.

KOHLBERG, L. (1976). Moral stages and moralization. In T. LICKONA (Ed.), *Moral Development and Behaviour*. New York: Holt, Rinehart & Winston.

KONECNI, V.J. (1972). Some effects of guilt on compliance: a field replication. *Journal of Personality & Social Psychology*, **23**, 30 – 32.

KONECNI, V.J. and EBBESEN, E.B. (1975). Effects of the presence of children on adults' helping behaviour and compliance: two field studies. *Journal of Social Psychology*, **97**, 181 – 193.

KONECNI, V.J., LIBUSER, L., MORTON, H. and EBBESEN, E.B. (1975). Effects of a violation of personal space on escape and helping responses. *Journal of Experimental Social Psychology*, **11**, 288 – 299.

KORTE, C. and KERR, N. (1975). Response to altruistic opportunities in urban and non-urban settings. *Journal of Social Psychology*, **95**, 183 – 184.

KORTE, C., YPMA, I. and TOPPEN, A. (1975). Helpfulness in Dutch society as a function of urbanization and environmental input level. *Journal of Personality & Social Psychology*, **32**, 996 – 1003.

KRANTZ, M. and ANDREWS, D. (1979). Reward deservedness and children's sharing behaviour. *Journal of Psychology*, **103**, 241 – 247.

KRAUT, R.E. (1973). Effects of social labelling on giving to charity. *Journal of Experimental Social Psychology*, **9**, 551 – 562.

KREBS, D. (1978). A cognitive – developmental approach to altruism. In L. WISPÉ (Ed.), *Altruism, Sympathy, and Helping*. New York: Academic Press.

KRISS, M., INDENBAUM, E. and TESCH, F. (1974). Message type and status of interactants as determinants of telephone helping behaviour. *Journal of Personality & Social Psychology*, **30**, 856 – 859.

KROLL, H.W. and MOREN, D.K. (1977). Effect of appearance on requests for help in libraries. *Psychological Reports*, **40**, 129 – 130.

LANGER, E.J. and ABELSON, R.P. (1972). The semantics of asking a favour: how to succeed in getting help without really dying. *Journal of Personality & Social Psychology*, **24**, 26 – 32.

LATANÉ, B. and DABBS, J.M. (1975). Sex, group size, and helping in three cities. *Sociometry*, **36**, 180 – 194.

LATANÉ, B. and DARLEY, J.M. (1970). *The Unresponsive Bystander: Why Doesn't He Help?* New York: Appleton-Century-Crofts.

LEAHY, R.L. (1979). Development of conceptions of prosocial behaviour: information affecting rewards given for altruism and kindness. *Development Psychology*, **15**, 34 – 37.

LERNER, M.J. (1970). The desire for justice and reactions to victims. In J. MACAULAY and L. BERKOWITZ (Eds.), *Altruism and Helping Behaviour*. New York: Academic Press.

LERNER, R.M. and FRANK, P. (1974). Relation of race and sex to supermarket helping behaviour. *Journal of Social Psychology*, **94**, 201 – 203.

LERNER, R.M., SOLOMON, H. and BRODY, S. (1971). Helping behaviour at a bus-stop. *Psychological Reports*, **28**, 200.

LESK, S. and ZIPPEL, B. (1975). Dependency, threat, and helping in a large city. *Journal of Social Psychology*, **95**, 185 – 186.

LEVITT, L. and KORNHABER, R.C. (1977). Stigma and compliance: a re-examination. *Journal of Social Psychology*, **103**, 13 – 18.

LINCOLN, A.J. (1977). Effects of the sex of the model and donor on donating to Amsterdam organ grinders. *Journal of Social Psychology*, **103**, 33 – 37.

LONDON, P. (1970). The rescuers: motivational hypotheses about Christians who saved Jews from the Nazis. In J. MACAULAY and L. BERKOWITZ (Eds.), *Altruism and Helping Behaviour*. New York: Academic Press.

LONG, G.T. and LERNER, M.J. (1974). Deserving, the 'personal contract', and altruistic behaviour by children. *Journal of Personality & Social Psychology*, **29**, 551 – 556.

LOWE, R. and RITCHEY, G. (1973). Relation of altruism to age, social class, and ethnic identity. *Psychological Reports*, **33**, 567 – 572.

LUCK, H.E. (1978). Aspects of a transnational theory of prosocial behaviour. In L. WISPÉ (Ed.), *Altruism, Sympathy, and Helping*. New York: Academic Press.

LYNCH, J.G. and COHEN, J.L. (1978). The use of subjective expected utility theory as an aid to understanding variables that influence helping behaviour. *Journal of Personality & Social Psychology*, **36**, 1138 – 1151.

MACAULAY, J. (1970). A shill for charity. In J. MACAULAY and L. BERKOWITZ (Eds.), *Altruism and Helping Behaviour*. New York: Academic Press.

MACAULAY, J. and BERKOWITZ, L. (Eds.) (1970). *Altruism and Helping Behaviour*. New York: Academic Press.

MASON, D. and ALLEN, B.P. (1976). The bystander effect as a function of ambiguity and emergency character. *Journal of Social Psychology*, **100**, 145 – 146.

MCGUIRE, J.M. and THOMAS, M.H. (1975). Effects of sex, competence, and competition on sharing behaviour in children. *Journal of Personality & Social Psychology*, **32**, 490 – 494.

MCKENNA, R.J. (1976). Good samaritanism in rural and urban settings: a non-reactive comparison of helping behaviour of clergy and control subjects. *Representative Research in Social Psychology*, **7**, 58 – 65.

MCMILLEN, D.L. (1971). Transgression, self-image, and compliant behaviour. *Journal of Personality & Social Psychology*, **20**, 176 – 179.

MCMILLEN, D.L. and AUSTIN, J.B. (1971). Effect of positive feedback on compliance following transgression. *Psychonomic Science*, **24**, 59 – 61.

MCMILLEN, D.L., JACKSON, J.A. and AUSTIN, J.B. (1974). Effects of positive and negative requests on compliance following transgression. *Bulletin of the Psychonomic Society*, **3**, 80 – 82.

MERRENS, M.R. (1973). Non-emergency helping behaviour in various sized communities. *Journal of Social Psychology*, **90**, 327 – 328.

MERRITT, C.B. and FOWLER, R.G. (1948). The pecuniary honesty of the public at large. *Journal of Abnormal & Social Psychology*, **43**, 90 – 93.

MIDLARSKY, E. (1971). Aiding under stress: the effects of competence, dependency, visibility, and fatalism. *Journal of Personality*, **39**, 132 – 149.

MILGRAM, S. (1970). The experience of living in cities. *Science*, **167**, 1461 – 1468.

MILGRAM, S. (1974). *Obedience to Authority*. London: Tavistock.

MILGRAM, S., MANN, L. and HARTER, S. (1965). The lost-letter technique: a tool of social research. *Public Opinion Quarterly*, **29**, 437 – 438.

MILLER, A.G. (1972). *The Social Psychology of Psychological Research*. New York: Free Press.

MILLER, D.T. and SMITH, J. (1977). The effect of own deservingness and deservingness of others on children's helping behaviour. *Child Development*, **48**, 617 – 620.

MILLER, R.L. and SULS, J. (1977). Helping, self-attribution, and the size of an initial

request. *Journal of Social Psychology*, **103**, 203 – 207.
MOORE, B.S., UNDERWOOD, B. and ROSENHAN, D.L. (1973). Affect and altruism. *Developmental Psychology*, **8**, 99 – 104.
MORGAN, C.J., LOCKARD, J.S., FAHRENBRUCH, C.E. and SMITH, J.L. (1975). Hitch-hiking: social signals at a distance. *Bulletin of the Psychonomic Society*, **5**, 459 – 461.
MORIARTY, T. (1975). Crime, commitment, and the responsive bystander: two field experiments. *Journal of Personality & Social Psychology*, **31**, 370 – 376.
MORRIS, S.C. and ROSEN, S. (1973). Effects of felt adequacy and opportunity to reciprocate on help seeking. *Journal of Experimental Social Psychology*, **9**, 265 – 276.
MORRIS, W.N., MARSHALL, H.M. and MILLER, R.S. (1973). The effect of vicarious punishment on prosocial behaviour in children. *Journal of Experimental Child Psychology*, **15**, 222 – 236.
MOSS, M.K. and PAGE, R.A. (1972). Reinforcement and helping behaviour. *Journal of Applied Social Psychology*, **2**, 360 – 371.
MURRAY, E.J. and VINCENZO, J. (1976). Bystander intervention in a mild need situation. *Bulletin of the Psychonomic Society*, **7**, 133 – 135.
MUSSEN, P. and EISENBERG-BERG, N. (1977). *Roots of Caring, Sharing and Helping*. San Francisco: Freeman.
NADLER, A., FISHER, J.D. and STREUFERT, S. (1976). When helping hurts: effects of donor – recipient similarity and recipient self-esteem on reactions to aid. *Journal of Personality*, **44**, 392 – 409.
NEWMAN, C.V. (1979). Relation between altruism and dishonest profiteering from anothor's misfortune. *Journal of Social Psychology*, **109**, 43 – 48.
NISBETT, R.E. and WILSON, T.D. (1977). Telling more than we can know: verbal reports on mental processes. *Psychological Review*, **84**, 231 – 259.
O'BRYANT, S.L. and BROPHY, J.E. (1976). Sex differences in altruistic behaviour. *Developmental Psychology*, **12**, 554.
OLWEUS, D. (1979). Stability of aggressive reaction patterns in males: a review. *Psychological Bulletin*, **86**, 852 – 875.
PAYNE, F.D. (1980). Children's prosocial conduct in structured situations and as viewed by others: consistency, convergence, and relationships with person variables. *Child Development*, **51**, 1252 – 1259.
PEARCE, P.L. (1980). Strangers, travellers, and Greyhound terminals: a study of small-scale helping behaviours. *Journal of Personality & Social Psychology*, **38**, 935 – 940.
PENNER, L.A., DERTKE, M.C. and ACHENBACH, C.J. (1973). The 'flash' system: a field study of altruism. *Journal of Applied Social Psychology*, **3**, 362 – 370.
PENNER, L.A., MICHAEL, D.E. and BROOKMIRE, D.A. (1979). Pro- and anti-social behaviour as a function of cost estimates and personality and situation variables. *Multivariate Clinical Experimental Research*, **4**, 111 – 124.
PENNER, L.A., SUMMERS, L.S., BROOKMIRE, D.A. and DERTKE, M.C. (1976). The lost dollar: situational and personality determinants of a pro- and anti-social behaviour. *Journal of Personality*, **44**, 274 – 293.
PETERSON, L. (1980). Developmental changes in verbal and behavioural sensitivity to cues of social norms of altruism. *Child Development*, **51**, 830 – 838.
PETERSON, L. HARTMANN, D.P. and GELFAND, D.M. (1977). Developmental changes in the effects of dependency and reciprocity cues on children's moral judgements and donation rates. *Child Development*, **48**, 1331 – 1339.
PILIAVIN, I.M., PILIAVIN, J.A. and RODIN, J. (1975). Costs, diffusion, and the stigmatized victim. *Journal of Personality & Social Psychology*, **32**, 429 – 438.
PILIAVIN, I.M., RODIN, J. and PILIAVIN, J.A. (1969). Good samaritanism: an under-

ground phenomenon? *Journal of Personality & Social Psychology*, **13**, 289 – 299.
PILIAVIN, J.A. and PILIAVIN, I.M. (1972). Effect of blood on reactions to a victim. *Journal of Personality & Social Psychology*, **23**, 353 – 361.
PLINER, P., HART, H., KOHL, J. and SAARI, D. (1974). Compliance without pressure: some further data on the foot-in-the-door technique. *Journal of Experimental Social Psychology*, **10**, 17 – 22.
POMAZAL, R.J. and CLORE, G.L. (1973). Helping on the highway: the effects of dependency and sex. *Journal of Applied Social Psychology*, **3**, 150 – 164.
POMAZAL, R.J. and JACCARD, J.J. (1976). An informational approach to altruistic behaviour. *Journal of Personality & Social Psychology*, **33**, 317 – 326.
POULOS, R.W. and LIEBERT, R.M. (1972). Influence of modelling, exhortative verbalization, and surveillance on children's sharing. *Developmental Psychology*, **6**, 402 – 408.
PRESBIE, R.J. and COITEUX, P.F. (1971). Learning to be generous or stingy: imitation of sharing behaviour as a function of model generosity and vicarious reinforcement. *Child Development*, **42**, 1033 – 1038.
RAVIV, A., BAR-TAL D. and LEWIS-LEVIN, T. (1980). Motivations for donation behaviour by boys of three different ages. *Child Development*, **51**, 610 – 613.
RAYMOND, B.J. and UNGER, R.K. (1972). 'The apparel oft proclaims the man': cooperation with deviant and conventional youths. *Journal of Social Psychology*, **87**, 75 – 82.
REGAN, D.T., WILLIAMS, M. and SPARLING, S. (1972). Voluntary expiation of guilt: a field experiment. *Journal of Personality & Social Psychology*, **24**, 42 – 45.
RICE, M.E. and GRUSEC, J.E. (1975). Saying and doing: effects on observer performance. *Journal of Personality & Social Psychology*, **32**, 584 – 593.
ROSENBAUM, M. and BLAKE, R.R. (1955). Volunteering as a function of field structure. *Journal of Abnormal & Social Psychology*, **50**, 193 – 196.
ROSENHAN, D.L., UNDERWOOD, B. and MOORE, B. (1974). Affect moderates self-gratification and altruism. *Journal of Personality & Social Psychology*, **30**, 546 – 552.
ROSENHAN, D.L. and WHITE, G.M. (1967). Observation and rehearsal as determinants of prosocial behaviour. *Journal of Personality & Social Psychology*, **5**, 424 – 431.
ROTTON, J. (1977). Sex, residential location, and altruism. *Psychological Reports*, **40**, 102.
RUBIN, K.H. and SCHNEIDER, F.W. (1973). The relationship between moral judgment, egocentrism and altruistic behaviour. *Child Development*, **44**, 661 – 665.
RUSHTON, J.P. (1975). Generosity in children: immediate and long-term effects of modelling, preaching, and moral judgment. *Journal of Personality and Social Psychology*, **31**, 459 – 466.
RUSHTON, J.P. (1978). Urban density and altruism: helping strangers in a Canadian city, suburb, and small town. *Psychological Reports*, **43**, 987 – 990.
RUSHTON, J.P. (1979). Effects of prosocial television and film material on the behaviour of viewers. In L. BERKOWITZ (Ed.), *Advances in Experimental Social Psychology*, Vol. 12. New York: Academic Press.
RUSHTON, J.P. (1980). *Altruism, Socialization, and Society*. Englewood Cliffs: Prentice-Hall.
RUSHTON, J.P. (1981). The altruistic personality. In J.P. RUSHTON and R.M. SORRENTINO (Eds.), *Altruism and Helping Behaviour*. Hillsdale: Lawrence Erlbaum (In press).
RUSHTON, J.P. and CAMPBELL, A.C. (1977). Modelling, vicarious reinforcement and extraversion on blood donating in adults: immediate and long-term effects. *European Journal of Social Psychology*, **7**, 297 – 306.

RUSHTON, J.P. and LITTLEFIELD, C. (1979). The effects of age, amount of modelling, and a success experience on seven-to-eleven year old children's generosity. *Journal of Moral Education*, **9**, 55 – 56.
RUSHTON, J.P. and OWEN, D. (1975). Immediate and delayed effects of TV modelling and preaching on children's generosity. *British Journal of Social & Clinical Psychology*, **14**, 309 – 310.
RUSHTON, J.P. and WHEELWRIGHT, M. (1980). Validation of donating to charity as a measure of children's altruism. *Psychological Reports*, **47**, 803 – 806.
RUTHERFORD, E. and MUSSEN, P. (1968). Generosity in nursery school boys. *Child Development*, **39**, 755 – 765.
SAMEROTTE, G.C. and HARRIS, M.B. (1976). Some factors influencing helping: the effects of a handicap, responsibility, and requesting help. *Journal of Social Psychology*, **98**, 39 – 45.
SATOW, K.L. (1975). Social approval and helping. *Journal of Experimental Social Psychology*, **11**, 501 – 509.
SCHAPS, E. (1972). Cost, dependency, and helping. *Journal of Personality & Social Psychology*, **21**, 74 – 78.
SCHIAVO, R.S., SHERLOCK, B. and WICKLUND, G. (1974). Effect of attire on obtaining directions. *Psychological Reports*, **34**, 245 – 246.
SCHNEIDER, F.W. (1973). When will a stranger lend a helping hand? *Journal of Social Psychology*, **90**, 335 – 336.
SCHOPLER, J. and BATESON, N. (1965). The power of dependence. *Journal of Personality & Social Psychology*, **2**, 247 – 254.
SCHOPLER, J. and THOMPSON, V.D. (1968). Role of attribution processes in mediating amount of reciprocity for a favour. *Journal of Personality & Social Psychology*, **10**, 243 – 250.
SCHREIBER, E. (1979). Bystander's intervention in situations of violence. *Psychological Reports*, **45**, 243 – 246.
SCHWARTZ, S.H. (1977). Normative influences on altruism. In L. BERKOWITZ (Ed.), *Advances in Experimental Social Psychology*, Vol. 10. New York: Academic Press.
SCHWARTZ, S.H. and GOTTLIEB, A. (1976). Bystander reactions to a violent theft: crime in Jerusalem. *Journal of Personality & Social Psychology*, **34**, 1188 – 1199.
SCHWARTZ, S.H. and GOTTLIEB, A. (1980). Bystander anonymity and reactions to emergencies. *Journal of Personality & Social Psychology*, **39**, 418 – 430.
SECHREST, L. and FLORES, L. (1974). Surplus and sharing in a prison sample. *Journal of Social Psychology*, **94**, 33 – 44.
SHAFFER, D.R. and GRAZIANO, W.G. (1980). Effects of victims' race and organizational affiliation on receiving help from blacks and whites. *Personality & Social Psychology Bulletin*, **6**, 366 – 372.
SHAFFER, D.R., ROGEL, M. and HENDRICK, C. (1975). Intervention in the library: the effect of increased responsibility on bystanders' willingness to prevent a theft. *Journal of Applied Social Psychology*, **5**, 303 – 319.
SHEMBERG, K.M., LEVENTHAL, D.B. and ALLMAN, L. (1968). Aggression machine performance and rated aggression. *Journal of Experimental Research in Personality*, **3**, 117 – 119.
SHOTLAND, R.L., BERGER, W.G. and FORSYTHE, R. (1970). A validation of the lost-letter technique. *Public Opinion Quarterly*, **34**, 278 – 281.
SHOTLAND, R.L. and STRAW, M.K. (1976). Bystander response to an assault: when a man attacks a woman. *Journal of Personality & Social Psychology*, **34**, 990 – 999.

SILVERMAN, L.J., RIVERA, A.N. and TEDESCHI, J.T. (1979). Transgression-compliance: guilt, negative affect, or impression management? *Journal of Social Psychology*, **108**, 57 – 62.

SIMON, A. (1976). Chivalry on the road: helping stalled drivers. *Psychological Reports*, **39**, 883 – 886.

SIMON, W.E. (1971). Helping behaviour in the absence of visual contact as a function of sex of person asking for help and sex of person being asked for help. *Psychological Reports*, **28**, 609 – 610.

SIMON, W.E. and GILLEN, M.J. (1971). Return rates of 'lost' letters as a function of whether the letter is stamped and amount of money apparently in the letter. *Psychological Reports*, **29**, 141 – 142.

SISSONS, M. (1981). Race, sex and helping behaviour. *British Journal of Social Psychology*, **20**, 285 – 292.

SKOLNICK, P. (1977). Helping as a function of time of day, location, and sex of victim. *Journal of Social Psychology*, **102**, 61 – 62.

SNYDER, M. and CUNNINGHAM, M.R. (1975). To comply or not to comply: testing the self-perception explanation of the 'foot-in-the-door' phenomenon. *Journal of Personality & Social Psychology*, **31**, 64 – 67.

SNYDER, M., GRETHER, J. and KELLER, K. (1974). Staring and compliance: a field experiment on hitch-hiking. *Journal of Applied Social Psychology*, **4**, 165 – 170.

SOBLE, S.L. and STRICKLAND, L.H. (1974). Physical stigma, interaction, and compliance. *Bulletin of the Psychonomic Society*, **4**, 130 – 132.

SOLE, K., MARTON, J. and HORNSTEIN, H.A. (1975). Opinion similarity and helping: three field experiments investigating the bases of promotive tension. *Journal of Experimental Social Psychology*, **11**, 1 – 13.

SOLOMON, H. and HERMAN, L. (1977). Status symbols and prosocial behaviour: the effect of the victim's car on helping. *Journal of Psychology*, **97**, 271 – 273.

SOLOMON, L.Z. and GROTA, P. (1976). Imitation of a helpful model: the effect of level of emergency. *Journal of Social Psychology*, **99**, 29 – 35.

SPRAFKIN, J.N., LIEBERT, R.M. and POULOS, R.W. (1975). Effects of a prosocial televised example on children's helping. *Journal of Experimental Child Psychology*, **20**, 119 – 126.

SROUFE, R., CHAIKIN, A., COOK, R. and FREEMAN, V. (1977). The effects of physical attractiveness on honesty: a socially desirable response. *Personality & Social Psychology Bulletin*, **3**, 59 – 62.

STAUB, E. (1978). *Positive Social Behaviour and Morality*, Vol. 1. New York: Academic Press.

STAUB, E. and BAER, R.S. (1974). Stimulus characteristics of a sufferer and difficulty of escape as determinants of helping. *Journal of Personality & Social Psychology*, **30**, 279 – 284.

STAUB, E. and SHERK, L. (1970). Need for approval, children's sharing behaviour, and reciprocity in sharing. *Child Development*, **41**, 243 – 252.

STEELE, C.M. (1975). Name-calling and compliance. *Journal of Personality & Social Psychology*, **31**, 361 – 369.

STEFFENSMEIER, D.J. and STEFFENSMEIER, R.H. (1977). Who reports shoplifters? Research continuities and further developments. *International Journal of Criminology & Penology*, **5**, 79 – 95.

STEFFENSMEIER, D.J. and TERRY, R.M. (1973). Deviance and respectability: an observational study of reactions to shoplifting. *Social Forces*, **51**, 417 – 426.

SWINYARD, W.R. and RAY, M.L. (1979). Effects of praise and small requests on receptivity to direct-mail appeals. *Journal of Social Psychology*, **108**, 177 – 184.

TESSLER, R.C. and SCHWARTZ, S.H. (1972). Help seeking, self-esteem, and achievement motivation: an attributional analysis. *Journal of Personality & Social Psychology*, **21**, 318 – 326.

THAYER, S. (1973). Lend me your ears: racial and sexual factors in helping the deaf. *Journal of Personality & Social Psychology*, **28**, 8 – 11.

TIDD, K.L. and LOCKARD, J.S. (1978). Monetary significance of the affiliative smile: a case for reciprocal altruism. *Bulletin of the Psychonomic Society*, **11**, 344 – 346.

TILKER, H.A. (1970). Socially responsible behaviour as a function of observer responsibility and victim feedback. *Journal of Personality & Social Psychology*, **14**, 95 – 100.

TIPTON, R.M. and BROWNING, S. (1972a). Altruism: reward or punishment? *Journal of Psychology*, **80**, 319 – 322.

TIPTON, R.M. and BROWNING, S. (1972b). The influence of age and obesity on helping behaviour. *British Journal of Social & Clinical Psychology*, **11**, 404 – 406.

TIPTON, R.M. and JENKINS, L. (1974). Altruism as a function of response cost to the benefactor. *Journal of Psychology*, **86**, 209 – 216.

TUCKER, L., HORNSTEIN, H.A., HOLLOWAY, S. and SOLE, K. (1977). The effects of temptation and information about a stranger on helping. *Personality & Social Psychology Bulletin*, **3**, 416 – 420.

UNDERWOOD, B., FROMING, W.J. and MOORE, B.S. (1977). Mood, attention, and altruism: a search for mediating variables. *Developmental Psychology*, **13**, 541 – 542.

UNGAR, S. (1979). The effects of effort and stigma on helping. *Journal of Social Psychology*, **107**, 23 – 28.

URANOWITZ, S.W. (1975). Helping and self-attributions: a field experiment. *Journal of Personality & Social Psychology*, **31**, 852 – 854.

VALENTINE, M.E. (1980). The attenuating influence of gaze upon the bystander intervention effect. *Journal of Social Psychology*, **111**, 197 – 203.

VALENTINE, M.E. and EHRLICHMAN, H. (1979). Interpersonal gaze and helping behaviour. *Journal of Social Psychology*, **107**, 193 – 198.

WAGNER, C. and WHEELER, L. (1969). Model, need, and cost effects in helping behaviour. *Journal of Personality & Social Psychology*, **12**, 111 – 116.

WALKER, M., HARRIMAN, S. and COSTELLO, S. (1980). The influence of appearance on compliance with a request. *Journal of Social Psychology*, **112**, 159 – 160.

WALKER, N. and ARGYLE, M. (1964). Does the law affect moral judgments? *British Journal of Criminology*, **4**, 570 – 581.

WAXLER, C. Z., YARROW, M.R. and SMITH, J.B. (1977). Perspective-taking and prosocial behaviour. *Developmental Psychology*, **13**, 87 – 88.

WEGNER, D.M. and CRANO, W.D. (1975). Racial factors in helping behaviour: an unobtrusive field experiment. *Journal of Personality & Social Psychology*, **32**, 901 – 905.

WEINER, B. (1980). A cognitive (attribution)-emotion-action model of motivated behaviour: an analysis of judgments of help-giving. *Journal of Personality & Social Psychology*, **39**, 186 – 200.

WENER, B.D. and PISANO, R.L. (1977). Relationship between altruism and aggression using behavioural measures. *Psychological Reports*, **40**, 673 – 674.

WEST, S.G. and BROWN, T.J. (1975). Physical attractiveness, the severity of the emergency, and helping: a field experiment and interpersonal simulation. *Journal of Experimental Social Psychology*, **11**, 531 – 538.

WEST, S.G., WHITNEY, G. and SCHNEDLER, R. (1975). Helping a motorist in distress: the effects of sex, race, and neighbourhood. *Journal of Personality & Social*

Psychology, **31**, 691 – 698.

WEYANT, J.M. (1978). Effects of mood states, costs, and benefits on helping. *Journal of Personality & Social Psychology*, **36**, 1169 – 1176.

WHITE, G.M. and BURNAM, M.A. (1975). Socially cued altruism: effects of modelling, instructions, and age on public and private donations. *Child Development*, **46**, 559 – 563.

WICKER, A.W. (1969). A failure to validate the lost-letter technique. *Public Opinion Quarterly*, **33**, 260 – 262.

WILSON, D.W. and DONNERSTEIN, E. (1976). Legal and ethical aspects of non-reactive social psychological research. *American Psychologist*, **31**, 765 – 773.

WILSON, D.W. and KAHN, A. (1975). Rewards, costs, and sex differences in helping behaviour. *Psychological Reports*, **36**, 31 – 34.

WISPÉ, L.G. and FRESHLEY, H.B. (1971). Race, sex, and sympathetic helping behaviour: the broken bag caper. *Journal of Personality & Social Psychology*, **17**, 59 – 65.

WISPÉ, L. and KIECOLT, J. (1980). Victim attractiveness as a function of helping and non-helping. *Journal of Social Psychology*, **112**, 67 – 73.

WUNDERLICH, E. and WILLIS, F.N. (1977). The youth of victims as a factor affecting the probability of receiving aid. *Journal of Psychology*, **97**, 93 – 94.

WYER, R.S., DION, K.L. and ELLSWORTH, P.C. (1978). An editorial. *Journal of Experimental Social Psychology*, **14**, 141 – 147.

YAKIMOVICH, D. and SALTZ, E. (1971). Helping behaviour: the cry for help. *Psychonomic Science*, **23**, 427 – 428.

YARROW, M.R., SCOTT, P.M. and WAXLER, C.Z. (1973). Learning concern for others. *Developmental Psychology*, **8**, 240 – 260.

YARROW, M.R. and WAXLER, C.Z. (1976). Dimensions and correlates of prosocial behaviour in young children. *Child Development*, **47**, 118 – 125.

ZELNIO, R.N. and GAGNON, J.P. (1977). The viability of the lost letter technique. *Journal of Psychology*, **95**, 51 – 53.

ZINSER, O., PERRY, J. and EDGAR, R.M. (1975). Affluence of the recipient, value of donations, and sharing behaviour in preschool children. *Journal of Psychology*, **89**, 301 – 305.

CHAPTER 8

Intergroup Conflict and Cooperation*

John C. Turner

8.1 Introduction

This chapter reviews the experimental research on the social psychology of intergroup behaviour. The central objective of this work is to discover the social psychological causes of conflict and harmony between social groups, and its main preoccupation is to investigate basic processes in intergroup cooperation and competition. The chapter will summarize the important research findings and ideas in this area and discuss their implications for the aetiology of intergroup conflict.

The following two sections describe work relevant to the two dominant themes in contemporary studies: the effects of cooperative and competitive social interaction on intra- and intergroup relations and the role of social categorization in intergroup discrimination. The next section brings these themes together in a more speculative discussion of theoretical issues related to the resolution of intergroup conflict. The final section summarizes the main conclusion and identifies some directions for future research.

Some terms need to be defined at the outset. *Ingroup favouritism* describes any tendency to favour ingroup over outgroup members on perceptual, attitudinal or behavioural dimensions. It includes partisan intergroup attitudes, sociometric preferences for the ingroup, discriminatory intergroup behaviour and more favourable evaluations of the products and performances of the ingroup than the outgroup. *Ingroup bias* describes instances of ingroup favouritism which seem to be unreasonable or unjustifiable in that they go beyond the objective evidence or requirements of the situation such as derogatory outgroup attitudes which have no veridical basis or discriminatory intergroup behaviour which does not directly benefit ingroup members. Thus its use always implies some interpretative judgement on the part of the researcher. *Intergroup discrimination* and *differentiation* indicate mutual favouritism between groups. Where these terms are distinguished, the former specifies behavioural or quasi-behavioural and the latter perceptual and attitudinal responses. Later in the chapter differentiation is used in a theoretical sense to

* This chapter is a slightly modified version of Chapter 3 in J.C. Turner & H. Giles (Eds.), *Intergroup Behaviour* (Oxford: Basil Blackwell, 1981), reproduced by permission.

describe any form of favouritism motivated by a desire for positively valued distinctiveness for one's own group and thus can include discrimination.

8.2 Cooperative and Competitive Interaction between Groups

The pioneering research on this issue was conducted by the Sherifs and their colleagues. Their work was important because it demonstrated experimentally the role of intergroup relations in social conflict, identified social and psychological consequences of intergroup competition and also presented a specific theory of intergroup behaviour.

Three field studies were carried out in 1949, 1953 and 1954 in the USA with young male subjects at summer camps (Sherif, 1951; Sherif and Sherif, 1953; Sherif *et al.*, 1955; Sherif *et al.*, 1961). They were similar in basic design and comprised four stages in the development and reduction of intergroup conflict. In the first stage, the subjects engaged in sports and outdoor activities on a camp-wide basis, and normal friendships developed. In the second, they were divided into two groups through the separation of their living arrangements and camp activities; close friends were assigned to different groups. The groups gradually evolved status and role differentiations between their members and shared social norms. In the third stage, the camp authorities (the researchers) instituted an organized competition between the groups embracing sports contests and other camp activities. In consequence, overt hostility developed between them both within and outside the organized contests. The last study included a final stage which provided the warring groups with *superordinate goals*: compelling objectives desired by them both but which neither could achieve without the help of the other. They were placed in settings where collaborative action was necessary such as a lakeside outing where they had to join forces to rescue a truck which was to bring them food. A series of such encounters reduced mutual antipathy and led to favourable intergroup attitudes.

The researchers interpreted their observations as support for the following hypotheses (Sherif, 1967):

1. Where individuals interact under conditions that embody common goals requiring cooperatively interdependent activities for their attainment, a definite group structure will emerge, consisting of differentiated status and role positions and shared social norms.
2. Where two groups come into contact under conditions that embody a series of incompatible goals — where both groups urgently desire some objective which can be attained only at the expense of the other — competitive activity towards the goal changes over time into hostility between the groups; also:

   (a) unfavourable attitudes and images (stereotypes) of the outgroup come into use and become standardized, placing the outgroup at a definite social distance from the ingroup;

(b) intergroup conflict produces an increase in solidarity within the groups and other changes in intragroup relations;
(c) increased solidarity and pride in one's own group lead to ingroup biases which overevaluate the characteristics and performances of ingroup members and underevaluate those of outgroup members.

3. Where conflicting groups come into contact under conditions that embody a series of superordinate goals, cooperative activity towards the goal has a cumulative impact in improving intergroup relations: in reducing social distance, dissipating hostile outgroup attitudes and stereotypes, and making future intergroup conflicts less likely.

These hypotheses constitute a functional theory of intergroup behaviour. They imply that functional interdependence (positive or negative) between individuals or groups for the achievement of their goals, leads directly to cooperative or competitive social interaction, and also that cooperative or competitive interaction directly produces cohesive (solidary, friendly, etc.) or antagonistic social attitudes between the participants. Thus the social relations between individuals or groups are primarily determined by their functional or goal relations.

The important predictions are that objective conflicts of interests (incompatible goals) cause intergroup conflict and superordinate or collaborative goals induce social harmony. The theory explains the formation of social groups as an outcome of the same processes which reduce social distance between conflicting groups: cohesive social relations and group structure emerge from cooperative social interaction for interdependent goals. Thus it implies that conflict resolution is partly a process of weakening group boundaries and that competitive interaction should tend to consolidate ingroup–outgroup divisions.

The next major research programme on intergroup behaviour helped to corroborate some of the Sherifs' ideas. Blake and Mouton (1961, 1962) conducted a series of quasi-experimental, laboratory studies in which discussion groups of 9 – 12 adult members met over 10 – 14 days periods. Pairs of groups created solutions to human relations problems and compared their products on a win or lose basis to assess their problem-solving effectiveness.

The introduction of a competitive intergroup orientation had several consequences. Ingroup biases in the perception of the groups and their products (and even third parties) were enhanced and consolidated. Intergroup attitudes became extremely partisan and led to deadlocks in negotiations between the groups. Where the groups were provided with opportunities to discuss their respective solutions, they tended not to exchange objective information but to attack and attempt to discredit each others' views. Moreover, their communications were marred by perceptual distortions whereby agreements in the solutions were minimized and disagreements enhanced. Intragroup relations became more cohesive and organized and conformity pressures upon group members increased. Finally, competitive victory tended to increase the power of group leaders and enhance cohesiveness, cooperativeness and work motivation, whereas defeat had the opposite effects.

These results support the hypothesis that intergroup competition produces a syndrome of interrelated effects tending to strengthen social relationships within groups and disrupt them between groups. It is not so evident that they confirm the theory that competition is determined by extrinsic group interests. Blake and Mouton report that the provision of a win – lose orientation (and not incompatible goals) was sufficient to elicit the dynamics of competitive behaviour. In other words, their subjects were competitive because they wanted to win, and they wanted to win, not to achieve some extrinsic objective, but simply because they were in a competition. The implication is that intergroup competition may often be intrinsically and not extrinsically motivated. In this case, the most obvious explanation is that self-evaluative social comparisons between the groups to assess their problem-solving abilities led directly to a mutual desire to win.

The research of Wilson and his colleagues (Wilson, *et al.*, 1965; Wilson and Kayatani, 1968; Wilson and Robinson, 1968; Wilson and Wong, 1968) also suggests that social processes can contribute directly to competitive intergroup behaviour. In these studies pairs of dyads made cooperative or competitive choices to divide monetary rewards in an experimental game (see Chapter 5): the members made both inter- and intragroup choices. The important point is that the reward structure or payoff matrix and hence the functional relations between players were identical on both kinds of trials. Nevertheless, intergroup choices were approximately twice as competitive as intragroup choices. Team partners were also rated more favourably than members of the other team, especially on sociometric and motive traits relevant to the game-playing situation. Thus intergroup behaviour seems to be inherently more competitive or discriminatory than intragroup behaviour.

There is however an alternative interpretation of these results. The experimental game employed by Wilson normally leads to predominantly competitive responses even between individual players. In the above studies, intergroup relations may have reflected whereas intragroup relations may have counteracted this baseline tendency. Members of the same dyad had to cooperate to make joint decisions about inter-team choices. Hence there were differences in both degree and kind between social interaction within and between groups. These differences could and should have led to more attraction and understanding *within* than *between* dyads (as the subjects reported) and so encouraged cooperativeness (Billig, 1976, pp. 208 – 210).

This alternative explanation is interesting in its own right because it makes the simple but easily forgotten point that differential interpersonal relations can account for some forms of ingroup favouritism. We need not assume competitive or hostile intergroup relations to recognize that there are many variables such as social interaction, proximity, familiarity and attitudinal similarity which tend to ensure more interpersonal attraction *within* than *between* groups. We can also suppose that individuals naturally tend to have different information about ingroup and outgroup members and appraise their actions from different perspectives. Any individual tends to be more aware of the intra-than intergroup actions of ingroup members and the inter- than intragroup actions of outgroup members. These constant discrepancies between intra- and intergroup relations should cause ingroup favouritism under the most minimal conditions of group formation and need not imply prejudiced outgroup attitudes. Thus where there is more face-to-face interaction with ingroup than outgroup members we should not assume that favouritism represents bias: it may reflect a sociometric preference for ingroup members based on real differences in contact and information.

Other research during the two decades following the Sherifs' studies tended to corroborate the functional theory (Avigdor, 1953; Bass and Dunteman, 1963; Diab, 1970; Fiedler, 1967; Harvey, 1956; Johnson, 1967; Sussman and Weil, 1960). But more recent experiments have created difficulties. The Sherifs and Blake and Mouton confound functional interdependence with cooperative and competitive social interaction. Later studies compare the effects on intergroup attitudes of cooperation, competition and coaction (functional independence with face-to-face contact) under conditions where intra- and intergroup interaction are controlled or manipulated. They find that the early work is probably correct about the different effects of cooperative and competitive interaction but may be incorrect in its implicit stress on the importance of functional interdependence *per se*.

Doise *et al.* (1971, 1972) and Brewer and Silver (1978) excluded both anticipated and actual social interaction within and between groups, and measured intergroup attitudes before and after subjects make cooperative or competitive, or cooperative, competitive or independent decisions about rewards for ingroup and outgroup members. There were no significant differences between the effects of the different forms of intergroup behaviour. Before and after intergroup behaviour subjects evaluated ingroup more favourably than outgroup members.

Doise also found ingroup bias in a control condition where intergroup behaviour was not even anticipated, but to a lesser degree than in the experimental conditions. It appears then that a simple ingroup – outgroup division with neither face-to-face contact nor social interaction between group members can create ingroup bias and that the mere expectation of intergroup behaviour increases this bias to the same level as that obtained after intergroup behaviour.

In contrast to these two studies which manipulated intergroup behaviour unconfounded with intergroup interaction, Kahn and Ryen (1972) and Doise and Weinberger (1973) explored the effects of expected intergroup interaction. Under conditions without face-to-face contact between subjects, the former found ingroup bias with expected cooperation but less than with expected competition. Under conditions of face-to-face contact between ingroup and outgroup dyads, the latter found bias with expected coaction and competition but not cooperation.

Three studies manipulated cooperative interaction within groups. Rabbie and de Brey (1971) measured intergroup attitudes before and after intragroup task interaction under conditions of some face-to-face contact between cooperating or competing groups. The subjects preferred the ingroup to the outgroup on cohesiveness measures and more so after interaction. Performance ratings are more complex. There is little or no bias before interaction and, in fact, competing groups favour the outgroup over the ingroup. Interaction increased ingroup bias for both cooperating and competing groups, but more so for the latter subjects. Under similar conditions, Rabbie and Wilkens (1971) found no significant differences between intergroup coaction and competition. Both conditions produced bias in ratings of the groups as collective entities before and after task interaction, but interaction did increase ingroup bias in evaluations of individual group members. Janssens and Nuttin (1976, Experiment 2) found that verbal interaction increased ingroup bias in performance ratings for both competing and isolated, independent groups. Intergroup competition was associated with more bias than independence only under conditions of intragroup interaction.

Finally, four studies held constant some degree of intragroup interaction and face-to-face contact between groups. Rabbie *et al.* (1974) found that ingroups are preferred to outgroups on cohesiveness measures and that this preference was greater with anticipated intergroup competition than cooperation especially where the groups had strong bargaining positions. Intergroup competition also produced more negative outgroup attitudes than cooperation on other measures, especially where the groups had weak bargaining positions. Ryen and Kahn (1975) reported that ingroup bias increases from intergroup coaction to cooperation to competition. Worchel *et al.* (1977) found that attraction to the ingroup increases, and attraction to the outgroup decreases, from intergroup cooperation to coaction to competition. Janssens and Nuttin (1976, Experiment 1) also observed that coacting groups are less biased than competing ones.

These experiments make several important points. First, intragroup interaction increases ingroup favouritism. Second, ingroup favouritism or bias seems to be the rule rather than the exception under conditions of intergroup competition, coaction or independence, or cooperation. Even the anticipation of intergroup behaviour, with or without intragroup interaction, seems sufficient for ingroup bias. Only one study (Doise and Weinberger, 1973) found that anticipated cooperation actually eliminates ingroup bias. There is also evidence that simply being divided into groups without social interaction, face-to-face contact or anticipated intergroup behaviour can create ingroup bias (Doise *et al.*, 1972; see also the next section).

Third, not only does intergroup cooperation tend to produce biases, but it sometimes does so to the same extent as competition. To explain this we need to remember that any intergroup orientation implies both an ingroup – outgroup division and cooperative intragroup interaction and thus should tend to encourage ingroup favouritism. Intergroup competition should tend to accentuate this effect because: (i) it should enhance the salience of the ingroup – outgroup division; (ii) it should motivate or lead to the expectation of more cooperative intragroup interaction; and (iii) actual or expected competitive intergroup interaction should increase hostility towards outgroup members. Likewise intergroup cooperation should normally attenuate the effect by reducing the salience of the ingroup – outgroup division and/or promoting as much or more cooperative interaction with outgroup as ingroup members. Thus the differences between intergroup cooperation and competition might tend to disappear where intergroup behaviour takes place under experimental or real-world conditions which maximize the salience of the ingroup – outgroup distinction and minimize social interaction.

This analysis is consistent with the conditions of those studies which do not find the expected difference between cooperation and competition (Brewer and Silver, 1978; Doise *et al.*, 1972; and Rabbie and deBrey's 1971 pretest results). It also explains why cooperation eliminated bias in Doise and Weinberger's (1973) study, since these researchers provided as much face-to-face contact and anticipated interaction between as within groups.

Thus cooperative and competitive relations *per se* do not necessarily produce different intergroup attitudes. Their different effects are probably mediated by their implications for the perceptual or cognitive salience of ingroup – outgroup membership and social interaction.

Fourth, coaction or independence does not seem to represent a unitary psychological orientation. It sometimes produces as much bias as competition and sometimes less than cooperation. There seems little doubt that coaction can sometimes develop spontaneously into competition through intergroup comparisons to evaluate task performance or some other characteristic (e.g. Rabbie and Wilkens, 1971; Turner, 1975a). It may also be the case at the other extreme that coacting subjects sometimes have a minimal awareness of themselves as members of a distinctive social unit. Thus the experiments may produce different results depending on whether their specific conditions encourage or impede group formation and intergroup comparisons.

The main conclusions to be drawn from this section (cf. Dion, 1979; Hinkle and Schopler, 1979; Rabbie, 1974) are as follows:

1. Cooperative intragroup interaction tends to increase ingroup favouritism.
2. Competitive intergroup interaction tends to increase intragroup cohesiveness, morale, cooperativeness, work motivation, conformity pressures, status and leadership differentiations and develop into mutual hostility accompanied by ingroup – outgroup biases.
3. Cooperative intergroup interaction tends to decrease social distance and ingroup – outgroup biases.
4. The different effects of cooperative and competitive intergroup behaviour tend to disappear when social interaction is minimized and the salience of the ingroup – outgroup division maximized: under these conditions all forms of anticipated and actual intergroup behaviour seem sufficient for ingroup – outgroup biases.

The functional theory seems partly correct in its prediction about the effects of cooperative and competitive interaction, but partly incorrect in that social interaction seems to matter more for intergroup attitudes than functional interdependence. Under some circumstances for example, cooperative relations do not improve intergroup attitudes even when there has not been history of previous conflict. Its major difficulty is that ingroup – outgroup membership sometimes seems to cause intergroup differentiation when there is neither cooperative interaction *within* nor competitive relations *between* groups. The next section considers this issue directly.

8.3 Social Categorization and Intergroup Discrimination

During the 1960s and early 1970s several studies reported results which openly challenged the functional theory. They found that incompatible group goals were not necessary and that ingroup – outgroup membership *per se* seemed sufficient for intergroup competition (Doise, 1969; Ferguson and Kelley, 1964; Kahn and Ryen, 1972; Rabbie and Horwitz, 1969; Tajfel *et al.*, 1971).

The results were most clear in the research of Tajfel and his colleagues (1971). These investigators explored whether *social categorization per se* was sufficient for intergroup discrimination. A social categorization is a discontinuous cognitive division or classification of individuals into distinct groups. They divided subjects into two groups on the basis of a trivial, *ad hoc* criterion and had them make decisions about monetary rewards for anonymous members of the ingroup and the outgroup. There was no conflict of interests nor history of hostility between the groups; no utilitarian link between intergroup discrimination and subjects' self-interest; no face-to-face interaction within or between groups and group membership was anonymous. Thus social categorization or the ingroup – outgroup division was isolated from all other variables which normally determine cohesiveness within groups or antagonism between them. It was even explained that the recipients of the monetary sums were identified by their group affiliation solely for administrative convenience.

Nevertheless, the basic result was that subjects discriminated in their decisions in favour of ingroup and against outgroup members. Moreover they were competitive: not only did they give more money to ingroup than outgroup members but they were willing to give them less than was possible in absolute terms in order to give them relatively more than outgroup members. These findings have been extensively replicated (see Turner, 1980).

It is also worth noting there is no evidence that the data are artefactual. Post-experimental enquiries do not reveal the subjects to believe that they are expected to discriminate, to share any notion of how they should behave or to be trying to please the experimenter (Billig, 1972; Turner, 1975b). There are three relevant experiments. Tajfel and Billig (1974) suspected that subjects' responses might be due to their unfamiliarity with and hence anxiety about the experimental setting. Contrary to hypothesis, familiarizing subjects with the setting increased intergroup discrimination. Billig (1973) hypothesized that subjects were behaving in terms of what they perceived to be the appropriate social norms. He allowed subjects who were about to make their decisions to discuss the study with those who had already discriminated, assuming that the latter would communicate their normative expectations and so increase discrimination by the former. Again contrary to hypothesis, the second set of subjects discriminated less than the first. Thus if normative expectations were communicated, they seem to work against rather than explain the usual data. Both these experiments illustrate that subjects in the minimal group paradigm (as the experimental setting is described) do not always conform to researchers' expectations. Nevertheless, it has been argued that their actions reflect 'demand characteristics'. St. Claire and Turner (in preparation) reasoned that if this were true, then observer subjects exposed to the same experimental cues as categorized subjects should be able to predict the latter's responses. In fact they overestimated their fairness. There was also evidence, in line with Billig's study, that fairness was perceived as the socially desirable strategy. Thus subjects' responses do not seem to be based on the subjective strangeness of the setting, cultural norms or demand characteristics, but seem to be a genuine psychological effect of the ingroup – outgroup division.

This discriminatory effect seems to generalize across independent and dependent variables and methodological paradigms. Billig and Tajfel (1973) demonstrated that it does not depend upon criterial classification, but is obtained even when division into groups is explicitly random. Other studies illustrate that social categorization *per se* also causes perceptual and attitudinal biases and differential attraction to ingroup and outgroup members (Brewer and Silver, 1978; Brown and Turner, 1979; Doise *et al.*, 1972; Turner, 1978a). The experiments cited at the beginning of this section report findings similar to those of Tajfel *et al.* (1971) in different settings. Since they were published there has been continual flow of research results all tending to confirm their initial implications (e.g. Brewer, 1979; Doise, 1978; Tajfel, 1978; Turner, 1975a, 1980). Thus far, the more carefully researchers have examined whether social categorization *per se* or ingroup – outgroup membership is sufficient for intergroup discrimination, the more the answer has been clearly in the affirmative. The conclusion must needs be that there are social psychological processes intrinsic to or stimulated merely by ingroup – outgroup divisions which tend to create discriminatory social relations.

One process which has been proposed, the cognitive balance principle, will not be discussed here: first, because there are both consistent and inconsistent data (Hinkle and Schopler, 1979; Rabbie and Horwitz, 1969; Worchel *et al.*, 1975); second, because what seems to be its central proposition, that discriminatory intergroup behaviour simply reflects differential ingroup – outgroup attraction, seems to be untrue. There is no direct relationship between differential attraction and discriminatory biases in terms of either independent or dependent variables (e.g. Dion, 1973; Kennedy and Stephan, 1977; Turner *et al.*, 1979; cf. Rabbie and Huygen, 1974). Intragroup attraction does have effects, but in ways that can be accounted for by other theories. Third, the principle seems somewhat *ad hoc* and partly vacuous; its derivations in this field tend to be non-distinctive and leave explanatory gaps; thus it may be cognitively consistent to favour members of an arbitrary ingroup over members of an arbitrary outgroup, but it is not obvious why this should be true. Fourth, there seems to be no direct evidence that ingroup favouritism is mediated by a need for cognitive consistency.

There are two processes which do seem plausible.

8.3.1 The Categorization Process

Tajfel (1969, 1972; Tajfel and Wilkes, 1963) proposes a categorization process such that the systematic superimposition of a classification upon a stimulus dimension leads to the perceptual accentuation or intra-class similarities and inter-class differences on that dimension. He assumes that the criterial or defining attributes of a class are inferred from the correlated characteristics of its members and that these criterial attributes tend to be assigned to all members of the class as common properties. In consequence, imposing classifications upon stimuli tends to transform continuous but correlated similarities and differences into perceptual discontinuities between classes. He also assumes that the process operates in social perception to produce stereotyping: the assignment of characteristics to individuals on the basis of their group membership.

Doise (1978) considers that the process causes intergroup discrimination: social categorization *per se* induces individuals to perceive themselves and others in terms of their group memberships; therefore, they perceive themselves as similar to ingroup members (or ingroup members as similar to themselves) and different from outgroup members; these cognitive distinctions produce differential intergroup behaviour and attitudes.

There are several data consistent with Doise's analysis. First, social categorization (the independent variable) seems to be the effective cause of intergroup discrimination. Some studies have unconfounded it from similarities and differences between the subjects (as antecedent conditions not consequent effects). Billig and Tajfel (1973, cf. Billig, 1973) assigned similar or different code numbers to subjects on the basis of a criterion or explicitly randomly under conditions where they were either divided into groups or not consistent with their code numbers. Both the criterial and the arbitrary social categorization, but neither criterial nor arbitrary similarities and differences *per se*, were sufficient for intergroup discrimination. Brewer and Silver (1978) also found that both criterial and arbitrary social classifications cause attitudinal biases. Allen and Wilder (1975) divided subjects into groups on the basis of a trivial criterion and manipulated explicit similarity in beliefs to ingroup and outgroup members. There was discrimination in all conditions, which increased with similarity to ingroup members. Thus the ingroup – outgroup division was sufficiently powerful that subjects favoured dissimilar ingroup members over similar outgroup members. These experiments suggest that it is not just similarities and differences but the discontinuous similarities and differences produced by the categorization process which are crucial to favouritism.

Two studies indicate that intergroup discrimination depends upon subjects perceiving each other as representatives of their group. Wilder (1978) provided information which 'individuated' outgroup members so that they could be perceived as differentiated persons instead of as anonymous group members. In consequence, intergroup discrimination decreased. Brown and Turner (1979) asked subjects to estimate the performances of ingroup and outgroup members with whom they had some degree of face-to-face contact as individual persons and found no discrimination. Under similar conditions where two ingroup – outgroup divisions were criss-crossed, subjects seemed to resort to intergroup as opposed to interpersonal evaluations because the former were more informative: intergroup discrimination reappeared and was most pronounced where members of two ingroups were judged in relation to members of two outgroups.

Second, there is direct evidence that social categorization *per se* induces the perception of intragroup similarities and intergroup differences. (Allen and Wilder, 1979; Doise *et al.*, 1978; Hensley and Duval, 1976, as discussed in Brewer, 1979). Research on stereotyping also produces supportive data (cf. Tajfel, 1969, 1972; Tajfel and Wilkes, 1963).

Third, manipulating the salience of social categorization increases ingroup bias. Doise (1978) reports that 'symbolic' encounter between ingroup and outgroup members (making subjects aware that they must rate outgroup as well as ingroup members) tends to enhance differentiation, as does 'collective' encounter (interaction between more than one representative of the ingroup and outgroup). Turner (1978a) investigated self-favouritism where group membership was either salient or not. Under the latter conditions, subjects favoured themselves over both ingroup and outgroup members, but less against ingroup and more against outgroup members in the former conditions.

Finally, intergroup differentiation is sometimes enhanced by common fate, proximity and social interaction and similarities and differences (Rabbie and Horwitz, 1969; Rabbie and Huygen, 1974; Allen and Wilder, 1975; Hensley and Duval, 1976). These variables can be conceptualized as cognitive criteria for social categorization which help to define individuals as members of a distinct social unit.

Thus the categorization process may be one reason for the effects of social categorization *per se*: subjects may discriminate because they tend to stereotype themselves as similar or different on the basis of their group memberships. Even under conditions of arbitrary social categorization, there is a distinctive subjective correlation between the salient aspects of the self-concept and ingroup – outgroup membership and hence a basis for attributing similarities and differences.

8.3.2 The Social Comparison Process

Tajfel and Turner (1979) propose that social categorization *per se* stimulates a self-evaluative social comparison process. They assume that social categorizations tend to be internalized to define the self in the social situation and hence contribute to self-evaluation. They further assume that one's self-esteem as a group member depends upon the evaluative outcomes of social comparisons between the ingroup and the outgroup. Since it can be supposed that individuals desire positive self-esteem, they conclude that there is a tendency to seek positive distinctiveness for the ingroup in comparison with the outgroup. Thus their hypothesis is that self-evaluative social comparisons directly produce competitive intergroup processes which motivate attitudinal biases and discriminatory actions.

The most direct evidence for this analysis is that intergroup discrimination seems to contain a competitive component even under conditions of functional independence. The tendency to maximize the differences in relative outcomes for ingroup and outgroup members seems the most important single motive in the minimal group paradigm (Turner, 1980). Brewer and Silver (1978) found that both independent and competitive groups adopt this 'winning' strategy. Turner *et al.* (1979) demonstrated that it is maintained even where it conflicts directly with subjects' self-interest. Studies in other paradigms also report a spontaneously competitive element in intergroup differentiation and implicate social comparison as the cause (Doise and Weinberger, 1973; Ferguson and Kelley, 1964; Rabbie and Wilkens, 1971).

Three experiments have attempted to manipulate the social comparison process. Turner (1978b) found that stable status similarities between groups produce more ingroup bias than stable status dissimilarities. Turner and Brown (1978) reported some complex results generally consistent with the idea that secure (stable and legitimate) status differences between groups tend to minimize and insecure differences to enhance competitive biases. Turner *et al.* (1979) found that subjects are less fair and more discriminatory towards relevant than irrelevant comparison outgroups, especially where they distribute high monetary rewards. Thus at least under some conditions both spontaneous and manipulated social comparisons seem to increase ingroup bias.

More evidence is that there seems to be a definite motivational bias for positive self-esteem in intergroup behaviour. Oakes and Turner (1980) confirmed the prediction that minimal intergroup discrimination would increase self-esteem compared to a control condition in which categorized subjects were not able to discriminate. Alternative explanations of the result are possible, but it is consistent with the positive distinctiveness principle. There is also the fact, of course, that ingroups are usually fvoured over outgroups. Even where there are prior evaluative differences between groups it is not the case, as the categorization process predicts, that these correlated differences tend to be directly accentuated; evaluative superiorities tend to be enhanced and evaluative inferiorities minimized (Brewer, 1979; Van Knippenberg and Wilke, 1979).

The rôle of the self-evaluative motive is also supported by the effects of status differences on intergroup behaviour. Status differences represent the outcomes of intergroup comparisons conferring positive or negative distinctiveness and also the antecedent conditions for different social strategies (individual mobility, social creativity, social competition, etc.) directed at the maintenance or protection of self-esteem (Tajfel, 1978, Tajfel and Turner, 1979). Their effects can be complex but there seems little doubt as the social comparison process expects that they are important determinants of competitive intergroup biases (Tajfel, 1978).

Turner and Brown (1978) manipulated whether status differences were perceived as secure or insecure. High status groups tended to discriminate when either a legitimate superiority was threatened or an illegitimate superiority was perceived as stable; when an illegitimate superiority was also unstable, they tended to stress alternative status dimensions. Low status groups tended to discriminate when their inferiority was illegitimate and especially when it was also unstable. Thus, as one might expect, there are different reactions to status differences according to whether the groups are seeking to preserve or restore positive distinctiveness.

These data make it difficult to explain discrimination on the basis of in group – outgroup divisions solely in terms of cognitive processes; motivational factors need to be superimposed (cf. Brewer, 1979; Turner, 1975a). The simplest solution is to assume that the categorization and the social comparison process are complementary. There are many possible complexities in such complementarity. but we shall do no more than suggest that the former is the necessary and the latter the sufficient condition for competitive intergroup differentiation (see Fig. 8.1). The categorization process produces the perceptual accentuation of intragroup similarities and intergroup differences and thus makes salient or perceptually prominent the criterial or relevant aspects of ingroup – outgroup membership. In this way it selects the specific dimension for self-evaluation and social comparison in the given setting. It also ensures that intergroup comparisons focus on perceptual discontinuities between ingroup and outgroup members so that positive differences (distinctiveness) and not similarities contribute to self-esteem. The social comparison process transforms simple perceptual or cognitive discriminations into differential attitudes and actions favouring the ingroup over the outgroup. It motivates the competitive enhancement of criterial differences between the groups and other strategies apart from direct discrimination to achieve positive distinctiveness.

This hypothesis can be described as the *Social Identity Principle* since it stresses that social categorization *per se* causes intergroup discrimination through its impact on self-perception. Both Doise and Tajfel and Turner assume that individuals tend to perceive and define themselves in terms of the superimposed social categorization. Tajfel (1972; see Turner, 1982) uses the term 'social identity' to describe aspects of the self-concept based upon group memberships. The principle states: *that the systematic superimposition upon individuals of a cognitive division into ingroup and outgroup tends to cause the perceptual accentuation of stereotypical intragroup similarities and intergroup differences and self-evaluative social comparisons in terms of these similarities and differences.* It can be assumed that these effects depend upon the salience and normative relevance of the social categorization for social behaviour.

To summarize this section: much recent experimentation indicates that social categorization *per se* can cause intergroup discrimination; the hypothesis which provides the most plausible theoretical explanation of this and other

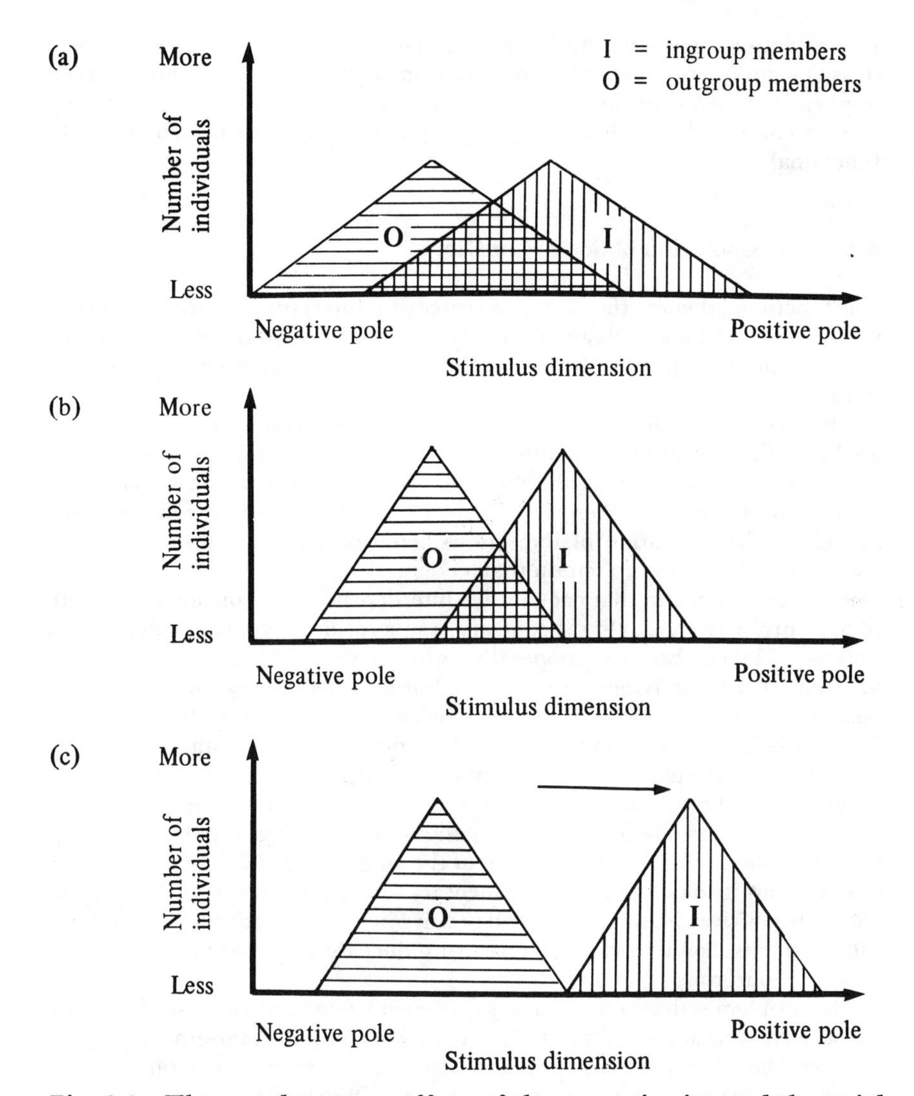

Fig. 8.1 The complementary effects of the categorization and the social comparison process on intergroup differentiation. (a) The baseline distribution of stimulus values displaying the modal (average, representative, typical, dominant, etc.) characteristics of ingroup and outgroup members. (b) The effect of the categorization process. The groups are perceptually differentiated in that fewer individuals occupy the overlapping area but their modal characteristics have not changed. (c) The effect of the social comparison process. The ingroup differentiates itself from the outgroup on a perceptually salient dimension in such a way as to increase the distance between their modal characteristics.

related data suggests that under appropriate conditions, ingroup – outgroup divisions can directly motivate competitive intergroup behaviour through their implications for self-evaluation. In the next section we consider how this conclusion charges the analysis of intergroup conflict bequeathed to us by the functional theory.

8.4 The Resolution of Social Conflict

The functional theory offers a simple remedy for intergroup conflict: the provision of superordinate goals and the development of cooperative interaction. To what extent does this hypothesis remain plausible in the light of the preceding research?

The first basic point is that cooperative interdependence (superordinate goals) conflicts whereas competitive interdependence (conflicts of interest) correlates with ingroup – outgroup divisions. If we assume that the latter create competitive tendencies, then it seems likely that there is an asymmetry in the functional determination of intergroup behaviour. Intergroup competition should be much easier to obtain than cooperation.

This does not mean that cooperative interdependence is incompatible with positive distinctiveness. On the contrary, a superordinate goal often demands a division of labour between cooperating groups, the differentiation and coordination of their activities into separate but complementary work-roles. The enactment of such distinctive work-roles should provide each group with favourable intergroup comparisons at the same time as the common objective engenders consensual social values. In consequence, a social consensus could develop that the groups share a series of complementary superiorities and inferiorities across relevant status dimensions. Since each group should be able to admire the distinctive superiorities of the outgroup and derive positive self-esteem from its own, these complementary status differences should help to reconcile positive distinctiveness with positive intergroup attitudes. Such social arrangements should tend to eliminate or reduce the negative consequences of ingroup – outgroup divisions.

The problem is that cooperative inderdependence may not be sufficient for cooperative interaction. Since it tends to conflict with the ingroup – outgroup division, the latter may counteract its effects and prevent cooperative interaction. In this case, complementary status differences may not emerge to neutralize the negative effects of group boundaries. It is not evident as yet that cooperative interdependence automatically lowers the salience of ingroup – outgroup divisions. As we saw in the first section cooperative interdependence and even cooperative behaviour unconfounded with social interaction did not reduce biased intergroup attitudes compared to competitive inter-dependence.

The picture seems to be the reverse for competitive interdependence. Since it tends to be congruent with group boundaries, it seems likely to be sufficient for competitive interaction and may also tend to increase the salience of the social division. Given a salient division into groups, competitive relations may be the natural state of affairs. This does not bode well if conflict resolution is to depend upon the effects of superordinate goals.

The obvious objection to this analysis is that the functional theory is also a theory of group formation. It states that a group structure tends to emerge where mutually cooperative interaction between a number of individuals has become sufficiently stabilized. The determinants of social cooperation are functional relationships. Thus group formation is basically an effect or symptom of cooperative interaction. Its special characteristics are merely the development of social roles and norms and shared values which coordinate and regulate goal-related activities. It follows that cooperative interactions between groups, once initiated, must inevitably tend to reduce and ultimately eliminate ingroup – outgroup divisions. The implication is that cooperative interaction, even if not cooperative interdependence *per se*, does automatically and is the basic means of decreasing the salience of group boundaries.

The Sherifs's research demonstrates that this can be true under certain conditions. There is evidence that their superordinate goals fused the conflicting groups into one (cf. Doise, 1971). However, these data may represent a special case, since these groups came into existence and were defined solely in terms of their activities in the summer camp. There was no external criterion by which they could maintain their differences during cooperative interaction. The general validity of the hypothesis that social cooperation causes group formation needs to be considered.

To do so, it is useful to bring out the tacit assumptions which the functional theory shares with the mainstream conceptualization of the social group in experimental social psychology. Turner (1982) describes these assumptions, or perhaps emphases is better, as the Social Cohesion model. It is important to point out that specific theorists such as the Sherifs might not endorse some of these emphases and indeed would almost certainly reject a few. However, our discussion is concerned with the functional theory in its most simple, and we would argue most general, form, not as the property of any specific individual.

The model can be summarized as follows. Motivational (or functional) interdependence for the satisfaction of needs, achievement of goals, or consensual validation of attitudes and values between persons leads to their social and psychological interdependence. The main expressions of the latter are mutual interpersonal influence and attraction and affiliative social interaction. Over time, social relations tend to become stabilized, organized and prescribed through the development of a system of status and role relationships, social norms and shared values (social structure). Individuals become psychologically attached to the group through the development of cohesive social relationships. 'Cohesiveness' stands for the degree to which members are attracted to each other as individual persons, to the characteristics of the group as a whole, and to group activities. In practice, it indicates interpersonal attraction since, implicitly or explicitly, it is denied that attraction to the group can be more than attraction to its members and assumed that the latter reflects the extent to which they satisfy one's needs, directly (e.g. attitudinal similarity) or indirectly (e.g. cooperative goal locomotion). Lott and Lott (1965) define cohesiveness as that group property which is inferred from the number and strength of mutual positive attitudes between group members. The fundamental criterion for group formation, therefore, is not group structure (which, although important, is derivative) but the development of affective or emotional bonds between persons based on their motivational interdependence.

There is little argument that group behaviour tends to be characterized by mutual cooperation, attraction and influence between members. However, it is not so evident that group-belongingness is based upon motivational interdependence and interpersonal attraction. This theory is difficult to square with the effects of social categorization *per se* and other data to be discussed presently. To discuss these data, it is useful to formulate an alternative set of assumptions, the Social Identification model (Turner, 1982).

This theory makes the cognitive component of self-attitudes not the affective component of interpersonal attitudes the basis for group behaviour. What matters for group-belongingness is not individuals' social relationships and attitudes to others but how they perceive and define themselves. A social group is defined as two or more individuals who perceive themselves to be members of the same social category or share a common social identification of themselves. The latter is some social categorization which has been internalized as a part of their self-concepts. Others are reacted to as group members in so far as they are included within and exemplify some self-defining social category. The theory explains group formation in terms of the formation and internalization of social categorizations into self-conception.

It is worth noting that this model does not deny group cohesiveness but sees it as a symptom and not a determinant of social identification. It distinguishes between interpersonal and inter-member attraction: liking for others as differentiated, individual persons and as representatives of the common characteristics of the group. The latter is assumed to be a product of the mutual stereotypical similarities perceived between group members due to the operation of the categorization process.

There are at least three strands of evidence for the analysis of group formation as a process of social identification.

8.4.1 *Interpersonal Attraction and Group Formation*

Does group formation depend upon interpersonal attraction? The main evidence is that variables which determine positive interpersonal attitudes (attitudinal similarity, common fate, shared threat, social interaction, proximity, cooperation and competition, etc.) are known to increase intragroup cohesiveness.

Sole *et al.* (1975) conducted three field experiments on altruism. They manipulated degrees of opinion similarity between subjects and a stranger who needed help. The basic result was that attraction to the stranger tended to increase directly with similarity, but that helping depended on total similarity which allowed the stranger to be categorized unambiguously as a member of the 'we-group'. Thus if altruism indicates group formation, this depended upon the cognitive and not the affective consequences of similarity. As similarity increased, it passed some critical threshold whereby the subjects perceived not merely similarity to but identity with the stranger, a discontinuous social categorization was formed. The implication is that similarity may contribute to group formation as a cognitive criterion for social categorization.

The same may be true of the other variables mentioned above. They all seem to have in common the capacity to generate cognitive boundaries between people, to create social discontinuities, which may define them as members of distinct 'perceptual units' (Dion, 1979). They may increase cohesiveness because they directly promote interpersonal attraction or because, as determinants of social identification, they enhance inter-member attraction. It cannot be assumed that their effects in this respect necessarily support the social cohesion model.

This is especially so since there is direct evidence that interpersonal attraction is not necessary for group formation. The experiments in the last section demonstrate that social categorization *per se*, even on an explicitly random basis, is sufficient for group behaviour in that the subjects display similar or collective reactions to others consistently related to their own and the others' group affiliations. This would have been just as true if they had favoured outgroup members over ingroup members. Thus group formation takes place in the complete absence of interpersonal relationships or any variables which might predict interpersonal attraction. These studies also show that social categorization *per se* causes intragroup attraction, despite the fact that subjects have no idea of the specific persons in their group. They seem to like individuals as and because they are group members, not because of their personal characteristics. In other words this seems to represent inter-member attraction produced by the perception of assumed stereotypical similarities.

Other experiments in different paradigms make the same point more dramatically. They point to group formation and resultant cohesiveness under conditions where there are or should be negative interpersonal relations and attitudes between group members. It seems that shared threat engenders favourable attitudes to group members despite racial prejudice against them (Burnstein & McRae, 1962; Feshbach & Singer, 1957). Proximity and social interaction create intragroup cohesiveness despite strong and relevant attitudinal disagreements between members (Rabbie & Huygen, 1974). Prejudiced whites include black supporters within their reference groups for some normative judgements but not others (Boyanowsky and Allen, 1973; Malof and Lott, 1962). Intergroup competition and intragroup cooperation induce positive attitudes towards group members who are, in fact, frustrating and detrimental to the collaborative effort (Kalin & Marlowe, 1968; Myers, 1962). And low cohesive dyad members, who dislike and compete with each other as individuals, rate their group as favourably as a collective entity as high cohesive dyad members (Dion, 1973). In these studies individuals seem to be defined as group members despite their negative personal attributes and, once so defined, they are liked. These data suggest that one can like people as group members at the same time that one dislikes them as individual persons.

It is noticeable that the same experiments which create problems for the social cohesion model indicate the central role of social categorization. In the studies immediately above the relevant variables, shared threat, proximity, common fate, etc. can easily be construed as determining perceptual unit formation. Other researchers have come to the same conclusion that cognitive factors play an important role in group formation (Brewer, 1979; Dion, 1973, 1979; Rabbie & Huygen, 1974; Sole *et al.*, 1975; Worchel, 1979). Thus social categorization and not interpersonal attraction may be necessary and sufficient for group behaviour. Individuals may become a group simply because they perceive themselves to share some form of discontinuous homogeneity.

This conclusion, we should remind ourselves, does not imply that social groups do not tend to be cohesive. They should be so for several reasons consistent with the social identification model: social categorization directly produces inter-member attraction; social categorization and interpersonal attraction may sometimes be correlated effects of the same variables, and because of the need for positive self-esteem, individuals should tend to define their group attributes positively, and be more likely to perceive inclusive similarities between themselves and attractive than unattractive others.

8.4.2 The Effects of Group Failure on Cohesiveness

If cohesiveness depends upon motivational interdependence or mutual need-satisfaction, then it should be the case that groups which mediate rewards for their members, which succeed in reaching their goals, should be more cohesive than those which do not. Failure, defeat, deprivation, or other negative outcomes related to group membership should reduce intragroup cohesiveness. This is perhaps the central prediction of the social cohesion model: individuals come together for cooperative success not failure. There is much supportive evidence, but also some disconfirmations of the prediction (Lott & Lott, 1965).

One recent example will suffice. Kennedy and Stephan (1977) manipulated the success or failure of dyad members on a task under conditions of intragroup cooperation or competition. They expected cooperative success to increase cohesiveness. One might also have expected competitive success to reduce cohesiveness, since an antagonistic relationship produces positive consequences. The opposite results were obtained: cooperative failure led to more ingroup bias than success, and competitive success more than failure. These data are obviously problematic for a theory which makes cooperative reward-mediation the basis for cohesive social attitudes.

Lott and Lott (1965), who are reinforcement theorists, accept that instances in which shared threat and failure do not reduce and even increase group cohesiveness pose a serious difficulty for the reward or need-satisfaction perspective. Their solution is twofold. First, they assume that failure is sometimes attributed to factors external to the group (bad luck, temporary difficulties, etc.) and so reinterpreted as shared, external threat. Second, they suggest that where group effort can defeat the threat, it will motivate increased cooperation (and so cohesiveness). Thus they deny that failure *per se* can increase cohesiveness: shared threat stimulates intragroup cooperation precisely to avoid failure and achieve success.

This is a plausible hypothesis in many circumstances and yet, theoretically, it is not fully satisfactory. It tends to assume what it needs to explain. Why should individuals react to failure as a shared threat to the group, or believe that they can cope with the threat through group action, unless they remain cohesive? The whole issue is to explain why the actual or expected costs of group membership do not make them less cohesive and so less likely to adopt such tactics. A possible solution (which does not necessarily reject Lott and Lott's specific hypothesis) is to assume that shared threat and failure can have a positive impact on social identification and that the latter mediates cohesiveness.

There are two available hypotheses. First, shared threat and failure are forms of common fate which should directly enhance the salience of group boundaries. Whether positive or negative, common fate induces perceived homogeneity between group members and so social identification. The more salient and distinctive the fate, the more cohesiveness. Thus the relative impact of success and failure would vary with their relative distinctiveness in specific settings (importance, frequency, novelty, the degree to which they differentiated between groups, etc.).

Rabbie and Horwitz (1969) provide some relevant data. They imposed differential, common fate on pairs of groups by rewarding one and depriving the other. Positive and negative fate increased ingroup bias. Deprivation could have been externally attributed, but it was nevertheless final: so it is difficult to interpret cohesiveness as instrumental to future rewards. The parsimonious explanation is to assume that reward and deprivation worked in the same way as shared experiences which highlighted the ingroup – outgroup division.

Second, if social identification represents a self-attitude, then it should tend to change as do other attitudes. There seem to be two basic inducements to attitude change: as a result of direct social influence from others, and as a reaction to one's own overt behaviour. Social identification could change in both ways. In the former case, individuals may be directly persuaded to define themselves in terms of certain social categories by attractive or credible others, as when, perhaps, subjects are categorized by prestigious experimenters. We shall concentrate on the latter case.

Research indicates that private attitudes tend to follow public behaviour (cf. Wicklund & Brehm, 1976). Therefore, it may be that simply acting as group members is sufficient for individuals to define themselves as such. Three relevant processes have been identified, reinforcement or incentive effects, cognitive dissonance, and causal attribution. The important point is that only the incentive theory expects more attitude change when overt behaviour produces positive outcomes. The latter two can both predict the opposite. Cognitive dissonance theory states that where individuals engage in counter-attitudinal behaviour with a sense of personal responsibility for their actions (high choice, commitment, awareness of possible negative consequences, etc.), they need to change their attitudes to justify their actions; the need for justification, to maintain cognitive consistency, is greater where there are negative outcomes. Attribution theory states that individuals may tend to explain their behaviour in terms of internal factors such as attitudes to the degree that they cannot explain it in terms of external factors such as the situation, role demands or rewards. Thus some data indicate (cf. Harvey and Smith, 1977) that where subjects are rewarded for activities which they would normally perform, their intrinsic motivation decreases since they now explain their actions in terms of the extrinsic rewards.

If we apply these ideas to social identification, we can suppose that under some conditions individuals will tend to justify and explain their actions more in terms of their self-definition as a group member the more negative the outcomes, whereas under other conditions, there will be more self-attitude change with positive outcomes. Thus both group success and failure could increase and decrease social identification depending on the circumstances in which they occurred.

Turner *et al.* (in preparation) conducted two experiments to test the dissonance hypothesis. They predicted that where subjects engaged in self-discrepant, group behaviour, with personal responsibility, group failure would create more social identification than success, but that the opposite would be true without personal responsibility (the incentive effect). They assumed that social identification would increase cohesiveness.

In the first study subjects had high or low choice about doing a group task on which they expected to and did succeed or fail. With high choice, there was more cohesiveness after failure than success, but less after failure than success with low choice. In the second study, subjects either committed themselves or not to staying in their group for the duration of an intergroup competition and either won or lost on the first task. Committed groups became more cohesive and biased against the outgroup after defeat than victory. They also developed *higher* self-esteem and attributed their performance more *internally* after defeat than victory. The reverse results were found in the uncommitted groups. The self-esteem and attribution data seem to rule out Lott and Lott's explanation in this instance and provide some evidence that changes in self-attitudes are taking place. It looks as if once subjects identify, they evaluate their group and hence themselves positively, whether or not they were successful. It is also worth noting that both the high choice, success and the committed, winning groups showed remarkably low levels of cohesiveness. There is a strong implication that self-attribution processes were at work: these subjects did not seem to need to feel part of their group, since the extrinsic rewards were a sufficient explanation of their group actions. Thus it may be that cooperative success sometimes provides extrinsic rewards which decrease intrinsic social identification.

In general, the above studies suggest that group cohesiveness is not simply a matter of mutual need-satisfaction. There is a sense in which under appropriate conditions individuals cannot but see themselves as group members for good or ill.

8.4.3 *The Effects of Cooperative and Competitive Interaction*

Is it the case that cooperative and competitive interaction themselves directly produce positive and negative intergroup attitudes? One might think that this could be taken for granted. However, we suggested above that they might determine social attitudes indirectly as cognitive criteria for social categorization. Other researchers have come to very similar conclusions. They argue that cooperation and competition reduce or enhance the salience of we/they distinctions and that the latter are the important determinants of intergroup biases.

Dion (1973, 1979) describes this as the cognitive differentiation hypothesis. He conceptualizes social groups as 'perceptual units' and considers that intergroup competition contributes to unit formation because it induces perceived homogeneity (common fate and similarity) within the ingroup and perceived heterogeneity (opposed fate and dissimilarity) between ingroup and outgroup members. So, too, Brewer (1979) argues that explicit competition can serve to clarify ingroup – outgroup boundaries where the cognitive distinction might otherwise be ambiguous, and Worchel (1979) states that it draws clear boundaries, accentuates we/they differences and makes these groupings a salient feature of the situation.

It can be presumed that intragroup cooperation has the same effects as intergroup competition, and that intragroup competition and intergroup cooperation tend to blur and even redraw group boundaries. There is in fact a definite implication that ingroup – outgroup formation is more important than intergroup relations in determining intergroup attitudes. Thus intragroup cooperation and competition could be more effective in increasing and decreasing ingroup biases than intergroup competition and cooperation. An experiment which seems to illustrate this, but which can also be explained to some extent by the social cohesion model, is reported by Goldman *et al.* (1977). They manipulated both intragroup and intergroup cooperation or competition. Both variables produced definite behavioural effects, but the former was much more important for social attitudes. Ingroup ratings were more favourable with intragroup cooperation (5.64) than competition (0.77), but outgroup ratings were only non-significantly more favourable with intergroup cooperation (2.59) than competition (1.56). Thus the consequence is that intragroup cooperation led to ingroup favouritism and intragroup competition to outgroup favouritism, independently of the functional relationship with the outgroup.

Worchel (1979) draws the important inference from the cognitive hypothesis that the best way to reduce intergroup conflict is to remove or reduce salient differences between the groups, and that cooperative interaction mitigates conflict only to the degree that it can and does accomplish this result. In other words, to produce lasting positive attitudes, intergroup cooperation has to eliminate the ingroup – outgroup distinction and tend towards intragroup cooperation. Worchel outlines several variables which may maintain group boundaries despite cooperative encounters: distinctive physical or visible differences between ingroup and outgroup members, cooperative failure, the intensity of previous conflict, the infrequency of and limited duration of cooperative encounters, disparities in power and status between the groups, etc. He reports two experiments to support his analysis that such variables mitigate conflict reduction despite intergroup cooperation.

Worchel *et al.* (1977) hypothesized that the effects of cooperative intergroup interaction would depend upon whether previous interaction had made the ingroup – outgroup division salient. In the first stage of the study, they manipulated intergroup cooperation, independence or competition; attraction to the outgroup decreased in that order. In the second stage, the same groups now all cooperated and either succeeded or failed. Cooperative success increased attraction to the outgroup, but cooperative failure increased it only where the groups had not previously competed and decreased it where they had. In other words, the groups which had previously cooperated or been independent reacted to the outcomes of later cooperation as if they were one common group: either success or failure increased cohesiveness. The previously competitive groups reacted as if they were still separate entities, willing to distance themselves if cooperation was unsuccessful. This experiment makes two clear points. First, that cooperative interaction can function to redefine cognitive boundaries. It is impossible to explain the qualitatively different effects of previous cooperation and competition on reactions to success and failure if we assume that they merely created more or less attraction to the outgroup. The data imply the elimination or maintenance of a social division. Second, that where cooperative interaction does not eliminate the ingroup – outgroup division, it does not necessarily improve intergroup attitudes: in this case, its effects may depend at the least on whether it results in success or failure.

Worchel *et al.* (1978) investigated the effects of distinctive visible differences on the results of intergroup cooperation. The design of this experiment was similar to that above except that ingroup and outgroup members also either wore identical or distinctive laboratory coats (both white or white and red). Similarity of dress produced a strong main effect: cooperation led to more intergroup attraction when the groups dressed identically than when distinctively. It also interacted with the other variables. Differences in dress retarded conflict reduction when cooperation ended in failure, regardless of the type of previous interaction. They also inhibited intergroup attraction for previously competitive groups when cooperation ended in success, but not for previously cooperative groups. These results support the hypothesis that intergroup attitudes are a function of salient intergroup differences and that cooperation does not reduce conflict where such differences are maintained. They also help to confirm the interpretation of the first experiment. So long as a visible difference maintained the ingroup – outgroup division, even previously cooperative groups reacted to cooperative failure like the competitive groups.

These two elegant experiments provide evidence that the role of cooperative and competitive interaction may be to define individuals as members of the same or different social categories or to minimize or accentuate the salience of existing social categorizations. They may not produce very different effects on intergroup attitudes unless they have these cognitive consequences.

8.4.4 *An Alternative Perspective: Group Formation as a Determinant of Social Cooperation*

If the social identification analysis is valid, then group formation is not merely a symptom of cohesive social attitudes developed through cooperative interaction. There are at least three classes of determinants: (i) social or physical variables which induce individuals to perceive themselves as defined by distinctive common attributes and experiences; (ii) social action on the basis of such attributes producing positive or negative outcomes; and (iii) other processes of direct social influence aimed at persuading people to change their self-attitudes towards self-definition in terms of some social category. Social cooperation is an important empirical determinant of group formation because it can and does operate through these processes. However, there is no intrinsic theoretical link. The ingroup – outgroup division may not be reduced or eliminated during intergroup cooperation because there may remain distinctive differences between the groups, joint action may be attributed to or justified by the extrinsic outcomes and not explained in terms of common group membership; and group members may adhere to social norms of ingroup – outgroup identification. The ingroup – outgroup division may then tend to reproduce negative intergroup attitudes as soon as the immediate demands of collaborative action are at an end.

Before drawing conclusions from this section, there is one more important point to be made. Much social cooperation may not reflect objective functional relations at all, but may be a direct effect of group formation. It seems likely that the social group can be an independent variable in the perception of cooperative and competitive interdependence. This can be understood through the operation of the social identity principle. In many cases individuals should tend to perceive their goals, needs or motives as correlated with their group membership; thus their interests should become stereotypical characteristics of the group as a whole. The categorization process, therefore, predicts that individuals should tend to perceive themselves as having similar or identical goals to members of their own group and different or opposed goals to members of other groups. This should provide a powerful basis for intragroup cooperation since group members should perceive their interests not merely as interdependent but as literally identical. Through common category membership we should assign others' goals to ourselves and assume that our goals are shared by others. Some evidence comes from the research of Hornstein (1972, 1976) and his colleagues on altruism. They find that individuals' motivational systems can become linked to the needs of others through common group membership, i.e. individuals act (altruistically) as if the goals of other group members have become motives for their own behaviour.

We can assume too that social groups tend to evaluate and compare themselves in terms of their distinctive stereotypical goals and locomotion towards them. The social comparison process predicts that such locomotion should tend to be perceived as competitively interdependent between different groups. Again there is some consistent evidence that social groups seem to be more competitive and perceive their interests more competitively than individuals under the same functional conditions (Brown & Deschamps, in press; Doise, 1969; Doise & Giraud, cited in Doise, 1978; Doise & Sinclair, 1973; Doise & Weinberger, 1973; Dustin & Davis, 1970; Janssens & Nuttin, 1976; McKillip *et al.*, 1977; Wilson & Kayatani, 1968, and Wilson's other studies previously cited; see too Brewer & Silver, 1978).

Thus we can derive from the social identity principle the hypothesis that, under conditions where objective functional relations are ambiguous, indirect or mixed cooperative and competitive (as they often are in real life), social categorization *per se* should cause individuals to perceive their interests as cooperatively linked within groups and competitively linked between groups. The implication is that the formation of a common or superordinate group tends to induce and stabilize cooperative behaviour in the same way that an ingroup – outgroup division elicits competitive tendencies: not merely through the need for positive distinctiveness. but more basically, because social categorization directly influences individuals' perceptions of their goals.

To conclude this section we can summarize the main difficulties with the functional hypothesis that intergroup conflict is resolved through superordinate goals and state the alternative perspective. The difficulties are as follows:

1. Superordinate goals need to be perceived to be acted on; yet, the social group may constitute an independent variable determining members' perception of their objective interests. The very fact of a salient social division into groups may create tendencies to perceive competitive instead of cooperative interdependence between them.
2. Even where superordinate goals are recognized and intergroup cooperation takes place, the crucial issue for long-term conflict resolution is whether the latter leads to the formation of a common or superordinate social group in the ways already discussed. Cooperative interaction has no special theoretical status as a determinant of group formation and may be counteracted in this respect by other variables that may obtain in specific contexts.
3. Where the ingroup – outgroup division is maintained, intergroup cooperation may nevertheless take place and be continued for purely instrumental reasons. However, there is no reason to assume in this case that this will produce lasting improvements in intergroup relations. On the contrary the expected rewards may provide external justifications of the intergroup behaviour which make changes in private intergroup attitudes unnecessary. As soon as the immediate goal is achieved, the

ingroup – outgroup division may tend to reproduce perceived conflicts of interests and partisan social attitudes between the groups.

The evident alternative strategy for conflict resolution is to take Worchel's hypothesis to its logical conclusion, i.e. to attempt directly to minimize and ultimately eliminate ingroup – outgroup distinctions. The most effective social psychological approach may be not so much to seek to manipulate intergroup relations as to encourage their transformation into intragroup relations through the creation of common or superordinate social identifications perceived as relevant to the given social context. The establishment of more salient common identifications between conflicting groups should tend to produce cohesiveness and the perception of cooperative interests between members of the erstwhile subgroups as a direct consequence. The specific measures necessary to achieve this end could include intergroup cooperation, but this would depend upon an analysis of the social forces maintaining group boundaries in the concrete situation. The fundamental point is that the processes implicated in group formation *per se* may also tend to dictate the cooperative and competitive orientations characteristic respectively of intra- and intergroup relations.

8.5 Conclusion

The chapter began with the Sherifs's basic proposition that functional relations determine social relations (the character of social interaction and thus the formation of social groups and the relations between them). We have seen that this proposition has proved extremely fruitful in generating research and ideas and that its chief empirical insights into the effects of cooperative and competitive interaction seem still to be valid. However, what is much less certain is any direct impact of functional relations *per se* on intergroup attitudes (Section 8.2), the hypothesis that conflicting interests are necessary for competitive intergroup behaviour (Section 8.3), and the theoretical construal of group formation and conflict resolution as simple effects of social cooperation (Section 8.4). Ingroup – outgroup membership seems to be an important independent variable in determining cooperation and competition. Thus the recent research argues that in some respects the Sherifs's proposition needs to be reversed: individuals' social relations understood as their social group memberships seem able to determine their functional relations in the sense of their *perceived* goals and hence the character of their social interaction and attitudes. Not objective interests but social identity may be the most predictive social psychological variable for understanding the development and resolution of intergroup conflict.

This conclusion is almost certain to be misunderstood. At least two caveats are in order. First, there is no doubt at all that people's objective interests (economic, political, etc.) play a major role in social conflict. The argument is that, at least at the social psychological level of analysis, their effects are probably mediated by their impact on social identifications. There is also no doubt that individuals' goals or purposes do contribute to group formation and, perhaps even more important, are likely to be critical determinants of the situational salience of specific identifications. However, our theoretical analysis means that we cannot assume any simple one-to-one correspondence between people's objective interests and their group memberships nor make the former a direct psychological theory of the latter.

Second, there is no implication that social conflict is an inevitable and universal consequence of ingroup – outgroup divisions. Our discussion suggests that at least some processes associated with social categorization produce a *social psychological tendency* to competitive intergroup behaviour. This tendency may at times be counteracted in the real world by other social psychological or more macro-social processes. The identification of the systematic conditions under which the tendency holds is a large research task to do both with the improvement of social psychological theory and the ascertainment of the boundaries of such theory in relation to other social sciences.

At the moment the usefulness of the present conclusion depends upon the extent to which it helps to stimulate new directions in basic research and provide a fresh perspective for applied work. It is beyond the scope of the chapter to discuss applied implications, but in general terms, the emphasis upon social group membership as an independent or intervening variable in social behaviour would seem to provide a promising perspective from which to consider policies for conflict resolution (or intensification). As regards basic research, there are many issues. Perhaps the three most important areas to which attention needs to be directed are: (i) the determinants of group formation, in particular to consider the adequacy of its analysis as a process of social identification or interpersonal attraction; (ii) the role of group membership as an antecedent process for social cooperation — the impact of social categorization on group members' perceptions of their needs, goals and motives; and (iii) the personal and situational factors that control which of the many social groups to which any individual belongs becomes psychologically salient or prepotent in a specific social encounter.

In general, our conclusion argues that future work needs to be conducted within the context of a wider theoretical interest in basic group processes, and also that the social psychology of the social group needs to confront the questions raised by intergroup behaviour. There seems every hope that research located at the interface of intergroup behaviour and the general psychology of the social group should make a valuable and timely contribution to both fields.

References

ALLEN, V.L. and WILDER, D.A. (1975). Categorisation, belief similarity, and group discrimination. *Journal of Personality and Social Psychology*, **32**, 971 – 977.

ALLEN, V.L. and WILDER, D.A. (1979). Group Categorisation and attribution of belief similarity. *Small Group Behaviour*, **110**, 73 – 80.

AVIGDOR, R. (1953). Etude expérimentale de la génèse des stéréotypes. *Cahiers Internationaux de Sociologie*, **14**, 154 – 168.

BASS, B.M. and DUNTEMAN, G. (1963). Biases in the evaluation of one's own group, its allies and opponents. *Journal of Conflict Resolution*, **7**, 16 – 20.

BILLIG, M.G. (1972). Social Categorisation and Intergroup Relations. Unpublished Ph.D. Thesis, University of Bristol.

BILLIG, M.G. (1973). Normative communication in a minimal intergroup situation. *European Journal of Social Psychology*, **3**, 339 – 343.

BILLIG, M.G. (1976). *Social psychology and intergroup relations*. European Monographs in Social Psychology, No. 9, London: Academic Press.

BILLIG, M.G. and Tajfel, H. (1973). Social categorisation and similarity in intergroup behaviour. *European Journal of Social Psychology*, **3**, 27 – 52.

BLAKE, R.R. and MOUTON, J.S. (1961). Reactions to intergroup competition under win – lose conditions. *Management Science*, **7**, 420 – 435.

BLAKE, R.R and MOUTON, J.S. (1962). The intergroup dynamics of win – lose conflict and problem-solving collaboration in union-management relations. In M. SHERIF (Ed.), *Intergroup Relations and Leadership*, New York: Wiley, Ch. 5, pp. 94 – 140.

BOYANOWSKY, E.O. and ALLEN, V.L. (1973). Ingroup norms and self-identity as determinants of discriminatory behaviour. *Journal of Personality and Social Psychology*, **25**, 408 – 418.

BREWER, M.B. (1979). Ingroup bias in the minimal intergroup situation: a cognitive-motivational analysis. *Psychological Bulletin*, **86**, 307 – 324.

BREWER, M.B. and SILVER, M. (1978). Ingroup bias as a function of task characteristics. *European Journal of Social Psychology*, **8**, 393 – 400.

BROWN, R.J. and DESCHAMPS, J-C. Discrimination entre individus et entre groupes, *Bulletin de Psychologie* (In press).

BROWN, R.J. and TURNER, J.C. (1979). The criss-cross categorisation effect in intergroup discrimination. *British Journal of Social and Clinical Psychology*, **18**, 371 – 383.

BURNSTEIN, E. and MCRAE, A.V. (1962). Some effects of shared threat and prejudice in racially mixed groups. *Journal of Abnormal and Social Psychology*, **64**, 257 – 263.

DIAB, L.N. (1970). A study of intra-group and intergroup relations among experimentally produced small groups. *Genetic Psychology Monographs*, **82**, 49 – 82.

DION, K.L.(1973). Cohesiveness as a determinant of ingroup-outgroup bias. *Journal of Personality and Social Psychology*, **28**, 163 – 171.

DION, K.L. (1979). Intergroup conflict and intra-group cohesiveness. In W.G. AUSTIN and S. WORCHEL (Eds.), *The Social Psychology of Intergroup Relations*. Monterey, California: Brooks/Cole.

DOISE, W. (1969). Les strategies de jeu à l'intérieur et entre des groupes de nationalité différente. *Bulletin du C.E.R.P.*, **18**, 13 – 26.

DOISE, W. (1971). Die experimentalle Untersuchung von Beziehungen zwischen Gruppen. *Z. Experimentalle-Angewandte Psychologie*, **18**, 151 – 189.

DOISE, W. (1978). *Groups and Individuals: Explanations in Social Psychology*. Cambridge: Cambridge University Press.

DOISE, W., CSEPELI, G., DANN, H.-D., GOUGE, G.C., LARSEN, K. and OSTELL, A. (1971). *Intergroup Relations — preliminary report*. Report from the 3rd European Summer school for Experimental Social Psychology, Konstanz, 4 – 31 July 1971.

DOISE, W., CSEPELI, G., DANN, H.-D., GOUGE, C., LARSEN, K. and OSTELL, A. (1972). An experimental investigation into the formation of intergroup representations.

European Journal of Social Psychology, **2**, 202 – 204.

DOISE, W., DESCHAMPS, J-C. and MEYER, G. (1978). The accentuation of intra-category similarities. In H. TAJFEL (Ed.), *Differentiation between Social Groups*. London: Academic Press.

DOISE, W. and SINCLAIR, A. (1973). The categorisation process in intergroup relations. *European Journal of Social Psychology*, **3**, 145 – 157.

DOISE, W. and WEINBERGER, M. (1973). Représentations masculines dans différentes situations de rencontres mixtes. *Bulletin de Psychologie*, **26**, 649 – 657.

DUSTIN, D.S. and DAVIS, H.P. (1970). Evaluative bias in group and individual competition. *Journal of Social Psychology*, **80**, 103 – 108.

FERGUSON, C.K. and KELLEY, H.H. (1964). Significant factors in over-evaluation of own group's products. *Journal of Abnormal and Social Psychology*, **69**, 223 – 228.

FESHBACH, S. and SINGER, R. (1957). The effects of personal and shared threats upon social prejudice. *Journal of Abnormal and Social Psychology*, **54**, 411 – 416.

FIEDLER, F.E. (1967). The effect of inter-group competition on group member adjustment. *Personnel Psychology*, **20**, 33 – 44.

GOLDMAN, M., STOCKBAUER, J.W. and MCAULIFFE, T.G. (1977). Intergroup and intragroup competition and co-operation. *Journal of Experimental Social Psychology*, **13**, 81 – 88.

HARVEY, J.H. and SMITH, W.P. (1977). *Social Psychology: An Attributional Approach*. Saint Louis: C.V. Mosby Co.

HARVEY, O.J. (1956). An experimental investigation of negative and positive relations between small groups through judgemental indices. *Sociometry*, **19**, 201 – 209.

HENSLEY, V. and DUVAL, S. (1976). Some perceptual determinants of perceived similarity, liking and correctness. *Journal of Personality and Social Psychology*, **34**, 159 – 168.

HINKLE, S. and SCHOPLER, J. (1979). Ethnocentrism in the evaluation of group products. In W.G. AUSTIN and S. WORCHEL (Eds.), *The Social Psychology of Intergroup Relations*. Monterey: California, Brooks/Cole.

HORNSTEIN, H.A. (1972). Promotive tension: the basis of prosocial behaviour from a Lewinian perspective. *Journal of Social Issues*, **28**, 191 – 218.

HORNSTEIN, H.A. (1976). *Cruelty and kindness: A New Look at Aggression and Altruism*. Englewood Cliffs, New Jersey: Prentice-Hall.

JANSSENS, L. and NUTTIN, J.R. (1976). Frequency perception of individual and group successes as a function of competition, coaction and isolation. *Journal of Personality and Social Psychology*, **34**, 830 – 836.

JOHNSON, D.W. (1967). Use of role reversal in intergroup competition. *Journal of Personality and Social Psychology*, **7**, 135 – 141.

KAHN, A. and RYEN, A.H. (1972). Factors influencing the bias towards one's own group. *International Journal of Group Tensions*, **2**, 33 – 50.

KALIN, R. and MARLOWE, D. (1968). The effects of intergroup competition, personal drinking habits and frustration in intra-group co-operation. *Proceedings of 76th Annual Convention A.P.A.*, **3**, 405 – 406.

KENNEDY, J. and STEPHAN, W. (1977). The effects of co-operation and competition on ingroup-outgroup bias. *Journal of Applied Social Psychology*, **7**, 115 – 130.

KNIPPENBERG, A. VAN and WILKE, H. (1979). Perceptions of collegiens and apprentices re-analysed. *European Journal of Social Psychology*, **9**, 427 – 434.

LOTT, A.J. and LOTT, B.E. (1965). Group cohesiveness as interpersonal attraction: a review of relationships with antecedent and consequent variables. *Psychological Bulletin*, **64**, 259 – 309.

McKillip, J., Dimiceli, A.J. and Luebke, J. (1977). Group salience and sterotyping. *Social Behavior and Personality*, **5**, 81 – 85.

Malof, M. and Lott, A.J. (1962). Ethnocentrism and the acceptance of negro support in a group pressure situation. *Journal of Abnormal and Social Psychology*, **65**, 254 – 258.

Myers, A. (1962). Team competition, success and the adjustment of group members. *Journal of Abnormal and Social Psychology*, **65**, 325 – 332.

Oakes, P.J. and Turner, J.C. (1980). Social categorisation and intergroup behaviour: does minimal intergroup discrimination make social identity more positive? European Journal of Social Psychology, **10**, 295 – 301.

Rabbie, J.M. (1974). *Effects of Expected Intergroup Competition and Co-operation*. Paper presented to Annual Convention, A.P.A., New Orleans, August, University of Utrecht.

Rabbie, J.M., Benoist, F., Oosterbaan, H. and Visser, L. (1974). Differential power and effects of expected competitive and co-operative intergroup interaction on intragroup and outgroup attitudes. *Journal of Personality and Social Psychology*, **30**, 46 – 56.

Rabbie, J.M. and de Brey, J.H.C. (1971). The anticipation of intergroup co-operation and competition under private and public conditions. *International Journal of Group Tensions*, **1**, 230 – 251.

Rabbie, J.M. and Horwitz, M. (1969). Arousal of ingroup-outgroup bias by a chance win or loss. *Journal of Personality and Social Psychology*, **13**, 269 – 277.

Rabbie, J.M. and Huygen, K. (1974). Internal disagreements and their effects on attitudes towards in- and outgroup. *International Journal of Group Tensions*, **4**(2), 222 – 246.

Rabbie, J.M. and Wilkens, G. (1971). Intergroup competition and its effect on intragroup and intergroup relations. *European Journal of Social Psychology*, **1**, 215 – 234.

Ryen, A.H. and Kahn, A. (1975). Effects of intergroup orientation on group attitudes and proxemic behavior. *Journal of Personality and Social Psychology*, **31**, 302 – 310.

Sherif, M. (1951). A preliminary experimental study of inter-group relations. In J.H. Rohrer and M. Sherif (Eds.), *Social Psychology at the Crossroads*, New York: Harper.

Sherif, M. (1967). *Group Conflict and Co-operation*. London: Routledge and Kegan-Paul.

Sherif, M., Harvey, O.J., White, B.J., Hood, W.R. and Sherif, Carolyn W. (1961). *Intergroup Conflict and Co-operation. The Robbers Cave Experiment*. Norman, Okla.: University of Oklahoma Book Exchange.

Sherif, M. and Sherif, C.W. (1953). *Groups in Harmony and Tension*. New York: Harper.

Sherif, M., White, B.J. and Harvey, O.J. (1955). Status in experimentally produced groups. *American Journal of Sociology*, **60**, 370 – 379.

Sole, K., Marton, J. and Hornstein, H.A. (1975). Opinion similarity and helping: three field experiments investigating the bases of promotive tension. *Journal of Experimental Social Psychology*, **11**, 1 – 13.

St. Claire, L. and Turner, J.C. *The Role of Demand Characteristics in the Minimal Group Paradigm*. University of Bristol. In preparation.

Sussman, M.B. and Weil, W.B. (1960). An experimental study on the effects of group interaction upon the behaviour of diabetic children. *International Journal of Social Psychiatry*, **6**, 120 – 125.

Tajfel, M. (1969). Cognitive aspects of prejudice. *Journal of Social Issues*, **25**, 79 – 97.

TAJFEL, H. (1972). Social categorisation. English ms. of 'La catégorisation sociale' in S. MOSCOVICI (Ed.), *Introduction à la Psychologie Sociale*. Vol. 1. Paris: Larousse, Chapter 8, 272 – 302.

TAJFEL, H. (Ed.) (1978). *Differentiation Between Social Groups: Studies in the Social Psychology of Intergroup Relations*. London: Academic Press.

TAJFEL, H. and BILLIG, M.G. (1974). Familiarity and categorisation in intergroup behaviour. *Journal of Experimental Social Psychology*, **10**, 159 – 170.

TAJFEL, H., FLAMENT, C., BILLIG, M.G. and BUNDY, R.F. (1971). Social categorisation and intergroup behaviour. *European Journal of Social Psychology*, **1**, 149 – 177.

TAJFEL, H. and TURNER, J.C. (1979). An integrative theory of intergroup conflict. In W.G. AUSTIN and S. WORCHEL (Eds.), *The Social Psychology of Intergroup Relations*. Monterey, California: Brooks/Cole.

TAJFEL, H. and WILKES, A.L. (1963). Classification and quantitative judgement. *British Journal of Psychology*, **54**, 101 – 114.

TURNER, J.C. (1975a). Social comparison and social identity: some prospects for intergroup behaviour. *European Journal of Social Psychology*, **5**, 5 – 34.

TURNER, J.C. (1975b). Social Categorisation and Social Comparison in Intergroup Relations. Unpublished Ph.D. Thesis, University of Bristol.

TURNER, J.C. (1978a). Social categorisation and social discrimination in the minimal group paradigm. In H. TAJFEL (Ed.), *Differentiation Between Social Groups: Studies in the Social Psychology of Intergroup Relations*. London: Academic Press.

TURNER, J.C. (1978b). Social comparison, similarity and ingroup favouritism. In H. TAJFEL (Ed.), *Differentiation Between Social Groups: Studies in the Social Psychology of Intergroup Relations*. London: Academic Press.

TURNER, J.C. (1980). Fairness or discrimination in intergroup behaviour? A reply to Braithwaite, Doyle and Lightbown. *European Journal of Social Psychology*, **10**, 131 – 147.

TURNER, J.C. (1982). Towards a cognitive redefinition of the social group. In H. TAJFEL (Ed.), *Social Identity and Intergroup Relations*, Cambridge and Paris: Cambridge University Press and Editions de la Maison des Sciences de l'Homme.

TURNER, J.C. and BROWN, R.J. (1978). Social status, cognitive alternatives and intergroup relations. In H. TAJFEL (Ed.), *Differentiation Between Social Groups*. London: Academic Press.

TURNER, J.C., BROWN, R.J. and TAJFEL, H. (1979). Social comparison and group interest in ingroup favouritism. *European Journal of Social Psychology*, **9**, 187 – 204.

TURNER, J.C., HOGG, M., OAKES, P.J. and SMITH, P.M.. *Group Formation as a Process of Self-attitude Change: The Effects of Success and Failure on Group Cohesiveness*. University of Bristol (In preparation).

WICKLUND, R.A. and BREHM, J.W. (1976). *Perspectives on Cognitive Dissonance*. Hilsdale, NJ: Lawrence Erlbaum.

WILDER, D.A. (1978). Reduction of intergroup discrimination through individuation of the outgroup. *Journal of Personality and Social Psychology*, **36**, 1361 – 1374.

WILSON, W., CHUN, N. and KAYATANI, M. (1965). Projection, attraction, and strategy choices in intergroup competition. *Journal of Personality and Social Psychology*, **2**, 432 – 435.

WILSON, W. and KAYATANI, M. (1968). Intergroup attitudes and strategies in games between opponents of the same or of a different race. *Journal of Personality and Social Psychology*, **9**, 24 – 30.

WILSON, W. and ROBINSON, C. (1968). Selective intergroup bias in both authoritarians and non-authoritarians after playing a modified Prisoner's Dilemma Game. *Percep-*

tual & Motor Skills, **27**, 1051 – 1058.
WILSON, W. and WONG, J. (1968). Intergroup attitudes towards co-operative versus competitive opponents in a modified Prisoner's Dilemma Game. *Perceptual & Motor Skills*, **27**, 1059 – 1066.
WORCHEL, S. (1979). Co-operation and the reduction of intergroup conflict: some determining factors. In W.G. AUSTIN and S. WORCHEL (Eds.), *The Social Psychology of intergroup relations*. Monterey, California: Brooks/Cole.
WORCHEL, S., ANDREOLI, V.A. and FOLGER, R. (1977). Intergroup co-operation and intergroup attraction: the effect of previous interaction and outcome of combined effort. *Journal of Experimental Social Psychology*, **13**, 131 – 140.
WORCHEL, S., AXSOM, D., FERRIS, F., SAMAHA, C. and SCHWEITZER, S. (1978). Factors determining the effect of intergroup co-operation on intergroup attraction. *Journal of Conflict Resolution*, **22**, 429 – 439.
WORCHEL, S., LIND, E.A. and KAUFMAN, K. (1975). Evaluations of group products as a function of expectations of group longevity, outcome of competition, and publicity of evaluations. *Journal of Personality and Social Psychology*, **31**, 1089 – 1097.

CHAPTER 9

Anthropological and Cross-Cultural Perspectives

Douglas W. Bethlehem

Cooperation and competition are at the basis of the philosophy of society, since people must find some accommodation of their diverse interests and of their conflict over scarce resources, and some way of coordinating efforts towards mutually desired ends, if society is to exist. Human life without some form of society is impossible.

Despite the long, if tangential, interest of philosophers in cooperation and competition among people, empirical studies began only fairly recently. In 1937 Margaret Mead, the doyenne of American social anthropologists, edited a volume whose aim was to examine a large number of simple societies, to assess the extent to which individuals in each society were typically cooperative, competitive, or individualistic, and to see whether these typical behaviours were related to other aspects of their cultures or their environments. The study was of some interest, as it did prove possible to classify cultures as leaning more to cooperative, competitive, or individualistic modes of behaviour. Of course, allowance must be made for possible unreliability, both of the ethnographers' reports and of the assessment of the cooperativeness, competitiveness, or individualism of the culture: this source of error is one to which anthropologists have traditionally been blind. Mead's study was far from seminal, however: no anthropological studies specifically devoted to cooperation and competition followed. The words rarely appear in the indexes of anthropological textbooks and monographs. Partly this was because no relation between cooperativeness and competitiveness and any other variable, cultural or ecological, emerged. Partly it was due to the confusion arising from the inadequate operational definition of the concepts. Cooperation was defined as working together to a mutually desired goal, and competition as pursuing a goal also desired by another person, or other people, and which only one person (or a limited number of people) could attain. Now these concepts are not contradictory: there are interesting modes of behaviour relating to relations between people pursuing goals which are neither cooperation nor competition. Mead was forced to grapple in her comments with such concepts as helping and rivalry (the desire to worst another person, without necessarily gaining anything oneself), which seem distinct from cooperation and competition. It was not until the growth of interest in game theory (see Chapter 5), which came into psychology by way of mathematics, that social science began interesting itself in cooperation and competition again. The late 1960s saw a sucker of Mead's study growing, in the form of experimental studies of cooperation and competition across cultures.

In this article I shall examine some relatively simple cultures, to show how they can be said, in some cases at least, to place their main emphasis on co-operative, competitive, or individualistic behaviour. Then I shall briefly review some experimental work in the field.

9.1 Cooperation and Competition among Primitive Peoples*

It has already been remarked that all individuals need at least a minimum of help and cooperation from others. (In this section, distinctions between co-operation, helpfulness, altruism, etc., and between competition, rivalry, etc., will not be too closely insisted upon.) No baby can survive without help from adults, and no group of people can permit its members to commit murder whenever they feel somewhat out of sorts, though some societies are more lax in this respect than others. With these thoughts in mind, let us examine some societies, and illustrate that the degree of cooperativeness, competitiveness, and individualism does differ in their cultures.

9.1.1 Cooperative Societies

The cultures of sub-Saharan Africa are frequently cooperative in nature, and the mildness and gentleness of the people are striking to a European visitor. This characteristic is changing as the cultures become Westernized (see below). But here we are concerning ourselves with stabilized traditional cultures, in the manner of traditional anthropologists.

Two of Africa's most attractive peoples are the Bushmen of the Kalahari Desert in Botswana and Namibia (Thomas, 1960) and the Mbuti of the Ituri forest in Zaire (Turnbull, 1963, 1965). They have much in common: both have been written about with great affection by anthropologists who visited them; both are physically small people; and both are hunters and gatherers who live in relatively small bands. The environment of the Bushmen provides a hard living for the small number of people who live in it. Surface water is very scarce, and the game is not prolific, so that Bushmen have to resort to infanticide in times of hardship. The Ituri forest, on the other hand, is much more bountiful, and want is not a problem. Both peoples are nomadic, moving around in small and fluid bands. Both have seen Western culture, and seen that despite any material advantages it has – and both peoples love tobacco, Western clothes, and the detritus of Western culture – the warmth, helpfulness, friendliness and cooperativeness of their traditional life is far more valuable to them than

* This subheading is a homage to Mead's exploratory volume. The term 'primitive' is not polite today, except as applied to the visual arts, where its vogue is laudatory.

the material advantages 'civilization' has to offer. That is not to say their lives are without tensions: the instability of the nomadic bands is partly due to the tendency of one party to a serious quarrel simply to leave one band and move with another, at least temporarily.

Among the Mbuti and the Bushmen, hunting is most efficiently done in cooperative groups. But this does not in itself guarantee the sharing of food which is so characteristic within bands, and even between bands when they meet. Food could be divided, for instance according to the investment in effort or material goods — hunting nets or arrows — contributed, as among the Ifugao (see Barton, 1949). In fact, both groups regard helpfulness and sharing as the norm. It would be unthinkable for a Bushman to eat while others present went without. There is no formal system of sharing, as among the Chins of Burma, for example, where giving feasts is a way of gaining prestige and obligations to share are specified down to the very cut of meat due to prominent others (Stevenson, 1943, pp. 132 – 134, 140). Similarly, they help each other in other ways, as for example in the building of huts, though there is no formal system of labour exchange such as we shall encounter below. It is simply that the Mbuti and the Bushmen value helpfulness and cooperativeness, and dislike the strife and noise to which jealousy and meanness give rise. 'No Bushman wants prominence,' remarks Thomas (1960, p. 167), and similarly no Bushman would accumulate goods which others might envy, preferring to give away a fine possession to enduring the ill-feeling that would result from his keeping it.

Lest it should appear that hunting and gathering peoples are the only cooperative peoples, it will be worth mentioning briefly some Bantu cultures. Swaziland is a small kingdom bordered by South Africa and Mozambique. It is characterized by a centralized political leadership and a well-defined social and political organization, right down to village level. The Swazis are a settled people who grow crops and keep cattle, which are a source of prestige and a repository of wealth, rather than a commodity (Kuper, 1947, 1952, 1964). The Chewa are a much less centrally organized set of people, living in Zambia, Mozambique, and Malawi, who subsist mainly on agriculture, with cattle coming to play a more prominent part in their economy than formerly (Marwick, 1965). The former are patrilineal, the latter matrilineal. The Swazis live in villages or homesteads, and usually choose to live in a homestead with kinsmen. Their clans are supposed to be exogamous (that is, marriages take place between members of different clans), which has the function of extending social ties. Men are divided into age classes, a class being named every five or seven years. Members of a household — a man, his wives, and their children — naturally cooperate. But cooperation is much more widely organized. Headmen organize work parties for large enterprises. Participants are not paid a wage, though they can expect food and beer as well as the comradeship of the party. Groups of kinsmen from different homesteads, and neighbours, work together to help a kinsman or neighbour who cannot cope with a task on his own or with members of his own household, again expecting only a meal with beer, and help when they need it, from the host. In general, his Swazis value obedience and good manners in people, and dislike and suspect ambition and competitiveness. As among the Chewa, excessive ambition and accumulation of unshared wealth leads to unpopularity and can bring upon a person accusations of witchcraft. Among the Chewa, the matrilineage (the group of people who are descended from a known female ancestor and are related to one another through female links) is a basic unit of social structure, and a village may have several matrilineages in it. But for day-to-day purposes the unit is the household, which consists of a matrilocally extended family, that is to say, a group of relatives, including those more distant than members of the basic family unit, who live in the home of a senior female relative. It is they who grow crops together and share a common budget, and in this family, as in all basic family household groups, cooperation is the norm. The system is looser than among the Swazis. Men have a duty to help their sisters when they are in need. But most cooperation in clearing fields, weeding, hut building, and so on, is done by working parties not made up exclusively of kinsmen, who are normally given food and beer while working on someone's behalf, and who can expect help from that person when they need it. The Chewa are a pacific people, who, despite harking back to a time when savage punishments kept law and order, in contrast to the anarchy of today, value cooperativeness and meekness of spirit.

It can be seen that among the peoples mentioned, who are not atypical in this respect of sub-Saharan Africa, cooperation, sharing, a respect for the rights and feelings of others, generosity, meekness, sociality, mutuality among people, are valued. President Kaunda of Zambia has elevated this spirit, perhaps exaggerating it somewhat, into his philosophy of humanism (Kaunda, 1966, 1970). And certainly it is heartening to know that this kind of spirit can exist. The Plateau Tonga of Zambia may look upon their cousins from the Gwembe Valley, ascending to the plateau during times of extreme famine, with the same enthusiasm with which they regard a plague of locusts (Colson, 1960, p. 56), but they do feed them until the famine conditions in the valley pass.

9.1.2 Competitive Societies

Asia provides us with some nice examples of competitive societies, which are also to be found in many other parts of the world.

One of the most competitive cultures is that of the Ifugao of northern Luzon, in the Philippines (Barton, 1969, 1977; Hoebel, 1954). Ifugao society is class ridden, and wealth and prestige are the rungs of the social ladder. Three classes are recognized: the lowest are the *nawatwat* (those who will become hungry), who do not own rice land; the middle class are known as *natumok*, and consists of people who own enough rice land to provide for themselves and their households in normal years; and the highest class are *kadangyang*, who have sufficient rice land to produce a surplus. Since rice is the best and preferred food, and land is limited, it is the *kadangyang* who can sell surplus produce, or let rice land superfluous to their immediate needs, and accumulate capital. Probably the most significant cause of the extreme competitiveness of the Ifugao is just this shortage of rice land (a rich man may own 8000 square metres of land), because their neighbours, the Kalingas, do not suffer such a shortage of land, and, though sharing many of the features of Ifugao culture, are less single-mindedly competitive (see Barton, 1949). It should be explained that Ifugaoland is extremely mountainous, and terraces on which to grow rice have to be laboriously built on the sides of the steep mountains. Other forms of food are available: shell fish in the paddy fields are available to everyone, and the *nawatwat* have as a staple a kind of sweet potato. But the latter is a despised food, which indicates the low status of the eater.

The Ifugao household is a nuclear family group, sometimes with dependants, and kinship is counted equally on the man's and on the woman's side. Members of the household cooperate with each other, share a budget, and have certain obligations to near kin not in the household when feuds arise. But otherwise competition is the universal practice. To be a *kadangyang* one must acquire wealth. Theoretically, the rank is available only to those who are born to it, but every man can find an ancestor somewhere in his past, on his father's or his mother's side, who was of that rank, and it is wealth that actually confers the status. To validate oneself as a *kadangyang*, one must build oneself a lounging bench before one's house, and give a series of expensive feasts, and make a large number of expensive sacrifices. Only the (relatively) very wealthy can afford these feasts and sacrifices. In fact, the real difference in wealth between a *kadangyang* and a *natumok* or *nawatwat* is not large: it is the prestige that differs. The sons of a *kadangyang* are only recognized as *kadangyang* if they in their turn acquire sufficient wealth.

So everyone is always striving for wealth and prestige. Wealth is acquired only minimally through inheritance. The surest way to wealth is shrewdness and good management of one's paddy fields, so that a surplus of rice can be acquired, lent out at usurious rates of interest (100% for a short loan, 300% or 400% for longer term loans), and further surpluses acquired which can be lent out, or used to purchase land. This land can then be share-cropped: a poor man will be given seed and allowed to use the land, in return for giving a large proportion of his crop to the owner. People will do this because rice is so prized as a food. Debts pass on to a person's heirs, and an Ifugao cannot afford to allow a debt to go uncollected, for he would lose in prestige. One can go so far as to kidnap a person or his kinsman to enforce repayment of a debt. Headhunting traditionally gained a man prestige, and encouraged other people not to be slow in repaying debts owed to a renowned headhunter.

Hunting is cooperatively organized, but the cooperation is done only as far as is absolutely necessary. A kill is shared according to the number of dogs a person contributes to the hunt. Headhunting is done in groups, but is competitive to the extent that the man who actually takes the head is the principal gainer of prestige and admiration.

Life among the Ifugao is a constant struggle to gain rank, and, once gained, to keep it, for a man who loses his wealth through bad luck or illness (which requires ruinously expensive sacrifices) loses his rank. Once joined in the struggle, no one can afford to relax, to allow himself to show weakness in enforcing his rights or in coming to the aid of a near kinsman in a blood feud.

For then he would be taken advantage of, and would find it hard to accumulate or maintain wealth. There are no policemen among the Ifugao; a man has to enforce the rights accorded by custom law himself.

A less fiercely competitive people are the Kachins of highland Burma. Their famous ethnographer, Leach (1954), was concerned to show that the fiction underlying most anthropology — that a society is a stable and balanced unity, and that ethnographic accounts are best presented as 'snapshots' of the society at a moment in time, not an account of its development — is inimical to the understanding of societies. This is not the place to discuss the point, but it is of interest because he presents the Kachins as a chronically unstable political grouping. There is a continuum of centralization of authority represented among different groups of Kachins, going from centralized authority (*gumsa*) at one end of the continuum, to complete egalitarianism (*gumlao*) at the other. In fact, he is at pains to emphasize, the difference is not great in practice. According to Leach, Kachins try to climb the social scale by the acquisition of riches and the giving of lavish feasts, though the pursuit of wealth is not so cut-throat as among the Ifugao. Once wealth is acquired, evidence of descent from a noble ancestor can be cooked up to validate the higher status to which a person aspires. Again Leach tells us, all Kachin chiefs and headmen aspire to be autocratic chieftains. It is not clear precisely how autocracy is cemented, but it is a gradual process, in which a chief arrogates status and wealth to himself, emphasizing the ritual position of a chief which entitles him to material and spiritual tributes from ordinary people. He has no real power, however, and when his demands become too great, a 'revolution' — or social reorganization — takes place, in which people remove themselves from the authority of the chief, and the policy becomes the *gumlao*, or egalitarian, one. But this *gumlao* policy is itself unstable. The very language used, Leach tells us, in regard to marriage, works against equality. *Mayu* lineages (i.e. lineages from which a person's lineage has taken brides) in the connotations of the language they use, are of a higher status than *Dama* (lineages into which females of a person's lineage have recently married). The inequality implied in the very terminology used, with the tendency to personal ambition and the openness of high status to anyone who is cunning and energetic and lucky, leads a *gumlao* polity to shift towards a *gumsa* one, which itself is unstable, and crumbles into a *gumlao* one again.

9.1.3 Individualistic Societies

The nadir to which almost untrammelled individualism can drop people is illustrated by Turnbull's (1973a, 1973b) account of the Ik of East Africa. Here is Hobbes's state of nature come alive. Among the Ik there are 'no arts, no letters, no society . . . and life is solitary, poor, nasty, brutish, and short'. Turnbull, who wrote with such affection of the pygmies of the Ituri Forest, was disconcerted and appalled by the Ik. He had expected to find them like most Africans, welcoming, warm to kin and distant strangers, and with a reasonably rich culture. Instead he found only selfishness and malice, a society barely coherent, in which everyone acted almost exclusively for him- or herself. He wrote about it while his feelings were still raw from the experience of living among the Ik, and for that reason may have exaggerated somewhat. It is almost as hurtful for us who can afford kindness and altruism to read about Turnbull's seared feelings, as it is for us who can afford more food than we need and who have perfect security, to read about the Ik's hunger.

The Ik, referred to on tribal maps of the area as the Teuso, were traditionally a hunting and gathering people. The government took the most fecund part of their traditional hunting range for a game reserve, and the loss of this range combined with the infertility of their mountain homeland, and frequent severe droughts, has destroyed their source of food, and with it their culture, their love, and their cooperativeness. They numbered only about 2000 individuals when Turnbull visited them.

As Turnbull describes it, the Ik live in villages, but merely from habit, since the villages are not coherent units; they are merely aggregates of people. A man, his wife, and children typically live together. Little love is shown for children, who are socialized brutally into their brutal world, being given minimal food and instruction. By three or four, children are expected more or less to fend for themselves. This they do by literally taking food from the mouths of the aged and weak. The misfortunes of others are a source of amusement. When food is got in time of hardship — through a famine relief organization, for example — it may reluctantly be shared with a spouse, but otherwise it is consumed alone if possible, and none saved, since it may be lost if it is not consumed immediately. When rains do come, little effort is made to cultivate properly or store the produce adequately, so demoralized are the people. The aged and the young are helped little. The old, a burden, are considered better out of the way, and Turnbull describes how parents deliberately starved to death a feeble-minded girl by walling her up in a hut. There is no trust between people. People other than members of a nuclear family do sometimes cooperate on hunting expeditions for example, but only for the shortest period of time and for the most immediate gain for themselves.

But the old remember a time when there was love and cooperation and trust. Even now, people sit together for company, though they interact little. And they observe the rule that if someone finds another with food, the latter must share it with him or her: hence their tendency to eat in secret and gorge on what they have. They occasionally make a gesture towards dimly remembered traditions, such as the feast that should go with a funeral: but these are only gestures. And, individualistic, selfish, and frequently malicious as they are, they do not often murder or assault one another, nor often fight, even over food. As Turnbull describes it, there is little aggression, no competition, and little passion of any kind, and the Ik's life is an obstinate but apathetic attachment to survival, a corpse's hand in rigor mortis gripping a fissure on a mountainside. (One cannot help wondering what the Ik thought of Turnbull, who did not share all *his* food, and indeed found himself — to his own horror — developing their selfish attitudes.)

Much less severely individualistic — they have comparative plenty — are the two peoples known as the Iban (or Sea Dayaks) (Freeman, 1955a, 1955b, 1955c; Sutlive, 1978) and the Land Dayaks (Geddes, 1961) of Sarawak, on the island of Borneo. Indeed, they are on the boundary of being cooperative. Both the groups have a *bilek* family — essentially a nuclear family occasionally with aged parents or adopted children — as the basic unit of social organization. The *bilek* is the room used by the family in the longhouse in which they live. The longhouse is essentially a lot of *bileks*, built on stilts, with their verandahs, lofts, etc., built side by side so that the verandahs form a long continuous street, in some cases 300 metres long. The *bilek* family has privacy in its *bilek*, and the verandah serves as a village street, community hall, meeting place, and lounging area. Though they may seem to a cursory glance to be very communally organized, in fact the *bilek* families are very individual. They do cooperate to clear jungle, work in fields, and so on, but each day's labour received by a *bilek* family from a member of another *bilek* family is repaid. The whole ethos is individualistic and egalitarian, and permissive, trusting and generous. *Bilek* families with a surplus will help neighbours with a deficiency of rice. There is no strong chief, and, since there has never been a shortage of virgin jungle to clear, no competition for rice land. The longhouse is barely a corporate body. All land, rights to fruit trees, etc., are owned by the *bilek* family which planted them. All *bilek* families have an equal right to virgin jungle, apportionment of which, when new plots are to be cleared, is decided at a general palaver in the longhouse. Kills at hunting are shared reciprocally. Fishing is done communally, by poisoning lengths of a river, but each fish belongs to the *bilek* family whose member picks it from the water.

In general both the Iban and the Land Dayaks are cheerful, friendly, relaxed, egalitarian, classless peoples. The Land Dayaks are rather more gentle and trusting than the Iban, who veer more towards a competitive spirit. This tendency is not surprising in historical perspective: the Iban are fairly recent settlers in their present territories, who gained their territories by driving the former people out. Both sets of people were traditionally headhunters (the Iban being the keener on this form of sport than the Land Dayaks) until the government put a stop to it. The Iban value personal prestige, young men often making long journeys to do migrant work to gain money and prestige. While they do not strive very hard to gain the edge on other Iban, they are unwilling to see another Iban prosper unduly. This attitude is causing difficulty as Westernization encroaches.

9.1.4 Ethnographic Conclusions

President Kaunda of Zambia (1966, 1970) considers that humanism, a respect for others, sharing, trust, and a cooperative spirit, is what Africa has to offer the world. And indeed these qualities do seem typical of sub-Saharan Africa, though not universal even there; and they can be exaggerated even when considering societies where they do predominate. Warfare among southern

African peoples has not been uncommon, particularly since Chaka, King of the Zulus, ascended his bloody throne.

No improvement seems possible on Mead's conclusions that there is no simple relationship between ecological or sociological characteristics of small-scale societies on the one hand, and tendencies to be cooperative, competitive, or individualistic on the other. No doubt a shortage of essential resources predisposes people to competition, but this predisposition is not overriding. The Ifugao compete for scarce rice land, and are competitive : but so are the Kalingas, the Chins, and the Kachins — though not so fiercely so — who are comparatively wealthy. Moreover, it is not just rice land the Ifugao compete for, but the high rank it bestows. The Swazis have a class system of sorts, but competition does not occur, probably partly because most important offices are open only to members of the royal clan, and individuals are appointed to high office by the hereditary king. Hunters and gatherers might be thought to be predisposed to being cooperative, and indeed it may be that members of very small groups usually are; though scarcity of food and potable water in the Kalahari might have been expected to engender competition for it, or at least selfishness. This cooperative spirit can be stretched beyond breaking at least sometimes, as witness the catastrophe among the Ik. One wonders what would happen among the Iban if resources became insufficient for all to have a reasonable minimum. One hopes that this will never happen, for even if they cannot go on clearing virgin forest for much longer, they will adapt to a modern economy.

We are left with three thoughts. One is that even in the most competitive or individualistic society, everyone needs some primary group — usually based on ties of kinship and marriage — that he or she can trust, share with, and cooperate with. Even the Ik in their crisis retain marriage and care to a degree for the children of their marriages. Another is that in this field, as in others, culture determines thought and behaviour to a remarkable degree. The Iban, the Swazi, the Chewa, could compete fiercely, but they do not, because that is not the way things are done among them, and they are socialized into behaving non-competitively, without giving much thought to the alternatives.

A third thought is that the terms used are ungainly. Tweedledum was fighting with Tweedledee, to their mutual satisfaction, and to the mutually shared goal of impressing Alice. The Melanau of Sarawak produce sago, which is sold through Chinese middlemen, who sell consumer goods to the Melanau on credit (Morris, 1953). When the Chinese traders need sago, they withdraw credit facilities from a family until sago is produced. This symbiotic relationship probably does not look like cooperation to the participants, but from a distance it does look cooperative. The Chinese and the Melanau both want goods; neither can get them without the other; and the mechanism of chronic debt and the withholding of credit serves to procure for each of them what they want and could not get independently.

We will be seeing in the following section that cooperation and competition can take many guises, and when examined in the laboratory, need a film of finer grain.

9.2 Experimental Comparisons

It has been remarked that the terms cooperation and competition are not contradictories: that is, that it is possible to behave in regard to others in a way that is neither cooperative nor competitive; and that the terms are themselves imprecise. A number of different motives have been distinguished under these umbrella terms. Some of these can be specified a little more clearly (in two-person contexts) as follows.

Competitive motives

1. Maximizing relative gain. This means the desire to win more than the other, without regard to the absolute size of the gain of either person.
2. Maximizing the other's loss. This is what has been termed 'rivalry'.

Cooperative motives

3. Maximizing joint gain. Here the desire is that the sum of the person's and the other's gains should be as large as possible, without regard to whether one or the other gets more.
4. Equality. The desire that, however much is won or lost, both should end with an equal amount.
5. Altruism. The desire to maximize the other's gain without regard to one's own gain.

Individualistic motives

6. Maximizing own gain. That is, the person tries to gain as much as possible for himself, without regard to what the other gains.
7. Minimizing relative loss. Messick and Thorngate (1967) have shown that even though people may sometimes not want to *win*, they may not like being made to *lose* relative to another.

The position is complicated, because these motives are often mixed and because many experimental techniques are used, few of which seem to involve these motives in even a fairly pure way.

9.2.1 Experimental Techniques

Some of the experimental methods that have been used in making cross-cultural comparisons are outlined below.

1. The marble pull game (Madsen, 1971). Children sit at opposite ends of a device along which runs a wooden holder with an indentation for a marble. Each child can pull the marble towards him by a string. The marble holder is in two halves, held together by a magnet. If both children pull against each other (i.e. compete) the holder splits, and the marble drops out, so neither gets a marble. A cooperative strategy is to take turns pulling, so that each one gets a marble in turn.

2. The Madsen board. This test, invented by M.C. Madsen (1967) consists of a square board with eyelets at each corner, through which strings run, each one

held by a child. The strings are attached to a pen at the centre of the board, and the targets, usually small circles or the players' initials, are pencilled on to the board. The object is for each child to pull the pencil in such a way as to mark his or her circle or initials. If all four pull simultaneously with equal force (i.e. compete) the pen is at the resultant of the forces, and does not move. Cooperating involves coordinating the pulling and releasing of their strings, so that each child's target is marked in turn. Rewards are proportional to the number of times the pen has marked the child's target.

3. The circle matrix (Kagan & Madsen, 1971). This is a square board on which a 7 × 7 matrix of circles is drawn. A marker is placed on the centre circle (or sometimes there are two markers) and two children move the marker one circle at a time, in turn. The circles at the ends of the centre columns are marked with the children's initials, and a child gets something each time the marker reaches his or her target circle. Cooperation consists of moving the single marker towards each child's target in turn, or not blocking the other's moves in the case of two markers. If the children compete, their markers simply oscillate in the centre of the board, and neither gains anything.

4. Experimental Games. The Prisoner's Dilemma Game (PDG) and Maximizing Difference Game (MDG) are described elsewhere in this volume (see Chapter 5). In the latter, defecting or competing reflects a desire to make a relative gain, or a lack of trust, or both. Cooperation involves trusting the other person to do the same. Both games are influenced by the relative values of the cells. The validity of the PDG as an index of cooperation has been attested by Deutsch's (1962) finding that people asked to behave cooperatively, competitively, and individualistically, do play as expected. Other evidence that the PDG has construct validity as a measure of competitiveness is provided by correlations of competitiveness in the PDG with pencil-and-paper measures of dominance (Sermat, 1968), cynicism and authoritarianism (Deutsch, 1960; Wrightsman, 1966), expectation that others are likely to defect (Dawes *et al.*, 1977), and (negatively) with level of moral judgement (Pilburn, 1977).

5. The social behaviour scale (Knight & Kagan, 1977a, 1977b). This, with some variation, is the most direct way of comparing motives that has been used in cross-cultural research. It consists simply of a choice of one of four possible alternatives, each one involving a constant reward to the person but a varied reward to the other (see Fig. 9.1). Knight and Kagan (1977b) found that children behave similarly whether another child is physically present or not. Even here, motives are confounded: the last cell, for instance, confounds altruism and maximizing joint gain; the first one maximizing other's loss (rivalry) and maximizing relative gain.

9.2.2 Experimental Results

Here are some of the results that have accumulated in comparing persons of different cultures. In each case the more *cooperative* groups are placed *first*. The techniques used to assess cooperativeness appear in brackets, and are

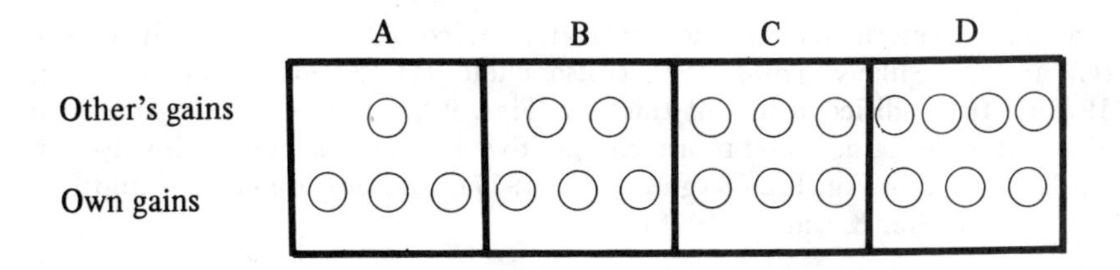

Fig. 9.1 The social behaviour scale. The person's own outcome is represented in the bottom row, the other's in the top. The person chooses A, B, C, or D.

abbreviated MP (marble pull), MB (Madsen board), CMB (circle matrix board), PDG (Prisoner's Dilemma Game), MDG (Maximizing Difference Game) and SBS (social behaviour scale).

Rural, poor, Mexican children were found to be more cooperative than urban middle class Mexican children (Madsen, 1967, MB); Mexican children in a small town in Mexico than white children in Los Angeles (Madsen, 1971, MP); rural Mexican children than Los Angeles Mexican-American, white, or black American children (Madsen & Shapira, 1970, MB); small town Mexican children than Mexican-American children, who were in turn more cooperative than white American children (Kagan & Madsen, 1971, CMB); less Western-educated Kpelle people in Liberia than more Western-educated (Meeker, 1970, PDG); rural Tonga adults little touched by Westernization in the Gwembe Valley in Zambia than Westernized Tonga adults, or than Tonga or Asian students at the University of Zambia (Bethlehem 1975, PDG); traditional Aboriginal Australian young people than somewhat Westernized Aboriginals, who were more cooperative than white Australians (Sommerlad & Bellingham, 1972, MB); rural Korean children than urban Korean children (Madsen & Yi, 1975, MB); semi-traditional rural Kikuyu children in Kenya than American white children (Munroe & Munroe, 1977, CMB); Cook Island and rural Maori children than urban Maori children and white New Zealand children (Thomas, 1975, MB); rural Colombian children than urban (Marin *et al.*, 1975); Belgian boys, Mexican-American children, white American children, Greek children, and Japanese children, in that order, though it is not clear whether all differences between the groups were significant (Toda *et al.*, 1978; McClintock & Nuttin, 1969, MDG); Indian university students in Delhi than Canadian students (Carment, 1974, MDG); Cuban-American children in Miami than white, native American children (Concha *et al.*, 1975., MB); Israeli kibbutz children than urban Israelis, urban West German, or urban American children, using in one experiment (Madsen & Shapira, 1977) a modified marble pull game (Shapira & Madsen, 1969; Shapira, 1976; Madsen & Shapira, 1977, MP, MB).

Using the social behaviour scale (see above, Fig. 9.1) it has been found that Mexican American children, particularly less Westernized ones, are less likely than white Americans to make the rivalry choice (A) and the eqaulity choice (C), and more likely to make the altruism choice (D) (Knight & Kagan, 1972a, 1972b). In modified forms of this test (Figs. 9.2 and 9.3), white American children were found to be more 'competitive' only on the choices involved in cards 1 and 2 in Fig. 9.2 (Kagan *et al.*, 1977), and only on cards 2 and 3 in Fig. 9.3 (Avellar & Kagan, 1976).

None of these choices involves loss to the chooser himself as a price for making the other lose, and the earlier finding (Kagan & Madsen, 1972a) that white Americans cause loss to themselves in order to make others lose, was thus not replicated.

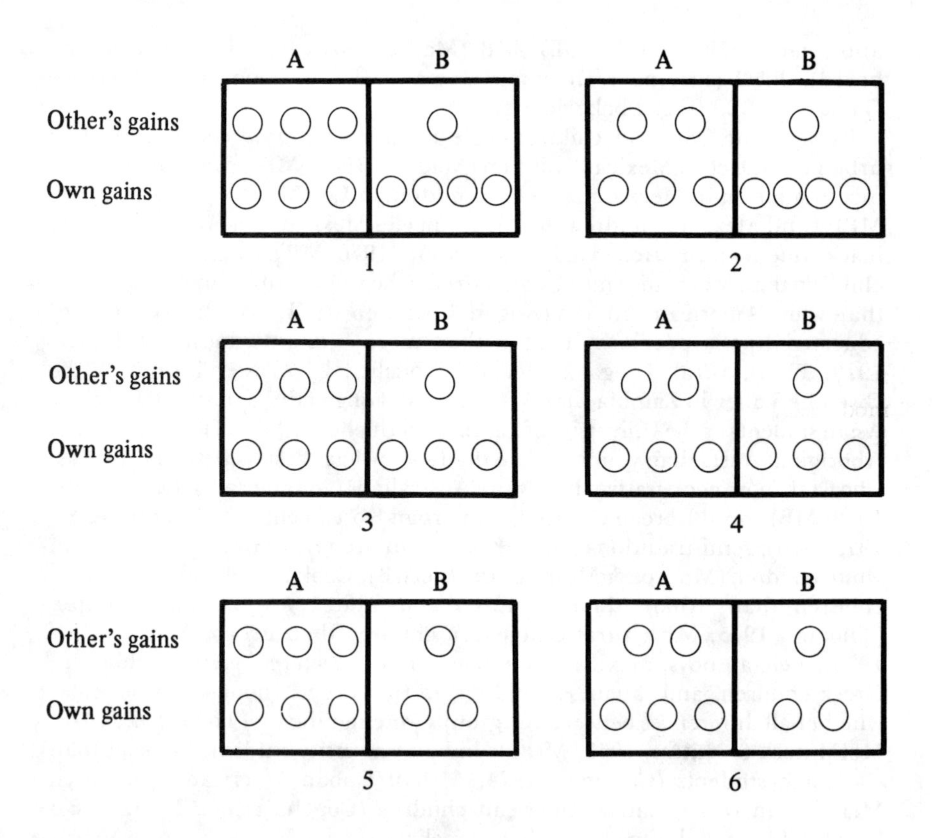

Fig. 9.2 Choice cards in the modified social behaviour scale used by Kagan *et al.* (1977). One card at a time is presented to the person, who chooses between the two possible responses A and B. The person's own outcome is represented in the bottom row of each card, the other's in the top.

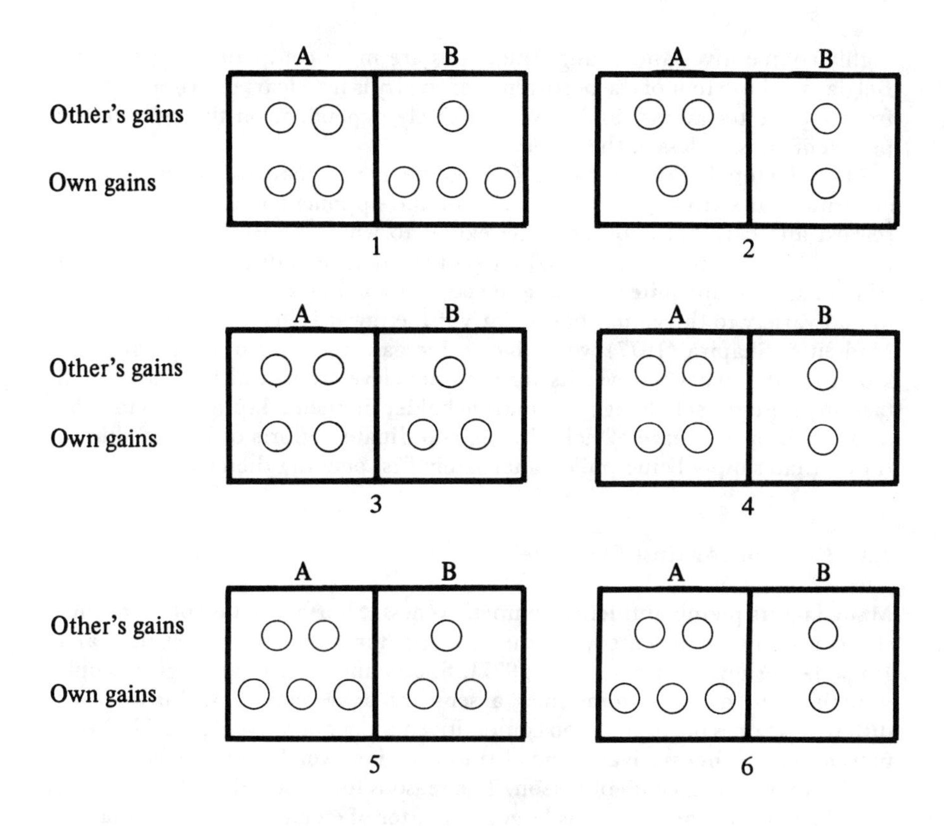

Fig. 9.3 Choice cards in the modified social behaviour scale used by Avellar and Kagan (1976). One card at a time is presented to the person, who chooses between the two possible responses A and B. The person's own outcome is represented in the bottom row of each card, the other's in the top.

9.2.3 Conclusions of Experimental Studies

Some clear conclusions, and some speculations and questions, emerge from the above. It is plain that cultures differ in the degree to which their members co-operate and compete in novel situations: and the differences in experimental techniques, which have found essentially the same things, give us confidence in that conclusion. By and large people whose culture enjoins cooperation, such as rural and traditional people and kibbutz children in Israel, act cooperatively; urban, Westernized people act competitively. Other, perhaps idiosyncratic, cultural differences also appear: for instance, the Japanese sample was highly competitive, and young Americans are more competitive than young Belgians. The extent of the occurrence of rivalry is not clear: it no doubt varies from sample to sample, and must be heavily dependent on the price to the person of causing loss to the other.

Many factors besides culture affect the degree of cooperativeness in these experimental settings. The behaviour of the opponent is one, the level of reward another. Yet another is the extent to which a task is interesting or boring. Many tasks, like repeated plays of the marble pull game, or repeated trials of a PDG, are quite tedious, and people are tempted to vary responses just to add variety to the game, particularly if the rewards involved are not high. Madsen & Shapira (1977) were able to increase the level of cooperation in kibbutz children beyond even its normally high level by making the marble pull task an interesting challenge (the marble holder, in their adaptation, had to be negotiated over a maze of holes by the coordinated efforts of both children, rather than simply being pulled alternately first one way then the other).

9.3 Everyone Against Everyone?

Many factors plainly influence competitiveness. Shortage is one of them, but shortages can be invented, as the struggle for status in universities and Ifugaoland show (Barton, 1969, 1977). Sports and board games give people something to do, and sometimes a sense of achievement. Cultures place different degrees of emphasis on competitiveness, cooperativeness and individualism, on selfishness, rivalry and altruism, and on which sort of behaviour to display to which category of person. The reasons for these cultural differences must be regarded at present as largely a matter of chance. It appears that all the non-Western cultures sampled in experimental studies are cooperative in orientation: certainly there is independent evidence to the effect that the cultures of the Gwembe Tonga, the Maoris, and the traditional Mexicans are. It would be of interest to test traditionally competitive people like the Ifugao *kadangyang* (if their culture has not been too much disturbed by modernization), or individualistic people like the Ik. Barton (1949) observes that the Kalingas, the competitive neighbours of the Ifugao, took very readily to gambling when it was introduced by Americans.

Westernization, or modernization, is leaving few peoples untouched. I was surprised, and somewhat disconcerted (for like many social psychologists, I am a milk-and-water liberal) to find the Zambian children in Lusaka not only as competitive as white children in Zambia and America, but keen to maximize relative gain or exhibit rivalry (Bethlehem, 1973). On consideration, it is easy to see why: Zambian children in towns have a very hard life. They are poor, and the only way up that they can see is through education. But at the time when the experiments were done, there were not even enough primary schools, so competition for vitally important places was very stiff. Even so, the behaviour of Zambian children in the experimental game was more varied than that of the whites: some were very competitive, and some rather cooperative, indicating that traditional cultural norms of cooperation still exerted an influence. It proved hard to find Zambian adults little touched by Western culture, but when they were found they proved, as expected, to be trusting and cooperative, whereas Westernized Zambians living in villages after years in towns, or those who had received more than a bare Western education, Zambian university students, Asian students in Zambia, and so on, were all competitive, despite the fact that they were playing for real money. The big difference between the co-operative groups and the others in the PDG was what happened when one of them made a defecting or competitive response: Westernized groups were inclined to respond tit-for-tat, but traditional Zambians were inclined to go straight back to cooperating. Conflict is unwelcome to them: as it is to the Mbuti pygmies, the Bushmen, the Chewa, and so on. Kagan and Madsen (1971, 1972b) found that Mexican and Mexican-American children playing the circle matrix board game tended, when not actually cooperating, to avoid overt and direct conflict, as by moving the marker sideways: that is, not actually helping the other, but not blocking him or her either.

Western culture enjoins competition. Conspicuous wealth is admired and envied, and so are achievements such as winning races, even when there is no reward other than victory itself. Once people get Western aspirations – for ever more possessions, security, comfort, and so on – competition cannot be avoided, though it can be engaged in to a greater or lesser degree. Traditional life is undemanding, but dull and uncomfortable to modern eyes; modern life is dynamic, but noisome and frenetic to traditional cooperative eyes.

Yet cooperation is never wholly absent, even in competitive Western culture. Competing commercial companies are often in a symbiotic relation to one another; boxers compete for titles, but need each other like Tweedledum and Tweedledee. Hobbes long ago pointed out that life would be intolerable, a war of everyone against everyone, if we did not form a society with rules to contain conflict substantially, and enforce some cooperativeness on even unwilling co-operators. Marwick (1965) emphasizes the role of sorcery in maintaining harmony among the Chewa, and what struck Barton (1969, 1977) when he visited the Ifugao and the Kalingas, was how well they had developed custom law to limit the conflict engendered by competition. So, if life often seems to be a multi-person PDG, we have legal institutions, governments, and moral principles to keep defectors to a bearable minimum. And we need (and need to like) one another, even if we are Ik. See Chapter 11 for a further discussion of this point.

People cooperate without even knowing it. Experiments on the minimal social situation have demonstrated this in a laboratory: people reward each other, because each person's own reward is intimately connected with others' rewards (see Chapter 11). Robert Frost has a poem recording how, when turning grass in a field alone and feeling an essential loneliness, he came across a tuft of flowers which had carefully been left by the man who had scythed the grass. The poem joyously concludes:

> 'Men work together,' I told him from the heart,
> 'Whether they work together or apart.'

References

AVELLAR, J. and KAGAN, S. (1976). Development of competitive behaviors in Anglo-American and Mexican-American children. *Psychological Reports*, **39**, 191 – 198.

BARTON, R.F. (1949). *The Kalingas: Their Institutions and Custom Law.* Chicago: University of Chicago Press.

BARTON, R.F. (1969). *Ifugao Law.* Berkeley and Los Angeles: University of California Press. (Originally published 1919.)

BARTON, R.F. (1977). *The Half-Way Sun.* New York: AMS Press. (Originally published 1930.)

BETHLEHEM, D.W. (1973). Cooperation, competition and altruism among school-children in Zambia. *International Journal of Psychology*, **8**, 125 – 135.

BETHLEHEM, D.W. (1975). The effect of westernization on cooperative behaviour in Central Africa. *International Journal of Psychology*, **10**, 219 – 224.

CARMENT, D.W. (1974). Indian and Canadian choice behaviour in a maximizing difference game and in a game of chicken. *International Journal of Psychology*, **9**, 213 – 221.

COLSON, E. (1960). *Social Organization of the Gwembe Tonga.* Manchester: Manchester University Press.

CONCHA, P., GARCIA, L. and PEREZ, A. (1975). Cooperation versus competition: a comparison of Anglo-American and Cuban-American youngsters in Miami. *Journal of Social Psychology*, **95**, 273 – 274.

DAWES, R.M., MCTAVISH, J. and SHAKLEE, H. (1977). Behavior, communication, and assumptions about other people's behavior in a commons dilemma situation. *Journal of Personality and Social Psychology*, **35**, 1 – 11.

DEUTSCH, M. (1960). Trust, trustworthiness and the F Scale. *Journal of Abnormal and Social Psychology*, **61**, 138 – 140.

DEUTSCH, M. (1962). Cooperation and trust: some theoretical notes. In M.R. JONES (Ed.), *Nebraska Symposium on Motivation*. Lincoln: University of Nebraska Press.

FREEMAN, J.D. (1955a). *Iban Agriculture*. London: HMSO.

FREEMAN, J.D. (1955b). *Report on the Iban of Sarawak. Volume 1. Iban Social Organization.* Sarawak: Govt. Printing Office.

FREEMAN, J.D. (1955c). *Report on the Iban of Sarawak. Volume 2. Agriculture, Land Usage, and Land Tenure among the Iban.* Sarawak: Govt. Printing Office.

GEDDES, W.R. (1961). *Nine Dayak Nights.* London: Oxford University Press.

HOEBEL, E.A. (1954). *The Law of Primitive Man.* Cambridge, Mass.: Harvard University Press.

KAGAN, S. and MADSEN, M.C. (1971). Cooperation and competition of Mexican, Mexican-American, and Anglo-American children of two ages under four instructional sets. *Developmental Psychology*, **5**, 32 – 39.

KAGAN, S. and MADSEN, M.C. (1972a). Rivalry in Anglo-American and Mexican children of two ages. *Journal of Personality and Social Psychology*, **24**, 214 – 220.

KAGAN, S. and MADSEN, M.C. (1972b). Experimental analyses of cooperation and competition of Anglo-American and Mexican children. *Developmental Psychology*, **6**, 49 – 59.

KAGAN, S., ZAHN, G.L. and GEALY, J. (1977). Competition and school achievement among Anglo-American and Mexican-American children. *Journal of Educational Psychology*, **69**, 432 – 441.

KAUNDA, K.D. (1966). *A Humanist in Africa*. London: Longman.

KAUNDA, K.D. (1970). *Kaunda's Guidelines*. (Selected by Titus B. Mukupo.) Lusaka: TBM Publicity Enterprises.

KNIGHT, G.P. and KAGAN, S. (1977a). Acculturation of prosocial and competitive behaviors among second- and third-generation Mexican-American children. *Journal of Cross-Cultural Psychology*, **8**, 273 – 284.
KNIGHT, G.P. and KAGAN, S. (1977b). Development of prosocial and competitive behaviors in Anglo-American and Mexican-American children. *Child Development*, **48**, 1385 – 1394.
KUPER, H. (1947). *An African Aristocracy.* London: Oxford University Press for the International African Institute.
KUPER, H. (1952). *The Swazi.* London: International African Institute.
KUPER, H. (1964). *The Swazi: A South African Kingdom.* New York: Holt, Rinehart, and Winston.
LEACH, E.R. (1954). *Political Systems of Highland Burma.* London: G. Bell and Sons.
MADSEN, M.C. (1967). Cooperative and competitive motivation of children in three Mexican sub-cultures. *Psychological Reports*, **20**, 1307 – 1320.
MADSEN, M.C. (1971). Developmental and cross-cultural differences in the cooperative and competitive behavior of young children. *Journal of Cross-Cultural Psychology*, **2**, 365 – 371.
MADSEN, M.C. and SHAPIRA, A. (1970). Cooperative and competitive behavior of urban Afro-American, Anglo-American, Mexican-American, and Mexican village children. *Developmental Psychology*, **3**, 16 – 20.
MADSEN, M.C. and SHAPIRA, A. (1977). Cooperation and challenge in four cultures. *Journal of Social Psychology*, **102**, 189 – 195.
MADSEN, M.C. and YI, S. (1975). Cooperation and competition of urban and rural children in the Republic of South Korea. *International Journal of Psychology*, **10**, 269 – 274.
MARIN, G., MEJIA, B. and DE OBERLE, C. (1975). Cooperation as a function of place of residence in Colombian children. *Journal of Social Psychology*, **95**, 127 – 128.
MARWICK, M.G. (1965). *Sorcery in its Social Setting: a study of the Northern Rhodesian Cewa.* Manchester: Manchester University Press.
MCCLINTOCK, C.G. and NUTTIN, J.M. (1969). Development of competitive game behavior in children across two cultures. *Journal of Experimental Social Psychology*, **5**, 203 – 219.
MEAD, M. (Ed.) (1937) *Cooperation and Competition among Primitive Peoples.* New York: McGraw-Hill.
MEEKER, B.F. (1970). An experimental study of cooperation and competition in West Africa. *International Journal of Psychology*, **5**, 11 – 19.
MESSICK, D.M. and THORNGATE, W.B. (1967). Relative gain maximization in experimental games. *Journal of Experimental Social Psychology*, **3**, 85 – 101.
MORRIS, H.S. (1953). *Report on a Melanau Sago Producing Community.* London: HMSO.
MUNROE, R.L. and MUNROE, R.H. (1977). Cooperation and competition among East African and American children. *Journal of Social Psychology*, **101**, 145 – 146.
PILBURN, M.D. (1977). Teaching about science and society: moral judgment and the prisoner's dilemma. *Theory and Research in Social Education*, **5**, 20 – 30.
SERMAT, V. (1968). Dominace – submissiveness and competition in a mixed-motive game. *British Journal of Social and Clinical Psychology*, **7**, 35 – 44.
SHAPIRA, A. (1976). Developmental differences in competitive behavior of kibbutz and city children in Israel. *Journal of Social Psychology*, **98**, 19 – 26.
SHAPIRA, A. and MADSEN, M.C. (1969). Cooperative and competitive behavior of kibbutz and urban children in Israel. *Child Development*, **40**, 609 – 617.
SOMMERLAD, E.A. and BELLINGHAM, W.P. (1972). Cooperation – competition: a

comparison of Australian European and Aboriginal children. *Journal of Cross-Cultural Psychology*, **3**, 149 – 157.

STEVENSON, H.N.C. (1943). *The Economics of the Central Chin Tribes*. Bombay: Times of India Press.

SUTLIVE, V.H. Jr. (1978). *The Iban of Sarawak*. Illinois: AHM Publishing Corporation.

THOMAS, D.R. (1975). Cooperation and competition among Polynesian and European children. *Child Development*, **46**, 948 – 953.

THOMAS, E.M. (1960). *The Harmless People*. London: Readers Union and Secker & Warburg.

TODA, M., SHINOTSUKA, H., MCCLINTOCK, C.G. and STECH, F.J. (1978). Development of competitive behavior as a function of culture, age, and social comparison. *Journal of Personality and Social Psychology*, **36**, 825 – 839.

TURNBULL, C.M. (1963). *The Forest People*. London: The Reprint Society of London.

TURNBULL, C.M. (1965). *Wayward Servants*. London: Eyre & Spottiswoode.

TURNBULL, C.M. (1973a). Human nature and primal man. *Social Research*, **40**, 511 – 530.

TURNBULL, C.M. (1973b). *The Mountain People*. London: Cape.

WRIGHTSMAN, L.S. (1966). Personality and attitudinal correlates of trusting and trustworthy behaviors in a two-person game. *Journal of Personality and Social Psychology*, **4**, 328 – 332.

III Implications

CHAPTER 10

Cooperation, Competition and Moral Philosophy

*J. L. Mackie**

It may be thought that the topics discussed in the earlier chapters in this book have no bearing at all on ethics. Ethics, it may be said, is autonomous; there is no way of arguing validly from 'is' to 'ought', from any truths or plausible hypotheses about the 'natural' facts to any moral prescriptions or judgements of value. However, this would be a mistake. All that Hume himself claimed (in Section I of his *Enquiry Concerning the Principles of Morals*) is that what he calls 'reason' cannot alone, by itself, establish moral distinctions, not that it has no bearing on them at all. Although, he says, the 'final sentence' which pronounces moral judgements depends on some feeling or sentiment, much reasoning has to pave the way for that sentiment and give a proper discernment of its object; distinctions have to be made, conclusions drawn, comparisons formed, relations examined, and general facts ascertained. Even actions and passions can be irrational if they are based on false beliefs, either about simple matters of fact or about causal relations (see Hume's *Treatise of Human Nature*, Book II, Part iii, Section 3, and Book III, Part i, Section 1). Or, to approach the issue from a different side, even if some ultimate or basic ethical principles are autonomous, the derivation from them of practical moral precepts must take facts and causal relations into account.

Even someone who held, therefore, that there are objectively valid ethical principles, discoverable by some sort of intuition, some independent moral awareness or understanding, would still have to pay attention to the topics of those earlier chapters in working out the details of his moral theory. But their significance is much greater for someone who holds, as I do, that morality is a human product, that it is a system of thought and evaluation and control of conduct into which human feelings, desires, instincts, social interactions and reciprocal pressures enter, along with knowledge and beliefs of various sorts (Mackie, 1977, 1980). Sociobiology, aspects of which are discussed in Chapters 1 and 2 of this book, and the theories of games and of collective action (see Chapters 4 and 5), are then relevant to morality in two distinct ways. On the one hand they may help to explain already-existing moralities, by outlining the contexts in which they have arisen and identifying some of the forces and mechanisms that have produced them. On the other hand they may indicate constraints on any workable systems of morality, constraints which must be

* Deceased.

taken into account in any intelligent advocacy of moral principles or any worthwhile proposals for the reform of existing moral attitudes and ideas.

10.1 The Explanation of Existing Moralities

Sociobiology is the offspring of a marriage between game theory and the neo-Darwinian theory of evolution. Genetically determined behavioural features, including elements of social behaviour, will be favoured by evolutionary selection in so far as they help the individuals that display them to propagate the genes that determine those features, typically in situations in which those individuals are in relations of mixed competition and cooperation with other members of the same species. It is important that the key process is gene selection, not group selection : there is no general principle that features which promote the well-being or flourishing of a group will be evolutionarily favoured. Tendencies which, if they became widespread, would thus help a group may well be defeated, in competition within the group, by tendencies which are relatively harmful to the group as a whole but are more likely to enable the individuals that display them to propagate their own genes. Thus altruism directed indiscriminately towards all group members will lose out in competition with more selfish behaviour. Yet it would be almost equally wrong to speak of individual selection, since the characteristics that are favoured are not necessarily ones that help the individuals that have them to flourish: an individual's genes may be propagated best by behaviour in which that individual sacrifices itself in helping its offspring or other near relatives to survive and reproduce. In consequence it is not purely egoistic behaviour that we can expect to result from evolutionary selection, but a mixture of egoism with self-referential altruism — that is, altruism directed towards individuals who are somehow related to the agent. But such altruism need not be directed only towards blood-relations: reciprocal altruism can also be favoured by evolutionary selection (Trivers, 1971). If, conditionally upon A's helping B in some way, B will do something that helps A to flourish and have offspring, then there will be an evolutionary pressure in favour of A's helping B — and B need not even be a member of the same species as A.

Of particular interest in relation to morality is the way in which retributive tendencies can be selectively favoured. This is most obvious for hostile retribution. Suppose that an animal is injured by another, either of the same or of a different species, where the first is able to do some harm to the second which the second can associate with its own initial aggression. The aggressor will then be discouraged from repeating the attack, so the retaliation which discourages it will tend to benefit the retaliator. More generally, where such situations constantly recur there will be two related selective pressures: among the potential victims of aggression, in favour of retaliation, and among the potential aggressors, against aggression towards retaliators. Of course there need not be any calculation or deliberate choice by either party; it is rather that the mechanism of natural selection mimics purposiveness, producing instinctive behaviours which resemble those that might well result from intelligent calculation. Thus we can understand how there could come to be instinctive spontaneous retaliatory tendencies, in much the same way as we can understand the development of reciprocal altruism and instinctive spontaneous mutual assistance. Kindly retributive tendencies — a disposition to display 'gratitude' for benefits, which is not quite the same thing as systematic mutual assistance — could in principle be developed in a corresponding way to hostile ones, but it would not be surprising if hostile retribution were in general stronger and more widespread than kindly retribution, simply because occasions on which it is likely to be beneficial will tend to occur more often. This is particularly significant in so far as morality itself can be seen as an outgrowth from retributive (especially hostile retributive) tendencies, as will be shown below. It is hostile retributive *behaviour* that is initially explained in this way; but creatures that have a high level of consciousness will naturally also develop retributive *sentiments*, such as anger and resentment, accompanying and sustaining the behaviour.

A central sociobiological concept is that of an evolutionarily stable strategy. A strategy — that is, a genetically determined behavioural tendency — is evolutionarily stable, relative to a certain context and to certain alternative strategies, if in that context it, rather than any of the alternatives, will be favoured by natural selection in the competition between these rival tendencies within a group of members of the same species (see Chapters 1 and 2 in this volume). As was suggested above, indiscriminate altruism will not, in most contexts, be evolutionarily stable in relation to a more 'selfish' strategy. But what is thus evolutionarily stable may be a mixed strategy or a mixture of strategies rather than a single uniform strategy. Consider (borrowing an example from Dawkins, 1976) a situation where members of the same species repeatedly come into conflict, perhaps over food or mates or territory, and consider just the two alternative strategies of aggression and conciliation. When two aggressors meet, they fight and in general both suffer a certain amount of injury, while only one of them eventually gets the item in dispute. When an aggressor meets a conciliator, the conciliator gives way without fighting and without being hurt, while the aggressor gets the goods. When two conciliators meet, they peaceably share the wanted item. Now while aggressors clearly do better against conciliators than other conciliators do, it may well be that aggressors will do less well against other aggressors than conciliators. This will be so if the damage sustained in fighting is considerable in proportion to the value of the items in dispute — both reckoned in terms of the tendency to decrease or increase the propagation of one's genes. If the average value of a 50% chance of getting the item in question is less than the average disvalue of the injuries, then the average payoff to an aggressor in dispute with another aggressor will be negative, whereas the payoff to a conciliator in dispute with an aggressor is merely zero. Now if this is so, if aggressors do better against conciliators than conciliators do, while conciliators do better against aggressors than aggressors do, then neither of these two strategies on its own will be evolutionarily stable. A population consisting wholly of conciliators could be successfully invaded by aggressor genes, but equally one consisting wholly of aggressors could be successfully invaded by conciliator genes. The evolutionarily stable strategy will be some mixture of the two. The precise ratio will depend on the average values and disvalues of the various possible results: for example, if the average disvalue of the injuries sustained in fighting is equal to the average value of getting the item in dispute, the stable ratio will be equality between aggression and conciliation. But this ratio may be realized in either a mixture of strategies or a mixed strategy. That is, it may be sustained either by there being just as many pure aggressors as pure conciliators, or by each individual being disposed to be aggressive half the time and conciliatory half the time, or, indeed, by some combination of these. Of course, this is only a simple illustration; what is evolutionarily stable may well be a more complicated mixture of strategies that are themselves more complicated (for example, by including various conditionalities) than simple conciliation or aggression.

So far we have been thinking of genetically determined behaviour — instinctive, spontaneous, uncalculating. But the formal character of these developments depends solely on the fact that the genes involved are self-replicating items which cause behaviour which in turn reacts favourably or unfavourably on the frequency of their replication, but whose replication is not always perfect: some mistakes in copying — mutations — occur, and these mistaken copies can in turn produce copies of themselves. Anything with these formal features is a possible subject of evolution by natural selection. Now in human (and in some non-human) populations there can arise self-replicators of another sort, cultural traits or, as Dawkins (1976) calls them, 'memes', which include tunes, ideas, fashions, and techniques. Provided that such items can reproduce themselves (fairly faithfully, but with occasional variations) by memory and imitation, and can cause behaviour which then reacts on their own propagation, they too and the behaviour they produce will be subject to evolutionary pressures which work in the same way as those that result in gene selection. Memes, no less than genes, will be selected on account of their tendency to produce behaviour that favours their own propagation — which is not necessarily behaviour beneficial either to the individuals or to the societies in which these memes take root. That some idea or belief or practice has a social function is neither necessary nor sufficient in itself to explain its persistence or its spreading. Its performance of a social function may be part of such an explanation, if it can be shown that its having this function helps to propagate it; but a trait which is socially neutral or harmful may also have the power to propagate itself. Just as infectious diseases can spread among the bodies of a population, harmful ideas can flourish and spread among their minds.

One sort of cultural item which both performs a social function and in doing so contributes to its own reproduction is what we can call a convention. Conventions can arise to solve problems of two sorts, problems of coordination and of partial conflict.

A problem of coordination arises where the interests of the parties do not diverge, but where their independent choices of action may or may not maximize the fulfilment of their interests. (The formal properties of 'pure coordination games' are discussed in Chapter 5.) A typical problem of this sort occurs when each of two or more people wants to meet the other(s), but each has to decide independently where to go and when to do so. For example, in a primitive setting, people may want to meet to barter their respective products. A suitable convention might be that they should meet at the foot of a certain tall tree on the morning after each full moon. It is easy to see how such a convention establishing a regular market place and market day could grow up even without any explicit agreement. If by chance two or three people met, with significant advantage to each, at some striking and therefore memorable place and time, they would be likely to associate that success with that place and time, and so tend to return to the same place at a corresponding later time — say, after the next full moon. Once two or three started meeting regularly, others who happened to find out about it would tend to join in: the advantage of the incipient convention to each joiner would provide a force sufficient to spread and maintain it.

Less obviously, a convention can arise to solve problem of partial conflict — say, something of the form of a prisoners' dilemma (see Chapter 5). Suppose that there are two families, one of which catches fish and the other collects edible fruits and roots. They are too much afraid of each other to meet and barter, although each would do better if they exchanged some of their products than if each consumed only its own products, and both families know this. But if each family has to decide independently what to do, each will do better by consuming all of its own products, whether or not the other family gives the first some of what it produces. Since neither family can trust the other, it looks as if no exchange can take place. But suppose that some time when the fishermen have had a good catch they say to one another : 'We might just try leaving two or three fish well in view on that rock that the fruit gatherers often pass, and see what happens'. Of course, it may not work; the fruit gatherers may just take the fish and leave nothing, and then it is likely to be some time before the experiment is repeated. On the other hand, the fruit gatherers may take the fish and leave some fruit in return, and then come back to see what the fishermen do the next day. In favourable circumstances a virtuous spiral could be set up, with each family encouraging the other, rewarding it when it repeats or increases its gifts, but reducing its own offering if the other family reduces its. With such reciprocal sanctioning, a convention of regular exchanges of produce could grow up and be maintained without any explicit bargaining or agreement, and without any prior principles of agreement-keeping or mutual trust between these parties. In fact this sort of convention maintained by reciprocal sanctioning is a more basic social relation than agreement or contract; indeed, even in a society where there is full communication the making and keeping of agreements can itself be seen as a particular example of this sort of convention. For the main motive that each party has for keeping the agreement lies in the fact that if it fails to do so it is less likely to be trusted another time. Nor need this be a consciously calculated motive: rather, the tendency to keep agreements rather than break them can be automatically 'reinforced' by the rewards of honesty and the penalties for dishonesty, so that each agent develops a spontaneous inclination to keep agreements.

Situations of partial conflict, where the prior interests of the parties diverge to some extent, and yet where each will do better in terms of those prior interests if they cooperate, each making some concessions, than if each pursues his own interests directly, need not be symmetrical: one party may have an initial advantage over another. Such a situation of unequal partial conflict can still be resolved by the growth of a convention in much the same way as one of equal partial conflict, but the convention that emerges is likely to be differentially advantageous to the party that starts in the stronger bargaining position. Conventions that arise in this way and are sustained by reciprocal sanctioning will thus include 'norms of partiality' as well as 'prisoners' dilemma norms'. The ways in which prisoners' dilemma norms, coordination norms, and norms of partiality arise from the corresponding problem situations are fully discussed in Ullman-Margalit (1977).

In speaking of 'norms' as well as of 'conventions', we are recognizing that what arise in this way are not only patterns of behaviour but also rules or principles of action which are 'internalized' by the participants. The association of moral sentiments with the practices, in particular disapproval of violations, the feeling that they are wrong or not to be done, and a sense of guilt about one's own transgressions, is a major part of such internalization. Only when this stage is reached can we speak properly of a morality, though as we have seen there can be pre-moral tendencies to behave in ways that coincide with or come close to those that are characteristically supported by moral thinking. But where does the notion of wrongness come from? We have already sketched a possible genetic explanation of hostile retribution and resentment of injuries. We have also seen how cooperation can arise and be maintained either by genetic selection or by the corresponding social evolution of a certain kind of meme, namely conventions. Putting these two together, we can understand how there can come to be cooperation in resentment, where all or most members of a group jointly react against injuries to any of them. Among human beings in particular, certain *kinds* of behaviour can be recognized and can become the objects of cooperative resentment. This may be the source of the characteristic 'disinterestedness' and 'apparent impartiality' of the moral sentiments — only apparent impartiality, since the conventions which are 'impartially' observed and enforced may themselves be norms of partiality, differentially more advantageous to some kinds of persons than to others. The notion of moral wrongness includes three main elements: what is thought wrong is seen as being harmful generally (not just to this or that particular person), as being intrinsically forbidden (not merely forbidden by this or that authority, but in itself simply not to be done), and as calling for a hostile response (again not merely from a particular person: it is rather that a hostile response from *somewhere* is needed). All three of these elements can be understood in the light of the above-outlined genetic and social mechanisms, as projections of the sentiments associated with cooperative resentment and hostile retribution. And this notion of wrongness is the central moral notion: other moral ideas fall easily into place around it. A sense of duty, for example, is the feeling that failure to act in such and such a way would be wrong in this sense. The view that morality is an outgrowth from the 'retributive emotions' was put forward by Westermarck (1932). I have discussed and developed it elsewhere (Mackie, in press).

Existing moralities vary between societies and even within one society. And even one morality will commonly recognize quite a collection of diverse requirements or values — for example, such virtues as courage, temperance, perseverance, honesty with regard to property, veracity, promise-keeping, loyalty to friends, patriotism, marital fidelity, parental devotion, chastity, modesty (in two different senses), piety, cheerfulness, compassion, tolerance, fairness, sportsmanship, and so on. And what has to be explained is not only the recognition of these as virtues but also the fact that people maintain a partial, but only partial, conformity to them. The content of moral thought and moral conduct is complex, and an adequate explanation of morality would have to cover much more than a bit of general benevolence and some rules about sexual behaviour. But what I have outlined here is the beginning of such an explanation: we can see how this sort of approach could account for the complex reality that we actually find. We have referred both to genetic (sociobiological) mechanisms and to sociological ones. We have found possible sources of self-referential altruism and reciprocal altruism, and of cooperation within groups guided and sustained by various conventional norms, including coordination norms, prisoners' dilemma norms, and norms of partiality. We have traced a possible development of retributive behaviour and retributive sentiments growing into cooperation in resentment and thence into the central moral concept of wrongness. This account of the origin of morality is closely related to that of Hume in his *Treatise*, Book III.

Is there some competition between the genetic and the cultural accounts? If so, it can be easily resolved. It will be reasonable to ascribe to biological evolution those pre-moral tendencies to care for children and close relatives, to enjoy the company of fellow-members of a small group, to display reciprocal altruism and both hostile and kindly retribution, which we share with many non-human animals, but to ascribe to cultural evolution the more specifically moral virtues which presuppose language and other characteristically human capacities and relations, such as honesty, veracity, promise-keeping, fairness, modesty as opposed to arrogance, and so on, as well as those detailed moral principles which vary from one human society to another.

I want to guard especially against two possible misunderstandings, both of which would make my account of morality seem more egoistic than it is.

First, I would stress that none of the above-mentioned mechanisms requires calculation, let alone calculation in terms of self-interest, on the part of the agents concerned. With the 'lower' animals there is no question of motives, but simply of genetically determined behaviour, self-referentially altruistic, retributive, and so on. Even among those animals, including humans, to whom we can ascribe motives, we have explained altruism, resentment, gratitude, norm-following, moral disapproval, a sense of duty, and the like as *direct* motives. From the agent's point of view the corresponding actions are not done as a means to anything else. It is only that both the genetic and the convention-forming mechanisms can mimic purposiveness, and so can give the agents direct, spontaneous, motives which lead them to act in ways which in fact promote what we can see as their pre-existing interests.

Second, even those pre-existing interests are not to be taken as being purely egoistic. At the genetic level, what we can describe, speaking behaviourally, as the selfishness of genes is not equivalent, even behaviourally, to the selfishness of individual organisms. And at the social level the pre-existing interests that create the problems of coordination or partial conflict, prisoners' dilemmas and the like, from which conventions may emerge, are not necessarily, and in fact will not be, exclusively egoistic. The human individuals enter into these situations already with their various direct motives of self-referential altruism (concern for children, relatives, friends, and so on as well as for themselves) and the joint purposes of already cooperating groups, as well as motives of pride, self-respect, honour, and the like. Prisoners' dilemmas, it must be emphasized, can arise whenever the parties have partly divergent purposes of whatever sort — even if, for example, both parties are aiming at the general happiness, but have different views about how it can best be promoted — and are not produced only by a clash of selfish aims.

A wide variety of moral rules and principles could be understood as having developed by the operation of mechanisms of these sorts in different concrete circumstances, and the fact that what is evolutionarily stable — either genetically or, by analogy, socially — may be a mixture of strategies could explain the coexistence within a single society, even in a stable environment, of different norms with regard to the same sort of choice, and of different degrees of conformity to a norm. Yet despite such diversity and indeterminacy there are some significant common features of the behavioural tendencies and moral principles that might emerge in these ways.

Except where individuals sacrifice themselves for the sake of their own children or close relatives, we should not expect there to be principles of complete sacrifice of the agent; but there could be principles of joining, when others do so too, in enterprises which carry some risk of the agent's being killed or suffering some other serious harm. We should not expect there to be principles of pure altruism or pure benevolence directed unconditionally towards the well-being of a whole community, of loving all your neighbours literally as yourself; the social insects are a striking exception, but their behaviour is covered by the above-mentioned proviso, since with them all members of the hive or nest are indeed close relatives. Equally, we should not expect to find people guided by the pure abstract principle of doing as you would be done by; we can expect them to follow rather the Hobbesian variant of this, to be willing to cooperate and make concessions *when others are so too*. One is not to do to or for others whatever one *would like* them to do to or for oneself absolutely or unconditionally, but only in so far as there is or can be established such a practice in which others as well as oneself will join. That is, what we should expect to develop and flourish are norms of cooperation and reciprocation, including asymmetrical ones that reflect the unequal bargaining strengths of different kinds of participants, not norms that enjoin that each agent should do whatever is most likely to promote the general happiness. And in fact we find that the norms that really do the work of controlling people's behaviour are of the sorts that this approach would lead us to expect. People generally feel that it is wrong to kill or assault others, and usually refrain from doing so, provided that those others are not a threat to them; they respect private property and keep mutually beneficial agreements; but they do not feel obliged to decide whether each such act or forbearance is likely to do more than its opposite to promote the general happiness. In an election, though one's individual vote is almost always causally inefficacious, one takes credit for having voted for the right party if it wins the election, and one puts a 'Don't blame me . . . ' sticker on one's car window if it loses; that is, we feel that all those who participate in an activity deserve a share of the praise or blame for its results, even if each person's action on its own was causally irrelevant.

Or consider people's moral feelings with regard to leaving litter at beauty spots. If the place is free from litter when you arrive, there is a fairly strong moral pressure against leaving the first beer can. One does not think 'Just one can won't make a significant difference', but rather 'It wouldn't be fair for me to make a mess when other visitors have taken the trouble to leave it all so clean'. Even if there is rubbish everywhere already, one may well not say 'One more can will make no difference', but rather 'If I throw my can away, I shall share the responsibility for all this filth'. Thus the norms that do the work include such ones as these:

Join in enterprises that promote public goods in which you will share, and play your part in them.

Join others in refraining from activities that would produce public harms from which you, along with others, would suffer.

Take a share of the credit for any good results of enterprises in which you have joined, and a share of the blame for any bad results of activities in which you have taken part, without calculating the differential effects of your participation; give credit and blame similarly to others.

Such norms as these are different from the utilitarian one:

Act so as to maximize the expected production of general good.

They are also different from the Kantian one:

Act only on a maxim which you can will to be a universal law of nature.

In short, the moral principles which we find flourishing and effective in controlling people's actions are of the sorts which we should expect to find if we assumed that morality has developed through the biological and social mechanisms outlined above; and they are significantly different from the ones recommended by some influential schools of philosophical moralists. The most vital differences are that the operative principles involve concrete relations of reciprocity, cooperation, and joint practices whereas the philosophically advocated ones are more abstract or appeal to merely hypothetical considerations, and therefore build less on each agent's pre-moral motives and offer him less chance of a reward.

10.2 Constraints on Moral Development and Reform

If it is agreed that already-existing moral systems can be accounted for in these ways, we may go on to the question whether — and, if so, to what extent — these genetic and social mechanisms place constraints on any workable and therefore rationally recommendable moral systems.

It is sometimes asked whether we can escape from our own biology. Indeed Dawkins himself, in the final chapter of *The Selfish Gene*, suggests that 'We are built as gene machines and cultured as meme machines, but we have the power to turn against our creators. We, alone one earth, can rebel against the tyranny of the selfish replicators' (Dawkins, 1976, p. 215). But this is a misleading way of putting it. We are, and will remain for the foreseeable future, what biological evolution over millions of years has made us. But on that practically unalterable basis, cultural evolution has already erected a far more complicated set of superstructures: we obviously do not behave *just* in ways that are biologically determined. The interesting question is how much freedom of movement is left for the development of still further superstructures, which will start from and yet may modify the existing culturally determined ways of behaving and thinking, much as cultural evolution has started from and yet modified the biologically determined patterns.

For example, we may sensibly enquire whether we could develop a morality of pure altruism or pure rational benevolence, which might replace the existing norms which prescribe more specific kinds of conduct and which are characterized, as we have seen, by reciprocity and (sometimes asymmetrical) cooperation. Such a morality would, of course, require each individual to be ready to sacrifice not only himself but also those close to him for any greater advantage to others, however remote. Such a replacement is most unlikely, for three reasons. First, this morality would frequently have to oppose strong genetically ingrained tendencies of egoism, self-referential altruism, reciprocal altruism, and retribution as well as strong culturally developed traits and traditions of similar sorts. Second, if this kind of morality did begin to flourish among some considerable number of people, it would lay them open to exploitation, to being used by those who diverge not only from this morality but also from the traditional one of reciprocity and conditional cooperation in the direction of pure selfishness. In Dawkins's (1976) terms, the more 'suckers' there are, the more 'cheats' will flourish. Or, as Hutcheson said long ago, to do away with reciprocation and a right to the fruits of one's labour 'exposes the industrious as a constant prey to the slothful, and sets self-love against industry' (Hutcheson, 1725, see Selby-Bigge, 1897, p. 165). Third, this sort of morality suffers from a radical indeterminacy in its object. As was demonstrated in Chapter 4, there simply are no natural and obvious ways of measuring the 'general welfare', or of eliciting a 'collective choice' or 'group preference' from the set of divergent preferences of the members of a group. Not even something as apparently neutral and uncontroversial as the Pareto principle is really acceptable in all circumstances (Sen, 1970). And of course this indeterminacy provides further opportunities for exploitation, for people to represent what are really their own selfish purposes as the promotion of the elusive general welfare.

It is true that we may distinguish between a practical, working morality, which guides or controls conduct fairly directly, and a higher level, critical moral theory in terms of which philosophers may evaluate and seek to modify the practical, working morality. All three of our objections tell against the possibility of developing a working morality of pure altruism or general benevolence, but the first two would not tell against the philosophical use of a moral theory based on general benevolence : the points that they make are ones that our critical philosophers would properly take into account in deriving a working morality from their higher level theory. But the third objection tells even against this philosophical use of general benevolence: if there is no satisfactory way of adding up interests or eliciting a collective choice from individual preferences or measuring general welfare, then there will be something spurious about any purported derivation of working moral principles from these concepts.

There may, then, be constraints which exclude moralities of the utilitarian type. If there are, I see no reason to regret the fact. As I have argued elsewhere (Mackie, 1978), a morality based on the assigning of rights to each individual would in itself be more attractive, even apart from the fact that it would fit in better with the suggested constraints of reciprocity and conditional cooperation.

Another question is this: Do these constraints imply that a workable morality can take account of the interests only of those who are able to compete and to cooperate, and can show no respect for non-human animals, for example, or for seriously and permanently handicapped human beings?

It is true that the mechanisms sketched so far would not in themselves generate moral sentiments in favour of such non-competitors. But they do not positively require that there should *not* be such sentiments, in the way they do tell against a morality of pure altruism or benevolence. Hume, in referring to this question in his *Enquiry* (Section III, Part I), suggested that considerations of what he called 'justice' would not arise between us and creatures, human or non-human, that were permanently unable to compete with us, but that 'we should be bound, by the laws of humanity, to give gentle usage to them'. Hume's use of the word 'justice' to refer only to moral principles of a quasi-contractual sort may be a bit misleading; but we can understand what he meant. But how are we to explain the sentiments of 'humanity'? Surely as Hume himself did, as a product of 'sympathy' and 'imagination'. Once we have developed, in the ways already outlined, a morality that assigns rights to those other human beings who are participators in the mixture of competition and cooperation that is the ordinary and inevitable human condition, and have acquired dispositions to show some respect for their interests and to feel compassion for their sufferings, it is not difficult for us to extend these attitudes to other creatures, human or non-human, in so far as we see them as being like ourselves and like those towards whom we have already developed respect and compassion. It is true that there is no necessity about this. It is perfectly possible for people to combine the finest moral sensitivity in relation to their fellows with extreme inhumanity towards 'brute beasts' and defective human beings, or indeed to non-defective human beings whom they see as in some way alien to themselves and their associates. All I am saying is that the contrary is also possible, and is the more likely to come about the more people are imaginatively aware of the similarities between themselves and the non-participators. The constraints we have been considering do not rule out a morality that includes an element of humanity in this sense. On the other hand, they do set some limits to its influence. The kind of humanity which we can expect to be effective will fall far short of the equal concern for all sentient beings, proportionate only to their capacity for feeling pain and pleasure, which seems to be a consequence of utilitarian principles. We cannot expect such equal concern for the interests even of other fully active human beings, even those with whom the agent is acquainted. Putting it bluntly, we can expect people in general to display humanity only when they can do so without the certainty of too great a cost to themselves and to those close to them, though, as I have said, they may be willing to *risk* the final sacrifice.

We have seen that where, in the mixture of competition and cooperation, there are parties with unequal bargaining power, the conventions which resolve such problems are likely to include norms of partiality, rules or principles which are differentially advantageous to what was already the stronger party. Any explanation of existing moralities would have to include such a mechanism, since nearly all actual moral systems have been of this biased sort. Duties and rights have been assigned unequally between peasants and noblemen, slaves and freemen, blacks and whites, Brahmins and untouchables, citizens and non-citizens, owners and workers, party-members and non-party-members, men and women. But is this widespread and easily explained feature an unavoidable constraint on any workable morality? Must any morality that actually controls human conduct merely reflect and perpetuate differences of strength that arise from other forces and relations in society? Of course there have been and are egalitarian moral *theories*; but the question is whether these can actually operate in practice.

As with our previous problem, we can see how sympathy and imagination can generate egalitarian moral sentiments; but egalitarian, like humanitarian, sentiments are likely to control people's conduct only when the cost to the agents themselves and those close to them is not certain to be too great. And, in general, the giving of more equal rights to important classes of those who are fellow participators in the mixture of competition and cooperation would cost more than the displaying of a moderate degree of humanity to non-participators. On the whole, then, we can expect norms of partiality to be replaced by norms of impartiality only in so far as the previously disadvantaged groups find non-moral sources of strength that improve their bargaining position. Otherwise egalitarian moral sentiments will either not arise at all or, if they are generated by sympathy and imagination, will remain largely at the level of theory, and not develop into a genuine working morality. This may seem to be a pessimistic conclusion; but something like it has, I believe, been reached through trial and error by many of those who have been actually engaged in campaigns for racial (etc.) equality. It is also only a generalization of the traditional Marxist thesis that capitalism cannot be reformed by the moral conversion of capitalists: as long as the 'relations of production' are unchanged an individual capitalist who attempts to give up exploitation is merely replaced by someone else who plays his social role more efficiently.

In raising this last problem, we have already touched upon the area where there is not only the greatest need for further developments of morality but also the greatest difficulty in devising them, that of the political applications and extensions of morality (cf. Mackie, 1977, pp. 235 – 9, and Mackie, 1980, pp. 113 – 18). Devices for compromise and adjustment of conflicts between individuals have grown up, largely automatically but with some help from deliberate invention, over many thousands of years, and have been widely accepted into moral thinking and into various legal systems. But corresponding devices for compromise and adjustment of conflicts between politically organized groups are relatively rudimentary, and though some principles of international justice are vaguely recognized, they form as yet only a weak system of international morality. Here, I am afraid, I have no specific suggestions to offer, but only a plea that the problems should be considered, and that they should be considered in the light of the understanding of morality in general, and the constraints upon it, that we have been developing. Here, as in all human affairs, the concrete situation is inevitably one of partial conflict, of a mixture of competition and cooperation, of partly coincident and partly divergent interests, but also, and importantly, of unequal and unstable concentrations of power. We cannot reasonably hope for effective principles of political and international morality based merely on abstract ideals. We need principles of adjustment which both allow for and are themselves sustained by the very forces which they try to control.

Hume (in his *Enquiry*, Section III, Part I, note) quotes from Cicero a passage which, as Hume rightly says, anticipates Hobbes's picture of the state of nature, the condition of men in the absence of laws and governments, as a state of war. The quotation (from *Pro Sestio*, 42) concludes thus:

> The difference between this civilized and humane life, and that monstrous one, depends upon nothing so much as upon the difference between law (or justice, *ius*) and force (or violence, *vis*). If we are unwilling to use one of these, then we must use the other. Do we want to eliminate force? Then it is necessary that law should flourish — that is, legal proceedings (*iudicia*) in which all law is contained. Do we not want legal proceedings, or not have them? Then it is necessary that force should rule. Everyone can see this.

This is, however, only part of the truth. We need not only *ius* but also *mores*, morality as well as law, and they must be in reasonable harmony with one another. Besides, we need the right sort of *ius* and the right sort of *mores* to contain the forces that would otherwise break out as *vis*. The problem is to find out what these are. The first step towards solving the problem is to see that this *is* the problem. Regrettably, not everyone has seen this, and many thinkers divert attention from it by posing questions about moral philosophy in less illuminating ways.

References

DAWKINS, R. (1976). *The Selfish Gene.* Oxford: Oxford University Press.

HUTCHESON, F. (1725). An inquiry concerning moral good and evil. In L.A.SELBY-BIGGE (Ed.), *British Moralists*. Oxford: Oxford University Press. Vol. I, 1897.

MACKIE, J. (1977). *Ethics: Inventing Right and Wrong*. Harmondsworth: Penguin.

MACKIE, J. (1978). Can there be a right-based moral theory? *Midwest Studies in Philosophy*, **3**, 350 – 359.

MACKIE, J. (1980). *Hume's Moral Theory*. London: Routledge & Kegan Paul.

MACKIE, J. (in press). Morality and the retributive emotions. In T.D. STROUP (Ed.), *Essays on Edward Westermarck*. Helsinki: Acta Philosophica Fennica.

SEN, A.K. (1970). *Collective Choice and Social Welfare*. Edinburgh: Oliver & Boyd.

TRIVERS, R.L. (1971). The evolution of reciprocal altruism. *Quarterly Review of Biology*, **46**, 35 – 57.

ULLMANN-MARGALIT, E. (1977). *The Emergence of Norms*. Oxford: Oxford University Press.

WESTERMARCK, E. (1932). *Ethical Relativity*. London: Routledge.

CHAPTER 11

Conclusions

Andrew M. Colman

11.1 Language and Cooperation

Previous chapters of this book have focused on the social behaviour of *either* human *or* non-human species; the authors have commented only occasionally and in passing on the similarities and differences between human and animal behaviour. But it is of obvious practical importance to know whether, and to what extent, theories and empirical findings pertaining to animal behaviour can help us to understand conflict and conflict resolution in human societies. This is a controversial question to which no simple clear-cut answer can be given; but it is possible to eliminate certain popular fallacies and to make some progress towards an answer.

Berryman (Chapter 3) has provided a comprehensive summary of what is known about animal communication. In some species of animals remarkably complex and sophisticated communication systems have evolved, but most people realize intuitively that even the most elaborate forms of animal communication differ qualitatively from human language. The crux of the difference, which has important implications for the comparative study of cooperation and competition, can be elucidated by an analysis of some of the major functions of language.

Karl Bühler (1934, pp. 24 – 33) developed a useful theoretical framework for analysing the functions of language; his *Sprachtheorie* is fairly well known in Germany but is seldom referred to by English-speaking psychologists and linguistic theorists. He distinguished between three levels or functions of language as follows. At the lowest level is the expressive function (*Kundgabefunktion*); next in the hierarchy is the signalling or releasing function (*Auslösefunktion*); and at an even higher level is the descriptive function (*Darstellungsfunktion*). Popper (1963, 1972) added a fourth function, the highest in the hierarchy, which he called the argumentative function.

This list does not exhaust the possible functions of language. But it is hierarchical in so far as a communication cannot serve any of the functions without simultaneously serving all of the functions below it in the hierarchy, whereas the lower functions can exist without the higher ones. An organism can *express* its physical, emotional, or cognitive state without provoking or intending to provoke another organism to respond, that is, without signalling; but it cannot signal without at the same time expressing itself. The signalling function is thus above the expressive function in the hierarchy. Similarly, an organism can *signal* danger (say) without describing the danger; but it cannot describe without also signalling and expressing itself. Finally, a person can *describe* a state of affairs without commenting on the truth or falsity or validity or invalidity of his own or someone else's statements, that is, without arguing; but he cannot *argue* without simultaneously describing, and signalling to anyone who is there to receive the message, and expressing himself.

According to Bühler (1934), all forms of animal communication are confined to the lower two functions. This is probably not strictly true since the bees (for example) seem to have evolved a rudimentary capacity to describe certain simple states of affairs, and some non-human primates can apparently be taught to do so (see Chapter 3). But there is little doubt that most forms of animal communication are merely expressive or signalling systems, and that none possesses the argumentative function. Even human language is not always used argumentatively : all children pass through a stage of linguistic development during which they merely describe things, and among both adults and children verbal exclamations can be simply expressive. But human language is often argumentative, whereas animal communication can serve only expressive, signalling, and perhaps occasionally descriptive functions. Psychologists, biologists, and linguistic philosophers, especially those who are influenced by behaviourist theories, tend to ignore the higher functions of language, presumably because the lower functions are invariably present in any communication that serves the higher functions. This has led to a deplorable blurring of the distinction between animal and human communication and to the propagation of demonstrably inadequate theories of human language (Popper, 1963).

What are the implications of the analysis of language functions outlined above for our ourstanding of cooperation and competition in human and animal groups? There are many circumstances in which the collective interest of a group or an entire society calls for joint cooperation. In some cases cooperative behaviour is also in the individual interests of the group members, and in these circumstances the goal of joint cooperation can be achieved by a natural evolutionary process which will be discussed in the following section, without the use of the higher language functions. But in other cases it is in the group members' individual interests to behave competitively; they will generally cooperate only if they are constrained to do so by some form of agreement or social contract backed up by sanctions (see Chapter 5), and such an agreement or contract presupposes a communication system that incorporates the higher functions.

Consider the problem of inducing people to contribute towards the cost of a national broadcasting network. The British Broadcasting Corporation is financed by the revenue from television licences, and the viewing public is required by law to buy these licences. If the purchase of licences were not compulsory, it would be possible for people to enjoy the benefits of television without contributing towards its cost, but if no one paid up, then unless an alternative source of revenue were found the service would have to be disbanded, and most people would wish to avoid this outcome. The British public is evidently generally in favour of compulsory licences : they regularly vote into office governments which perpetuate the system. It would be quite impossible, through a system of communication that lacked the descriptive and argumentative functions, to persuade people to support a binding agreement or social contract of this kind, or even to formulate it. A simple social contract has the form 'If we cooperate, we shall all be better off than if we pursue our individual interests selfishly, therefore let us as a community agree to enforce universal cooperation'. An individual would have insufficient incentive to cooperate unless he knew that the community as a whole had endorsed the social contract, but no one could indicate his endorsement of it without describing it, or persuade others to do so without arguing against competitiveness and in favour of enforced cooperation.

It is clear, therefore, that certain forms of cooperative behaviour, which depend for their existence and maintenance on social contracts, are impossible to establish without some system of communication resembling human language. Since animal communication systems invariably lack one or both of the higher functions, we can deduce that the only forms of cooperation to be found among animals are those in which individual and collective interests happen to coincide. In these cases, primitive forms of communication may facilitate cooperation, but as we shall see, cooperative behaviour can sometimes emerge and be maintained by a sort of invisible hand without any communication between group members. After a discussion of the natural evolution of cooperation in circumstances in which individual and collective interests coincide, the problem of binding agreements and the social contract will be examined in greater detail in Section 11.4.

11.2 Biological and Cultural Evolution

One of the most striking differences between human beings and less highly evolved animals is the relatively smaller degree to which human behaviour is constrained by genetic factors. The social behaviour of certain insects such as bees, wasps, and termites, for example, though extremely complex, is none the less genetically programmed in fine detail and is therefore stereotyped, whereas the social behaviour of human beings is strongly influenced by non-genetic factors and is much more variable. (Many of the non-genetic sources of human social behaviour have been specified in Chapters 4 to 9.) This may seem too obvious a point to merit comment, but it is one that is often ignored by overzealous sociobiologists who subscribe to the dogma that evolutionary models suitable for explaining innate social behaviour in insects and other animals can be applied, without modification of the fundamental ideas, to human social behaviour (see for example Lumsden & Wilson, 1981). It is true that the 'primary' facial expressions of happiness, sadness, surprise, disgust, and fear are innate in humans — they are recognizably similar in isolated cultures, and infants born blind and deaf display them in a more-or-less conventional way (Eibl-Eibesfeldt, 1972; Ekman *et al.*, 1972). It is reasonable to suppose, therefore, that this form of non-verbal communication, in which the lower expressive and signalling functions are present without the higher descriptive and argumentative functions, has evolved through natural selection. But there is no evidence of any genetic component in most other forms of human social behaviour, including most forms of cooperation and competition. The doctrine that *all* forms of human social behaviour have necessarily arisen through the mechanism of natural selection tends to raise the hackles of social anthropologists and others who are alive to the dangers of anthropomorphism (the hackles of Leach, 1982, Ch. 3, for example, are fully erect).

In many species of animals there are forms of cooperative and altruistic behaviour that are apparently innate. Huntingford (Chapter 1) has discussed numerous examples from the behaviour of insects, minnows and other small fish, ring doves, groove-billed anis, male turkeys, Florida scrub jays, ground squirrels, lions, savanna baboons, and other animals. Lazarus (Chapter 2) has added several examples of animal conflict in which the combatants avoid using their weapons to full advantage : deers look antlers and push each other around but seldom try to pierce each other's bodies, rattlesnakes wrestle but do not bite, many species engage in ritualized displays without actually coming to blows, and so on. At first sight, these patterns of behaviour are difficult to reconcile with the theory of evolution because a mutant individual that behaved non-cooperatively would seem to have a better chance of survival and reproduction than its cooperative conspecifics, so one might expect such a mutation to invade and spread through the population by natural selection. But this is not necessarily so : Huntingford and Lazarus have convincingly demonstrated that the evidence is in perfect harmony with a contemporary interpretation of natural selection based on the idea of inclusive fitness. This conclusion, which owes a great deal to the application of game theory to behavioural evolution, is surprising and interesting; but it cannot be generalized straightforwardly to human social behaviour for the reasons outlined in the previous paragraph.

Mackie (Chapter 10) has argued, however, that the theory of natural selection can be applied in a modified form to the evolution of non-instinctive social behaviour in human societies. The idea of applying the principles of natural selection to non-biological entities can be traced through the writings of Dawkins (1976) and Popper (1961) to Samuel Butler (1872), the author of *Erewhon*. The fundamental idea of cultural evolution can be summarized as follows. Like genes, memes (conventional patterns of social behaviour, theories, moral principles, techniques, fashions, tunes, and the like) are capable of self-replication. In certain circumstances they tend to produce multiple copies of themselves, but small variations, akin to genetic mutations, are apt to occur in the process of replication. A new meme — a new pattern of behaviour, for example — that satisfies human needs or desires in a particular society is likely to invade and spread through the population by memory and imitation, driving out its less beneficial competitors. Social practices and conventions may therefore be interpreted as the products of a kind of cultural evolution which can, of course, proceed much more rapidly than genetic evolution because it is not limited by the reproductive rate of the species. Mackie has shown how various cooperative behaviour patterns can be explained in this way, and how the theory limits the range of moral conventions that can evolve.

Cooperative agreements play no part in the natural evolution of social behaviour, whether by gene or meme selection. According to the theory, rattlesnakes avoid biting one another's bodies during wrestling matches, not because they have agreed to act cooperatively, nor because they understand the benefits to the species of mutual cooperation, but because it is in their long-term individual interests — measured in units of inclusive fitness — to do so; this pattern of behaviour is the product of straightforward natural selection. And, again according to the theory, people generally try to keep promises, not because they are bound by contract to do so, but because it is in their long-term individual interests to maintain their reputations for trustworthiness; the convention of honouring promises is a product of cultural evolution through meme selection. Cooperation is thus interpreted as a by-product of the pursuit of individual self-interest. It will be argued in Section 11.4 that the mechanism of meme selection cannot suffice to solve some of the most pressing problems of cooperation in human societies. But first, in order to show how cooperation *can* sometimes evolve by meme selection in the absence of cooperative agreements and intentions, let us examine the intriguing case of the minimal social situation.

11.3 The Minimal Social Situation

Consider the following hypothetical problem. Mr. Jones and Mr. Smith commute to work every weekday on the same train. They always sit in adjacent compartments, and during the winter the compartments are always uncomfortably cold. Each compartment has a lever marked 'heater', but it is unclear whether it should be turned to the left or the right to increase the temperature. In fact there is a fault in the electrical wiring of the train : moving the lever to the left increases the temperature and moving it to the right decreases the temperature in the *adjacent* compartment. Thus if Mr Jones turns his lever to the left, Mr Smith's compartment warms up, and if he turns it to the right, Mr Smith has an especially cold journey; Mr Jones's comfort is similarly controlled by Mr Smith's lever.

The commuters obviously cannot directly influence their own physical comfort by manipulating the levers; their comfort is entirely in each other's hands, though neither of them realizes this. But they would none the less both benefit if both turned their levers to the left at the beginning of every journey. The following interesting question arises : Can they learn to cooperate in this way in spite of their ignorance of their mutual dependence and even of each other's existence? If so, it is clearly possible for cooperative behaviour to evolve unintentionally in the absence of cooperative agreements.

The commuters' problem is isomorphic with the minimal social situation originally devised by Sidowski and his colleagues (Sidowski *et al.*, 1956;

Sidowski, 1957). Experimental evidence has provided an unambiguous answer to crucial question. Yes, the subjects can, and generally do learn to cooperate by choosing 'left' on every occasion or on most occasions.

In the original experiments, the appropriate conditions of mutual fate control (as it is often called) were engineered as follows. Pairs of subjects were seated in separate rooms, unaware of each other's existence, and electrodes were attached to their bodies. Each subject faced an apparatus fitted with a pair of buttons marked *L* and *R* and a digital display showing the cumulative number of points scored. Their instructions were to choose a button on each trial and to press it, and their objective was to try to accumulate rewards (points) and to minimize punishments (shocks). The electrical wiring was arranged in such a way that an *L* choice always resulted in a point and an *R* choice a shock to the *other* subject. The experimental set-up is obviously identical at a formal level to the commuters' problem, and Sidowski's (1957) results revealed that the frequency of cooperative (*L*) choices tends to increase over trials.

Kelly *et al.* (1962) showed that these findings can be explained by what they called the *win — stay, lose — change* principle, which is really just a version of Thorndike's (1911) law of effect. According to Thorndike, responses that 'are accompanied or closely followed by satisfaction [are] more firmly connected with the situation' and those that 'are accompanied or closely followed by discomfort . . . have their connections with the situation weakened' (p. 244). Let us assume that both commuters in the above example obey the law of effect by adopting the win — stay, lose — change principle. On the very first journey each commuter chooses 'left' or 'right' at random, and on every subsequent journey repeats his previous choice if it was accompanied by satisfaction (if his compartment warmed up) and switches to the alternative option if it was accompanied by discomfort (if his compartment got colder).

The commuters' initial choices are random, so there are three initial combinations to be considered : both may choose 'left' (*LL*), both may choose 'right' (*RR*), or one may choose 'left' and the other 'right' (*LR* or *RL*). In the first case, both will repeat their initial choices indefinitely on subsequent journeys because the combination of choices is mutually satisfying:

$$LL \rightarrow LL \rightarrow LL \ldots$$

If both initially choose 'right', then both will switch to 'left' on the second journey (because the initial choices are mutually discomforting) and repeat the 'left' choices on all subsequent journeys:

$$RR \rightarrow LL \rightarrow LL \rightarrow LL \ldots$$

Finally, if one commuter initially chooses 'left' and the other 'right', then the former experiences discomfort and the latter satisfaction. On the second journey, the former will therefore switch to 'right' and the latter will stay with 'right'. On the third journey, both will switch to 'left' and repeat these choices on all subsequent journeys:

$$LR \rightarrow RR \rightarrow LL \rightarrow LL \rightarrow LL \ldots$$

or

$$RL \rightarrow RR \rightarrow LL \rightarrow LL \rightarrow LL \ldots$$

To summarize: whatever choices the commuters make on the first journey, by the third journey at the latest they will both be turning their levers to the left, and this cooperative pattern of behaviour will persist indefinitely. This theoretical deduction follows logically from Kelley *et al.*'s (1962) model of the minimal social situation, and it must be true provided that the model's sole assumption — that people's behaviour obeys the law of effect — is psychologically valid.

Kelley *et al.*'s (1962) theoretical model, in effect, specifies a mechanism of meme selection through which a cooperative pattern of behaviour can evolve in a dyad without any agreement or social contract between the group members, and without any cooperative intentions on their part. The model also yields a number of more specific predictions, one of the most unexpected of which is the following. Except in the relatively unlikely event of the commuters both hitting upon the 'left' choice on the very first journey — the probability of this happy accident is $\frac{1}{4}$ — they are bound to suffer a mutually discomforting (*RR*) journey before the mutually satisfying (*LL*) pattern of behaviour can become established. This prediction was strongly confirmed by Kelley *et al.*'s experimental results : almost every run of *LL* combinations was immediately preceded by an *RR* combination (see also Burnstein, 1969). It suggests a possible strategic basis for the belief, common in the criminal underworld, that a quarrel or a fight is necessary to 'clear the air' before mutual trust can develop between two people, and for Braiker and Kelley's (1979) assertion that conflict often enhances interpersonal intimacy.

In practice, experimental subjects do not adhere rigidly to the win — stay, lose — change principle (Kelley *et al.*, 1962; Rabinowitz *et al.*, 1966; Burnstein, 1969). In the minimal social situation, cooperative *L* choices exceed chance frequency after a few trials and continue to increase in frequency thereafter; but after 100 trials only about 75% of choices are cooperative. According to the model, of course, 100% cooperation should occur after three trials at most, and the discrepancy between theory and empirical observation can only be due to the fact that people do not conform strictly to the win — stay, lose — change principle, or to put it differently, that the law of effect is not strictly valid. But cooperative behaviour does tend to evolve, and it is not unreasonable to suppose that similar processes occur naturally in multi-person groups or even in whole societies. In a society composed entirely of commuters travelling in trains with crossed wires, the practice of switching the heaters on by turning the levers to the left could spread very quickly through memory and imitation without any agreement or social contract ever being formulated, and without people understanding the social consequences of their actions. This example may be a trifle artificial, but the underlying idea is widely applicable.

11.4 The Social Contract

Sections 11.2 and 11.3 were devoted to forms of cooperative behaviour that optimize the evolutionary fitness or satisfy the individual desires of the animals or people that practise them. Under these conditions, cooperation can evolve through natural selection or through an analogous mechanism of cultural evolution without any agreement or social contract between the group members. Evolution can thus mimic intelligent social engineering in the same way that it often mimics intelligent physical engineering — many people find it difficult to believe that the intricate biological structures in the world were not deliberately designed by a superior intelligence. But cooperation can evolve through gene or meme selection only in circumstances in which individual and collective interests happen to coincide and, as pointed out in Section 11.1, they often do not. This problem is ubiquitous in modern industrial societies : contribution to the cost of public services; conservation of scarce resources; restraint in wage bargaining; and nuclear disarmament are just four of the most familiar social dilemmas in which individual rationality is at loggerheads with collective rationality (see Chapter 5). In each case, joint cooperation, which is in everyone's interest, cannot be fashioned by the invisible hand of biological or cultural evolution because the selfish pursuit of individual interests leads inexorably to universal competition. This important discovery of game theory is overlooked or ignored by many conservative political scientists and economists whose misplaced faith in the benevolence of the invisible hand was originally inspired by Adam Smith (1776).

Where natural evolutionary processes tend to produce socially undesirable effects, human beings, armed with a descriptive and argumentative language (see Section 11.1), can sometimes take steps to achieve mutually beneficial cooperative solutions. This problem was tackled by Thomas Hobbes (1651) in Chs. 13 to 17 of *Leviathan* and by Rousseau (1762) in *Du Contrat Social*. According to Hobbes, the natural desire for self-preservation and a decent life gives people a reason to seek cooperative solutions to social problems. But in circumstances in which selfish motives generate competitive behaviour, there is insufficient incentive to cooperate unless there is a general agreement to limit competition; and even if such an agreement exists, no one has a strong motive to abide by it unless it is backed by some coercive mechanism of enforcement. This, Hobbes argued, must be a political sovereign whom everyone undertakes to obey, and who is invested with the necessary power to punish non-cooperators. Hobbes imagined a state of nature — 'a condition of Warre of every one against every one' (Ch. 14) — in which people came together to set up a civil society based on a social contract backed by a sovereign power. Rousseau's version of the social contract is a more democratic conception : 'a form of association that defends and protects, with the whole common force, the person and goods of each member, and in which each, by uniting with all, obeys only himself and remains as free as before' (Bk. I, Ch. vi). According to Rousseau, 'the undertakings that bind us to the social body are obligatory only because they are mutual, and their nature is such that in fulfilling them we cannot work for others without also working for ourselves' (Bk. II, Ch. iv). When Rousseau says that 'man is born free, and everywhere he is in chains' (Bk. I, Ch. i), he means that binding agreements can have a liberating effect by promoting the collective interest of those who enter into them; bemused translators who have substituted 'but' for 'and' in this quotation have evidently missed the point and conveyed exactly the opposite meaning. For a fuller discussion of Rousseau's ideas in the context of game theory, see Colman (1982, Ch. 13).

In circumstances in which selfish behaviour, if universal, is ultimately self-defeating, the social contract provides a mechanism for protecting everyone's interest. 'Mutual coercion mutually agreed upon' (Hardin, 1968, p. 1247) sounds harsh and authoritarian, but in fact it is the basis of every democratic legal system. Most motorists obey traffic lights and the rule of the road, contribute to road maintenance and bridge building, and buy third-party insurance precisely because they are obliged to do these things in terms of the laws of the land; and if there were no inducement to behave in these ways, life would be more difficult for everyone.

For the reasons outlined in Section 11.1, this method of solving social problems is possible only in human societies in which the higher functions of language have evolved. Even in societies blessed with descriptive and argumentative languages, however, there are social problems that cannot easily be solved. For example, there is no world government with the power to enforce cooperative multilateral nuclear disarmament, so technologically advanced nations continue to pursue individual strategic military interests to the collective detriment of humanity. The humble creatures of this earth may yet prove fitter in terms of long-term survival than the human species.

References

BRAIKER, H.B. and KELLEY, H.H. (1979). Conflict in the development of close relationships. In R.L. BURGESS and T.L. HUSTON (Eds.), *Social Exchange in Developing Relationships*. New York: Academic Press. Pp. 135 – 168.

BÜHLER, K. (1934) *Sprachtheorie*. Jena: Fischer.

BURNSTEIN, E. (1969). The role of reward and punishment in the development of behavioral interdependence. In J. MILLS (Ed.), *Experimental Social Psychology*. London: Macmillan. Pp. 341 – 405.

BUTLER, S. (1972). *Erewhon*. London.

COLMAN, A.M. (1982). *Game Theory and Experimental Games: The Study of Strategic Interaction*. Oxford: Pergamon (In press).

DAWKINS, R. (1976). *The Selfish Gene*. Oxford: Oxford University Press.

EIBL-EIBESFELDT, I. (1972). Similarities and differences between cultures in expressive movements. In R.A. HINDE (Ed.), *Non-Verbal Communication*. Cambridge: Cambridge University Press.

EKMAN, P., FRIESEN, W.V. and ELLSWORTH, P. (1972). *Emotions and the Human Face*. Elmsford, NY: Pergamon.

HARDIN, G. (1968). The tragedy of the commons. *Science*, **162**, 1243 – 1248.

HOBBES, T. (1651). *Leviathan, or the Matter, Forme and Power of a Commonwealth, Ecclesiasticall and Civill*. London.

KELLEY, H.H., THIBAUT, J.W., RADLOFF, R. and MUNDY, D. (1962). The development of cooperation in the 'minimal social situation'. *Psychological Monographs*, **76**, Whole No. 19.

LEACH, E. (1982). *Social Anthropology*. London: Fontana.
LUMSDEN, C.J. and WILSON, E.O. (1981). *Genes, Mind and Culture: The Evolutionary Process*. Cambridge, Mass.: Harvard University Press.
POPPER, K.R (1961). Evolution and the Tree of Knowledge, Herbert Spencer Lecture delivered in Oxford, 30 October. Reprinted in K.R. POPPER, *Objective Knowledge: An Evolutionary Approach*. Oxford: Clarendon, 1972, Pp. 256 – 284.
POPPER, K.R. (1963). Language and the body-mind problem. In K.R. POPPER, *Conjectures and Refutations: The Growth of Scientific Knowledge*. London: Routledge & Kegan Paul. Pp. 293 – 298.
POPPER, K.R. (1972). Of clouds and clocks: an approach to the problem of rationality and the freedom of man. In K.R. POPPER, *Objective Knowledge: An Evolutionary Approach*. Oxford: Clarendon, 1972, Pp. 206 – 255.
RABINOWITZ, K., KELLEY, H.H. and ROSENBLATT, R.M. (1966). Effects of different types of interdependence and response conditions in the minimal social situation. *Journal of Experimental Social Psychology*, **2**, 169 – 197.
ROUSSEAU, J.-J. (1762). *Du Contrat Social ou Principes du Droit Politique*. Paris.
SIDOWSKI, J.B. (1957). Reward and punishment in the minimal social situation. *Journal of Experimental Psychology*, **54**, 318 – 326.
SIDOWSKI, J.B., WYCKOFF, L.B. and TABORY, L. (1956). The influence of reinforcement and punishment in a minimal social situation. *Journal of Abnormal and Social Psychology*, **52**, 115 – 119.
SMITH, A. (1776). *An Inquiry Into the Nature and Causes of the Wealth of Nations*. Reprinted in an edition edited by E. CANNAN, London: Methuen 1904. Vol. I.
THORNDIKE, R.L. (1911). *Animal Intelligence: Experimental Studies*. New York: Macmillan.

Index

This index contains major references to names and subjects. Names not appearing in the index can be found in the lists of references at the end of each chapter.

Printed and Bound in Great Britain by
Robert Hartnoll Limited, Bodmin, Cornwall.

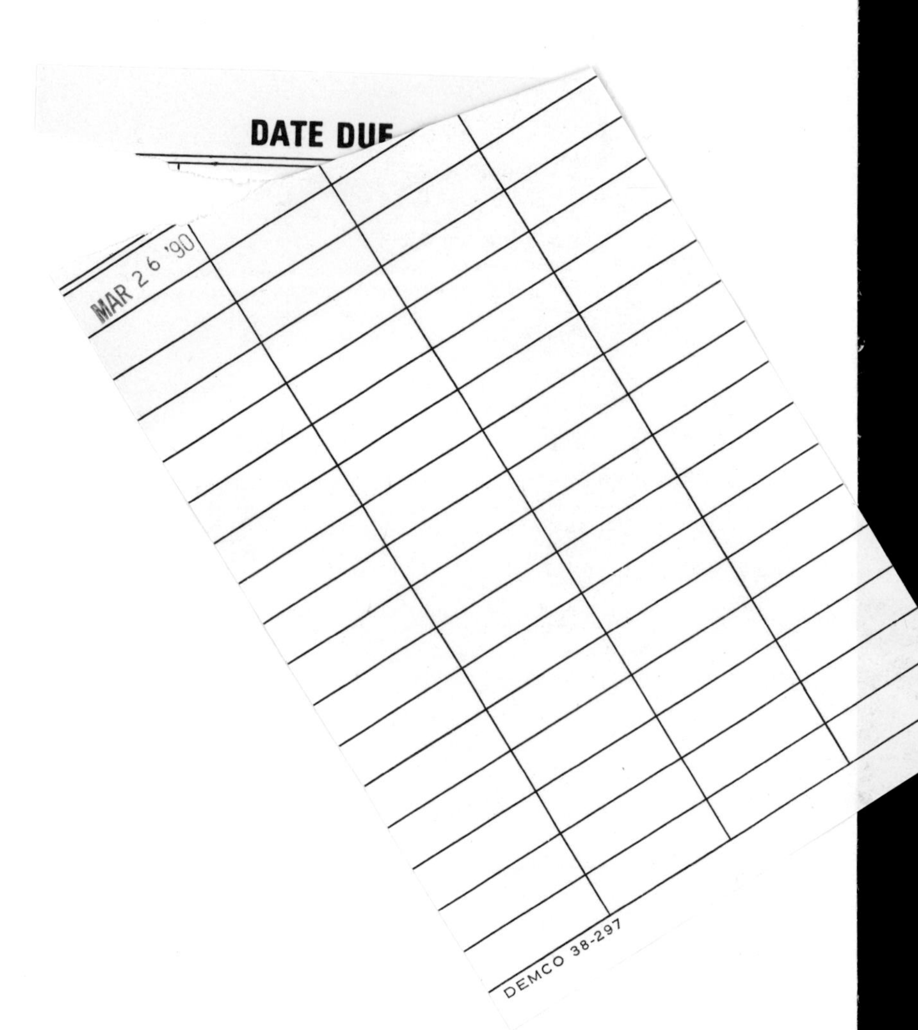
DATE DUE
MAR 26 '90
DEMCO 38-297